SUPERVISION FOR BETTER SCHOOLS
fifth edition

John T. Lovell
University of Tennessee

Kimball Wiles

Prentice-Hall, Inc., Englewood Cliffs, New Jersey 07632

Library of Congress Cataloging in Publication Data

Wiles, Kimball
    Supervision for better schools.

    Bibliography: p.
    Includes index.
    1. School supervision.   I. Lovell, John Thomas.
1921-   .   II. Title.
LB2805.W5 1982   371.2'013   82-15066
ISBN 0-13-876169-8

Editorial production/supervision
    and interior design by Virginia Livsey
Cover design by Zimmerman/Foyster Design
Manufacturing buyer: Ronald Chapman

Printed in the United States of America

10 9 8 7 6 5 4 3 2 1

ISBN 0-13-876169-8

Prentice-Hall International, Inc., *London*
Prentice-Hall of Australia Pty. Limited, *Sydney*
Editora Prentice-Hall do Brazil, LTDA, *Rio de Janeiro*
Prentice-Hall Canada Inc., *Toronto*
Prentice-Hall of India Private Limited, *New Delhi*
Prentice-Hall of Japan, Inc., *Tokyo*
Prentice-Hall of Southeast Asia Pte. Ltd., *Singapore*
Whitehall Books Limited, *Wellington, New Zealand*

DEDICATED TO OUR STUDENTS
WHO WERE OUR TEACHERS
AND
TO OUR TEACHERS
WHO CONTINUED TO BE STUDENTS

CONTENTS

PREFACE

This book is the second revision of *Supervision for Better Schools* since the tragic and untimely death of the original author, Kimball Wiles. The revision of any book is a difficult process. Decisions concerning what to add, delete, rewrite, update, or reorganize are excruciatingly difficult; in this revision the process was even more difficult since the author of the first three editions was not available for consultation, help, fresh ideas, new insights, and critical questions. Fortunately, the first four editions of *Supervision for Better Schools* were developed from a stated theoretical frame of reference. Such a statement facilitated the revision process since an evaluation of the basic assumptions, theoretical formulations, and research findings of the fourth edition provided direction for the development of the fifth edition. The revision process has resulted in the addition of several new chapters as well as extensive revision and reorganization of other parts of the book. However, every effort has been made to maintain the quality and style of earlier editions.

The book is based on the assumption that instructional supervision is an organizational behavior system that interacts with the teaching behavior system to improve the quality of education for students. As an organizational behavior system, instructional supervision can be studied and generalizations can be reached concerning the possible consequences of various supervisory practices, procedures, methods, and approaches. Readers are introduced to concepts, theoretical formulations, and research findings from many fields of study that are assumed to have implications for behavior in the supervisory process. It is hoped that practitioners can use the conceptual tools to study the particular behavior systems of which they are a part and to develop their own behavior to meet the needs of their unique situations.

Practical ideas for action are discussed throughout the book. An attempt is made to maintain consistency with the general conceptual framework. Readers are urged to check this for themselves and to evaluate these action ideas in terms of their own situation.

The first section of the book defines the boundaries and distinctive characteristics of supervisory behavior, presents the theoretical framework, and provides historical perspective.

The second section of the book defines and discusses concepts, theoretical formulations, and research findings from the studies of leadership, communication, releasing human potential, and the change process, and explains their implications for educational supervision.

Instructional supervisory behavior is assumed to have the functions of facilitating instructional improvement, curriculum development, and human development in the educational organization. The nature and delivery of these anticipated outcomes of supervisory efforts are developed in the third section of the book.

The allocation and organization of the instructional supervisory support at both the central office level and local school level are presented in the chapters of the fourth section. Finally, in the last section an attempt is made to apply the meaning of the book to the special problems of the beginning supervisor.

Help with the revision came from so many sources that it is impossible to mention specific individuals. Students and colleagues were most helpful in reading and reacting to the manuscript. The secretarial staff of the Department of Educational Administration and Supervision was especially helpful in the preparation of the manuscript. A special note of thanks is due Angela Fryer, who helped with the final editing as well as with reading and reacting to the manuscript.

John T. Lovell

1

INSTRUCTIONAL SUPERVISION
Organizational Behavior System

This is a book about instructional supervision in educational organizations. Its study requires not only a careful conceptualization of instructional supervision, but also an equally careful consideration of the environment with which it interacts. The study and practice of instructional supervision in educational organizations has been confused, hampered, constrained, and distorted by the lack of an adequate conceptualization of instructional supervision including its nature, purpose, organizational structure, and the roles and responsibilities of persons occupying instructional supervisory positions. The purpose of this chapter is, first, to clarify the nature, purpose, and function of instructional supervision and, second, to develop a rational system for the organization of personnel to fulfill the requirements of instructional supervision. An attempt is also made to present the theoretical framework that gave direction to our study and analysis of instructional supervisory behavior.

Supervision has many different meanings. Persons who read or hear the word interpret it in terms of past experiences, needs, and purposes. A supervisor may consider it a positive force for program improvement; a teacher may see it as a threat to individuality; another teacher may think of it as a source of assistance and support.

Teachers' feelings about supervision differ because of the various ways in which supervisors the teachers have known have interpreted the supervisory role.

During the past half century, supervision has been in a state of rapid evolution. One supervisor may hold to a philosophy and use procedures that are in direct conflict with those of another supervisor. Any teacher with several years of experience has probably encountered several types of supervisors.

At one time, supervision was a directing and judging activity. In the 1910s and 1920s, the writing in the field of supervision recommended directing and telling people what to do and then checking to see whether people had done as they were directed. It is easy to see one reason for this emphasis. Teachers were not trained then as they are now. Some started teaching as soon as they had left high school, with very little preservice education.

In the 1930s, the emphasis was on "democratic supervision." A survey of the literature reveals, however, that this term meant different things to different people. To some it meant a type of manipulation in which teachers were to be treated kindly and maneuvered into doing what the supervisor wanted to do all along. To others it meant a hands-off approach where teachers could do as they pleased. But to others it meant involving teachers in cooperative instructional improvement.

This emphasis continued until 1957, the year of Sputnik. At this point, the national government became interested in improving the quality of education, especially in the sciences, mathematics, and foreign languages. Large curriculum projects were developed through the National Science Foundation and with funds made available under the National Defense Education Act of 1958. Supervisors in subject matter fields were added to central office staffs and given the function of improving the program in the fields already mentioned here. Many conceived their task to be convincing teachers to adopt a national program and to develop the information and skills necessary to implement the program. Success was interpreted to mean changing teachers in the desired direction.

During the 1970s and the 1980s, the role of the supervisor has become increasingly confused. The supervisors with a specific mission to perform have seen themselves as directing the process of change, and their primary question has been one of strategy. Other supervisors, those who see themselves as helping professional people solve their instructional and curricular problems, have continued to work for improvement in the process of decision making, decision sharing, curricular change, and instructional improvement. But, the supervisor's role concept is not the only source of confusion.

A growing variety of positions in educational organizations are filled by "supervisors." Position titles include general supervisor, special supervisor, clinical supervisor, director, coordinator, consultant, assistant superintendent in charge of instruction, and many others. Instructional supervisors occupying these various positions often have different roles and different responsibilities in different organizations or the same organization. Much confusion exists. Lovell (1978 p. 44) described the confusion as follows: "The title of the position may not reflect the role of the position. The authority structure for the position may not be appropriate for the roles and responsibilities of the position." The administration may expect the supervisor to direct, control, and monitor the behavior of teachers. Teachers, on the other hand, may expect help and warm encouragement, free of threat. An administrator may expect the supervisor to work in the central office making applications for governmental projects or doing other administrative chores. Teachers may expect readily available help, service, and support for their teaching performance.

The result can be confusion, disappointment, or even alienation by all parties. There is a need to clarify the purpose and function of instructional supervision as an organizational behavior system and to develop a basis for the structure and coordination of the supervisory positions needed in a given organization to provide the services of instructional supervision (Lovell, 1978 pp. 44-45).

A CONCEPT OF INSTRUCTIONAL
SUPERVISORY BEHAVIOR*

It is helpful to think of educational organizations as subsystems of the society, which are expected to provide certain valued services. These valued services take the form of educational outcomes for students. Therefore, when we think of educational organizations, it is important to think of students as the central focus of our organizational thrust. In a general sense, the society specifies the nature of these expected educational outcomes and provides other "inputs" such as students, organizational personnel, and money.

In order to achieve its objectives (educational outcomes for students) the educational organization is itself composed of a cluster of interacting behavior systems that exist to contribute to the achievement of the goals of the super system (the educational organization). The student behavior system is the most important of these subsystems since all other systems exist to make a contribution to the achievement of the goals of the student behavior system. Students operating from their own conceptual base, including their skills, knowledge, views of the world, values, attitudes, and understandings, are expected to extend their conceptual bases through growth and development in directions consistent with their own needs and societal expectation.

In order to ensure that the goals of the student behavior system are achieved, the organization provides a teaching behavior subsystem to facilitate the achievement of student learning outcomes. Examples of teacher behavior systems include the faculty of an elementary school, the faculty of a social studies department, or a team of teachers who work with 150 elementary students. Thus, it is possible to conceptualize a behavior system formally provided by the organization to interact with the student behavior system. In order to achieve their goals, organizations have recognized the need for other behavior systems that contribute to the student behavior system in various ways. For example, the "administrative behavior system"

*This section is an extension of an earlier publication by the author. John T. Lovell, "A perspective for Viewing Instructional Supervisory Behavior," in Supervision: Perspectives and Propositions, ed. William H. Lucio, Washington, D.C.: A.S.C.D. 1967) pp. 12-27.

may develop policies, enforce rules, prepare budgets, present bond issues for facilities, and so on. The "student counseling behavior system" may function to help students cope with personal problems. Lovell (1967 p. 12) defined the instructional supervisory behavior system: "Instructional supervisory behavior, while external to the teacher-pupil system, is calculated to influence directly and purposefully teacher behavior in such a way as to facilitate student learning." The organizational subsystems are open systems in constant interaction with the organization and with each other, but they also have their own identity that is a function of their unique purpose or value to the organization. The achievement of a subsystem's purpose requires the specifications of objectives, the development of programs to achieve objectives, the definition of roles and competence to actualize the roles, and finally continuous implementation and evaluation of results.

The central focus of this book is the study of instructional supervision as a behavior system of the educational organization. The purpose of this behavior system has already been defined as a formally designated behavior system that interacts directly with the teaching behavior system in order to improve the probability that the goals of the teaching behavior system will be achieved. (Lovell, 1967 pp. 12-28). It is assumed that the following operational goals will provide direction for the effort to improve instruction (Lovell, 1978 p. 42):

1. Goal formulation, implementation, and evaluation
2. Curriculum development
3. Direct support and service for the teaching behavior system
4. Evaluation for personnel decisions
5. Inservice education
6. Evaluation of educational results

Figure 1-1 attempts to show the major components of this conceptual scheme for viewing supervisory behavior.

The educational organization is clearly portrayed as a changing system that is a subsystem of a society that is also in constant flux. The teacher behavior system is a subsystem of the organization and interacts with the student behavior system for the purpose of achieving the goals of the student behavior system. It is assumed that teaching behavior that facilitates the establishment of goals, the design and implementation of operations, and the evaluation of results will contribute to the effectiveness of the student behavior system.

Instructional supervisory behavior is assumed to be an additional behavior system formally provided by the organization for the purpose of interacting with the teaching behavior system in such a way as to maintain, change, and improve the design and actualization of learning opportunities for students. Individuals both from within the organization and outside the organization who are officially designated by the organization to work to improve teachers and/or teacher-student systems are working in the supervisory behavior system. Such a conceptual framework broadens the possible sources of supervisory behavior to include not only persons officially designated as supervisors (persons who spend all or most of their time working in supervision), but also to include persons within the organizations,

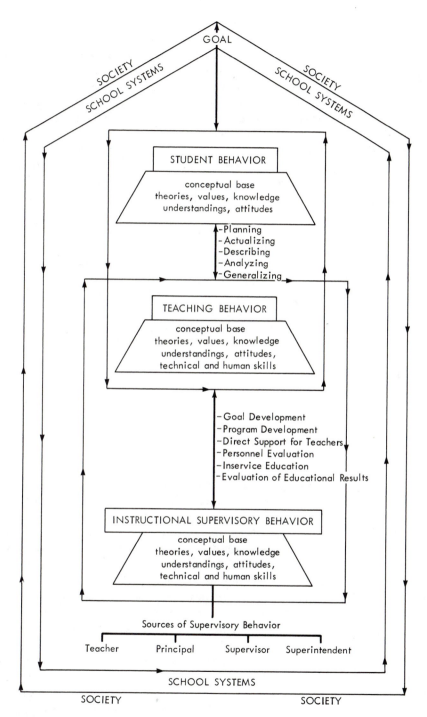

GOAL

SOCIETY
SCHOOL SYSTEMS

SOCIETY
SCHOOL SYSTEMS

STUDENT BEHAVIOR

conceptual base
theories, values, knowledge
understandings, attitudes

-Planning
-Actualizing
-Describing
-Analyzing
-Generalizing

TEACHING BEHAVIOR

conceptual base
theories, values, knowledge
understandings, attitudes,
technical and human skills

-Goal Development
-Program Development
-Direct Support for Teachers
-Personnel Evaluation
-Inservice Education
-Evaluation of Educational Results

INSTRUCTIONAL SUPERVISORY BEHAVIOR

conceptual base
theories, values, knowledge
understandings, attitudes,
technical and human skills

Sources of Supervisory Behavior

Teacher   Principal   Supervisor   Superintendent

SCHOOL SYSTEMS

SOCIETY   SOCIETY

FIGURE 1-1 Supervisory Behavior: A Conceptual Framework

SOURCE: This figure is based on an earlier work by John T. Lovell (1967).

5

such as teachers, principals, superintendents, and guidance counselors, who spend most of their time working in other organizational behavior systems. Such individuals can be used on an ad hoc basis according to special competence, willingness to help, and acceptability to those being helped. For example, a teacher who has developed exceptional competence in certain teaching strategies may be used to help other teachers who want to develop their competence in these strategies and are willing to utilize help from this teacher. A superintendent with exceptional competence in teaching mathematics could be used to help a small group of teachers evaluate their program.

Other individuals, such as students or university faculty members, or community members, such as social workers, medical doctors, nurses, or engineers, could be used according to competence, willingness to help, and acceptability to persons who need help.

Supervisors are persons formally designated as prime sources of help for the teaching behavior system. But the conceptualization just presented broadens their functions considerably. For example, they become developers of knowledge about who needs help and who is competent and willing to provide help. They use this knowledge to develop structures and facilitate the process through which a broad base of sources of supervisory behavior can be utilized.

Figure 1-2 (page 7) clearly shows that teaching behavior is assumed to have five distinctive but interdependent dimensions:

1. Planning
2. Actualizing
3. Describing
4. Analyzing
5. Generalizing

Planning is the dimension in which teachers develop goals and objectives, designs for operations or for engagement opportunities for students that are assumed to contribute toward achieving objectives, ways of verifying the operations that *were* provided, ways of analyzing "what happened," and ways of evaluating results.

The *actualizing dimension* is the process of putting the plan into operation. The *describing dimension* involves utilizing the plan to observe and record what actually happened during instruction. The *analyzing dimension* is the study and ordering of the observational data in order to understand what happened, why it happened, and how. What happened is related to the achievement of learning objectives. Finally, the *generalizing dimension* is making decisions about future plans and future actualization. It is important to understand that these dimensions are not steps that follow one after the other. They are dimensions of an ongoing process, which have been separated here for the sake of discussion and analysis. Actually, teachers may be in the actualization phase, become aware of new data, and make new strategy or content decisions on the spot.

It is our contention that the dimensions of teaching provide important points of interaction between teaching behavior and supervisory behavior. For example,

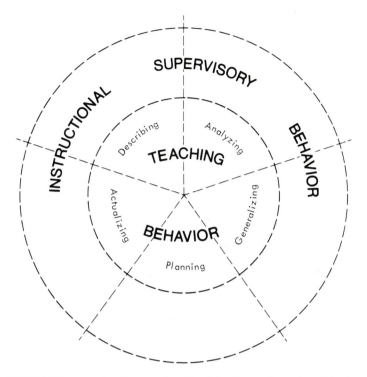

FIGURE 1-2 Interaction Between Teaching Behavior and Supervisor Behavior

teachers participating in planning behavior provide an excellent opportunity for supervisors to provide services. Teachers need someone who is competent, trustworthy, and caring as a source of ideas and support, and as a person who will listen and respond with enthusiasm. The same can be said for the other dimensions of teaching. Teachers need feedback, to use as a basis for improvement, which is based on competent observation and analysis of teaching. They need to collaborate on the introduction of new strategies, methods, and content. The provision of such services is the focus of the supervisory behavior system.

The operational goals of instructional supervision were identified in Figure 1-1 and provide the basis for clarifying the parameters of the supervisory behavior system in educational organizations.

THE OPERATIONAL GOALS
OF INSTRUCTIONAL
SUPERVISORY BEHAVIOR

The operational goals of instructional supervision provide the direction and define the dimensions of the instructional supervisory behavior system. It is our assumption that it is important for educational organizations to influence teaching behavior in certain ways (Lovell 1978, p. 42):

1. Goal formulation, implementation, and evaluation
2. Curriculum development
3. Direct support and service for teachers
4. Evaluation of personnel
5. Inservice education
6. Evaluation of educational results.

These operational goals are considered to function in interaction with each other and as parts of the same whole. They are separated here for purposes of discussion and clarification.

Goal Development, Implementation, and Evaluation

The conceptualization of the educational organization as a subsystem of a larger social system indicates that it must study and interpret the society's expectations for educational outcomes. These expectations must be translated into educational objectives for various student behavior systems. This is a task that is continuous; is carried out at the system level, school level, and teacher level; and demands the cooperative efforts of teachers, supervisors, and administrators. Societies change, educational expectations change, educational objectives need to change, and it is our contention that the processes through which teachers, administrators, and supervisors cooperate in this endeavor should be a function of the supervisory behavior system.

Curriculum Development

In order to achieve the objectives of the student behavior systems, it is necessary to plan, implement, and evaluate engagement opportunities for students, which are assumed to contribute to the achievement of certain outcomes. This planning effort must occur at the central office level, the local school level, the classroom level, and the student level. It is important for school systems to have an overall curriculum design for achieving their objectives. Such a general plan serves to show how various parts of the program fit together in terms of sequence, depth, and scope of coverage. Instructional supervisors must provide the leadership to involve teachers, administrators, and supervisors in the cooperative efforts to get this job done. The involvement of teachers is essential for two reasons. First, their competence is needed. They are specialists in their subject areas, and they have direct contact with students. Second, teachers are the primary implementers of the curriculum and, therefore, need both an understanding of and commitment to the overall curriculum design.

There are also overall educational goals at the local school level and the need for an overall curriculum design that is compatible with the system design. The local school needs continuous contact with curriculum planning at the system level, both to be aware of system expectations and to provide the system with feedback for needed change. The local school also needs considerable freedom to plan, operate, change, and improve the curriculum to meet the needs of its students and community. It is proposed that the instructional supervisory behavior system will be deeply involved in the coordination of curriculum development at the local school level.

Probably the most important curriculum development occurs at the classroom and student level. Certainly, teachers should have primary responsibility for curriculum development in their own classrooms. But, we believe it essential for supervisors and others participating in supervisory behavior to provide not only psychological and technological support to teachers, but also the needed coordination. Teachers are not autonomous units, but rather are parts of an instructional system. Each unit must be aware of what other units are doing and how the activities of other units are related to its own programs. There is a necessity for quality control to insure that individual units have goals and outcomes that are consistent with local school and system goals. These expectations are appropriate for the supervisory behavior system.

Direct Support and Service for Teachers

We think it is essential to provide support and service *directly* to teachers to help them improve their performance in working with a certain group of students. This kind of support makes it possible for teachers and supervisors to examine plans for instruction, and to observe and analyze instruction with reference to what was planned, what happened, and what results were achieved. These procedures provide the foundations for future instructional decisions and improvement. The process is essentially a problem-solving approach to improve a particular situation. It is our assumption that it is a critical dimension of supervisory behavior, and we discuss it in depth in Chapter 9.

In-service Education

Teachers and other professional personnel need an opportunity to continue to develop professionally and personally in-service. Their preservice preparation provided an opportunity to begin the process of developing the foundation for professional service. But, the organized body of knowledge from which teachers generate the content of the teacher-pupil learning environment is constantly expanding and changing. Teachers are busy as practitioners and need a competent and reliable source of help to keep up with new content developments.

New developments in the behavioral sciences and social sciences often have important implications for teaching methodology. Teachers need help and support in order to keep up with new ideas and, just as importantly, they need a readily available system of support to help with the implementation and evaluation of these ideas in the teaching process.

New teaching materials and media equipment are constantly being developed, and teachers and other professional personnel need to keep abreast of these events. New organizational structures, such as team teaching and mastery learning, call for new skills and understanding.

Psychological support for teachers and other professional personnel is an essential ingredient in any organization. Professional personnel need to know that there are other people who know about and are interested in what they are doing. Motivation of organizational members is at least partly a function of psychological support.

Teachers need to develop as fully functioning individuals. Their personal development will contribute to their approach to life and teaching, and to their effectiveness as members of their profession. In-service education is treated in Chapter 10.

Evaluation of Performance

Organizations consist of a pattern of interdependent parts, which it is assumed will work together to achieve certain organizational goals. One essential component of any educational organization is a professional staff that is willing and competent to contribute to the goals of the organization. Organizational members are recruited and selected to contribute to goal attainment in special ways. Naturally, they are selected on the assumption that they are competent and highly motivated. But, it is impossible to predict with complete accuracy the effectiveness of a professional worker. Sometimes an individual is employed without the necessary motivation and, or competence. Often organizations and position requirements change so that individuals must adapt or organizations must find new employees. In many cases individuals change and lose their effectiveness. These are some of the factors that make it essential for organizations to provide an effective and efficient system for the continuous evaluation of the performance of organizational members. Such a system should provide an effective system of support for individual improvement and a basis for personnel decisions. It is our assumption that the evaluation of personnel who work in or work to improve the instructional program is an appropriate operational goal for the instructional supervisory behavior system.

Evaluation of Educational Results

Educational organizations must take appropriate actions to determine their effectiveness in achieving their preferred outcomes. Results must be determined at the individual student level, the classroom level, the school level, and the system level. The results of the evaluation process can be used as a basis for planned improvements, for reporting educational outcomes to the community, and as a way of justifying the need for additional resources. It is logical for the organization to provide the supervisory behavior system with the personnel and other resources necessary to assume continuous evaluation of educational results.

SOME PROCESSES
OF INSTRUCTIONAL
SUPERVISION

Processes of instructional supervision are assumed to be categories of human interaction that are basic and persistent in the various supervisory operations that are used to improve the instructional program. The following processes are given special treatment in our study and analysis because they are so fundamental and persistent in the human interaction we call instructional supervision:

1. Releasing human potential
2. Change
3. Leadership
4. Communication

These processes are considered to be interdependent and would normally function together in basic supervisory operations. It is assumed that there is a strong scientific body of organized knowledge that has implications for the application of these processes in the delivery of instructional supervision. These processes will be discussed in depth in Chapters 3 through 6. They are identified here to communicate what we assume to be the basic processes through which the operational goals of instructional improvement are achieved.

WHAT IS A SUPERVISOR?

A supervisor is a person formally designated by the organization as "supervisor" to improve curriculum and instruction in order to improve the quality of learning of students. No assumption is made that individuals so designated are the sole contributors to the improvement of the teacher behavior system.

It is recognized that some individuals who spend most of their time in other organizational roles are often formally designated by the organization to work in the instructional supervisory behavior system. For example, a teacher may be designated as official leader of a curriculum committee to evaluate and improve the reading program for children in the first three grades. In this capacity the teacher is working as an instructional supervisor, but is still known as teacher since teaching is his or her primary responsibility. It is also recognized that there is an important informal support system. Teachers help other teachers. Students help each other and teachers. Ideas are shared and skills are developed through the informal behavior system.

It is our assumption that formally designated supervisors have an important role. They spend most of their time working to improve instruction. Their duties involve developing and evaluating educational objectives, programs, and instruction;

helping teachers develop professionally; providing support and assistance to teacher performance; and evaluating teacher performance. It is our belief that if the operational goals of instructional supervision are to be achieved, it is necessary to think of at least two categories of the structional supervisory role. Esposito, Smith, and Burbach (1975, pp. 63-67) defined four categories of supervisory tasks:

1. Indirect service to teachers
2. Direct service to teachers
3. Administrator
4. Evaluator

They concluded that is was possible to classify direct and indirect tasks under the general rubric "helping role," and administrator and evaluator tasks under the classification "administrative role." Supervisors working as "helpers" are the expediters. They help establish communication between persons who have similar problems and resource people who can help. They stimulate staff members to look at the extent to which ideas and resources are being shared and the degree to which persons are encouraged and supported as they try new ideas. They make it easier to carry out the agreements that emerge from evaluation sessions. They listen to individuals discuss their problems and recommend other resources that may help in the search for solutions. They bring to individual teachers, whose confidence they possess, appropriate suggestions and materials. They observe and analyze teaching and provide helpful feedback. They do demonstration teaching when appropriate. They help teachers design and implement innovations in their teaching. They sense, as far as they are able, the feelings that teachers have about the system and its policies, and they recommend that the administration examine irritations among staff members. They provide expertness in group operation, and provide the type of meeting place and structure that facilitates communication. They are, above all, concerned with helping people to accept each other, because they know that when individuals value each other, they grow through their interaction and will provide a better emotional climate for pupil growth. The role of the "helper" is basically supporting, assisting, and sharing, rather than directing. The authority of these supervisors has not diminished, but it is based on competence and used in another way. It is used to promote growth through responsibility and creativity, rather than through dependency and conformity.

The administrative instructional supervisors would manage, control, and coordinate programs. They would be responsible for quality control for the instructional program and would evaluate teacher performance for personnel decisions. The allocation of personnel, equipment, and materials would be matters of importance. They would coordinate policy development and implementation and would perform administrative duties related to the instructional program. The achievement of the tasks of the administrative supervisor will require an authority structure with more emphasis on formal authority. However, authority from competence and personality would still be crucial to the influence process.

Recognition of two categories of instructional supervisory behavior does not imply that organizations should or could define roles as being totally in one category or the other. But, it is felt that recognition of these different role dimensions may help organizations eliminate some of the past role confusion that has resulted in such negative consequences.

THE STUDY AND ANALYSIS OF INSTRUCTIONAL SUPERVISORY BEHAVIOR

In the earlier part of this chapter, instructional supervision was conceptualized as one of many behavior systems formally provided by the organization to interact with the teaching behavior system, for the purpose of improving instruction and thereby improving the possibility of achieving certain learning objectives of the student behavior system. The meaning of instructional improvement was clarified by the identification and discussion of its operational goals. *The purpose of this book is to help readers develop knowledge (concepts, theoretical formulations, empirical research findings, skills, and philosophical assumptions) that will help them participate more effectively and efficiently in the instructional supervisory behavior system.* A major purpose of the authors was to explicate the knowledge base from which we were operating and try to logically derive principles and practices of instructional supervision. As a result of our study of the literature, our own research, and many years of experience as supervisors and as teachers, we became convinced that there are many sources of knowledge that have implications for the understanding and practice of instructional supervision. Some of the most important sources of knowledge are identified as follows:

1. *The teacher or teachers with whom the supervisor is working.* Supervisors need knowledge about the needs, interest, concerns, maturities, and attitudes and self-concepts of the teachers with whom they work. Whether or not teachers have had positive experiences with supervisors in the past can be critical to decisions about supervisory approaches. If teachers have become self-directing, knowledgeable about supervision, and self-confident, and have developed trust and respect for the supervisor, the appropriate supervisory approaches may be quite different from those in situations that are not characterized by these teacher attributes. Supervisors must recognize the uniqueness of the individuals with whom they work if they expect to provide appropriate supervisory behavior.

2. *The social and psychological context in which the supervisory behavior occurs.* The organizational climate, administrative expectations and rewards, time provided for supervision, allocation of human resources for supervision, availability of materials and equipment, and administrative support for supervision are some of the factors from the social and psychological context that should be considered in the effort to provide appropriate supervisory services.

3. *The Supervisors.* The nature of the supervisors is an important consideration. Do they have the relevant knowledge and the skills to provide the needed services? Are they trusted and respected by teachers? Do they trust and respect teachers?

Do the supervisors believe in their own competence, ability to solve problems, potential for helping teachers, and capacity for self-determination and self-growth toward improvement? These considerations are representative of factors that should be examined as a basis for the determination of supervisory strategies and methods.

4. *Organized fields of study.* Our review of the literature indicated that there are a number of fields of study that have generated concepts, theoretical formulations, and research findings, which have implications for the study and practice of instructional supervision. No claim is made that these are the only fields of study. However, we have drawn heavily on the following fields of study in developing the rationale for the positions we have taken and recommendations we have made throughout the book:

1. Communication
2. Motivation
3. Change
4. Leadership
5. Mental health
6. Teaching and Learning
7. Group development
8. Organization

The preceding eight categories are some of the sources of knowledge from which supervisors can derive the conceptual and theoretical basis for their practice. In a sense, we are suggesting an inferred or contingency approach to practice, but also recognizing the need for an explicit statement of the basis of that practice. Such a basis for practice facilitates continuous evaluation and improvement of the basis for practice and the practice itself.

Figure 1-3 may help clarify the relationship of the various sources of knowledge to the instructional supervisory behavior system.

Instructional supervision is defined as a subsystem of the educational organization, which is formally provided by the organization to interact directly with teaching behavior to improve the effectiveness and efficiency of the teaching behavior. Since supervision interacts directly with teaching behavior, it has been concluded that supervisors need to be knowledgeable about the nature of the teachers with whom they interact.

It has also been concluded that supervisors must study themselves. They should know their values, maturities, skill development, feelings about teachers, and influence potential. The authors felt that the supervisor's self-knowledge should be a significant factor in drawing inferences about appropriate supervisory behavior.

Figure 1-3 clearly shows that supervisory behavior takes place in a complex social and psychological environment. Elements of this environment include students, teachers, supervisors, administrators, classroom organization, local school organization, systems organization, the educational community, and larger society. It is our assumption that supervisors need to be aware of the nature of the social and psychological context in which they work. This context not only affects what

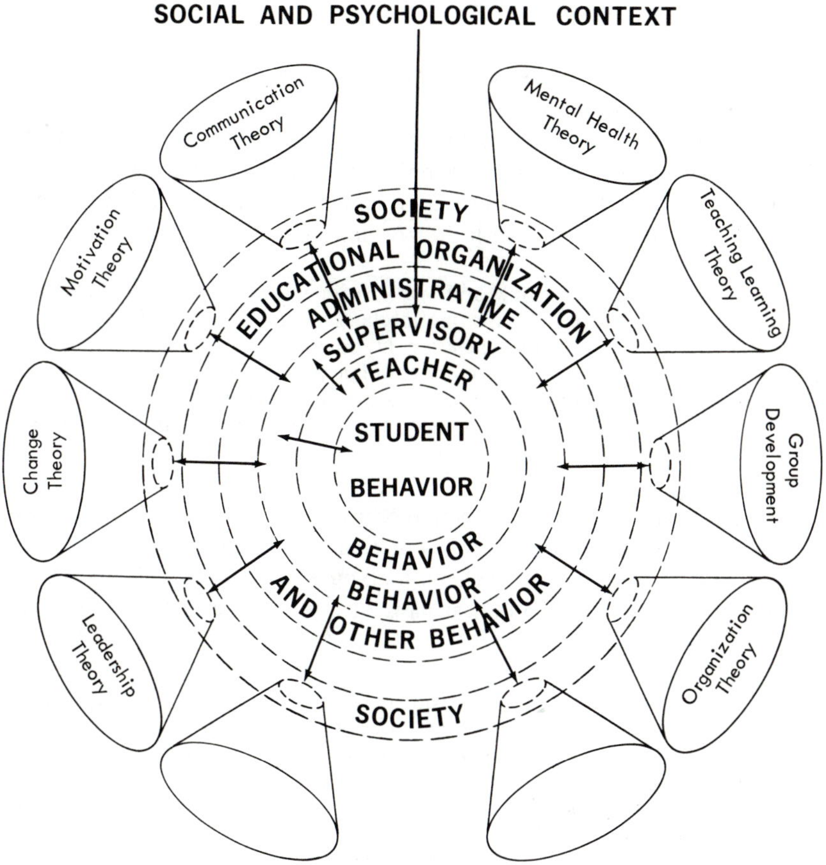

SOCIAL AND PSYCHOLOGICAL CONTEXT

FIGURE 1-3 Social and Psychological Context

Sources of relevant knowledge for the study and practice of instructional supervision. The authors wish to express appreciation to Dr. Ed Taylor for the art work and for suggestions for improving Figure 1-3.

supervisors can and cannot do, but is also subject to change through the efforts of supervisors.

In our review of the literature, we did not find a fully developed theory of supervision that would provide specific directions for supervisors. However, we did identify a number of well-established fields of study that have produced concepts, theoretical formulations, and research findings that have implications for the practice of instructional supervision. These fields of study are shown in Figure 1-3 as external to the educational organization, but as subsystems of the society. It is our contention that the findings from these fields of study have important implications for the conceptual base from which supervisors infer their strategies, methods, and techniques.

THE CONCEPTUAL FRAMEWORK

The definition of instructional supervision helps provide direction for the identification and organization of relevant knowledge that can be used as a basis for planning and implementing supervisory behavior to meet the needs of a particular situation. Supervisors always operate from a theoretical base. The question is whether or not to explicate our theoretical stance or leave it hidden somewhere within the channels of our own thinking. We agree with the position that Getzels (1960, p. 38) took:

> Always, however, we think and work from within some conceptual framework, some theoretical bias, some intellectual stance, which is, of course, to be held "lightly," but nonetheless held, however, provisionally, until a better one comes along. We are in a more strategic position to move forward both in our own thinking and in communicating with others if we make this bias explicit to ourselves and to others than if we keep it "implicit" under the guise of self-proclaimed neutrality.

We agree with Getzels and, therefore, make the following attempt to explicate the conceptual framework of our book on supervision. We invite evaluation, questions, and suggestions and believe that open discussion will contribute to improvement of both the theoretical basis of our practice and its effectiveness.

I. Assumptions
    A. Assumptions about professional workers in educational organizations
        1. Professional workers have worth and dignity.
        2. They possess the capacity to solve their problems and make effective decisions through cooperative action.
        3. They possess potential for growth in ability.
        4. As individuals, they are unique.
        5. They have motivation to improve their effectiveness as professionals.
        6. They have specialized competencies, and a desire and capacity to be self-directing.
        7. Organizational workers are an important source of originality, creativeness, intelligence, and technical skills and, therefore, they are important sources of organizational improvement (Miles, 1965, pp. 148–163).
        8. Professional workers in educational organizations have advanced preparation and considerable specialization as educators.
        9. Teachers are responsible for the efficiency and effectiveness of their teaching activities, and, therefore, must have the authority to develop the learning opportunities for a particular group of students.
      10. It is essential to involve a broad base of educational workers in curriculum development and policy formulation.
      11. People are emotional as well as rational, and their feelings are important and need consideration.
    B. Assumptions about educational organizations

1. Educational organizations are dynamic.
2. Organizations exist to serve students, parents, professional workers, and community.
3. Scientific inquiry is the most effective basis for organizational change.
4. The assumption of organizational members as human resources in the delivery of supervisory services has led us to the need for broadening the base of instructional supervisory behavior (Miles, 1965).
5. It is possible to enhance our understanding of the educational organization by the utilization of "social system theory."
6. Instructional supervisory behavior is a subsystem of the educational organization.
7. The educational organization is a subsystem of the society, and, therefore, the society provides "input," such as specification of educational goals, and human and material resources.
8. The society is the consumer of the output of the educational organization.
9. Educational organizations will become more dynamic with an increasing utilization of temporary systems to solve and identify problems. Instructional supervisors will be used as specialists both in the problem-solving process and in the coordination of the ad hoc systems (Bennis, 1966).
10. Educational organizations will become more concerned with their interaction with their environment (Campbell, 1977–78).
11. Organizations need member behavior characterized by reliability, conformity, and predictability, but organizations have an equally powerful need for member behavior characterized by creativity, unpredictability, and free response. There is a need to keep member behavior in some rational balance between these two sets of needs.

C. Assumptions about instructional supervisory behavior
   1. Instructional supervisory behavior is behavior that is officially designated by the organization for the purpose of directly influencing the "teaching behavior subsystem" in such a way as to facilitate the achievement of students' goals.
   2. The objectives of this behavior system are (Lovell, 1978 p. 42)
      a. Goal development
      b. Psychological and technical support for teachers
      c. Program development and actualization
      d. Evaluation of personnel performance
      e. Development of professional workers
      f. Evaluation of educational outcomes.
   3. The fundamental processes of instructional supervisory behavior are assumed to be
      a. Leadership
      b. Communication
      c. Releasing human potential
      d. Change.
   4. The limits of supervisory authority are defined by the responsibility and requirements of the task.

5. Reliance on scientific knowledge and scientific inquiry in problem-solving activities is the most effective approach.
6. The change process is fundamental, but there is recognition of the importance of stability.
7. It is possible to control to some extent the direction, quality, and amount of change in the "teaching behavior subsystems of the educational organization."
8. Concepts and theoretical formulations from various fields of inquiry can contribute to the formulation of a theory of supervision.
9. Some of the most valuable sources of concepts for understanding supervisory behavior are the behavioral sciences: psychology (with emphasis on learning, motivation, and mental health), social psychology (with emphasis on leadership, group development, and human relations), sociology (with emphasis on community power structure), and communication.
10. It is inappropriate to limit the supervisory behavior system to only those individuals who are formally designated as instructional supervisors.

D. Assumptions about teaching
1. The major components of teaching behavior include
   a. Planning
   b. Actualizing plans
   c. Describing the actualization
   d. Analyzing the actualization
   e. Generalizing back to future planning.
2. Each teacher cannot serve as an independent and autonomous unit in the teaching behavior system. Rather, the activities of teachers must be coordinated in terms of school and system goals.
3. The teaching behavior system must be "open" to input from external sources.
4. Organizations must develop a systematic procedure for the evaluation of the teaching behavior system and the evaluation of the effectiveness of each participant in the teaching behavior system.

II. Concepts, theoretical formulations, and empirical findings which have implications for the study and practice of instructional supervision.
A. Mental health, counseling, therapy
1. A person behaves in the manner that he or she believes best at the moment (Markey and Herbkersman, 1961).
2. People change their behavior as they change their perceptions of themselves, their role, or the situation (Glass, 1964), (Kay and Meyer, 1965), (Kitane, 1962), (Nelson, 1956).
3. The best single predictive indicator of future self-adjustment is the extent to which people are accurate in their knowledge of themselves and their purposes (McGrath, 1962), (Reader and English, 1947), (Tabachnick, 1962).
4. A person who feels worthy, wanted, and adequate is open to change, finds a wider range of facts and experiences significant, is learning, and is becoming more mature (Dowis and Diethelam, 1958), (Reader and English, 1947), (Stith and Connor, 1962).
5. Persons become more open as they live and work in a situation in which they are accepted, find it unnecessary to be defensive and closed, and have access to many new experiences (Ainsworth,

1958), (Feldhusen and Klausmeier, 1962), (Gaier, 1952), (Hallworth, 1961), (Mandler and Sarason, 1952), (Palermo, Castaneda and McCandance, 1956).

6. Persons are assisted in the process of change by others who convey a feeling of acceptance and a desire to be helpful to them in developing self-direction (Festinger and Hutte, 1954), (Markey and Herbkersman, 1961), (Reader and English, 1947), (Stith and Connor, 1962).

B. Learning

1. Human beings learn through their interaction with their environment (Bruner, 1961).

2. Individuals select from the environment the factors with which they will interact (Bahrick, 1954).

3. Persons learn what they perceive that interaction to be, and their perception is a product of their past experiences, their present needs, and their purposes (Bales, Strodtbeck, Mills, and Roseborough, 1951).

4. The individual's learning is affected by his or her emotions. Anxiety inhibits performance. (McKeachie, Pollie, and Speisman, 1955), (Montague, 1953), (Watson and Broomberg, 1965).

5. Learning by discovery, the process of rearranging and reinterpreting evidence to enable the individual to gain new insights, increases intellectual power, aids in retrieval, and brings satisfaction (Bruner, 1961), (Gagne and Brown, 1961), (Hale, 1961), (Kersh, 1958), (Kersh, 1962), (Kersh and Wittrock, 1962), (Kittrell, 1957).

C. Group Development

1. Group cohesiveness is developed through the interaction of individuals (Back, 1951), (Harrison and Lubin, 1965), (Polansky, Lippitt, and Redl, 1950).

2. An aggregation of individuals becomes a group when common goals, common values, and norms are developed (Kiesler, 1963).

3. Cohesive groups are satisfying to members (Festinger, Torrey, and Willerman, 1954), (Hebb, 1958).

4. Group members are influenced by the norms of the group to which they give allegiance (Horowitz, Lyons, and Perlmutter, 1950), (Nelson, 1956), (Strickland, Jones, and Smith, 1960).

5. The greater the prestige an individual attaches to a group, the stronger the influence of its norms on the individual (Festinger, Torrey, and Willerman, 1954).

6. In highly cohesive groups, members make more effort to reach an agreement, behavior is more influenced by the situation, and interaction is more effective in producing influence (Back, 1951), (Gilchrist, Shaw, and Walker, 1954), (Festinger, Torrey, and Willerman, 1954), (Hare, 1952), (Hebb, 1958).

7. Organized groups with past interaction quarrel with frustration, but remain cohesive (Moos and Speisman, 1962), (Myers, 1962).

8. Groups must develop a structure and organization to make and implement decisions (Larson and Mill, 1958).

9. High-incentive groups tend to learn faster and work more efficiently than low-incentive groups (Bahrick, 1954), (Phillips, 1955, pp. 161–164).

10. The behavior of an individual in a group is affected by the position

he or she has in it (Bavelas, 1950), (Beal, Rogers, and Bohlen, 1957), (Bovard, 1951), (McClintock, 1963), (Reeves and Goldman, 1957), (Shaw, 1954).

11. Peripheral members of a group are more susceptible to outside influences (Gilchrist, Shaw, and Walker, 1954), (Thibaut, 1950).

12. Individuals are much more likely to change their perception to accord with the judgment of the group in situations in which the group thinks together than in situations in which the leader dominates the group (Bovard, 1951).

13. High cohesiveness in groups is not necessarily related to high production. Cohesiveness is related to the susceptibility of group members to other group members (Barnett, 1962).

14. Acceptance of self helps the individual to accept others.

15. Valuing of differences enables each to develop his or her uniqueness (Lippitt and White, 1947).

16. Concern for feelings of others is an essential element of effective leadership (Hemphill, 1949).

17. Membership in cohesive supportive groups decreases the emotional instability of individuals (Tabachnick, 1962).

D. Leadership

1. Leadership is one of the functions in group operation that contributes to the formulation and attainment of group goals. An individual is a leader when he or she influences group behavior (Hemphill, 1949), (Jennings, 1950), (Markey and Herbkersman, 1961).

2. Leadership function is widespread and diffused throughout the group. A group has more than one leader. Many individuals within the group exert leadership for other group members (Carter, 1951).

3. The leadership function is fulfilled by different individuals as the situation changes. A group uses the leadership of individuals within it who can assist in the solution of the problem confronting it (Pryer, Flint, and Bass, 1962), (Sterling and Rosenthal, 1950).

4. Leadership is a group role, a product of interaction within the group (Cornell, 1954), (Hemphill, 1949), (Lewin, 1939), Markey and Herbkersman, 1961), (Shaw, 1963).

5. Leadership and followership are interchangeable. The characteristics that make an individual a good leader also make him or her a good follower (Jennings, 1950), (Sterling and Rosenthal, 1950).

6. The leadership exerted by an individual is determined by the extent to which group members can use an individual's contribution (Reger, 1962).

7. The extent to which groups are able to use the participation of individuals as a part of the leadership function is determined by its perception of them, their motives, and competency (Heinicke and Bales, 1953), (Horton and Wohl, 1956), (James, 1955), (Lippitt, Polansky, and Rosen, 1952), (Pascoe, 1963), (Reger, 1962), (Strickland, Jones, and Smith, 1960).

8. The leadership that a group uses is partly determined by norms of the group. If an individual violates the critical norms of a group, his or her participation will not be used as leadership by the group. Group members select for leaders, individuals they believe will

understand, accept, and maintain the group norms (Markey and Herbkersman, 1961), (Sterling and Rosenthal, 1950).

9. Other things being equal, the amount of leadership exerted by an individual is dependent upon the frequency of his or her inter-action with other group members (Hare, 1952), (Hemphill, 1949), (Shaw, 1963), (Wilkins and Decharms, 1962).

10. Qualities found in individuals who frequently contribute to the leadership function are exhibiting willingness to cooperate, com-municating feelings and information, empathizing (Cornell, 1954), (Jennings, 1950), (Wilkins and Decharms, 1962), suggesting new answers to problems, serving others, and demonstrating emotional stability (Hicks and Stone, 1962).

11. Leadership is exerted by individuals with and without official status (Baskin, 1962), (Lewin, 1939), (Shaw, 1963).

12. High-prestige individuals in a group are more spontaneous, make more direct attempts to influence others, and are more open to behavioral contagion than those with low prestige (Kallegian, Brown, and Weschler, 1953), (Myers, 1962), (Polansky, Lippitt, and Redl, 1950).

13. Leadership is behavior on the part of one or more individuals, which influences the behavior of other individuals in a predeter-mined direction (Bass, 1960).

14. The concepts of attempted leadership behavior, successful leader-ship behavior, and effective leadership behavior give direction to the study and practice of leadership behavior (Bass, 1960).

15. Certain personality characteristics are significant factors in the process of leadership (Stogdill, 1974, p. 81).

16. The evidence is strong that there is a positive relationship between follower-oriented leaders and production, and follower-oriented leaders and follower satisfaction. However, the review of the literature by Stogdill shows that there may not be one superior style of leadership behavior, but rather that the effectiveness of a certain style is a function of other factors (Stogdill, 1974).

17. Initiating structure behavior and consideration behavior are two fundamental parts of leadership behavior and are significant contributors to effective leadership (Halpin, 1966, pp. 126–127).

18. Current efforts to study leadership have not produced a complete understanding of leadership effectiveness. But, much is known and has important implications for the behavior of potential leaders (Stogdill, 1974, p. VII).

19. If supervisors wish to encourage staff members to attempt leader-ship, they should reinforce leadership attempts, reward goal accomplishment, and provide opportunities for staff growth (Hemphill, 1961, pp. 101–115).

20. To be successful leaders, it helps for supervisors to have formal authority, have knowledge in areas of group concern, and be esteemed by group members (Bass, 1961, pp. 3–9).

21. According to Doyle (1974), human-relations-oriented leaders are more likely to support group member ideas and are, therefore, more likely to have ideas generated by group members.

22. Fiedler (1976, pp. 6–16) reported that task-motivated leaders are

more likely to be effective in either highly favorable or highly unfavorable situations. Relations-oriented leaders will more often experience success in situations in which they have moderate control and influence. Leadership effectiveness is contingent on the fit between the personality of the leader and the situation.

23. There are at least four styles of leadership behavior.
    a. High task and high relationship
    b. High task and low relationship
    c. Low task and low relationship
    d. Low task and high relationship
    Any of these styles has the potential for being effective or ineffective, depending on the situation (Reddin, 1970), (Hersey and Blanchard, 1977).

24. Leadership behavior is at least partly a function of the maturity level of followers (Hersey and Blanchard, 1977).

25. The "power with" approach to the exercise of leadership is more likely to be effective in most situations involving supervisors and teachers.

E. Communication

1. Communication is never complete and accurate. Its degree of distortion depends upon the openness of the social situation and the desire of the individuals for complete communication (Goetzinger and Valentine, 1964).

2. Communication affects the efficiency at which groups perform and the ability of the groups to develop adequate organization (Bavelas, 1950), (Bavelas and Barrett, 1951), (Boag, 1952), (Cohen, 1958), (Cohen, 1962), (Goetzinger and Valentine, 1964), (Guetzkow and Dill, 1957), (Guetzkow and Simon, 1955), (Gustad, 1962), (Kelley, 1951), (Leavitt, 1951), (Shaw, 1955), (Shaw, 1954).

3. The communication pattern of a group affects its accuracy, emergence of leaders, organization, satisfaction of members, and efficiency (Back, 1951), (Bavelas, 1950), (Bavelas and Barrett, 1951), (Boag, 1952), (Cohen, 1958), (Goetzinger and Valentine, 1964), (Guetzkow and Dill, 1957), (Kelley, 1951), (Leavitt, 1951), (Read, 1962), (Shaw, 1955).

4. In communication patterns with a high, localized centrality, organization evolves quicker and is more stable, speed and accuracy in solving problems are increased, errors in performance are less, and morale tends to drop (Bavelas, 1950), (Bavelas and Barrett, 1951), (Gilchrist, Shaw, and Walker, 1954), (Guetzkow and Dill, 1957), (Leavitt, 1951), (Shaw, 1955), (Shaw, 1954).

5. In communication patterns where centrality is evenly distributed, there is high activity, slow organization, and high satisfaction (Bavelas and Barrett, 1951), (Guetzkow and Dill, 1957), (Leavitt, 1951), (Shaw, 1954).

6. Occurrence and utilization of insight will be found to drop rapidly as centrality becomes highly localized (Bavelas, 1950), (Guetzkow and Dill, 1957).

7. Increasing the amount of information initially available to an individual in a given position in a communication net has the effect of increasing the individual centrality index of that position

or the number of channels available to that position (Cohen, 1958), (Gilchrist, Shaw, and Walker, 1954), (Goetzinger and Valentine, 1954), (Kelley, 1961), (Shaw, 1954).

8. The positions that individuals occupy in a communication pattern affect their behavior while occupying those positions. An individual's position in the group affects the chances of his or her becoming a leader in the group, his or her satisfaction with the job and with the group, the quantity of his or her activity, and the extent to which he or she contributes to the group's functional organization (Bales, Strodtbeck, Mills, and Roseborough, 1951), (Bavelas, 1950), (Bavelas and Barrett, 1951), (Cohen, 1958), (Cohen, 1962), (Goetzinger and Valentine, 1964), (Guetzkow and Dill, 1957), (Kelley, 1951), (Leavitt, 1951), (Shaw, 1955), (Shaw, 1954), (Shaw, Rothschile, and Strickland, 1957).

9. A recognized leader in a task-oriented group will most probably emerge at the center of the communication pattern (Bavelas and Barrett, 1951), (Leavitt, 1951), (Shaw, 1954).

10. Communication isolation, a situation in which the individual acts without essential data, frequently alienates the individual from the group (Boag, 1952), (Cohen, 1958), (Goetzinger and Valentine, 1964), (Jenkins and Lippitt, 1951), (Kelley, 1951), (Read, 1962).

11. The completion of the circuit between sender and receiver (feedback) increases the accuracy with which information is transmitted (Goetzinger and Valentine, 1964), (Leavitt and Meuller, 1951), (Lysgaard, 1955).

12. The behavior of a group toward a person is affected by the credibility of that person as a source of information (Aronson and Godlen, 1962), (Bergin, 1962), (Eagle, 1959), (Hoveland and Weiss, 1951), (Runkel, 1956), (Zander and Cohen, 1955).

13. The message is distorted by feelings of superiority or inferiority of the individuals involved (Cohen, 1958), (Kelley, 1951).

14. The ability of highly anxious subjects to communicate is less than that of nonanxious subjects (Cohen, 1958), (Shaw, 1963), (Steiner, 1963).

15. Language that is apparently adequate for superficial communication may not be adequate for understanding deeper meanings (Bennett and McKnight, 1956), (Brown and Lenneberg, 1954), (Lionberger and Milton, 1957).

F. Community Power Structure
1. Each community has a power structure in which certain individuals make the decisions of others. In complex (competitive) communities, the power structure may be distributed in several peaks that represent the power figures of different segments of the population. In homogeneous (monopolistic) communities, the power structure may have only one peak and the decision making is concentrated in a very few individuals (Kimbrough, 1964).

2. The overt decision making is not necessarily the real decision making in a community (Kimbrough and Nunnery, 1971).

3. Decisions made and actions taken by legal bodies and community institutions reflect the decisions of the community power structure (Kimbrough, 1964), (Kimbrough, 1965).

G. Supervisory Behavior
1. It is possible and helpful to think of instructional supervision as a behavior system with two interdependent dimensions:
   a. The helping, supporting, and servicing dimension.
   b. The coordinating dimension (Esposito, Smith, and Burback, 1975), (Lovell, 1978).
2. The need for quality control for instruction and curriculum development will continue to be an important function of instructional supervision (Lovell, 1978).
3. Teachers desire and have a need for instructional services (Lovell and Phelps, 1977).
4. Direct services for teachers, to help them improve their performance with a particular group of students, will continue to grow in importance, and clinical supervision will continue as an important system for providing these services.
5. The inevitable conflicts between the needs of teachers and the needs of the organization means that the instructional supervisory behavior system must be geared to provide a climate and structure to deal with possible negative outcomes, such as poor teacher motivation or alienation.

H. Organizational Behavior
1. The behavior of members of educational organizations can be partly explained by the organizational expectations for member behavior and the need dispositions of individual members (Getzels, 1958).
2. An organization's effectiveness is at least partly a function of its structure, the needs of its members, its goals, and the way these factors relate to each other (Morse and Lorsh, 1970).
3. An important principle of organizational effectiveness is the integration of the needs of the organization's members and the organization's goals (McGregor, 1957).
4. The formal bureaucratic model is not adequate unto itself as a model for educational organizations.
5. Educational organizations need member behavior characterized by creativity, risk taking, high motivation, and competence. Organizational members need an opportunity to take risks, be original, and experience the satisfaction of outstanding performance and rewards for their performance.
6. Organizational effectiveness is at least partly a function of member opportunities to be self-directing, self-improving, and part of a self-directing group (Gyllenhammar, 1977, pp. 102–113).

I. Change
1. Changes in the external and internal environment of the educational organization provide forces that produce the need for continuous change. The initiation, support, and evaluation of change will continue to grow as an important function of instructional supervision (Lovell, 1978, p. 43).
2. Social systems can be described in terms of boundary, tension, equilibration-disequilibration, and feedback (Chin, 1976, pp. 90–101).
3. It is possible for supervisors and teachers to at least partly control the process in which old goals and processes are questioned and

new directions and procedures are instituted. Further, some external and internal forces can be influenced or activated so as to control to some extent the change process (Chin, 1976, pp. 99–102).

4. It is through the application of certain principles of leadership, communication, motivation, and problem solving that it is possible for teachers, administrators, and students to influence the change process in educational organizations.

5. It is our assumption that the three strategies for change defined by Chin and Benne (1976, pp. 22–45)—impirical-rational, normative, reeducative, and power—have relevance for the change process in educational organizations. However, the normative reeducative is the most effective approach for instructional supervisors under most circumstances.

6. It is possible and helpful to conceptualize three phases of the change process: unfreezing, moving, and refreezing. When driving forces for change or restraining forces against change are equal, the system will not change. Change occurs as a function of increasing driving forces and of decreasing restraining forces (Lewin, 1947, pp. 340–344).

7. Blake and Mouton (1976, pp. 48–68) discussed five intervention strategies: acceptant intervention, catalytic intervention, confrontation intervention, prescriptive and self-correcting approach. We believe all of these approaches may be appropriate, contingent on the demands of the situation. However, we believe the self-directing and self-improving approach is most effective in most situations in the practice of instructional supervision.

8. Rogers (1962) indicated the change process has three parts: antecedents, process, and results. The antecedents of change were theorized as the psychological dynamics of the innovator and the innovator's perception of the situation.

J. Motivation

1. Human potential in educational organizations is not fully utilized. It is important for the instructional supervisory behavior system to facilitate an organizational environment characterized by openness and opportunities for new experience (Lionberger, 1957).

2. It is important for organizations to have teachers whose behavior is characterized by authenticity. Since we develop as persons through our interaction with others, it is important for supervisors to attempt to facilitate a social climate for teachers in which teachers can develop a more positive self-concept and thus become more open to new experience (Rogers, 1971, p. 215).

3. Motivation is what an individual is willing to do in order to achieve some outcome.

4. Motivation is a function of the needs of the individual, the anticipated rewards associated with a particular goal, and the individual's estimate of the probability of achieving the goal (House, 1971, p. 321), (Hersey and Blanchard, 1977, pp. 51–81).

5. The lack of motivation in an educational organization is often a function of incompatibility between the needs of the organization and the needs of organizational members (Maslow, 1954), (McGregor, 1960), (Herzberg, 1959).

6. Important human needs include physiological, security, belonging, ego development, self-actualization (Maslow, 1954), freedom and autonomy (Kelly and Rasey, 1954, p. 103), competence (Morse and Lorsch, 1970, p. 67).

7. We have concluded that when teachers have an opportunity to participate in certain kinds of decision making, the result is an improvement in the organization, which contributes to improved satisfaction and motivation (Miles, 1965, pp. 148–163).

8. The motivation of professional workers in educational organizations is at least partly a function of the fit among the following factors:
   a. Formal structure
   b. Needs of people
   c. Tasks (Morse and Lorsch, 1970, pp. 61–66).

9. Successful performance contributes to a feeling of competence, which in turn contributes to the level of motivation (Morse and Lorsch, 1970, pp. 61–66).

10. Achievement, recognition, work itself, responsibility, and interpersonal relations with students are factors that have been shown to contribute to teacher satisfaction (Herzberg, 1959), (Savage, 1967), (Sergiovanni, 1967, pp. 66–82), (Holdoway, 1978, pp. 30–47).

11. Teacher participation in decisions related to the technical domain is related to the teacher's extrinsic and intrinsic satisfaction (Mohrman, Cooke, and Mohrman, 1978, pp. 13–29).

Throughout this book, these propositions will provide the basis for advancing hypotheses about the ways in which administrators, directors, supervisors, and resource personnel should work with faculties and individual teachers. Although each practice recommended has proved itself in some school system, it has also been tested against the integrated theory evolved by examination of the interrelationships of the selected concepts.

Each person who reads the book is encouraged to check the congruence of the recommended practices and the conceptual framework and to test the recommended practices against his or her experience. Where the reader finds differences, he or she is encouraged to explore the degree to which variation in results occurred as a product of divergence in assumptions.

Theory is the most practical instrument any professional has. It guides practice and inquiry. It enables the professional to engage constantly in a process of self-education.

2

THE EVOLVEMENT OF INSTRUCTIONAL SUPERVISION

The current status of the practice and theoretical development of instructional supervision is at least partly a function of its historical evolvement. The assumption on which Chapter 2 was developed is that a look backward provides perspective for analysis and understanding of the present as well as a basis for the development of new ideas, understandings, and practices for the future. There have been major thrusts in the development of instructional supervision, and it is possible in a general way to identify them chronologically. It is apparent that these major movements do not start and stop at some precise time and place. Rather, they tend to start gradually in many places and continue to persist so that threads of past practice can still be found in current practice.

It is assumed that through a study of the historical development of supervision it is possible to learn and profit both from past mistakes and past successes. This does not imply the acceptance of a cyclical interpretation of history. It does mean that there are present events that have similarities to events of the past. There are suggestions and recommendations for educational change that have been resurrected from the past. It is hoped that a study of the historical origin of these ideas will contribute to sound decisions regarding their current suitability. For example, the current cry for specification of behavioral objectives and educational accountability has roots in the "scientific management movement." This fact does not mean the ideas are good or bad. It does mean we may already have some relevant evidence.

Major developments in the study and practice of instructional supervision can be organized around the assumptions made about the human being to be supervised. March and Simon (1961, p. 6) have grouped propositions about organizational behavior in three broad classes as follows:

1. Propositions assuming that organization members, and particularly employees, are primarily passive instruments, capable of performing work and accepting directions, but not initiating action or exerting influence in any significant way.
2. Propositions assuming that members bring to their organizations attitudes, values, and goals; that they have to be motivated or induced to participate in the system of organization behavior; that there is incomplete parallelism between their personal goals and organization goals; and that actual or potential goal conflicts make power phenomena, attitudes, and morale centrally important in the explanation of organizational behavior.
3. Propositions assuming that organization members are decision makers and problem solvers, and that perception and thought processes are central to the explanation of behavior in organizations.

The periods of "administrative inspection" and later scientific management were characterized by the assumption of the employee as a passive instrument or tool of management who could be manipulated in such a way as to achieve the goals of the organization. The period of scientific management began in the early part of the twentieth century and is still an important factor in supervision. In the later part of the first quarter of the twentieth century, as a result of certain theoretical formulations and empirical studies, questions were raised about scientific management since it became apparent that it did not explain all events. This brought on the beginning of the "human relations movement," which is still a dominating factor in supervisory practice.

Currently, theorists are turning to the assumption of the rationality of people as well as their emotions and attitudes. This is beginning to influence supervisory behavior in educational institutions. Accordingly, Chapter 2 is organized around these major movements as they have affected instructional supervisory behavior in educational institutions.

ADMINISTRATIVE INSPECTION

Supervision during the early part of the eighteenth century was described by Burton and Brueckner (1966). Committees of citizens were appointed to inspect the plant and equipment as well as to check on pupil achievement. The primary focus of these committees was to determine the extent to which teachers were doing their job, based on the "inspection," and to take appropriate action. Several factors deserve special comment. First, the inspectors were lay citizens and therefore operating on the assumption that no special professional competence was required for supervisors. Second, there was no effort to improve teachers or teaching. There was an effort to determine whether children were learning. If a problem was identified, teachers were expected to improve, or else. There was no assumption of a science of teaching that could be taught or learned. Third, there is no evidence that these inspectors were particularly concerned about the emotions, feelings, attitudes, or morale of the teachers. Fourth, the inspectors, lay citizens, held the teachers accountable for the pupil achievement. It is interesting to note the current emphasis on accountability and lay participation.

As schools became larger and it was necessary to have multiple teachers, one teacher would often be singled out as the "principal" teacher and would be assigned certain managerial functions. But these building "principals" did not assume responsibility for improvement of the instructional program at this time (Burton and Brueckner, 1966).

During the nineteenth century, the schools were growing, population was growing, and people were beginning to crowd into urban centers. These changes called not only for multiple teachers but also for multiple schools. As a result of the growing complexity of school systems, the functions of lay boards or citizens' committees began to be placed in the hands of superintendents, and the improvement of teaching became an important function of these positions (Ayer and Barr, 1928, pp. 7–28). By the latter part of the nineteenth century, there were twenty-nine superintendents of schools in the United States, and the superintendents were seeking to improve teachers and teaching as well as to reject inadequate teaching (Lucio and McNeil, 1969, p. 4).

As school systems became larger with more and more teachers in more widely scattered facilities, superintendents found it increasingly difficult to meet their responsibilities for supervision of the instructional program. Therefore, they added additional professionals to their staffs, and these personnel became general supervisors and began to develop the role. Since these supervisors were appointed by the superintendent, it was natural that they worked from his or her office and as representatives of the superintendent. Thus, there was the development of a highly centralized system of supervision. This situation probably helps explain some of the relationship problems that developed between building principals and general supervisors, as well as difficulties the schools have experienced in developing the instructional leadership function of the school principal. As schools continued to grow, the highly centralized structure persisted.

Another significant development for supervision was the addition to the curriculum of certain new subjects that required special competence that teachers in the schools did not have. "Special teachers" were hired to teach these subjects. In some cases they became "regular" teachers for these subjects. But in other cases they became traveling teachers and taught the special subjects in different schools on different days. These "special teachers" began advising and working with the regular teachers, and under some circumstances the regular teachers taught the special courses under the supervision of the special teachers, who became special supervisors.

In summary, supervision during the period of "administrative inspection" was conducted on the assumption that the workers (teachers) were passive tools of the organization and would do, or had better do, what was expected of them. Supervision was telling, inspecting, rating, checking, and monitoring. It wasn't until the later part of the nineteenth century that improvement of teachers and teaching became a well-established function of instructional supervision.

SCIENTIFIC MANAGEMENT

At the beginning of the twentieth century the industrial revolution was a dominant factor in American life and the method of science was the major approach used by industry. Scientific management became the dominant theory for organizational improvement, largely through the creative and scholarly efforts of a relatively small group of organizational theorists (March and Simon, 1961). A spokesman for scientific management was Frederick Taylor, whose primary concern was to increase efficiency in industrial organizations. The assumption that the worker was a passive instrument who could be manipulated to achieve the goals of the organization was the same as the assumption for the practice of "administrative inspection," but the methods of science were applied to achieve the greatest possibly efficiency.

In the application of scientific management, people were assumed to be motivated by economic gain, and foremen "supervisors" established the conditions of work, the best methods for proceeding, and the overseeing of the job. Time and motion studies were used to determine the "one best way" of achieving a special task. Workers were expected to do it that way and supervisors were there to see that they did.

Scientific management had important implications for educational organizations and various educational leaders took up the gauntlet to make public schools more efficient. Cubberley (1916, p. 338) referred to the fact that industry was working to turn out a standard product and to produce it with the most efficient methods. This objective called for the scientific study of methods of production and the scientific measurement of the output. He advocated this model for the public schools, which were seen as factories with the children as the raw material to be changed according to the specifications of society and with the greatest efficiency. He called for the use of the methods of science to determine the most efficient methods of teaching and to measure the outcomes of student learning.

Bobbitt (1912) was one of the important advocates of scientific management for the schools. He was concerned with the elimination of waste, efficiency of workers, and continuous use of facilities. He was also concerned with finding the most efficient and effective educational methodology and utilizing supervisors to see that teachers carried it out. Kliebard (1971, p. 81) interpreted Bobbitt's writing as follows:

> . . . Extrapolating from this and other examples, Bobbitt went on to comment on the functions of specialized supervisors in schools in determining "proper

methods" and "the determination of more or less definite qualifications for the various aspects of the teaching personality." The supervisor of instruction occupied that middle-management function roughly comparable to the foreman in industry.

The move toward standardization and particularization of educational objectives and methods had important implications for the evolvement of educational supervision. After objectives had been predetermined and the best way of achieving them had been scientifically established, it was the function of supervision to see to it that the workers (teachers) carried out the specifications. The specifications were complete and there was little or no concern with the teachers as human beings except as instruments for getting the job done. Teachers were paid and were expected to perform with efficiency. If not, they were either taught to do so or relieved of their assignment. Supervision was telling, explaining, showing, enforcing, rating, and rewarding. In a general way this was the status of instructional supervision during the first quarter of the twentieth century. Naturally, there was a variety of patterns. Some systems operated on a laissez-faire pattern in which teachers were expected to produce and were left to their own resources. There were also rigid systems of inspection and rating, which had roots in the earlier period of "administrative inspection." But the fundamental assumption was that the teacher was an instrument who could be used and molded by the administration to facilitate the achievement of the goals of the educational organization. Little concern for the feelings, attitudes, and motivations of teachers was expressed. A combination of factors, including the development of theoretical formulations and empirical findings as well as certain social developments, set in motion a challenge to the "theory" of scientific management and laid the foundation for a growing concern with the psychological well-being of organizational members.

SUPERVISION AND HUMAN CONCERN
IN EDUCATIONAL ORGANIZATIONS

Instructional supervision during the second quarter of the twentieth century was characterized by a growing concern with the nature and needs of human beings in the educational organization. The assumption that human beings in the organization have their own goals, values, feelings, emotions, and needs, which affect their need to behave in certain ways, and that these factors are important determinants of the efficiency and effectiveness of worker behavior was a dominant factor in the theory and practice of supervision.

The famous Hawthorne Studies carried out by Elton Mayo and others (Mayo, 1933), (Roethlisberger and Dickson, 1947) led to serious challenges against the principles of scientific management. The finding that relationships between workers and supervisors could be a more potent factor in production than a variety of environmental conditions shook the scientific thinking about supervision of that day. The conclusion that the informal social system that workers form can be an important stimulant in setting standards for worker production led to a barrage of research and changes in the practice of supervision.

The study of social groups coming from the behavioral sciences also had a profound effect on the growing body of literature on instructional supervision as well as the practice. Lewin (1943, 1944, pp. 195-200), Homans (1950), Lippitt and White (1947), to name only a few, were significant contributors. The concept of group structure was verified. Subconcepts such as interaction, activity, and group sentiment were defined to describe the internal structure of groups. Research findings indicated that group members who participate in making group decisions are more likely to accept and act on these decisions. A person's position in the social group can be an important factor in behavior, including work production. Groups have norms of behavior for their members, and these norms are important factors in the behavior of group members. Those members most attracted to the group are more likely to act according to group norms.

The study of leadership behavior also had an important effect on educational supervision. Of particular significance were the works of Lippitt and White (1947), Stogdill (1948, pp. 35-71), Lewin (1930, pp. 21-32), Bavelas (1942, pp. 143-165) and many others. Through these studies, focus was placed on the importance of the behavior of organizational leaders. Questions were being posed and studied concerning the nature of leadership behavior and variables related to leadership effectiveness. The study of the "traits" of leaders and the attempt to correlate certain traits with certain criteria of leadership effectiveness were early approaches. The "styles" of leadership behavior were also studied. Findings indicated that the same groups or similar groups operating under different styles of leadership will develop different group structure and group production. Since the early studies were developed around democratic and authoritarian styles and since the democratic style came out with "favorable" results, "democratic supervision" took on a new significance.

The thirties was a period of depression, economic suffering, and disenchantment with the business community. Angry young men were speaking out against economic oppression and for human rights and democratic principles. Therefore, it is not surprising to find a strong trend toward introducing democratic principles in organizational governance. This factor became especially important in the literature and practice of educational administration and instructional supervision.

The impact of these various strands of thought on the body of professional literature of this period was significant. Even the titles of important textbooks of this period are indicative of the trends of the day:

1. John Bartky, *Supervision as Human Relations*
2. Charles Boardman, *Democratic Supervision in Secondary Schools*
3. William H. Burton and Leo J. Brueckner, *Supervision, A Social Process*

In an earlier edition of *Supervision for Better Schools* Wiles developed a concept of supervision around the subconcepts of skill in leadership, skill in group process, skill in evaluation, and skill in human relations. Emphasis was placed on building staff morale, release of the creative energies of group members, shared leadership, cooperative decision making, self-evaluation, and developing staff leadership. The central focus was on the behavior of the supervisor and his or her attempt to influence the behavior of teachers. Significant research was listed that provided the rationale of the book (Wiles, 1950).

Burton and Brueckner (1955) put strong emphasis on social process, social change, principles of democratic supervision, cooperative planning, and leadership, but also included the improvement of the educational program through the study of the learner, instruction, curriculum, and the use of materials of instruction.

It is clear that the professors of education had joined the "tide" of the human relations movement. A brief review of the literature and activities of the Department of Supervisors and Directors of Instruction, which later became the Association for Supervision and Curriculum Development, also revealed a strong and lasting influence of this movement. Democratic principles were defined and applied to the supervisory role. It was assumed that teachers were capable of participating in decisions on teaching and curriculum. The role of the supervisor was to provide a climate where this participation could happen. Much was written about group process, the importance of morale, cooperative problem solving, worth and dignity of the individual, leadership, and positive support. Less was written about supervision as maintenance and improvement of quality teaching and learning, and the necessity for responsibility and authority.

Even more important was the fact that the Association of Supervision and Curriculum Development emerged as a powerful and influential organization during the forties. Their national meetings were well attended by supervisors, and they were taught group process and democratic leadership, not only by the excellent literature and speeches of the organization, but also by having an opportunity to "live it" during these meetings. Topics were discussed in small groups according to principles of group process. Participants were involved, and the organization grew in strength and national prestige.

Things began to happen in the schools. The title "supervisor" (long associated with overseer or monitor) began to disappear and was replaced by "consultant," "resource person," "helping teacher," "coordinator," and others. The assumption was that it was essential for the needs of teachers to be met, and this practice sometimes became "keeping them happy." The approach was to provide a non-threatening source of help for teachers. Supervisors worked at developing a comfortable and facilitating climate. Often superintendents would announce that supervisors were "simply" resource people and had no authority in the organization. These approaches were quite a change from the first quarter of the century when there was a highly centralized system and supervisors came from the central office as personal representatives of the superintendent. During the period of "scientific management," courses of study were developed by "curriculum experts" in the central office, and the supervisors took the "word" to the local schools, where they checked to see that the "word" was being carried out. What a shift! The curriculum was now being defined as what happens to students under the direction of the school (Caswell and Campbell, 1935) and the basic agency for school improvement had shifted from the central office to the local school (Miel, 1946, p. 69). Supervisors were resource people, on call, waiting for requests for services.

Some supervisors became dispensers of happiness, using slaps on the back and offerings of coffee and cookies as important techniques. In some cases, supervisors were able to work effectively in this setting and maintain close contact with teachers and the instructional program. But in many situations, supervisors lost significant contact with local schools, teachers, and the instructional program. Problems developed. Teachers did not request services. Many principals of local schools were not trained, experienced, or inclined to assume responsibility for leadership for the instructional program. Roles, responsibility, and authority were unclear in many situations and contributed to poor communication and working relationships between central office supervisors and local school principals. There were also many incidences of poor working relations between supervisors and teachers. Services weren't requested. When they were, supervisors were often more interested in being "democratic" than in helping teachers identify and solve problems. Many teachers did not trust the new approach that supervisors were using and felt that they were still "supervisors." Some supervisors failed to live up to expectations of some teachers, who longed for the "old" supervisors.

The picture was not all rosy. There were serious problems, and it was becoming clear that the "human relations" approach was not the total answer. Practitioners were raising questions and demanding answers.

THE MOVEMENT TOWARD
INTERACTION THEORIES

During the last half of the twentieth century, several important developments emerged, which had important implications for instructional supervision. First, largely as a reaction to some of the dysfunctions of the human relations movement, organizational theorists, such as Etzioni, and March and Simon, developed a more structured view of organizations, referred to as "Structuralism." The challenge to formal bureaucracy continued with a renewed interest in the functional consequences of bureaucracy. Concern for humans in the organization persisted, but extended beyond "human relations" to recognition of organizational members as vital human resources who can make significant contributions as rational decision makers and problem solvers. The utilization of research and theory coming from the behavioral and social sciences continued and intensified, and there were significant efforts to define and explain instructional supervision.

Structuralism

The "structuralist" position is defined by Etzioni (1964, p. 41) as follows:

Having many sources but only one adversary, the Structuralist approach is a synthesis of the Classical (or formal) school and the Human Relations (or informal) one, drawing also on the work of Max Weber, and, to a degree, that of Karl Marx. But its major dialogue has been with the Human Relations approach. Its foundations are best understood through examination of the criticism it raised against this school. It is in exploring the "harmony" view of the Human Relations writers that the Structuralist writers first recognize fully the organizational dilemma: the inevitable strains—which can be reduced but not eliminated—between organizational needs and personal needs; between rationality and non-rationality; between discipline and autonomy; between formal and informal relations; between management and workers, or, more generically, between ranks and divisions.

Adherents of "scientific management" emphasized the formal organization, with a focus on specialization, and on clearly defined tasks and jobs, with enough formal authority to get the job done. The "human relations" movement recognized the informal organization and the importance of the human beings and their needs and feelings as significant factors in organizational efficiency and effectiveness. It was the structuralists who related these concepts and developed a new synthesis. They recognized and accepted the fact that organizations have goals and have needs for member behavior that is goal directed. But, they also saw that individuals in organizations had their own goals and needs, and that individual needs and organizational needs were not always in harmony. This conflict of needs often caused member dissatisfaction and even alienation. Therefore, the structuralists looked to organizational structure as a way of coping with member alienation.

The structuralists built on the concept of bureaucracy developed by Weber. Some of the essential characteristics of the bureaucratic model were identified by Blau (1956) as "hierarchy of authority, impersonalization of management, tasks achieved through fixed positions or structures and control maintained through general rules."

From inspection alone, it seems apparent that Weber's "ideal" type of organization and the structure of educational organizations are quite similar.

Careful observers such as Miles (1965, pp. 54-72), and Moeller (Moeller and Charter, 1966, pp. 444-65), reached similar conclusions. Kliebard (1971, p. 74) explored the influence of bureaucratic ideas in educational organizations:

The picture that emerges from the apparently frenetic educational activity during the first few decades of this century seems to be one of growing acceptance of a powerful and restrictive bureaucratic model for education which looked toward the management techniques of industry as its ideal of excellence and source of inspiration.

Many students of bureaucracy became increasingly concerned with the unexpected consequences of bureaucracy: Merton (1940, pp. 560–68), Selznick (1949), Gouldner (1954), Argyris (1961), Kliebard (1971), Arnstine (1971), Miles (1965), and Blau and Scott (1962), among others. Merton, for example, found that the demand for control, with the intended result of emphasis on reliability, also resulted in rigidity of behavior (unintended) and an amount of difficulty with clients (unintended). The difficulty with clients resulted in a greater felt need for defensibility of individual action, which leads to greater emphasis on reliability and more difficulty with clients.

Kliebard developed the thesis that the assumptions and needs of bureaucratic educational organizations lead to "dehumanization of education, the alienation of means from ends, the stifling of intellectual curiosity," and he describes this as a tragic paradox (Kliebard, 1971, p. 92). Arnstine developed the idea that intellectual freedom is a necessary ingredient in the educational process and that though it is possible to think about intellectual freedom without political freedom, it is never possible to actually have it. Since bureaucracy cannot tolerate political freedom, it is necessary to shake the shackles of bureaucracy in school governance in order to have an effective system of education (Arnstine, 1971, pp. 5–8). Blau and Scott (1962, p. 242) defined the following dilemmas of formal organizations: "1. coordination and communication; 2. bureaucratic discipline and professional expertness; 3. managerial planning and initiative."

McGregor compared two sets of contrasting assumptions that could serve as a frame of reference for the management of organizations. In theory X and theory Y, management was assumed to have the responsibility for organizing the elements of production to achieve certain economic ends. In theory X, however, people were assumed to be lazy, irresponsible, unresponsive, incapable and/or unwilling to be self-directing and self-controlling, and resistant to change. Therefore, it was necessary for management to direct, control, motivate, inspect, and modify the behavior of organizational members to fit the needs of management.

In theory Y, people are not assumed to be naturally lazy, unmotivated, and incapable of self-direction. Rather, they have become that way as a result of management practices. Therefore, it is the function of management to provide the structure in which organizational members can develop their talent, creativeness, and motivation through participation in decision making and problem-solving activities. It is assumed that people can achieve their own goals by self-directed work toward the goals of the organization (Bennis and Schein, 1966).

Much of the work on the study and analysis of the organizational environment has been done with focus on industrial organizations. Certainly, we take the position that such work has important implications for educational organizations. But, some work is being done in educational organizations. Halpin and Croft (1963, pp. 55–67) have made an important contribution to this body of literature. They developed the Organizational Climate Description Questionnaire as a way of describing the climate in various schools. The work resulted in the delineation of six distinctive school climates, which range from open to closed.

In the open climate the groups were extremely high on esprit and low on disengagement and hindrance. They were "with it" and worked well together without the need for great intimacy. The group leader's behavior was perceived as high on thrust and consideration, but low on aloofness and production emphasis. The formal leader was perceived as being highly motivated to work hard, but did not have to provide close supervision or emphasize production by subordinates.

The closed climate was characterized by high disengagement, hindrance, intimacy, aloofness, and production emphasis, and low esprit, thrust, and consideration. The other climates—autonomous, controlled, familiar, and paternal—were also described.

Halpin and Croft (1963, pp. 112-16) were much interested in the fact that they observed that the behavior of organizational members in the more open climates was much more "authentic" than behavior in the more closed climates. In the closed climate it almost appeared that people were playing a part in a play, whereas in the open climate the action was authentic.

Halpin's (1966, pp. 81-127) formulation of initiation of structure behavior and consideration behavior as two important predictors of leadership behavior was closely related to the effort to synthesize scientific management and human relations. Halpin demonstrated that effective leadership behavior is not just a function of structure or just a function of human relations, but that both variables make a contribution.

Getzels (1958, pp. 150-165) developed a model that explained "observed" behavior in organizational social systems as a function of two dimensions. The "nomethetic" dimension was defined as institutional expectations of behavior for the role incumbent. The "idiographic" dimension was defined as the individual's special need disposition to behave in certain ways. Thus, the behavior of the individual in an organization was explained as a function of the interaction of these two sets of forces.

It became increasingly apparent that the formal bureaucratic model had serious disadvantages for organizations in general, but was especially inadequate for the institution of education because of certain special characteristics:

1. The fact that the "work" of the organization is done by highly trained and specialized professionals
2. The difficulty of measuring and evaluating the "output" and "input" of the educational organization
3. The fact of "person" specialization rather than "task" specialization
4. The relative isolation of the teacher-pupil system and, therefore, the lack of a comprehensive system of "supervision"
5. The need for intellectual freedom
6. The nature of human relations in the learning process
7. The need for flexibility and adaptability.

It is true that in the educational organization there is a need for control, general rules, and consistency of response. But, there is also a need for creative response, initiative, adaptiveness, and freedom of movement. The effort to control sometimes leads to teacher dissatisfaction, rigidity, and defensiveness. These conditions tended to stifle creative problem solving, flexibility, and willingness to learn new skills and try new ideas. Communication channels were often blocked, and the opportunities for teachers to share ideas and learn from each other were often stifled. It became increasingly clear that educational organizations needed a structure that not only provided for coordination of personnel but also for psychological support growth and development, creative response, recognition of achievement, and nonthreatening opportunities to participate in school improvement through experimental and developmental activities.

Bennis (1976, pp. 84–101) related that a short while ago he had predicted that in twenty-five to fifty years we would experience the end of "bureaucracy." He now feels that his prediction is already a distinct reality. He identified the following problems with which organizations of the future must cope:

1. Integration
2. Social Influence
3. Collaboration
4. Adaptation
5. Revitalization.

These are the problems that organizations face, and it is the contribution of Bennis (1976) that "new" organizational arrangements will be developed and implemented. He proposed a new organizational arrangement, which he called "organic-adaptive structure." This concept will be discussed in the following section.

The preceding references are examples that were chosen from a growing body of literature that is concerned with both organizational goals and human goals and the way they relate one to the other. The need is for an organizational structure that recognizes

1. The organizational member's need to use his or her creative talents and the organization's need for those creative talents
2. The organizational member's need to be involved in decision making and problem solving and the organization's need to have decisions made and problems solved
3. The organizational member's need to be included in communication and contribute to it and the organization's need for communication
4. The organizational member's need to be authentic and the organization's need for authentic behavior
5. The organizational member's need for control and a chance to participate in the development of the control structure and the organization's need for a control structure
6. The organizational member's need for recognition, creative work, and satisfaction of work well done, and the organization's need for highly motivated workers.

Open Systems

According to Campbell (1977-78) the open-systems concept of organizations focuses on the organization's interaction with its environment. Part of the organization's environment is external to the boundary of the organization and part of it is internal. Therefore, the organization is not only concerned with inputs from the outside, but is also concerned with the interaction of various organizational subsystems.

According to Scott (1975, p. 18), when organizations are viewed as open systems, the following questions become important:

1. What are the parts of the system?
2. How do they relate one to the other?
3. What are the means for linking the parts together?
4. What are the goals of the system?

The parts of the systems were identified as the individual, the formal organization, the informal organization, status and role patterns, and the physical environment.

It is obvious that the parts of the system are interdependent in the effort to achieve certain goals. Scott (1975, p. 19) identified the linking processes of the organization as communication, balance, and decision making. He identified the goals of organizations as growth, stability, and interaction. Organizations as open systems must be able to change and grow to meet changing conditions in both the internal and external environments. However, there is also a strong need for stability, reliability, and conformity to provide a base of coordinated and directed energy to meet constantly changing needs.

Another important contribution in this area was the concept of human resources presented by Miles (1965, pp. 148-163). He made the assumption that organizational members are capable of making important contributions to the achievement of organizational goals. He also indicated that these human resources are not being utilized to their full potential and in fact represent important untapped resources. Therefore, it is important for organizational leaders to provide a structure that facilitates the utilization of the competence and creativeness of organizational members on important matters of organizational policy formulation and problem solving.

According to Bennis (1976, pp. 84-101), organizations of the future will be characterized by "adaptive, problem-solving, temporary systems of diverse specialists, linked together by coordinating and task-evaluating specialists in an organic flux." He calls such structures "organic-adaptive." He further points out the following conditions that will influence organizational life in the future: rapidly changing environment, highly educated organizational members who are highly committed to their positions, and organizational tasks that are technical, complex, and unpredictable.

Morse and Lorsh (1970, pp. 61-68) developed "contingency theory" as a possible explanation of organizational effectiveness and efficiency. They found in the study of several firms that effectiveness was a function of the fit among organizational arrangements, tasks, and the needs of organizational members. The implication is that there is not one best organizational arrangement, but rather the "best" arrangement for any organization is contingent on member needs, tasks to be accomplished, organizational arrangements, and the way these components relate one to the other.

Gyllenhammar's (1977, pp. 102–113) description of "How Volvo Adapts Work To People" is an example of one corporation's attempt to change. Volvo's management began with reorganizing production and technology to meet the needs of people. In one plant, for example, this effort involved car assembly in working groups of about twenty persons. Then management invested large sums of money to improve the work environment. The third change was an attempt to improve the jobs themselves by creating greater flexibility and phasing out or enriching unpleasant jobs. The fourth major effort toward change was to provide opportunities for the personal development of workers. It was believed that "productivity will continue to increase because the people who work here have better jobs."

Ouchi (1981) studied and compared American and Japanese industry. He concluded that it was possible to describe Japanese organizations as generally characterized by "life-time employment, slow evaluation and promotion, non-specialized career paths, implicit control mechanisms, collective decision making, collective responsibility and wholistic concern."

American organizations were seen in contrast as characterized by "short-term employment, rapid evaluation and promotion, specialized career paths, explicit control mechanisms, individual decision making, individual responsibility, and segmented concerns" (Ouchi, 1981, pp. 48–49).

Interestingly, he also identified certain organizations that had developed in the United States that had many features that were much like Japanese structures, but modified in ways that reflected American culture. He called these successful and well-managed companies *Theory Z* type organizations (Ouchi, 1981, p. 58).

According to Ouchi (1981), Theory Z organizations were characterized by consensual decision making, strong commitment to an organizational philosophy, strong emphasis on information but great reliance on human judgment, subtle forms of control based on the assumption of broad-based worker commitment to the organization. Individuals in the organization felt a sense of personal freedom even though they were conforming to organizational goals and expectations.

Theory Z organizations showed a basic concern for organizational members as people. Workers dealt with each other on a person to person basis with less emphasis on formal relationships. There was more emphasis on long-term employment, continuous training and retraining, team work, mutual trust and respect, and psychological and technological support. There was less emphasis on specialization, segmentation, individualization and even professionalism. The study of Theory Z type organizations has important implications for educational organizations and the practice of supervision in those organizations.

Campbell (1977-78) summarized his view of open systems as follows:

> One might take the position that whereas industrial management, human relations, and structuralism are rather definitive views of administration, open systems is simply chaos. While the concept of open systems may not be fully developed and even the name ascribed to it may not be a fortunate one, I think it is more than chaos. Only in an open systems view can one do full justice to the interaction between an organization and its environment.

RECENT DEVELOPMENTS
IN INSTRUCTIONAL SUPERVISION*

It is helpful to conceptualize instructional supervision as a behavior system formally provided to improve instruction. Improvement of instruction includes (Lovell, 1978, p. 42):

1. Direct psychological and technical support, service, and help for teachers
2. Curriculum developments, coordination, and evaluation
3. Organization for and development, coordination, and evaluation of instruction, including the provision of facilities, equipment, and materials
4. Development and evaluation of educational goals
5. Professional development of personnel
6. Evaluation of personnel performance
7. Evaluation of educational outcomes.

Review of the literature (Lovell, 1978, p. 43) revealed a growing emphasis on the initiation, support, and evaluation of change as an important function of instructional supervision. For example, changing societal expectations, changing students, teaching methods, materials, and equipment all have implications for change in the instructional program and process. There was also a growing expectation that instructional supervision would not only provide leadership for change but would also be a prime factor in the release of the creative energies of teachers and other personnel in the change process.

Ideas from the literature also established a strong need to maintain a system of support and quality control for ongoing programs. Organizations not only have needs for teachers with the freedom, motivation, and creativeness to change but also have a need for coordination, predictability, and control. An important function of educational supervision is to recognize and support both kinds of organizational needs while maintaining a proper balance.

*This section is based on an unpublished paper written by John T. Lovell, *Instructional Supervision: Emerging Perspective,* 1978, which was part of a larger paper, *The Roles and Responsibilities of Instructional Supervisors,* which was presented to the Association for Supervision and Curriculum Development (ASCD) as a report of the "Working Group on the Roles and Responsibilities of Supervisors." Members of the group included A.W. Sturgess, Chairman; R.J. Krajewski, J.T. Lovell, E. McNeil, and M.G. Ness.

Research studies (Puckett, 1963), (Carlton, 1971), (Lovell and Phelps, 1977, p. 8) indicated that teachers desired supportive and nonthreatening services that are relevant to the improvement of their performance. But the evidence was strong that teachers were dissatisfied with the support, service, and help that they were receiving. Many teachers felt that supervisors spent too much of their time working on administrative chores and that they should have been providing direct support for teachers.

There is growing recognition of the need to provide direct supervision to assist teachers in the improvement of their on-the-job performance. Clinical supervision has been proposed as an effective system for providing direct supervision to assist a particular teacher in improving his or her performance in a particular classroom. Much has been learned and communicated about the processes of preobservation behavior, observation behavior, and postobservation behavior. Much work still needs to be done if clinical supervision is to become a crucial factor in the practice of instructional supervision. Of special importance is the need to develop and implement new organizational structures that will make it possible to provide clinical supervision.

There is confusion and disagreement about the appropriate role structure for instructional supervisors. It is our position that there is a need to clarify the roles and responsibilities of instructional supervisors. We do not believe that it is possible or even appropriate to develop a universal role for supervisors. But, it is our assumption that roles need to be clearly defined in a flexible manner at the system level in an effort to eliminate as much of the confusion as possible. We also believe that it may be appropriate to develop broad categories of roles for instructional supervisors, which could give direction both for the preparation of supervisors and the development of role structures at the local system level. Esposito, Smith, and Burback (1975, pp. 63-67) developed the broad concepts of supervisor–helping role and supervisor-administrative role. If these concepts were used, it would be possible for local school systems to develop their supervisory role under these two general rubrics. Administrative instructional supervisors would be more involved in program management, coordination of personnel, evaluation of personnel, and so on. Consultative instructional supervisors would be more involved with providing support, service, and help for instructional personnel.

AN EMERGING POINT OF VIEW

Based on the research, theory development, and practice of instructional supervision during the past few years, certain key ideas are taking shape that could have important implications for the practice of instructional supervision. Since the shape and form of the chapters that follow are at least partly a function of these various threads of thought, an attempt will be made to identify them and briefly discuss their implications for instructional supervisory behavior.

Instructional supervision will continue to be seen and studied as an organizational subsystem that has the function of directly influencing teaching behavior in such a way as to facilitate student learning. The inevitable conflicts between the needs of individuals and organizational needs means that organizations must be concerned with providing special arrangements to deal with teacher alienation, lack of motivation, and poor performance. The instructional supervisory behavior system should make a significant contribution to those arrangements. Organizational members need to feel that they are a significant part of the organization, and thus need to be significantly involved in the processes of determining and achieving goals. As rational decision makers and problem solvers, they do in fact have a vested interest in organizational effectiveness and efficiency, and this concern provides a basis for self-determination of direction and self-discipline.

Rapid changes in the organizational environment provide the necessity for an organization that can change to maintain harmony with external and internal forces. It is our assumption that instructional supervision will be significantly involved in all ramifications of the change process. There is a need to gather and analyze data that can be used as feedback on organizational and organizational member effectiveness. Such a data base needs to be used to create member dissatisfaction and, therefore, provide a rational basis for change. It is assumed that scientific problem solving is an appropriate method to facilitate change that will result in improvement. We believe that the instructional supervisory behavior system will be expected to be a central agency in this process.

Since organizations will find it increasingly necessary to use various kinds of temporary systems as a basis for meeting quickly changing needs, it will be necessary to bring together teaching personnel with various specializations and need dispositions. Often these individuals will not have had a chance to get to know each other over time. Yet, they will be expected to "pull together" in an effective way to achieve their mission. It is our feeling that it will be a critical function of instructional supervision not only to pull these groups together, but also to provide the needed psychological and technological support required to keep them working efficiently and effectively.

Responsibilities, roles, and tasks of teachers and administrators will be constantly changing. Therefore, the relatively fixed role expectations and territorial boundaries will not apply. Workers will need to learn new skills and make decisions in unfamiliar territories. The instructional supervisory behavior system will be expected to provide the needed support, service, and help.

Since teachers and administrators will be thought of as critical human resources, a strong effort will be needed to use them as a creative source of problem solving and decision making. To apply the human resources wherever they are found to problems wherever they exist will require instructional supervisors who know the resources and who have the competence to provide the needed support.

Many factors indicate that there will be an increased emphasis on the specification (where feasible) of operational goals, definition of learning conditions, and evaluation of outcomes. With the recognition of the need for organizational members to be sensitive to overall organizational goals and the realization that one of the best methods to achieve this is through teacher involvement, it is apparent that instructional supervisors will be increasingly concerned with involving teachers in policy development, problem solving, and decision-making activities. These propositions are based on the assumption of teachers as professional educators with specialized expertise.

The motivation of teachers will continue to be a matter of grave concern to instructional supervisors, but relatively less emphasis will be placed on monetary rewards and working conditions and more emphasis will be placed on the teacher's need for recognition, creative experience, satisfaction of a job well done, belonging, and self-esteem. Supervisory activities will be provided for these kinds of needs.

Leadership effectiveness is not just a function of formal position, but is also a function of complex factors including appropriate specialized competence and level of esteem by colleagues. Since these attributes are broadly distributed among faculty members, it would be appropriate to broaden the allocation of formal supervisory authority to carry out certain kinds of supervisory behavior. Of course, it will also be the function of instructional supervision to identify and organize the personnel for these activities. Chapter 4 provides a study of leadership behavior to give focus to this important supervisory process.

The processes of coordination and quality control will become increasingly important, but greater emphasis will be placed on teacher participation in the development of organizational goals. There will also be greater emphasis on self-direction and self-evaluation. These processes involve the utilization and development of many kinds of instruments that will make it possible for teachers to have more definitive information about the outcomes of their teaching efforts. Interaction analysis, videotaping, and microteaching are examples of such procedures. Instructional supervisors will be expected to provide leadership in these activities. A discussion of direct supervision for the instructional program appears in Chapter 9.

The rapid expansion of knowledge both in subject matter content and teaching methodology has important implications for teaching. Even though teachers are assumed to be professionally competent, it is not appropriate to assume that they do not need a highly specialized support system. Changes in technology, behavioral sciences, curriculum, evaluation, and learning resources are important factors. The fact that teachers need to keep abreast of these changes and need help to do so represents an important challenge to instructional supervision.

The growing complexity of educational organizations, the development of specialization, teacher involvement in policy development and decision making, and difficulty of coordination emphasize the need for authentic communication, not only down, but also "up" and "sideways." To function as decision makers and problem solvers, teachers must have the total picture, and this requires quality communication.

In summary, educational organizations will continue to be concerned with the specification of learning outcomes, conditions for achieving the outcomes, and evaluation. These functions have been and will continue to be a primary function of instructional supervision. But, the growing concern for human beings in the organization will continue and intensify with a growing focus on teachers as problem solvers, decision makers, and change agents. A prime function of instructional supervision will be to involve, lead, and coordinate teachers in these kinds of activities. The salient need is to get the allocation of human resources, effort, authority, and expertise for the appropriate problems.

3

SUPERVISION IS RELEASING HUMAN POTENTIAL

Supervision is an organizational behavior system that has the function of interacting with the teaching behavior system for the purpose of improving the learning situation for children. The position has been developed that supervisory behavior is not just a function of supervisors but rather is a function of various roles, depending on the needed ability for a particular undertaking. The focus of the "supervisor's" roles is not so much to be competent in all areas and to be the "formal" leader in all situations but, rather, to facilitate the release of the human potential of organizational members that makes available a more competent staff to conduct the human interaction that is called education.

HUMAN POTENTIAL
IS NOT
FULLY UTILIZED

To determine how to be most helpful in the release of human potential, the supervisor needs to become well informed about human development, especially motivation and learning. Studies from anthropology, psychology, and human growth and development indicate that each person is born with more potential than is used. People are born with different capacities, but no matter how limited or how extensive the individual's potential, no one ever develops all that he or she has. Since no one ever fully develops all of his or her potential, there is, in effect, no ceiling. Even on the most limited person, there is a ceiling that is higher than will ever be reached.

A person's experiences determine which of the possible potentials will be developed and utilized. These experiences can build the kind of structure that is restrictive, which causes a person to see himself or herself as less adequate and therefore less able to explore new experiences and develop more potential; or they can build the opposite, an open structure.

The earlier one has experiences that will develop openness, the greater the possibility of developing additional potential. If early experiences are restrictive, they build structures that make it less possible to expand into other areas. As persons interact, they form structures of knowledge, concepts of self, concepts of other people, and concepts of the world. The concepts formed determine how extensive future experiences can be and how much persons can move in the direction of realizing potential.

Even though early experiences are very important, the human being continues to develop some potential all through life. The amount depends upon the quality of the environment in which he or she lives. If the person is fortunate enough to live in a heterogeneous, changing society that provides many positive experiences, more potential will be developed.

Lionberger and Milton (1957), in their study of how farmers change their habits of farming, found that it is much more difficult to bring about change in the farming process in a homogeneous community, where people live with others like themselves, than in a heterogeneous community, where many kinds of people live together. Interaction with people who are different provides challenge and a choice of patterns.

If the environment is a changing one, the individual knows it is possible to be an innovator and play a different role. The belief that change is possible affects the individual's freedom to try. If the society is one in which the patterns are fixed and little change is apparent, individuals develop only the potentials that are appropriate to their assigned roles. But if people believe they can be more than they are, they will dare to try to develop unused potential.

If, in interaction with other individuals in the society, a person has many positive experiences, he or she develops the kind of personality and knowledge structure that makes it possible to dare to seek new and different experiences that increase understanding and skills. Positive experiences are ones that bring satisfaction to the individual. Support! Expression of faith in ability! Success in achieving goals! Any experience that increases the individual's belief in his or her worth and his or her ability to solve the problems that confront him or her is a positive experience.

Carl Rogers (1971, pp. 215) posed the rhetorical question, "Can schools grow persons?" and answered with a definite "No." Rather, he indicated that only "persons can grow persons." Thus, it is through our interaction with others that we develop into the kind of persons we become. Rogers sees a person as having a strong set of values that give direction for living. He goes on to define a person as follows:

> A person is openly expressive of where he is, who he is. He does not live a facade or a role, hiding behind the convenient front of being a "teacher," a "principal," a "psychologist." He is real, and the realness shows through. Hence he is unique, and this means that there is enormous diversity in persons —diversity in philosophy, in approach to life, in opinions, in ways of dealing with students.

A person with sufficient positive experience develops a self-concept that enables him or her to be more open to experience. Because he or she feels adequate, he or she does not fear strangeness and welcomes new problems, sensations, opportunities, and challenges. He or she does not need to seek cover by retreating to the known, the tried, and the tested. There is courage to risk failure, rebuff, and self-evaluation. He or she feels like a person of worth and, therefore, like a person who can cope regardless of the consequences.

If a person with an adequate self-concept exists in a school in which inclusiveness rather than exclusiveness is valued, he or she does even more to develop potential. If exclusiveness is valued, the person with an adequate self-concept may never find the situations that produce challenge and growth. If inclusiveness is prized, the individual's contacts in a heterogeneous population with different ideas, values, and procedures will be sufficiently great to test his or her thinking and ability to resolve conflicts. An example of openness to experience follows:

> A consultant was working for a school in a Georgia town that had taken its first steps in school desegregation. He conducted the first integrated meeting of the professional staff of the school system. The black teachers entered first and pursued the strategy of taking seats throughout the room so that there would not be a black group and a white group. As the whites came into the room, they took seats among the blacks. The consultant made a presentation and asked the staff to break up into discussion groups to discuss it. He felt a resistance to his suggestion, so he designated the people who would be in each discussion group—he wanted to be sure each group was mixed. As they started to discuss, he observed the same phenomenon throughout the hall. If the blacks happened to be sitting in front, not a single black turned his or her chair around to talk to the whites behind, and the whites talked to the back of the blacks' heads. If the whites were in front, they did not turn around, and the blacks talked to the back of the whites' heads. After this behavior had gone on for about ten minutes, he noticed a black teacher who turned her chair halfway. A little bit later, she turned her chair all the way, and another black teacher turned her chair halfway. He walked over to them and said to the first black teacher, "How did you get the courage to do it?" She said, "Well, I thought I could profit by it."
> As the consultant was getting ready to leave, he asked if they would be interested in his reactions to what went on. When they agreed, he remarked he had noticed that when they moved into the discussion group where they had an opportunity to engage in the kind of professional experience that

many of them had not engaged in before, that only one person in the room really took advantage of it. He asked, "Why?" and began to talk about using opportunities for growth. After the session was over, at least 25 people came by and said to him, "I'm very thankful that you said what you did, because what you were doing was helping open the doors so that more of us felt free to be more open."

The black teacher provided the necessary leadership. Even in this kind of situation with 300 persons involved, one person who was more open to experience could take the initiative that then made it possible for other people to be more open and, therefore, extend their opportunities for growth and their opportunities for helping others grow.

Not all teachers were equally open to experience. The ones who needed to have the administration provide increased opportunities to develop openness did not utilize the situation presented.

A human being seeks to maintain existence and enhance self. The action taken depends upon the intrepretation of the situation and the individual perception of self and role. At any given moment, individuals behave in the manner that they believe is best. If their behavior is to be changed, their perceptions of self, skills, role, or the situation must be altered.

A CONCEPT OF MOTIVATION

The achievement of organizational and individual goals requires a high level of human motivation. But, what is human motivation? We start off with the assumption that all human behavior is purposeful. This assumption means that persons move, think, create, work, and play in order to achieve certain goals.

Behavior is directed toward multiple goals that can be either conscious or subconscious. For example, a teacher may be working toward the goals of an effective evaluation report in order to achieve tenure, success in meeting the needs of students, recognition by fellow teachers, marriage, and many others. Motivation is the level of effort an individual is willing to apply toward the achievement of a particular goal or motive (Hersey and Blanchard, 1977, p. 16). Naturally, some goals are more important to individuals than other goals at a given time, and the important goals provide the direction for behavior. It is our contention that the potency of a particular goal for an individual is at least partly a function of that individual's needs structure at that particular time. Thus, individuals tend to behave toward goals that will meet their needs. However, another important factor to help explain individual motivation was developed by House (1971, p. 322) as follows:

> Thus, according to this theory of motivation, an individual chooses the behaviors he engages in on the basis of (1) the valences he perceives to be associated with the outcomes of the behavior under consideration; and (2) his subjective estimate of the probability that his behavior will indeed result in the outcomes.

According to House, motivation is not just a function of the possibility of needs satisfaction, but also of the individual's feelings that the goal can be achieved. The application of this theory of motivation in educational organizations provides the basis of a possible dilemma. Individuals have their own needs and are willing to work toward goals they think will help satisfy those needs if the goals appear obtainable. However, organizations also have goals that require member behavior that may or may not be consistent with individual goals. If the goals of organizations and the high potency goals of organizational members are congruent, and if the paths toward the goals are clear and offer high probability of achievement, the chance for a highly motivated staff will be great. But, if the goals of the organization and the goals of individual members are not congruent, then this could lead organizations to *induce* member behavior that could lead to member frustration, alienation, avoidance, negativism, and poor motivation toward organization goals. Etzioni (1964, p. 2) described this organizational dilemma:

> Thus, to a degree, *organizational rationality and human happiness go hand in hand*. But a point is reached in every organization where happiness and efficiency cease to support each other. Not all work can be well-paid or gratifying, and not all regulations and orders can be made acceptable. Here we face a true dilemma.

The lack of congruence between the needs of the organization and the needs of organizational members has been a prime concern in the study of human motivation in organizations. An attempt will be made to review the literature on motivation and share our conclusions concerning the implications for the provision of an organizational structure that will facilitate the development of a highly motivated staff.

THE STUDY OF MOTIVATION

We described motivation as the level of effort an individual is willing to expend toward the achievement of a certain goal. We also said that goals are a function of needs and that the potency of a particular goal is dependent on the strength of the need. What are the needs of people and how are they related to human behavior directed toward goals?

Human Needs

Maslow (1954) has developed a hierarchy of human needs that consists of interdependent levels. The first level was defined as physiological. When man's need for air, water, or food is not satisfied, this need becomes a highly potent motivator of human behavior and continues to exist as a powerful influence on an individual until the need is met. But, when the first order of need is satisfied, then the next level of need becomes the focus of motivation for the behavior of the individual. Other levels of needs include security or safety, belonging, ego development, and finally, self-actualization. When members of the faculty are relatively well fed, clothed, and sheltered and feel safe and secure, there is the possibility of motivation to belong and become an accepted part of the organization, social groups, or professional group. The achievement of these needs contributes to the individual's concern for personal growth, professional growth, recognition, and esteem by fellow workers. These are powerful, pervasive, and continuing needs for organizational members. It is through the teacher's motivation at this level of need fulfillment that it is possible to release faculty energy to improve the quality of education for students.

The highest order of need in the Maslow formulation is the need for self-actualization. This is the "capstone" of man's attempt to become what he can become. The possible fruits are great personal accomplishment, creative problem solving, and exceptional dedication. The facade is removed and the human being is "open" to "become."

Maslow's formulation not only describes the needs of human beings, but also indicates the way these needs relate one to the other. It is not until the first order of need is satisfied that the second order of need can become a potent factor in behavior. As long as a faculty member has a first-order need of security, the potential for release of effort toward self-improvement could be limited. Teachers concerned with low salaries and morale problems will not be concerned with developing their ability as teachers. But, meeting the lower-order needs opens up the way for new goals concerned with self-improvement, professional achievement, and even creativeness and self-fulfillment.

Some writers have discussed the need for freedom and autonomy. Kelley and Rasey (1954, p. 103) discussed the powerful need that individuals have to be free and the equally powerful need individuals have for other people. They indicated that complete freedom may interfere with the freedom of associates who also need to be free and, therefore, individuals must reconcile their needs for freedom and for other people.

Teachers and supervisors who work in educational organizations need to be free to be creative, to try out new ideas, to do their own "thing." In these ways, people grow and become. They also need a sense of control over their own destinies. However, they must also be responsible for their own behavior and the effect it has on associates. Not to be responsible could result in being cut off from affiliation and esteem needs and could throw them back to behavior directed toward goals coming from a lower order of need.

Morse and Lorsch (1970, p. 67) developed the idea of competence motivation. They indicated that all human beings have a basic need "to achieve a sense of competence." They theorized that sense of competence continues to motivate even if a competence motive is achieved, because the achieved competence goal is replaced by another competence motive. We agree with Morse and Lorsch and feel that teachers and supervisors have a powerful need to be competent and that this need persists.

Human Motivation in Organizations

During the early part of the twentieth century, organization theory was dominated by the scientific management movement. Under this approach the worker in the organization was assumed to be a passive instrument of management. Motivation was not conceptualized as a serious problem since members of the organization were assumed to be motivated by the goal of economic gain. The idea was to pay the person what it took to get the job done.

The second quarter of the twentieth century was characterized by a growing concern with human motivation in organizations. As a result of the research coming out of the human relations movement, theorists were beginning to challenge the assumption that workers were *only* motivated by the desire for economic gain. For example, evidence from the famous Hawthorne Studies (Roethlisberger and Dickson, 1947), among others, led to the conclusion that the way workers felt about themselves, their fellow workers, and their organization were important factors in production effectiveness and efficiency. This did not mean that economic factors and production methods were not important, but it did establish the importance of the human dimension.

Miles (1965, pp. 148-163) challenged the human relations approach and advocated the human resources approach. Miles made the point that in the human relations model, management is involving members in order to achieve decisions that will be carried out in an efficient and effective way.

Miles (1965, pp. 148-163) indicated that the human resources model is built on the assumption of organization members as important sources of ideas, problem solvers, decision makers, and controllers. The purpose of participation is to utilize these important human resources and improve organizational decision making, performance, and control. He suggested that self-control and self-direction should grow in accordance with the growing competence of members of the organization.

The human resources model seems particularly appropriate for the educational organization, for many reasons. First, the workers (teachers) of the organization are highly trained professionals who normally operate from a broad base of experience. Second, they often have a great deal of autonomy and freedom to operate their classes in their own way. Third, they are held accountable for the results of their teaching activities. Fourth, a group of students provides for a dynamic and unique situation that requires a great amount of local control, creative decisions, and adaptations.

McGregor (1960 and 1957, pp. 1-9) developed the thesis that the nature of personnel management practices is largely the result of the assumptions that management makes about the human beings in the organization. He developed and compared two sets of contrasting assumptions that he labeled theory X and theory Y. In both theory X and theory Y, it was assumed that management had the responsibility to structure the elements of the organization so as to facilitate the achievement of organizational goals.

In theory X, it was assumed that management needed to direct, control, and modify the behavior of organizational members in order to meet the needs of the organization. It was assumed that without this active effort to control, coerce, manipulate, and closely supervise, workers would be passive, indifferent, or even actively alienated from the organization. This proposition was based on the following assumptions about people (McGregor, 1957, p. 2):

1. The average man is by nature indolent—he works as little as possible.
2. He lacks ambition, dislikes responsibility, prefers to be led.
3. He is inherently self-centered, indifferent to organizational needs.
4. He is by nature resistant to change.
5. He is gullible, not very bright, the ready dupe of the charlatan and the demagogue.

Theory X took a form ranging from the hard approach to the soft approach. The hard approach was more direct and aggressive and often involved coercion and threats of withholding rewards. The soft approach was indirect and permissive, with emphasis on harmony and happiness.

McGregor felt that the application of these practices "whether 'hard' or 'soft' " was often disfunctional and inappropriate and, in many instances, resulted in poor performance and reduced organizational effectiveness and efficiency.

McGregor (1957, p. 6) insisted that management operating under theory X assumptions was generally ineffective because of the attempt to motivate people through control, salary, fringe benefits, security, and threat of withdrawal or promise of increased rewards (based on assumption of predominance of physiological and security needs) when, in fact, these needs were largely satisfied and no longer strong motivators. Actually, people in organizations had reached a stage where their social esteem, and self-fulfillment needs were dominant and not being met and, therefore, they felt frustrated, discontent, alienated and poorly motivated. He advocated a different theory of personnel management based on different assumptions, which he called theory Y (McGregor, 1957, pp. 6-7):

1. Managment is responsible for organizing the elements of productive enterprise —money, materials, equipment, people—in the interest of economic ends.
2. People are *not* by nature passive or resistant to organizational needs. They have become so as a result of experience in organizations.
3. The motivation, the potential for development, the capacity for assuming responsibility, the readiness to direct behavior toward organizational goals are all present in people. Management does not put them there. It is a responsibility of management to make it possible for people to recognize and develop these human characteristics for themselves.
4. The essential task of management is to arrange organizational conditions and methods of operation so that people can achieve their own goals *best* by directing *their own* efforts toward organizational objectives.

Essentially, McGregor is advocating an approach to management based on the human needs of belonging, esteem, and self-actualization. It is the responsibility of management to provide the structure that will make it possible for people to feel accepted and valued, and to feel that they can best work toward their own goals by working toward organizational goals.

This approach is certainly consistent with the human resources approach advocated by Miles (1965). Both authors assume a broad base of human competence in the organization, which needs to be utilized. It is through the process of utilization of human potential that it is possible to achieve more effective decisions and implementation and, therefore, better-motivated and better-performing personnel. These assumptions are particularly appropriate to the educational organization since the management and work of the organization is done by highly trained professionals in a structure that provides autonomy, flexibility, accountability, and goals and processes that require creative and adaptive responses to a changing environment.

Morse and Lorsch (1970, pp. 61–66) studied four contrasting organizations and suggested a new set of assumptions that they called "contingency theory," which emphasized that there is *not* one best pattern of organization, but rather that organizational effectiveness is contingent on the fit among the organizational structure, the needs of the people involved and the nature of the task. They also found that individuals in the effective organizations showed significantly more feelings of competence.

We feel that it is important for educational organizations to develop organizational structures that are appropriate to the task and people. It is also essential to facilitate the process through which individuals can develop a sense of competence that is a possible motivator.

Herzberg (1959) made an intensive study of motivation in industrial organizations. Using a technique of content analysis of stories over periods of high and low morale of workers, he found that positive feelings workers have about their work come from the workers' sense of personal worth and self-fulfillment and that these positive feelings were related to achievement, work itself, recognition, and responsibility. Job dissatisfiers were found to be factors defining the context in which the work was done, such as physical surroundings, supervision, and company policies. The elimination of the dissatisfiers did not lead to high satisfaction since high satisfaction was a function of other factors.

Hahn (1961, pp. 280–282) did a similar study in the U.S. Air Force and got results that tend to support the Herzberg findings. The "stories" describing the "good day" situations tended to fall in the self-realization category and included such factors as "recognition," productive self-effort, sense of belonging, and cooperative effort. Dissatisfying experiences were generally associated with the general job environment category.

The studies of motivation of teachers have produced similar findings. Ralph Savage (1967) made a study of teacher satisfaction and dissatisfaction in the educational organization. His findings generally supported the findings of the Herzberg study. Achievement, recognition, and the work itself were found to be factors that lead to satisfaction for teachers. But, interpersonal relations with students was also found to be a factor in achieving satisfaction for teachers.

Sergiovanni (1967, pp. 66-82) found that achievement, recognition, and responsibility were statistically significant contributors to teacher satisfaction. The absence of these factors was not found to contribute to dissatisfaction. The factors that were found to be significantly related to teacher dissatisfaction include interpersonal relations with subordinates, superiors, and peers as well as with technical supervision, school policy and administration, and personal life.

Teacher participation in decision making has been broadly advocated as a process for improving the quality of decisions, decision implementation, and teacher satisfaction. Mohrman, Cooke, and Mohrman (1978, pp. 13-29) studied participation in decision making in educational organizations. They found that the multidimensional approach to teacher participation in decisions can improve job satisfaction. Participation in decisions related to the technical domain was related to greater extrinsic and intrinsic satisfaction of teachers as well as to less role ambiguity. However, participation in decisions related to the managerial domain was not found to be associated with intrinsic and extrinsic satisfaction. It appears that teacher satisfaction is not just a function of participation in decision making but, rather, depends on the nature of the decision under consideration.

Forsyth and Hoy (1978, pp. 80-96) did a study of isolation and alienation in educational organizations. They found that members who are isolated from any one of the following—persons in authority positions, influentials, friends, or respected coworkers—are likely to be isolated from the others. Supervisors were found to be less likely to be alienated than those individuals who were not in supervisory positions. Interestingly, isolation from formal control and perceived influentials was not related to work alienation. However, isolation from friends and isolation from respected coworkers were both related to work alienation. It appears that respected colleagues and friends are sources of recognition and help fulfill social and ego needs of teachers.

Holdaway (1978, pp. 30-47) did a study of a sample of teachers in Alberta, Canada, to determine the relationship between their overall job satisfaction and certain facets of their job situation. It was found that overall satisfaction was most closely related to achievement, career orientation, recognition, and stimulation. "Working with students" again appears as a major source of satisfaction. This item was most often included in the free responses. The study provided general support for the Herzberg studies.

IMPLICATIONS OF THE STUDY
OF MOTIVATION

There is considerable evidence that supervisors who seek to release the potential of organization members need to produce opportunities for teachers to feel more adequate as professionals, to see greater significance, possibilities, and responsibility in their role, and to perceive the situation as one in which improvement is not only possible but highly valued. Teachers need to feel that their contribution to the achievement of organizational goals is recognized and valued. A friendly pat on the back is nice, but far from adequate. What is essential is a positive logistical and psychological support system as the teachers "push out" to explore and test new approaches to teaching. When the effort is complete, a sense of personal achievement of a job well done is essential. Words of praise are not enough. Rather, definitive feedback on the outcomes of their teaching effort is required.

A sense of personal responsibility contributes to high satisfaction and motivation. An opportunity to participate in appropriate decision making and policy formulation contributes to a sense of responsibility to carry them through. Further, faculty should be used for official leadership responsibilities on an ad hoc basis, according to expertise, and with appropriate authority. Activities such as these contribute to the teacher's sense of worth, self-concept, and personal well being.

Supervisors and teachers need confidence in themselves. Psychology contains much evidence that scapegoats and the desire to belittle or to hurt others come from feelings of insecurity. When people are sure of themselves, of their ability to meet situations, of the value of their ideas and purposes, and of their value as persons, they do not feel a constant need to have other people tell them that they are important, valuable, and worthy. They don't have to build up feelings of superiority. They do not have to show themselves that they are better than someone else.

When supervisor and teachers accept their ability to deal with situations, they don't feel the need for being constantly on guard. They can treat others as equals and believe that all are working for the good of the school. They don't have to be afraid of other persons or feel a need to threaten them as a way of defending themselves. Persons who are not sure of themselves must watch the way situations are developing to see whether or not they will be capable of dealing with them when they arise. They often feel the need to take actions, often harmful to others, to keep situations in which they may fail from arising. To avoid feelings of insecurity, individuals must know their roles and must have the training that gives them the skill to perform them.

An example of insecurity caused by lack of understanding of the function of an official leader is the false assumption on the part of some principals that they should know more about the subject matter in all fields than the teachers working in each field. That is an impossibility. As a result of the insecurity arising from this assumption, they issue orders about the way subjects should be taught and about the content of courses; they give instructions without any consultation with the members of the staff involved. These principals avoid joint thinking, because they are afraid their lack of knowledge will be revealed. This unnecessary insecurity, with its resulting malpractice, occurs because these principals have not recognized that their function is one of coordination and that they are not expected to serve as the only technicians and specialists in the field.

If a supervisor can eradicate feelings of superiority, the sense of adequacy increases. This apparently contradictory statement is true. If the assumption that the formal leader is chosen because of superior intelligence and ability is eliminated, the necessity always to be better than any member of the group is also eliminated.

It becomes possible to admit mistakes, to ask for help, and to recognize and use superior skill in the group. If the official leader's function is helping the group to achieve unity and to release its inherent leadership, then a feeling of adequacy can be achieved by performing these tasks well.

Insecurity plagues some supervisors because they establish a stereotype of the way a person in a leader's position should act. They fail to recognize the need for being themselves, the need for accepting their own personalities as valid for leadership; they try to assume a dignity and a manner of behavior that are alien to them. As a result, they keep other people away from them in order to keep the falseness of their assumed personality from being detected.

But remaining secure involves more than accepting one's present status. In order to maintain self-confidence, it is necessary to continue to study and grow. Failure to keep abreast of the new developments in education can lead to rejecting new activities and those members of the staff who are participating in them.

It is also necessary to study the results of one's past actions and to recognize that mistakes can be learning experiences. If the leader looks upon mistakes as something to hide, performance becomes something that decreases self-confidence. Everyone makes mistakes. If mistakes are seen as a way to grow, failure in the present situation helps to build confidence for new situations that will arise.

When a leader is sure of self in the sense described, it is possible to stop analyzing situations to see whether they will make the leader feel successful and to study them to see whether or not they are going to make other people feel more adequate and become stronger persons. The leader's self-confidence increases the self-confidence of the staff. Compare the principal who is in perpetual fret, afraid the task will not be done on time, afraid superiors will not like the way the work is being handled, with the supervisor who is aware of all the difficulties, yet shows by every action that the situation is in control and that the staff will be able to do its part. No one likes to work for a worrywart or even a supervisor who gives the appearance of being one.

An official leader must believe in the worth of others—all others. It is important to believe that each principal, teacher, and child in the school has value and a contribution to make; that the failure of any individual to make a contribution is evidence that the group is not achieving its full potential. Such faith is basic to an environment in which everyone respects the worth of everyone else.

People tend to live up to what others expect them to be. If the supervisor does not believe that others are worthwhile, that they are trustworthy, that they have a real contribution to make, they won't profit from his or her leadership. If the leader has faith in them and believes in their potentialities, they will grow and mature through their interaction.

But the supervisor dares not make an exception. If the value of anyone in the situation is denied—principal, teacher, pupil, or parent—the stage is set for other persons to begin classifying as unworthy and unimportant individuals with whom they differ.

If some teachers have lost their enthusiasm and their desire to grow and be better teachers, it is possible that the situation has come about as a result of the supervisor's lack of faith in them or as a result of frustrations in the teaching situations that have led them to feel that the official leader does not believe they are important. An official leader can demonstrate lack of faith in many ways:

> In a large city high school the principal was speaking to the student honor society about types of service. To illustrate a negative kind of service, he said, "There are not more than twelve teachers on this staff who will assume new responsibilities or do anything for me unless I pay them overtime or give them a free period." The faculty members present immediately began to speculate on which twelve were the ones who would do the principal's bidding.

Not only did the principal, by a display of lack of faith, decrease the possibility of growth in the faculty by condemning them as unworthy, but he also increased the students' doubt of the teachers' worth. Such chance remarks are significant in two ways. They are indices to the kinds of relationships that exist in the school group and they intensify the emotions already aroused.

In attempts to help teachers, supervisors can act in such a way that the respect of staff members for each other is jeopardized. A substitute teacher cites the following experience:

> While I was taking over an English class for the day at a junior high school, the assistant principal in charge of English decided it was her day for showing up an underling. I was doing remedial reading work when Miss Brown stepped in, looked at me sourly, and exclaimed, "That's not the way it is done, Mrs. Jones." She then, in very audible and definite tones, corrected me in front of the students at every turn of the lesson. Every time I am observed, I think of the incident and feel like crouching under a seat.

In this action, the supervisor showed no respect for the worth of the substitute teacher. Such supervision has discredited the use of observation as a technique for improving instruction. It has separated supervisors from teachers. All other supervisors this teacher encounters are suspected and feared until they prove themselves. Improvement of teaching must start with respect for the personality and work of the teacher.

Teachers react negatively to an attempt to force a philosophy and procedure upon them. Attempted imposition makes clear that the supervisor considers himself or herself more intelligent than the teacher, and engenders active resistance by the more intelligent, aggressive staff members.

> In one school where the principal was trying to institute more progressive practices, the members of the staff who would not accept the newer theories were disregarded and their teaching practices were scorned. An older member of the staff, the head of the English department, suffered in silence and then began an opposition campaign. The faculty split and the principal became ineffective.
>
> A new supervisor entered the scene. He disregarded the philosophic differences altogether. He began working with each staff member on improving

the phase of teaching that seemed most important to that teacher. The results were vastly different. The head of the English department began a special study of ways to improve her teaching of remedial reading. Soon she was telling the faculty about specific programs she was carrying on that were far in advance of any practices in the school. The same reaction was observed in the other teachers in the areas of their special interests.

Teachers are not all alike. They do not have the same concerns, abilities, or maturity. If a supervisor believes in everyone's worth, there must be willingness to accept differences and to value each person for his or her special contribution. There must be recognition that the staff is richer because of the presence of each person, regardless of the limitations of the various staff members. Official leadership must make allowances for differences in the temperament and tempo of various individuals and must encourage the staff to do so as well. Attention must be centered on the special contribution that each staff member can make and on creating a situation in which the individual will want to make it.

There are tremendous differences among teachers in their openness to experience when looking at education and curriculum. Some are quite sure that there are no answers other than those demonstrated in the pattern of school that they attended, and they seek ways of working more effectively to fulfill the roles they saw their teachers perform. Some have a very narrow conception of what education should be or what it can be. They see education as restricted to certain disciplines and see curriculum improvement as consisting of revising the content of a subject. Others think that perhaps education can be better than it has been, and that they can be a part of its improvement. Others are completely open and say, "Let's forget the present pattern of education; let's see what it can be." There is a difference in what each of these kinds of teachers can do. Some see their function as innovators, and they view education as an innovative process. Others see their function as holding on to what has been, and they hunt for arguments to defend what they're already doing.

People are not equally responsive to the kind of supervisory structure that enables them to be more creative. As a result of previous experiences, people have different degrees of readiness for change. Supervisors need to give serious consideration to the uniqueness of each member of the faculty.

SUPERVISORY ACTION
TO RELEASE
HUMAN POTENTIAL

Supervisors must use the power of their position to create an environment conducive to the release of human potential. There are at least two basic sources of power. First, there is the authority that the supervisor has because of the official position held in the organization. This source of power normally manifests itself in control of a variety of resources that can be used to influence the behavior of organizational members. It is this source of power that makes it possible for the supervisor to call meetings, provide materials, provide consultants, and release teachers from normal duties and support their attendance at professional meetings.

Some persons question any use of authority, but we do not. Rather, authority is accepted as a legitimate factor in the interpersonal influence system. It is the use of authority according to the values of the supervisor that is good or bad. Since the release of human potential is assumed to be desirable, the use of authority to achieve that condition is also desirable.

In terms of what is known about interaction and the way people grow, the supervisor has a responsibility to use authority to hold people together until they can explore issues and alternatives and arrive at decisions that are acceptable to the group. It is necessary to develop and use the skill of helping people to examine alternatives in terms of values held and to test their values. The job is to see that people live by the existing policies that the faculty has established and to see that any one of these policies can be challenged and modified by the staff's thinking together intelligently about the policy.

A second source of power is the esteem that faculty members have for the supervisor. If they value the competence and trust the motives of the leader, they will value his or her suggestions, ideas, and desires and thereby increase the supervisor's power in the group. Conversely, if he or she has not earned their esteem through interactions in the past, there is little chance that the supervisor will be a highly influential person in the informal organization.

The supervisor who wishes to release human potential uses group power to create a working environment with the following elements:

1. *All persons have a sense of belonging.* Teachers want to feel that they belong to the group with which they work. Studies of work groups have found that this desire is one of the most important in determining how well a person produces. Desire to be accepted or to remain a part of the group is more powerful in conditioning the amount of work a person will do than is even take-home pay. A group may be a psychological one in which there is a lot of interaction, as in a departmental or grade-level group; members may also be in groups that drink coffee or beer together or bowl together. It has been discovered that these small psychological groups can be important factors in motivation. Supervisors have to be careful in fostering change and innovations, so that they do not destroy the psychological support of the groups that already exist.

In addition to existing psychological groups, there is need for a place where there can be free interaction in the exploration of a new area without reference to assigned tasks and present duties, a place where people may explore new frontiers in ideas and form cooperative projects to work together.

2. *Many stimuli are available.* Not all people have a common degree of readiness for an experience. Persons march to their own music. They set their own goals and they look for the elements in the environment that will enable them to move at their speed in the direction they desire. If all staff members are to find a stimulus to excite them and release their potential, the setting must contain many challenges and opportunities. Routine successes or intense failures will not suffice. Sufficient challenge to cause expenditure of effort must be present.

3. *All persons are encouraged to explore.* It is important for persons who are in official leadership roles to try to make some judgments about readiness for change in the members of the staff. They must not pretend that staff members are all alike. They should recognize that there are differences and try to be as accurate as possible in the assessment of those differences. The use of those differences should provide guidance in planning strategies to help people grow. Their job is placing the major portion of their energies in helping and facilitating the venturing, the innovating, and the exploring of the individuals who are most ready—not the ones who are least ready, but the ones who are most ready!

Some people are less willing to change than others because of firmer commitment to the values they hold. They find that anything that represents much change is threatening to them. The people who hold to the status quo are valuable people on the staff. They are the people that help keep the program stable, making it possible for other people to venture. This stabilizing group helps to determine the norms of the staff, and the innovation group, as it works, helps to shift the norms. Present group norms move in the direction of the venturing if the structure is such that it is possible for some people to venture. But the innovators must be valued and encouraged if the status quo adherents are not to create rigidity with little development of additional potentialities.

A strategy for change must be a strategy for releasing the potential of people; otherwise it becomes a change that decreases the possibility for continuing change. Some people who are very ready to change may, at present, be much less able professional people than some who are less ready to change. But if the release of potential is the strategy, the person who is ready to change will be more powerful and able to produce further change.

4. *Opportunity to explore is available.* All groups develop norms, and these norms determine the extent to which people may change and still remain a part of the group. Even though there is a degree of permissiveness within the norms of groups, there must be an administrative operation in which permissiveness is fostered and implemented.

The supervisor cannot tell people when to move; teachers have to take the step. The supervisor's major role is to make opportunities for participation possible. Almost every staff member should become a member of an innovative group where the norms are (a) how can we learn more about the educative process? and (b) how can we better implement what we know? The major norm must be one of constant improvement rather than one of holding to what exists.

Opportunities to explore are provided (a) by the administration indicating its desire for constant experimentation designed to lead to improvement, (b) by the provision of funds for research and dissemination, and (c) by the organization of study groups with common interests, who explore hypotheses concerning ways of reaching desired goals. If the staff believes that change is desired and possible, some members will seize the opportunity to explore.

5. *Individual interpretations are valued.* Potential is released if individuals are encouraged to develop their own judgments. Teachers are professionally trained, and their educations have prepared them to make professional judgments, not to be robots following a prescheduled routine. Little, if any, difference in professional education and experience exists between the supervised and the supervisor. Directives and demands that insist upon conformity decrease the competency of professionals by belittling their judgment and, thereby, undermining their confidence or by depriving them of the opportunity to increase their skill by experience. If supervisors want to release potential, they must value professional judgment, en-

courage questioning of existing policy and practices, and value the diversity of opinion that is the product of differing backgrounds.

6. *Heterogeneous staff is sought.* If a heterogeneous community is more conducive to change, and it seems to be, the supervisor should seek teachers with different education, experiences, and ways of looking at the educative process. Staff growth will occur through interaction, and the potential of both supervisor and teacher will be released if individual differences are valued and used.

The supervisor need not worry about the fact that people have different ideas. Each person's ideas will have to stand the test of the intellectual marketplace. If the supervisor can aid the faculty in reaching a norm where all feel responsible for becoming increasingly better students of the educative process, success will be impossible for any person who advocates a point of view without presenting evidence that it will provide the hoped-for growth in people. It is not the supervisor's role to stop any proposal, but rather to make sure that the group has an opportunity to examine it and the alternatives.

7. *The organizational structure and process promote communication.* The only way the potential of people is released is through communication—through interaction. An individual's potential is released as he or she interacts with people in such a way that visions are increased, horizons expanded, and his or her present limitations of thought changed. An organizational structure has value for releasing human potential only as it increases the possibility for deep and continuing communication.

8. *Help with personal problems is available.* People will grow intellectually and professionally through the interaction involved in solving educational problems if they are not too deeply troubled with personal problems. A person's potential for growth is not released if he or she is under emotional tension. Actions by supervisors to reduce tension contribute to the release of human potential.

Teachers are under tension. In American society, it has been estimated that one out of every twelve persons spends part of his or her lifetime in an institution for the improvement of mental health. Teachers are no exception. Such factors as specialized behavior standards for teachers and lack of acceptance and appreciation by the community serve to aggravate existing mental and emotional disturbances in members of the profession. Teachers need all the help they can get in maintaining their emotional health. Supervisors can help decrease the emotional tension of teachers by listening to the teachers' concerns and helping to provide appropriate resources to deal with those concerns.

9. *Broad participation exists in making decisions and implementing them.* Teachers and supervisors need more opporunity to participate in decision making with special emphasis on their own technical domains. Utilizing teachers and supervisors in decision making provides opportunities for the organization to improve the quality of decisions and their implementation. The improvement of the quality of decisions and the performance of members of the organization leads to more highly motivated and competent teachers and supervisors.

10. *Job enrichment is available to improve motivation.* Herzberg (1968, pp. 53–62) discusses the process of job enrichment. The purpose of job enrichment is to facilitate the process through which an individual can work toward and achieve certain important motivators such as personal achievement, responsibility, recognition, advancement, and growth and learning. Herzberg contends that it is possible to develop these motivators by removing controls, increasing accountability, giving direct feedback about job performance, and providing greater worker autonomy and opportunities to develop greater specialization. We agree with Herzberg and

believe this approach is particularly applicable to educational organizations. Teachers need and should have great autonomy in the teaching process, but should be held accountable for the results. Opportunities are needed for teachers to develop specialized competence with greater responsibility for serving as a resource to their fellow teachers. Certainly teachers need more definitive feedback on the results of their teaching efforts, which should contribute to their sense of achievement on the job.

11. *Human potential is utilized.* We recognize that according to our current level of knowledge, there is no one best approach to organizational management. However, it is our belief that educational organizations are generally more effective if the practice of supervision is based on the assumption of organizational members as important sources of ideas, creativeness, problem solving, and organizational control. The utilization of this human potential results in more effective decisions and a control that leads to greater motivation toward individual and organizational goals. The assumption is not made that all members have the capacity for self-control and self-direction, but rather, that they have the potential for self-control and self-direction and that it is the function of supervision to provide a structure in which human potential can be reached and utilized.

12. *Supervision is based on the assumption of human needs of belonging, esteem, and self-actualization.* It is our belief that physiological and security needs are no longer strong motivators for professional personnel in the educational organization. Rather, the needs for belonging, esteem, and self-actualization are more likely to be dominant, and continued emphasis on lower-level needs will lead to member frustration and poor motivation (McGregor, 1957). It is essential that supervisors provide opportunities for teachers to be accepted in the group and to achieve a sense of professional competence through professional performance with appropriate recognition and paths for new direction and growth.

4

SUPERVISION IS LEADERSHIP

Educational organizations need professional behavior that is characterized by creativeness, originality, adaptability, and a willingness and competence to take the risks of leadership. They also need behavior characterized by predictability, stability, and conformity. Instructional supervisors are expected to be prime contributors to the processes through which these needs are met. Instructional leadership for educational improvement is one of these processes. It is our assumption that instructional supervisors serve as educational leaders and should have the additional responsibilities of identifying and releasing leadership potential throughout the instructional staff.

A supervisor beginning work in the organizational behavior system needs a functional concept of leadership, a clear picture of the influence position he or she wishes to attain, and an explicit view of the way he or she plans to use this position to influence the behavior of others in the organization. Accordingly, it will be the purpose of Chapter 4 to develop a concept of leadership behavior as one aspect of instructional supervisory behavior. Further, certain theories of leadership behavior and empirical findings have been identified and later applied in the discussion of the leadership behavior of the supervisor.

THE NATURE OF LEADERSHIP

Researchers and theorists have defined leadership in many different ways. Stogdill (1974, pp. 7-15) classified leadership definitions under a wide variety of categories:

1. Leadership as a focus of group process
2. Leadership as a personality and its effects
3. Leadership as the art of inducing compliance
4. Leadership as the exercise of influence
5. Leadership as act or behavior
6. Leadership as a form of persuasion
7. Leadership as an instrument of goal achievement
8. Leadership as an effect of interaction
9. Leadership as a differentiated role
10. Leadership as the initiation of structure

Burns (1978, p. 18) said that, "Leadership over human beings is exercised when persons with certain motives and purposes mobilize, in competition or conflict with others, institutional, political, psychological, and other resources so as to arouse, engage, and satisfy the motives of followers." Leadership was recognized as a dimension of power but at the same time as separate and distinguishable from power. Power was conceptualized as the ability to activate the behavior of followers in certain directions, whether or not these directions were consistent with the motives and purposes of the followers. Leadership requires not only the consent of followers, but also consistency between the motives and purposes of the leader and the led. All leaders have real or potential power, but power holders are not necessarily leaders.

Burns (1978) defined two kinds of leadership: transactional and transformational. Transactional leadership is the interaction of leaders and followers in order to make an exchange of valued things. He compares this exchange to the bargaining process where the leaders and followers exchange valued items within the framework of consistent motives and purposes. Transforming leadership was described as a deeper and more enduring relationship in which the leader and follower motives and purposes are fused and become a basis for a higher level of behavior for both.

Etzioni (1964, p. 61) distinguishes between officials, informal leaders, and formal leaders. An official is a person whose power to lead is derived primarily from formal position in the organization. An informal leader's power is normative and is based on the respect of followers. The formal leader is an individual whose basis for leadership includes both his or her position in the organization and respect of followers.

Lippitt (1979, p. 399) identified four methods an instructional leader could use to influence the behavior of other people:

1. *Force*—the leader uses his or her control of means to *force* the choice of certain activities that he or she desires as goals.

2. *Paternalism*—the leader provides means and hopes for acceptance of his or her leadership out of loyalty and gratitude.
3. *Bargain*—the leader may arrive at a *bargain,* a more or less voluntary choice made by each party, to furnish certain means in return for certain other means.
4. *Mutual means*—the leader creates the situation in which certain activities of his or hers and of the group, if performed together, will serve as *mutual means,* means for each to satisfy his or her own (perhaps different) needs.

Lippitt's conceptualization is strikingly similar to Burns'. They both identify naked power or force as a method of controlling the behavior of followers without consent and without concern for the followers' motives or purposes. They both recognize bargain seeking (transactional leadership) as a method of leadership. Transformation (Burns) and mutual means (Lippitt) are similar in that there is a fusion or development of mutual means to satisfy compatible motives and purposes.

Our own view of leadership was partly derived from the ideas just discussed. We define leadership as behavior that is generated to cause certain other individuals to act, think, and feel in certain definable ways. The sources of the ability to influence can be force, paternalism, bargaining, or mutual means (Lippitt, 1979, p. 399). It is our belief that the establishment of mutual means is the most effective approach for supervisors to use in most situations.

Since leadership is behavior, it can be observed, studied, and learned. We also believe that behavior is a function of perception and that an individual perceives a leadership situation in terms of his or her experience, values, attitudes, and other personality characteristics. Therefore, leaders apply learned behaviors in terms of the way they perceive a situation. No leader can apply skills that are not in the leader's repertoire of behaviors, but neither should we expect the leader to apply a skill just because it is there.

Since in groups and organizations there are both formal and informal leaders, it is assumed that leadership behavior is not the exclusive property of any individual or group of individuals. Rather, supervisors (potential formal leaders), can attempt leadership, but so can supervisees (potential informal or formal leaders). From this frame of reference all members of the group or organization represent a source of leadership for organizational and individual improvement.

We believe that leadership effectiveness is not only a function of goal achievement, but is also a function of the well-being of the group. It may be possible for a supervisor to use "power" or "force" to control the activities of teachers and to achieve certain objectives in the "short run." But it is also possible, or even probable, that future potential of the teachers for achieving goals could be lost.

THE STUDY OF LEADERSHIP

One of the earliest approaches to the study of leadership was an attempt to find relationships between traits and leadership. Conclusions were generally negative. No strong positive correlations exist between intelligence and leadership, scholarship and leadership, or height and leadership, unless the trait gives the individual an advantage in the situation in which he or she exerts leadership.

Stogdill (1974, p. 81), after an extensive review of the research, concluded that leaders are characterized by a variety of attributes such as drive for responsibility, venturesomeness, self-confidence, and initiative in social situations. It was found that clusters of characteristics differentiated leaders from followers but individual characteristics held insignificant predictive value. These findings were not seen as a return to the traits approach, but were viewed as supportive of the importance of personality characteristics of leaders as significant factors in the dynamics of leadership.

The Styles of Leadership

Lewin and Lippitt (1938, pp. 292–300) and White and Lippitt (1960) did some of the earlier studies to investigate the effects of democratic, autocratic, and laissez-faire patterns of leadership on group climate and group achievement. A large number of studies followed these early studies of autocratic and democratic patterns of leadership. The results are mixed. Stogdill (1974, p. 370) concluded that the evidence does not show that democratic leadership increases production. However, the evidence is strong that democratic leadership is positively related to group member satisfaction. Some investigators compared group-members-centered and task-centered leadership. Out of 28 studies reported by Stogdill (1974, p. 380), nineteen showed a positive relationship between follower-oriented leaders and production, and nine studies showed either a zero or negative relationship. The evidence was even stronger in favor of follower-oriented leaders and the satisfaction of their followers. But there was still a large number of cases at variance with the follower-oriented theory of leadership. The evidence is beginning to form that there may not be one best style of leadership behavior.

Stogdill's (1974, p. 390) review of the literature on participative and directive leadership found that the number of studies that showed a positive correlation between directive leadership and production was about equal to the number of studies that showed a positive correlation between participative leadership and production. Group member satisfaction and group cohesion were found to be associated with participative leadership in significantly more studies, but even here there were some studies that indicated zero and negative correlations.

The Ohio State Leadership Studies identified "initiating structure behavior and consideration behavior as two critical dimensions of leadership behavior." Halpin (1966, pp. 126-127) summarized the results of his studies as follows:

> The evidence from these inquiries shows that effective leadership is characterized by high initiation of structure and high consideration. These two dimensions of leader behavior represent fundamental and pertinent aspects of leadership skill.

These findings were apparently consistent with the descriptions of democratic leadership as it was operationally defined in the Lewinian studies. Halpin (1966, pp. 123-124) verifies this notion as follows:

> In fact, it is our impression—and here we are speculating—that what ordinarily is referred to as democratic administration or democratic leadership is precisely what we have defined "operationally" as leadership behavior characterized by high initiation of structure and high consideration.

The fact that these independent investigators who were using distinctive methods came out with quite consistent results strengthened the generalization.

Blake (1964, p. 136) defined the following five leadership styles based on the leader's concern for people (consideration) and the leader's concern for production (initiation of structure): "Impoverished, Country Club, Task, Middle-of-the Road, Team."

The "impoverished style" is low on both concern for people and concern for production. The "country club style" is high on concern for people and low on concern for production. The "task style" is high on concern for production and low on concern for people. The "middle-of-the-road style" is midway, or medium, on both concern for production and people. The "team style" is high on both concern for production and people and is the style that Halpin's (1966) research indicated was most effective.

Stogdill (1974, pp. 393-397) reviewed the research on consideration and initiation of structure and group performance. The results were mixed. About half of the studies (eight) showed a positive correlation between group productivity and consideration. The relationship between group productivity and structure was positive in thirteen studies and zero in five studies. Group satisfaction and group cohesiveness were positively related to both consideration and structure in most of the studies, but there were still some studies that did not show a positive relationship. Stogdill (1974, p. 396) observed that, "several studies indicate that consideration and structure interact to influence productivity and satisfaction. The most effective leaders tend to be described as high on both scales."

Results from the "styles of leadership approach" to the study of leadership have been rewarding. The evidence is strong that the behavior of the leader is an important factor in group effectiveness. But research also shows that it is only one factor among many. For example, Fleishman, Harris, and Burtt (1955) found that freshly trained supervisors had a tendency to revert back to leadership behavior that was more consistent with the expectations of the situation.

Results from the traits and styles of leadership approaches have led to a different approach to the study of leadership. Marks, Guilford, and Merrifield (1959, p. 23) concluded, "We are almost forced to agree with the numerous reports . . . which view leadership from a behavioral and situational point of view . . . In essence, this view means that leadership is a function of the situation and its requirements, and of the followers and their expectations as well as of qualities of the leader."

The Study of Leadership Based on
Interaction Theories

Most modern theorists maintain that leadership effectiveness is a function not only of the characteristics and style of the leader, the maturity and expectations of followers, the nature of the task, or the nature of forces internal and external to the group and organization, but rather of all of these factors and more, with special concern for the interaction of these factors. There is apparently no full-blown general theory of leadership that can account for all variations of results. Simplistic prescriptions need to be examined with care and humility. Our position is well stated by Stogdill (1974, p. VII) as follows:

> Four decades of research on leadership have produced a bewildering mass of findings. Numerous surveys of special problems have been published, but they seldom include all the studies available on a topic. It is difficult to know what, if anything, has been convincingly demonstrated by replicated research. The endless accumulation of empirical data has not produced an integrated understanding of leadership.

But he goes on to indicate that much is known and that practice should be based on solid theory and research. We agree and will attempt to explore some of the modern theories and research findings. No attempt is made to be comprehensive. We leave this task to the scholars and proceed with "care" and "humility."

Bass (1961, pp. 3-9) developed a general theory of leadership based on the assumptions of behaviorism. He started with the idea that a group is a collection of individuals who are held together by the expectation of reward. In order to increase reward or avoid punishment, some members will attempt to change the behavior of other members. He called such actions attempted leadership behavior and theorized them to be a function of leader task orientation, self-orientation, interaction orientation, self-esteem, and self-accorded status.

Hemphill (1961, pp. 201-215) did a study of attempted leadership behavior. His studies strongly suggested that attempts to lead are related to rewards for goal achievement, expectations of group tasks accomplishment, member acceptance by other group members for leadership attempts, possession of superior and relevant knowledge, and previously acquired status as a leader.

Bass (1961, pp. 3-9) also theorized that successful leadership is a function of power and ability. Power is defined as the potential to coerce or grant permission and is acquired through status in the formal organization. Successful leadership is also a function of the ability of the leader to persuade members because of his or her perceived superiority to solve the group's problems. Ability is interdependent with esteem. When successful leadership results in greater group effectiveness, the leader achieves greater esteem and is more likely to be successful in the next leadership attempt.

According to Bass, it is necessary for supervisors to be where the interaction is and to accept the risks of leadership attempts. To be successful leaders, it helps to have position in the formal organization, but it is also necessary to have ability in the area of group concern and the esteem of group members. Esteem is earned by initiating successful leadership attempts that are rewarding to group members.

It is interesting to speculate that use of power without ability may result in group member compliance that is not rewarding and a deterioration of the leader's potential leadership.

Doyle (1974) supports the work of Hemphill and Bass by reporting that human-relations-oriented leaders were more likely to support the ideas of group members and, further, that support of member ideas was positively related to the generation of ideas by group members.

Piper (1974) found evidence that decisions made by group discussion and consensus, or decisions made by certain persons using the help of other group members are more "correct" than decisions made by individuals only. The evidence is strong that leader utilization of human resources in the group contributes to group efficiency and group effectiveness.

Fiedler (1976, pp. 6–16) developed the contingency model of leadership effectiveness. The theory holds that group or organizational effectiveness is contingent on the "fit" between the personality of the leader and the situation. The personality of the leader is defined as his or her motivational structure, including the goals and motives that are most important to the leader. Fiedler is not talking about leader behavior, but rather about personality characteristics from which behavior comes. The situation is defined as the amount of control the leader has over the outcomes of his or her decisions.

The personality of the leader was described as the high LPC (least preferred coworker) and the low LPC. The high LPC leader is a relations-oriented leader whose major concern is with his or her relations with subordinates. The low LPC leader is a task-motivated superordinate whose major concern is to get the job done.

The favorableness of the situation was high when the formal leader had strong control and felt that he or she could determine group outcomes. Fiedler and others (Fiedler reported that well over fifty studies had supported the contingency theory), using the contingency model of leadership effectiveness, have found that task-motivated leaders are more likely to experience good performance in either highly favorable situations or highly unfavorable situations. The relations-motivated formal leader is more likely to experience better performance in situations in which he or she has moderate control and influence.

Fiedler explained that it is possible to change group effectiveness either by changing the personality of the leader or the situation in which the leader works. He observed that it is very difficult to change personality, but relatively easy to change the situation by matching leader personality with the situation favorableness, or by changing the situational favorableness through organizational changes, or by helping the leader to develop skills that could be used to make the situation more or less favorable.

Fiedler (1976, p. 12) made the interesting point that leadership training can result in either more or less effective performance. For example, a relations-motivated leader may be experiencing good performance in a situation only moderately favorable. Through the development of leadership skills, it would be possible for the leader to develop a highly favorable situation that would be incompatible with his or her personality.

Based on Fiedler's findings, it would be appropriate to place supervisors in situations of high or low favorableness, depending on their personalities. But, it would also be helpful to use organizational structure (position authority, regulations) as a way of increasing or decreasing situational favorableness. It would also be possible to help instructional leaders develop group skills to either raise or lower their influence or control in a situation in a direction consistent with their personality needs.

Reddin (1970, pp. 11-17) developed the 3-D Theory of leadership, which is based on the assumption that task behavior and relationship behavior are the common dimensions of leadership behavior. He asserted that managers have a task to achieve and must get the job done through relationships with other people. He also assumed that the essential criterion of effectiveness for any formal leader was meeting the required job output.

Reddin (1970, pp. 12-13) defined four basic styles of leadership:

1. Related (high on relationship and low on task);
2. Integrated (high on relationship and high on task);
3. Dedicated (high on task and low on relationship); and
4. Separated (low on relationship and low on task).

Using these four styles, Reddin proposed that each style had an effective and ineffective potential, depending on the situation. Situational components that were assumed to be crucial to the effectiveness or ineffectiveness of a particular style include organization, technology, subordinates, superordinates, and coworkers.

Reddin's conceptual scheme is presented in Figure 4-1.

Each basic leadership style has an effective and ineffective potential, depending on the situational elements. The related style is characterized by concern for the needs of people. The manager is interested in subordinates and their development. Effective application of the related style is made by the "developer," who is primarily interested in utilizing, releasing, and developing the potential of subordinates. Ineffective application of the related style is made by the missionary manager, who takes care of human relationships at the cost of all other considerations.

The integrated style is highly concerned with tasks and relationships. Effective use of this style is by the executive leader. The effective utilization of personnel to achieve organizational goals is given high priority. A strong effort is made to integrate organizational needs and human needs. The ineffective use of this style is typified by a manager who is too concerned with cooperative decision making and is often perceived as not able to make a decision or provide decisive leadership.

The dedicated style is strong on task, which often means a driving and decisive decision maker and leader. The effective dedicated leader is the benevolent autocrat who directs the operation but with concern for people. The ineffective

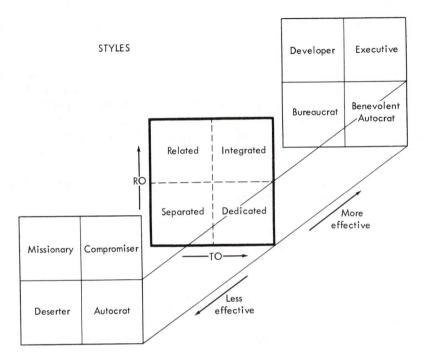

STYLES

Developer	Executive
Bureaucrat	Benevolent Autocrat

Related	Integrated
Separated	Dedicated

RO

Missionary	Compromiser
Deserter	Autocrat

——TO——→

More effective

Less effective

FIGURE 4-1 3-D Theory of Leadership

SOURCE: William J. Reddin, *Managerial Effectiveness,* New York: McGraw-Hill, 1970, p. 13.

dedicated leader is the autocrat who drives, dictates, makes decisions, and puts achievement of tasks above everything else.

The last basic style is the separated, which is low on task and relationship. The leadership is through rules and regulations, or anything to keep things impersonal. The effective separated leader is the bureaucrat. He or she knows organization policy and conforms. He or she plays the "game" and expects others to do the same. The ineffective style is typified by the deserter, who tries to maintain the status quo when change is needed. He or she is resistant to change and fights creativeness from others.

To be an effective supervisor it is necessary to read the situation and adapt your characteristic style. Reddin (1970, p. 46) does not suggest that a leader should or could change his or her dominant style. But, he does suggest adaptation of one's style, and he called this process style "flex" (Reddin, 1970, pp. 51-58). Our interpretation would be that though a leader could not change his or her dominant style very easily since it is a function of personality factors, it is possible to change behavior in order to be more consistent with the demands of the situation. For example, a related leader might make an autocratic decision to clear the building under threat of a bomb plant. This decision would be a change in behavior (flex) but not a basic change in leadership style.

According to Reddin, a supervisor working with a teacher needs to be sensitive to the situation and be able to "flex" style in order to maintain effectiveness.

For example, a supervisor who works from the related style could be perceived as ineffective (missionary) by a teacher who needs to learn a skill and is only getting psychological support. Conversely, an integrated style supervisor could be seen as ineffective (compromiser) by a teacher who needs an immediate definitive decision on a discipline problem.

Hersey and Blanchard (1977, p. 103) identified the following four styles of leadership behavior, which are similar to the four styles defined by Halpin (1966) and others:

1. High relationship and low task;
2. High task and high relationship;
3. High task and low relationship; and
4. Low task and low relationship.

They built on the work of Reddin (1970, pp. 104–105) and utilized his concept of the effectiveness dimension in conjunction with the concepts of task and relationship. Thus, they based their work on the assumption that leader effectiveness is a function of the interrelation of leader style and the situation. Therefore, any of the basic styles has the potential for being effective or ineffective, depending on the situation. They illustrated the possible effectiveness and ineffectiveness of the basic styles in Table 4-1.

TABLE 4-1   How the Basic Leader Behavior Styles May Be Seen by Others When They Are Effective or Ineffective

BASIC STYLES	EFFECTIVE	INEFFECTIVE
High Task and Low Relationship	Seen as having well-defined methods for accomplishing goals that are helpful to the followers.	Seen as imposing methods on others; sometimes seen as unpleasant, and interested only in short-run output.
High Task and High Relationship	Seen as satisfying the needs of the group for setting goals and organizing work, but also providing high levels of socioemotional support.	Seen as initiating more structure than is needed by the group and often appears not to be genuine in interpersonal relationships.
High Relationship and Low Task	Seen as having implicit trust in people and as being primarily concerned with facilitating their goal accomplishment.	Seen as primarily interested in harmony; sometimes seen as unwilling to accomplish a task if it risks disrupting a relationship or losing "good person" image.
Low Relationship and Low Task	Seen as appropriately delegating to subordinates decisions about how the work should be done and providing little socioemotional support where little is needed by the group.	Seen as providing little structure or socioemotional support when needed by members of the group.

Source: Paul Hersey and Kenneth H. Blanchard, *Management of Organizational Behavior: Utilizing Human Resources,* Third Edition (Englewood Cliffs, N.J.: Prentice-Hall, Inc., 1977), p. 107.

It is clear that any style can be seen as effective or ineffective, depending on the situation. But what are the significant factors in the situation that make a difference? Hersey and Blanchard (1977, pp. 133-137) built on the work of Reddin and developed the following environmental factors:

Leader's style   Leader's expectations
Followers' styles   Followers' expectations
Superiors' styles   Superiors' expectations
Associates' styles   Associates' expectations
Organization's style   Organization's expectations
                Job demands

They defined style as the consistent patterns of behavior utilized by the leader. Expectations were seen as the way individuals conceptualized the appropriate role behavior for themselves and others (Hersey and Blanchard, 1977, p. 135).

Hersey and Blanchard (1977, pp. 160-170) developed a theory of leadership behavior based on three interacting components of the situation: task behavior of the leader, relationship behavior of the leader, and maturity level of the followers. Even though they recognized that there are numerous factors in the environment that can contribute to the effectiveness of one of the basic styles, they emphasized the behavior of the leader in interaction with the followers. Hersey and Blanchard (1977, p. 161) justified this position in that followers determine the personal power base from which a leader operates. Maturity level of the followers was defined "as the capacity to set high but attainable goals (achievement-motivation), willingness and ability to take responsibility, and education and/or experience of an individual or a group" (Hersey and Blanchard, p. 161).

Situational leadership theory proposes that low maturity of followers suggests leadership behavior characterized by high task and low relationship. As the maturity level increases, the leader moves to high task and high relationship. As the group or individual achieves even greater maturity, the leader moves to a high relationship and low task style. The leadership behavior for highly mature groups is low relationship and low task. Figure 4-2 should help clarify the concept.

The bell-shaped curve means that as the maturity of followers is diagnosed to fall at a particular point on the maturity line, a perpendicular line drawn from that point to a point on the bell-shaped curve indicates the appropriate style of leadership. In Figure 4-2 the followers are relatively immature (M 1) and the line from the maturity line to the bell-shaped curve indicates that the appropriate leadership style should be high task and low relationship.

We like situational theory as developed by Hersey and Blanchard because of its strong theoretical context and simplicity and because we recognize the maturity level of followers as a significant factor in the situation. However, we feel that other factors in the environment are also significant and need to be considered in the diagnosis of the situation.

We also believe that it is more helpful to think of leadership style as a personality disposition to relate to the leadership situation in certain ways. Though leader-

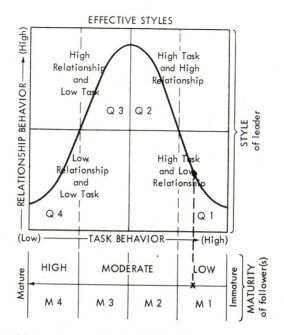

EFFECTIVE STYLES

STYLE of leader

FIGURE 4-2 Determining an Appropriate Leadership Style According to Maturity Level of Follower(s).

SOURCE: Paul Hersey and Kenneth H. Blanchard, *Management of Organizational Behavior: Utilizing Human Resources,* Third Edition (Englewood Cliffs, N.J.: Prentice-Hall, Inc., 1977), p. 167.

ship behavior is strongly influenced by one's style or personality, it is not the only influence. Therefore, it is possible for a leader to adapt or flex (Reddin, 1970, pp. 51-58) a style (change leadership behavior) to a situation without changing his or her dominant leadership style. We agree with Fiedler (1976, pp. 6-16) that a person's leadership style is his or her motivational structure or personality. Therefore, it is possible, but difficult, to change leadership style. Fiedler (1979, p. 395) suggests that it would be more appropriate to teach leaders to modify their situations than their leadership styles.

CONCLUSIONS FROM THE STUDY OF LEADERSHIP

In general the studies of leadership have investigated questions such as what is leadership? Who attempts leadership and why? Who is effective in what situation and why? The following conclusions have been reached:

1. *Leadership is behavior that is generated to cause certain other individuals to act, feel, and think in certain ways.* Formal leaders (influence from formal position and respect of followers) and informal leaders (influence from respect of followers)

must be concerned about the needs and motives of the persons with whom they work. We believe that leaders need to be concerned with achievement of group goals, but must also be concerned about maintaining the continuing strength of the group to solve future problems and achieve future group goals (Burns, 1978, p. 18).

2. *Leadership is behavior that can be observed and studied.* A person's leadership style is a disposition or tendency to behave in certain ways in particular situations. Therefore, it is possible to acquire leadership skills and apply them in some situations without basic changes in leadership style. A leader decides on behavior in terms of the interaction of his or her leadership style, repertoire of leadership skills, and perception of the needs of the situation. Leadership skills, and even the situation, can be changed more easily than leadership style, but all are subject to change.

3. *Leadership is a group role.* No one is a leader walking down the street alone. He or she is able to exert leadership only through effective participation in groups.

4. *Leadership, other things being equal, depends upon the frequency of interaction.* If a person usually shuts himself or herself behind the office door and does not have time to interact frequently with the staff, he or she will probably not exert much leadership in it (Bass, 1961).

5. *A person's effort to exert leadership in a group is more effective when the group members have enough values in common with the person attempting leadership to accept him or her as a member.* If he or she is an outsider, or so far ahead that the group feels that he or she does not have values in common with it, leadership will be more difficult to exert. A group turns for leadership to those people that it sees supporting its norms.

This leadership generalization raises one of the major problems for status leaders: If the person who is used by a group as a leader is a person who supports the norms of the group, how does a status leader who has an official responsibility for constantly improving the program work to challenge and raise the norms without losing leadership?

6. *Status position is only one of the sources of leadership potential.* Successful leadership is a function of both formal authority and earned esteem. The fact that a supervisor holds a formal position does not assure his or her effectiveness as a leader (Bass, 1961).

7. *Leadership in any organization is widespread and diffused.* The role of a status leader is not just leading a group, but also coordinating and focusing, as well as helping the group use the leadership that exists within it. A person who hopes to exert leadership for everybody is doomed to frustration and failure, because there are many different people within any organization or group who exert leadership for other people.

In his studies of the street-corner gang, Whyte (1943) found that gangs had more than one leader. Each gang had one leader who had two or three lieutenants, and these two or three lieutenants had people who followed them, not the gang leader. If the gang leader couldn't carry the lieutenants with him, he couldn't carry the gang with him.

A study was made of leadership among students in P.K. Yonge High School at the University of Florida. More than 240 students were asked these questions: If all the football equipment were destroyed, which person would you choose to head a campaign to raise funds to buy new equipment? If we were going on the radio to explain our school program to the public, which people would you choose to be on the panel? Seven types of activities were sampled. More than 200 out of the 240 were identified by their fellows as the persons they would choose.

8. *Persons who try to persuade too much or who give evidence of a desire to control are rejected for leadership roles.* Lippitt and White (1947) studied the effect of three different kinds of adult leadership on groups of fourteen-year-olds. One directed and told and used punishment to make people do what he wanted done. Another attempted to plan with people, encouraged members to work with people they liked to work with, and sought to help the group members evaluate with him the progress they were making. The third did practically nothing. He just sat back. He helped when he was asked. Lippitt and White found that the third type, the laissez-faire type, was the least effective. Authoritarian leadership was not as effective as the second type of leadership in getting people to work together. The authoritarian type of leadership produced thirty times more aggression in persons toward other persons in the group than the democratic type of leadership produced.

Lewin (1939, pp. 21–32) attempted to get people to eat different foods. In one type of situation, a home economist talked to people and told them they should eat certain new foods; only 4 percent of the people who listened changed their eating habits. In another situation, the same home economist sat with the members of the group as they talked about what they could do to further the war effort and made the same suggestion; 25 percent of the people made a change in their eating habits.

9. *The feeling that people hold about a person is a factor in whether they will use his or her behavior as leadership.* A person's behavior within a group must be such that people can accept him or her as a person of worth if they are going to give his or her contributions adequate consideration.

Helen Jennings (1950) reports a study of leadership among teenage girls in an institution for delinquents. She found that the leaders were the girls who were sensitive to the feelings of other people and who did not wear their own feelings on their sleeves. If an individual wants to exercise leadership with others, he or she must be concerned with their feelings and not be disturbed by the statements and actions of others. If supervisors want to be effective in working with teachers, they will work in terms of how teachers feel about action that is occurring

10. *Leadership shifts from situation to situation.* Sterling and Rosenthal (1950) found that if a group was being attacked by outside groups, the group turned to its more aggressive members for leadership; if it was going out to have a party and have fun, it turned to its fun-loving members for leadership. The group will use the leadership of people that it feels can contribute to a particular operation, unless the structural organization prevents it.

Cowley (1928, pp. 144–167) studied leaders in situations ranging from college campuses to prisons. He found that the same type of person is not a leader in different groups; that leadership isn't a common quality that makes it possible for a person to lead in any group, but that leadership is a group function and is determined by whether or not the person involved has qualities and values viewed as valuable by the group.

The research leads to the conviction that leadership is an element of group operation that enables a group to agree on and achieve goals; that it is a function to which many people contribute; and that the group selects which person's contribution will be used by that group for leadership.

11. *To be a leader, an individual must be willing to take the risks of attempted leadership behavior.* If leaders want other members of the group to attempt successful leadership, then they must give positive support for attempts and provide an opportunity for group members to develop relevant knowledge and status in the group (Hemphill, 1961, pp. 201–215).

12. *Groups can achieve more "correct" decisions by wise use of the human resources in the group* (Piper, 1974).

13. *The relations-oriented leader is more likely to function effectively when he or she feels a moderate ability to determine group outcomes. The task-oriented leader is more likely to be successful in situations when there is a strong feeling or very weak feeling of group control* (Fiedler, 1976, pp. 6–16).

14. *Leadership behavior can be affected by training.* It is possible for leaders to learn new skills that can be applied in leadership situations. But, learning such skills does not mean that they will be applied, since their application is a function of the style of the leader and the situation. It is also possible to change "leadership style" through training, but this is a more difficult process.

15. *Relations-oriented behavior and task-oriented behavior are the basic dimensions of leadership behavior.* Using these two dimensions of behavior, it is possible to think of leadership style characterized by high relationship and high task, high relationship and low task, low relationship and high task, and low relationship and low task. It is possible for any of these styles to be effective or ineffective, depending on the situation. However, we conclude that the high relationship and high task or the high relationship and low task are more likely to be appropriate and effective in the educational organization. We believe that a supervisor needs to read the situation and adapt his or her behavior accordingly (Halpin, 1966).

16. *Group satisfaction and group cohesion are generally positively correlated with leader behavior characterized by high structure and high consideration* (Stogdill, 1974).

17. *Leadership effectiveness is a function of the personality or style of the leader, the behavior of the leader, the maturity and expectation of the followers, and other elements internal and external to the situation.*

Apparently, if persons hope that their contributions will be used as leadership by the group, they will

1. *Exert initiative.* If they go into a situation and merely wait for people to come to them, people won't interact with them as frequently as they do with the persons who exert initiative. It's this willingness to take the needed steps that increases the possibility of exerting leadership.

2. *Communicate their feelings and their thoughts.* Probably no kind of individual is more disturbing to most people than "the great stone face" who sits like a sphinx and lets others wonder what he or she is thinking.

3. *Empathize with those they hope to lead.* They are able to put themselves in the other person's shoes to see how it feels there.

4. *Be creative or original.* They come up with an answer. The extent to which people are able to advance ideas that will be helpful to a group in solving a problem determines the extent to which their leadership is used.

5. *Be of service.* Some people think leaders dominate a group to get them to do what they want. Leadership research indicates that a person will be used as a leader more frequently when he or she has something that is of service to a group.

6. *Be knowledgeable about the area of group concern.* Such knowledge will increase the probability that successful leadership attempts will turn out to be rewarding to the group members and, thus, contribute to the esteem that group members have for the individual. This esteem increases the probability

that the next attempted leadership will be accepted by the group (Bass, 1961, pp. 3–9).

7. *Attempt to be perceived by followers both as considerate and "initiating of structure."* For the supervisor who wishes to be effective, expressing concern or even meeting the personal needs of fellow workers is important but not in itself sufficient. It is also necessary to be willing and able to initiate structure into group interaction, which is the "getting out the work" dimension of leadership behavior. It appears that these factors are independent of each other, but both are important contributors to leadership effectiveness (Halpin, 1966, pp. 81–127).

8. *Work to be perceived by teachers as putting great emphasis on both telling and listening or asking for information, raising questions, and reflecting.* This approach was verified in a study by Blumberg and Amidon (1965). When working with supervisors, teachers are likely to evaluate the interaction in a favorable way if the supervisors are both willing to tell and listen with a positive concern or if the supervisors are just reflective with concern and interest. But, if supervisors are perceived as just telling and criticizing or as relatively passive, teachers are likely to perceive the situation as relatively less productive.

Leadership is any contribution to the establishment and attainment of group purposes. It may be exercised by the supervisor or by any member of the staff. A definition that restricts leadership to persons in official positions is a denial of reality. Any person may make a contribution to the success of the group.

A group and leadership are mutually dependent. Neither exists without the other. A person cannot be a leader apart from a group. Neither can a group develop without leadership. Unity must be established; otherwise the group remains a collection of individuals. Someone must have a basic concern for developing group feeling and coordination. Leadership is a crucial force that someone must exert if a group is to come into being and continue to exist.

Leadership may be official or emerge from the group. Official leadership is appointed by some authority outside the group or elected from within the group by the group. Leadership may come from any member of the group; it is recognized as the group incorporates the contribution into its purposes or procedures.

Supervisors are official leaders and are almost always appointed by an authority outside the group in which the supervisors work. Throughout this book, attention is focused on formal and informal leaders and the way they provide the most helpful leadership for the staffs of the schools in which they work.

THE "POWER WITH" APPROACH TO LEADERSHIP

The "power with" approach to supervisory leadership is based on the assumption that followers have the potential for thinking, being creative, acting with maturity, and accepting responsibility. Therefore, it is also assumed that official leaders should not only seek to influence the behavior of followers, but should also attempt to release the leadership behavior of followers in planning and implementing action for educational improvement.

Under the "power with" approach to leadership, leaders are not concerned with getting and maintaining personal authority. Their chief purpose is to develop group power that will enable the staff to accomplish its goal. They do not conceive of their power as something apart from the power of the group. They are concerned with developing the type of working relationships that will give them power "with" the group.

If supervisors use the "power with" approach, they begin by assisting the group members to plan together. As problems arise in the organization of the group and in the steps taken to reach goals, supervisors expend effort in thinking of ways in which the group can attack the problem, instead of ways in which they can influence the group to accept their opinions. The chief questions for the group become: What is the job? How can we do it better? In answering these questions, the members of the group find that they are taking orders from the situation rather than from the supervisor.

If a faculty is governed by the situation, no one has power over anyone else. Decisions are made as to who will exercise which functions on the basis of skill and training. The supervisor participates in the discussion, exercises full intelligence, and gives the group the benefit of his or her best thinking. But the supervisor's ideas are tested just as carefully as is the thinking of any other member of the group.

An official ruling under such an approach becomes the statement of the staff's final decision. After a group has given full consideration to the ideas and the proposed solutions of all members, consensus is sought. Wherever possible, decision is delayed until consensus is reached. If time does not permit, as much agreement as possible is attained, and the dissenting members of the staff are asked to go along with the majority decision, with the understanding that the policy will be reconsidered if it appears unsatisfactory in the light of experience.

An executive decision is only a moment in the total process of the solution of the problem. It is the final statement of policy that the official leader is asked to administer. The solution begins with a clear definition of the problem, involves analysis of the factors of the situation, is based on procedure formulated by group decision, is stated as an official decision, and is implemented by the activities agreed upon by the group members as their responsibility in carrying out the decision.

In such a situation, authority and responsibility are derived from function, not from delegation or position. For example, if the faculty is confronted with a problem of mental hygiene, it calls in a specialist or refers the decision to the best-trained member of the staff. The staff accepts the decision, not because the one making the recommendation is the person vested with authority by right of position, but because the group respects his or her training and background and deems him or her the member best qualified to render an intelligent decision. Under such a procedure the official leader does not lose power. He or she is free to utilize all the resources of the staff. Authority is identified with training and information; it is used for "power with," not "power over." If the staff does not agree upon the best authority to accept, the question is open once more to group problem solving. Turning to the best-trained person is only a short cut in interpretation of data.

When a faculty operates on the basis of power "with" the supervisor, many persons have the opportunity to lead. Any contribution to the attainment of group goals is accepted as leadership. Each faculty member is called upon to exert leadership in proportion to his or her special skills and place in the faculty. Under such a method of operation, the supervisor's function is to coordinate the activities of the group. In other words, the focus is on the power of the group. The supervisor creates group power through coordination of activities.

Group power is the total capacity of the staff, centered upon the attainment of definite goals and operating through relationships built up under the guidance of the supervisor. A leader in this type of staff operation is the one who can help the group organize its knowledge, make it available to all members, and use it to exert the full power of the group in the solution of problems. An effective supervisor is one who can relate the different wills and abilities of group members so that they become a driving, unified force. The problem for the supervisor is to learn how to develop group power, not how to use his or her power to control others in the group.

A good leader helps the members of the group feel increased responsibility and enables teachers to attain importance by sharing with them responsibility for the program. He or she does not allow position to interfere with the opportunity for others to assume responsibility. Even though final responsibility rests with the supervisor, teachers and committees are given full authority to carry out their own tasks. As a result, all have joint responsibility. It is a shared responsibility, not a division of responsibility, among members of the staff. An official leader can share all of his or her responsibility and authority.

The question of delegated authority is less important under this approach. The total program of the school becomes the responsibility of the total staff, and the official leader is seen as chairperson of the group. When the school board or the community asks for an explanation of some phase of the school program, the official leader alone does not give it. The members of the staff who have primary responsibility for that phase of the program are used for the explanations. By such a procedure, the official leader does not lose power or increase the vulnerability of his or her position. He or she increases his or her strength because such actions have the full support of the staff. The full power of the group is back of the position taken by the leader. When the total staff makes decisions that represent the best efforts of group intelligence, the supervisor is in a stronger position than when he or she makes decisions alone and asks group members to carry them out.

Following the "power with" concept, the leader is able to build group loyalty, a sense of personal responsibility for the accomplishment of group goals, and a unity of effort that are impossible under the "power over" concept. He or she creates cooperative working relationships with the staff rather than personal control over the actions of individual members. Under the "power with" approach, there is actually greater control of individual staff members. If a group member decides to establish personal goals that oppose group purposes, the total pressure of group opinion is brought to bear. The opinion of fellow workers is a much more effective control than is any action that can be taken by an administrative or supervisory official.

When the official leader decides to work within the group, he or she is faced with the necessity of working cooperatively with people. In fact, he or she must become highly skilled in group processes in order to fulfill the major function of helping the group members to think, reach decisions, and take action together.

It must be recognized in all work with groups that a group does not start as a mature one. If the members of the staff have not had group work experience, the progress toward group maturity may be slow. Even where staff members are sophisticated in group processes, it will take time to develop group spirit and common concern. The more immature the group, the greater amount of direction it will be necessary for the official leader to exert. As quickly as possible, however, status leadership will want to pull into the background and allow group members to assume more and more responsibility. As more people have an opportunity to develop skill in group processes, the total group achieves more maturity.

A leader can tell whether the staff is attaining group maturity by the extent to which it moves toward developing a clear sense of direction, an ability to improve upon its own procedure, and a high degree of satisfaction from the work process and achievement of group goals.

How Should the Supervisor Begin?

A framework is necessary. The group members need to know the boundaries within which they can work and the extent of responsibility and authority the group has. The official leader should be very definite with the staff concerning the decisions he or she can and will share. He or she should make clear the boundaries of authority for staff members.

Operating under the "power with" concept, the supervisor shares the authority that is given in the situation. They cannot, in fairness to the group, share authority that they do not have. If they do, and if the group makes decisions that are reversed by outside controls, the group's confidence in itself and its power will be decreased. Supervisors cannot go beyond the rulings of the board of education or the state department of education. They cannot go beyond the mores of the community. It is possible, however, for the supervisor and the staff to decide what they want to recommend to governing boards or to the community. Recommendations issued as the result of the group thinking will be more effective in securing acceptance by outside authority than will be the declarations of a single individual. Cooperative thinking with other groups involved will be even more effective.

There may be areas of authority that official leaders are unwilling to share with staff. If they are afraid to risk the results of group thinking on certain problems, it should be made plain to the staff which decisions they are reserving and the reasons for imposing the restrictions. The staff may or may not accept the official leader's thinking, but the results will be less disastrous to group operation and staff growth than if the leader were to pretend he or she had no reservations about sharing decision-making authority and then vetoed a decision of the group.

Time must be provided for thinking together.   A staff does not become a group because a collection of individuals have been assigned to one building. It becomes a group as the members begin to develop common purposes and common values that tend to control the pattern of behavior of the individuals on the staff. Common concerns, purposes, and values are reached through sharing. There is no alternative. It takes time together. Official leaders must recognize that time spent on thinking together is not wasted; nor is it an indication that democratic processes are inefficient. It is the basis for effective and efficient work. The amount of time spent together can be decreased as the group continues as a unit, because the common concerns, purposes, and values will have been established and will need revision only in terms of new problems and solutions. But time together for solving group problems can never be completely eliminated as long as the staff remains a group.

However, discussion is only a part of a group's development. Experience together is an equally important element. The two must be combined. Without common experience to give common meanings, discussions may produce confusion through semantic difficulties. Action without time for analysis is likewise ineffective in developing a group. Unless there is opportunity to sit down together and interpret what is happening, the experiences may actually separate individuals because of the variety of interpretations. Experience provides common meanings only when there is analysis of it and agreement concerning it.

Let the staff know the method of work being used.   This suggestion may sound as though the supervisor is directing rather than allowing cooperative thinking. But it is essential that the staff know the procedures they are following. Teachers need to understand the processes if they are going to become enthusiastic participants in a group. The method of operation must be stated. Vagueness will lead to hesitation and drawing back. One way to achieve this understanding is for the official leader to suggest a way of working. He or she should then open the meeting to other members of the group to propose suggestions for improvement in the plan that has been outlined. Quite likely, if this experience is the first the staff has had with that official leader, no supplementary ideas or alternate plans will be suggested. The group, not trusting its official leader, may sit back and wait to see the operation.

The opportunity for change of procedure must be maintained.   Although group members may not suggest any variation from the plan of operation suggested by the status leader at the first meeting, these suggestions will come as soon as the members of the staff decide that the official leader can be trusted. Suggestions for change in procedure indicate that the group is beginning to accept the leader and develop maturity.

During the initial stage of group development, the official leader must be very careful to keep the word "I" out of the picture if he or she wants the staff to start thinking of itself as a group. The emphasis needs to be placed on cooperative work. The use of "we" instead of "I" leads to integration of interest. The use of "I" produces a division—"My staff and I"—and encourages other people to think in individual terms.

An absolute requirement for the initial staff decision making is that a group problem be attacked first.   A problem gives a collection of people a purpose. Without the purpose there is no need for the members of the group to continue to associate themselves. The problem's solution is the common enterprise that requires thinking together, planning together, and taking action together. The problem cannot be the supervisor's. It must be important to the staff if they are to be willing to spend time in solving it.

The supervisor must start where the staff is.   If the staff agrees on the most important problems facing it, the leader's task is an easy one. If there is lack of agreement on problems, time must be taken to help the staff reach agreement. As a temporary measure, the official leader should encourage the group to select a small problem in which there is general concern as a starting point for work. As the staff works together on the problem, the members will develop a greater number of common concerns. As individuals have experience together, agreement on importance and priority of problems increases.

Although it is well to proceed cautiously until the staff has learned that the official leader's suggestions are not a command, the supervisor, as a member of the group, needs to make his or her concerns known. His or her comments may lift to the level of consciousness a problem that is bothering the staff.

The supervisor must stress faculty-planning sessions as a place in which ideas can be advanced without fear of embarrassment. It is probable that certain members of the staff will be embarrassed by disagreement, because their experience has led them to believe it is a mistake to advance an idea that is not accepted by the group. The leader will want to take steps to assist the group to understand that if people accept each other and want to help each other, ideas can be tested without anyone's being hurt. If the staff has not had such an interchange of ideas, it is well to tone down criticism at first until people begin to feel safe with the official leader and with each other.

The supervisor should keep in mind that agreement on hypotheses is more difficult and less clear-cut in group thinking than in individual thinking.   Where forty or fifty people with different sets of values examine the same data, the chance of arriving at an agreement on a single hypothesis is much less than when one individual with one set of values examines the data. Group agreements on hypotheses contain a degree of compromise.

THE SUPERVISOR'S ROLE
IN THE GROUP

The study of leadership based on interaction theories has emphasized leadership behavior as the performance of needed group functions. Cartwright and Zander (1960, p. 492) have defined this approach as . . . "the performance of those acts which help the group achieve its preferred outcomes. Such acts may be termed 'group functions.' More specifically, leadership consists of such actions by group members as those which aid in setting group goals, moving the group toward its goals, improving the quality of the interactions among the members, building the cohesiveness of the group, or making resources available to the group."

Lippitt (1955, pp. 556-557) has described the functions of leadership as attempting "to discover what actions are required by groups under various conditions if they are to achieve their objectives and how different members take part in these actions."

Leadership behavior will vary among group members according to the demands of the situation, the expectations of followers, and the competence and esteem of group members. The supervisor or official leader would participate along with other group members in carrying out needed group functions; but according to Lippitt, the official leader has a special responsibility to be sensitive to the group's functional needs and to see that they are carried out. It isn't necessary or desirable for the supervisor to have all of the ideas or to do all of the pushing. However, it is crucial to see that problems are identified, ideas are generated, and action is implemented; and the supervisor has special responsibility in these areas.

As an official leader in the organization, the supervisor has certain prescribed authority, status, and position that others in the group do not have. It is important to use this source of power to provide a work climate that supports leadership attempts, questioning, information giving, and challenging from all members of the staff. It is true that such authority contributes to the leadership power of the supervisor. But, it is also true that if authority is used to threaten, cut people down, inhibit, and belittle staff members, it can reduce the effectiveness of the supervisor. This is because leadership success is partly a function of the esteem the group members hold for the supervisor, without which he or she can never achieve full potential as a leader.

If the supervisor acts in terms of evidence from leadership research, he or she uses influence to deepen teachers' insights into the methods of group thinking and into the importance of building solutions on the basis of scientific evidence gained through experimentation. He or she focuses on constant improvement, using the concerns of the group as the starting point.

In the process of improvement there is a constant effort to increase the unity of the group, to encourage diversity and the experimental approach, to enrich the group thinking, to build the security and self-confidence of the group, to help the group see clearly the boundaries of its authority, to increase interaction and sharing of experience, and to extend the opportunities for leadership.

As official leader, the supervisor wants to spread the leadership in the group, because it is recognized that sharing leadership helps the members grow in ability and thereby increases the strength of the group. He or she works to keep the organization of the group from concentrating responsibility in a few people.

One of the problems that a supervisor faces as attempts are made to spread responsibility is the manner in which certain staff members regard themselves. They glory in their leadership roles and want them. An attempt to give more people an opportunity to serve as leaders is a threat to those who yearn to monopolize the leadership roles. Other teachers feel inadequate and afraid. Out of a desire to shirk responsibility or a sincere belief that their leadership will not be sufficiently skillful, they try to avoid leadership roles by renominating the persons who have served before or by insisting that everything has been going so well it would be undesirable to institute any change.

The attitudes staff members have developed toward one another may also hinder the attempt to spread leadership. Any staff will have developed confidence in certain persons. Through the years, the staff will have come to respect their judgment and their ability to guide studies and committee work. Other staff members, through erratic and ill-timed statements, have lost the faith of their fellows. They are considered weak and inept. The probable success of an activity is enhanced or decreased by the person designated to lead it. If a person is selected whom the staff considers able, the other members will want to work with the committee and will give a fair hearing to the proposal that results. If a teacher who is considered unskilled, self-seeking, unintelligent, or shallow is selected as chairperson, the others will seek ways to avoid working with him or her, and the proposal that results will have less chance of acceptance.

The place defined for the official leader does not make him or her a less dynamic person, but increases his or her potential power. It allows a person with leadership to get into a position where he or she can use it. Qualities that generate enthusiasm and unity are wasted if preconceived ideas of status and organization prevent an official leader from using these qualities effectively.

A supervisor has the responsibility of helping a staff to establish or improve the organization necessary to study and improve the program. It may not be easy. The existing organization may not have made provision for curriculum study, research experimentation, or in-service education. The plan of organization may have been devised to provide for carrying out directives but not for participation in problem identification, decision making, or policy planning. The supervisor in many situations will find it necessary to take the initial steps to secure a modification in the organizational structure that makes possible wider participation in the leadership function. In some cases it will be necessary to suggest modification to the administrative leadership and in others to propose to the teaching staff participation in developing a new plan.

An organization cannot be forced on a group. Modification of any existing structure grows out of an attempt to decrease dissatisfactions. The first step of the supervisor is to provide opportunity for dissatisfactions to be stated and then to create the channel through which suggestions can be made concerning an organization that will decrease the dissatisfactions.

An effective organization of a group is a structure through which it can study and solve its problems. The supervisor can perform his or her official leadership role by creating sensitivity to the needs of the group and providing an opportunity for group members to plan and implement organizational structures appropriate to their needs.

LEADERSHIP PITFALLS

A pitfall in supervisory leadership comes in not recognizing the necessity for exerting initiative. But initiative should not be designed to control. It should be exerted to help people develop an organization through which they can make decisions that are to be implemented.

A second pitfall is not having an organization sufficiently defined and described, so that people know the functions that are performed by different individuals; know the channels through which to get a problem considered; know the procedures by which problems will be examined and studied; and know that when a decision is made, action will be taken to implement it. Moving into effective leadership does not mean moving away from structure. It means providing a kind of structure that implements the values that help people to grow.

A third pitfall is not moving in on a problem when it arises. Pretending that a problem will go away if it is ignored doesn't make it go away. If a vital problem is ignored by official leadership, feelings begin to build, and the acids of anger and fear begin to erode the objectivity of the participants.

The fourth pitfall is not emphasizing what is right instead of who. In any situation, the question should be, "In terms of our values and this situation, what is the right thing to do?" When this approach is taken, the individuals involved are controlled by their values and the situation rather than being controlled by personal power. Official authority is used to help the group apply the criterion and to implement the decision.

A fifth pitfall is not using the authority of the official position to hold the group together until decisions are reached. One of the primary uses of the legal authority of the status leader is to hold the group together until they reach a decision. In a deadline situation, the supervisor may say, "If we cannot reach a decision by December 1, I will have to make it." If it is possible for people who disagree to walk away from the conference table when they do not happen to agree with the way a decision is going, chaos results. The supervisor uses authority to hold together people who have different values, until the decision is made.

The sixth pitfall is not exercising executive authority to carry out policy. At times, the supervisor must say to some people who are not living up to policy, "This you must do." Leadership is not an abdication of the use of executive power, but the use of executive power to implement agreed-upon solutions to problems.

Another pitfall is not distinguishing clearly between policy-forming procedures and executive action. Many people say, "This supervisor took that action." Whether the action was democratic or undemocratic is not determined by whether the supervisor said something had to be done, but by how the decision that he or she was implementing was reached.

Another fault is not making clear to the group involved the limitation of its authority to make decisions. No one can share decisions beyond the authority that he or she has. Frustration is created within groups if the group is led to think it can make a decision that it doesn't have the authority to make. It is important for a supervisor who is sharing decisions to say, "Here is the limit to the kinds of decisions we have the authority to make."

Still another pitfall is for the supervisor not to share the information he or she has. It is important to keep both superordinates and subordinates informed of decisions and contemplated actions. The decision as to which information to share is hard to make. No one wants to clutter up the desks of the staff or supervisor with unnecessary information, but one also has the responsibility of keeping them fully informed if he or she hopes they will assume appropriate responsibility and action.

Another pitfall is not working within the expectations of the group. If a supervisor goes into a situation and works in a way that is contrary to what people expect of persons in his or her role, without taking time to talk through with them the process and their expectations, people may interpret the supervisor's actions as weak or inconsistent or manipulative.

The eleventh pitfall is not understanding that the supervisory role has many facets; the supervisor should recognize that in a role as official leader of a school, a person has responsibility for promoting group unity, for developing structure and policy, for contributing ideas, for implementing policy, for helping release the potential of the group for solving problems, and for developing better ways of working together.

5

SUPERVISION
IS
COMMUNICATION

The work of the supervisor is to influence teaching behavior in such a way as to improve the quality of learning for students. This objective can be achieved by working directly with teachers in the planning for teaching; the description, analysis, and evaluation of teaching; and the development and implementation of new approaches to teaching based on the evaluation. Supervisors also work with teachers in the development of general goals for school systems and local schools from which teaching objectives can be derived. Teachers and supervisors work together in the development of proposed learning engagement opportunities for students. All of these activities are instructional supervision, and effective communication is an essential ingredient in the process.

Communication has deep significance for human organizations since individuals make specialized contributions to the achievement of the overall goals of the organization. The degree of coordination, ability to use specialized expertise of members, and degree of group unity are at least partly a function of the quality of communication. In the most critical sense, communication is the basis of cooperative effort, interpersonal influence, goal determination, and achievement of human and organizational growth.

COMMUNICATION IN
AN ORGANIZATION

A communication system exists in any institution, whether it is a corporation, nation, family, or school system. It is the means of transmitting information, emotions, values, and insights. If it is used to develop cohesiveness and commitment among members of a group, depth as well as accuracy is important.

As far as group development is concerned, communication is necessary if a group is to be formed. Group cohesiveness depends upon common goals, so it is necessary for group members to communicate enough to discover what they hold in common and to identify the areas of difference that should be studied further. If group members are really to value each other through interaction, there is a necessity to have the type of communication that will get below the superficial layer of outward appearances. If group interaction is not an attempt to learn purposes, values, insights, understanding, and knowledge held by other group members, the group's bonds will be formed only by what people can observe.

Without depth communication, the people remain an organization without loyalty to each other or to a set of purposes. Each person is really alone. Each is controlled by the organizational structure that gives power to the person sitting at the crossing of the channels used for transmitting information. If organizations are to become cohesive groups, the communication must make it possible for group members to form adequate judgments about the worth of each other through having the opportunity to discover the real needs, motivations, and competencies of fellow members.

THE NATURE OF COMMUNICATION

Communication is more than talk. It is an attempt by the individuals involved to share their own feelings, purposes, and knowledge, and to understand feelings, purposes, and knowledge of the others. Gestures, facial expressions, posture, space arrangements, and time enter into the interaction. Between two people, communication is a two-way process. As more individuals are involved, the processes multiply.

Earl Kelly (1952, p. 78) defined communication as "the process by which one human being can to a degree know what another thinks, feels or believes. It is the means by which an individual's need for others can be satisfied. It is the source of all growth except body building, and the key to human relatedness."

It is obvious from this conceptualization that if the supervisor wishes to influence or be influenced by teachers, he or she must communicate. Communication is the means of learning and growth and, therefore, a fundamental element of the supervisor's effort. The facilitation of supervisor-teacher, teacher-teacher, and teacher-student communication must become a basic focus of the supervisory behavior system.

Berlo (1960, p. 32) defined six ingredients of communication that we feel are helpful in the understanding of communication in educational organizations:

1. The communication source
2. The encoder
3. The message
4. The channel
5. The decoder
6. The communication receiver

In Berlo's (1960, pp. 30-32) conceptualization, the *source* is the origin of the ideas, feelings, directions, suggestions, and descriptions of factors in the external environment that a communicator has a need to share. Such factors have to be expressed in some form that will transfer common meaning to potential receivers. This process requires *encoding* the raw material into a *message* through the use of symbols that potential receivers can understand. The *channel* is the method for transferring the message that must be *decoded* back to the original meanings by the *receiver* or *receivers* of the message.

Banki (1971, p. 31) included the sharing of ideas in addition to just sending them. We think interaction between the sender and receiver provides for the possibility of testing the congruence between the message the sender thought he or she was sending and the message actually received. Naturally, in the interaction process, when receivers respond to messages, they become senders and the original senders become receivers. Though we recognize that it is impossible to ever achieve absolute validity between the message intended by the sender and the message received, it is our position that interaction improves the potential for greater common perceptions of senders and receivers.

Kelly (1952, p. 78) put emphasis on the exchange of ideas, feelings, and beliefs (messages) among individuals (receivers and senders). Berlo (1960, pp. 30-32) added the concepts of the need for encoding, and decoding, and the method or channel for transmitting the message. Banki (1971, p. 31) was in substantial agreement with these definitions and explicated the idea of exchange between senders and receivers. We stress the idea that interaction between senders and receivers will enhance the possible degree of common understandings. Accordingly, we feel that it is helpful to think of the communication process as consisting of four major components: sender, receiver, message, and method of transmitting the message.

Sender.   The sender is the individual or group that wishes to transmit a message to a receiver. There are many factors that affect the message sent. The message will be affected by what the sender wishes to say and the purpose for saying it. The content of the message will be limited by the availability to the sender of symbols that convey the message. Such symbols must necessarily be selected on the basis of the sender's past experience and the stimuli in the external environment of which senders are aware.

The sender may also have certain things that he or she wishes to conceal. This concealment is a function of purpose, intent, self-concept, and external factors, and is conditioned by the sender's perception of the receiver. It is also true that the sender may reveal many things without knowing it.

The concept of self that the sender holds, and especially perceived relationships with the receiver of the message, could be important factors in the way the message is worded, what the sender is willing to reveal, what must not be revealed, and the expectations held for the receiver's response. For example, if the receiver is a superordinate of the sender, then an effort might be made to include only information that would tend to enhance the position of the sender. The message might also be worded in such a way as to express deference for the receiver. Such factors may be a function of either conscious or unconscious motivations of the sender.

The use of symbols to express feelings, emotions, or abstract ideas may be particularly difficult to put in a form that will be understood by the receiver. In some cases, senders may have to reach out for help in finding suitable symbols to convey intended meanings. There may be language barriers, socioeconomic differences among others, that could have a profound effect on the message received. In some cases, there may even be a need for a mutually agreed-on code between sender and receiver in order to protect the secrecy of messages sent. Such a system would require careful encoding by senders and decoding by receivers.

Message. The message is the symbol of the idea, event, information, or attitude that the sender is using to stimulate the receiver of the message in some specified way. The problem is that symbols are far from perfect representations of reality. They have to be interpreted and given meaning by humans. As messages become more complex, meanings and interpretation become more complicated and more dependent on a common field of understanding between senders and receivers.

Forms of the messages can be either verbal or nonverbal. Verbal messages can be either written or oral. Bulletin boards, morning reports, newsletters, written notes, letters, minutes of meetings, and written group reports are examples of written communication. Faculty meetings, conferences, classroom visits, intercoms, closed-circuit television, and informal contacts at lunch and other social situations are examples of oral communication. The form of the message that is used is an important factor in the effectiveness of the message.

McLeary (1968) found that principals relied heavily on classroom visits, conferences, and small group meetings to communicate with individual teachers. General faculty meetings and departmental meetings were used most often to communicate with the staff as a whole. A significant number of principals felt that increases in the size and complexity of schools made it more difficult to communicate effectively.

There is a need for teachers and administrators in an organization to communicate. In the past there has been a heavy reliance on informal face-to-face communication. But with the increase in complexity of the educational organization, the growth in size, and the growing tendency toward a separation of teachers and administrators, communication has become more difficult. It has been advocated and explained in other sections of this book that there is a need to broaden the base of supervisory behavior so that more and more teachers perform in the supervisory behavior system on an ad hoc basis. This procedure should contribute to the effectiveness of both oral and written communication among teachers and between teachers and administrators. Procedures such as cooperative teaching and cooperative evaluation should also help. The idea is to provide a structure in which teachers and supervisors can work together to improve teaching skills, the content of teaching, and the actualization of the instructional process. The utilization of procedures such as microteaching, collegial supervision, and "clinical supervision" should help to improve the flow of communication.

Methods of transmitting messages. Messages travel from sender to receiver through specified linking systems of transmission. In face-to-face communication, the channel is normally a direct line, but in some organizational communication, different kinds of networks develop and sometimes messages have to be interpreted and reformulated at different stations before the intended receiver gets them. The "wheel," the "circle," and the "all channel" are patterns of communication that have been defined and studied (Guetzkow and Simon, 1955).

In the chain each person in the network has direct contact with only two individuals. In the wheel, one individual has contact with all others, but they only have contact with the one individual. The individual in the center of the communication normally emerges as the leader. In the "all channel" all members of the network have contact with all other members. It was concluded from the study that the networks influenced group performance only in terms of influence on the group's ability to develop adequate organizations.

In educational organizations, formal messages flow downward and upward through the hierarchy. There are also horizontal linkages among peers. All of these directions of communication are important. However, in educational organizations, the normal flow is downward. Superintendents send messages to assistant superintendents, and assistant superintendents send messages to principals, and on through the channels to teachers and students. Even downward channels present problems since messages often change during their downward flow. This occurs as a result of misinterpretation, lost meaning, and blockages. Often it is to the advantage of official leaders to withhold information or change meanings to protect their own position within the organization.

Upward channels are even less effective in the educational organization, but quite important. It is essential for educational leaders to get feedback from students, teachers, supervisors, and principals. Students and teachers represent an important source of ideas for improvement. It is also necessary to know how policy statements, directives, and other kinds of messages are being received and acted on. This feedback is an important source of information about teacher satisfaction and dissatisfaction and is, therefore, an important factor in teacher motivation. But upward flow of communication can be threatening to formal leaders in the organization. It can also be threatening to students and teachers. Therefore, it is often distorted and inaccurate. Teachers say what they think the principal wants to hear, and principals say what they think the superintendent wants to hear. Sometimes principals block or distort information that they feel may make their performance look bad.

Horizontal patterns of communication have left a great deal to be desired. Teachers in classrooms that are on the same floor or even side by side often have little communication, thus depriving themselves of an opportunity to learn, get psychological support, or share expertise with each other. Team teaching, small group work, and cooperative problem solving can help. There is a grave need to improve the quantity and quality of horizontal communication in schools.

Keith Davis (1966, pp. 185–195) studied informal patterns of communication in organizations and identified the "single strand" and cluster chain. The single strand is a message that is passed along by a series of individuals. The cluster chain involves a network of informal groups that communicate with each other on a regular basis along with interconnecting links. If an individual understands these patterns, then it is possible to pass the word along to certain key individuals with the knowledge that it will make the rounds.

Davis indicates that the informal system of communication can cause trouble. It can start and spread untrue rumors, or true information that can disrupt the organization. But, nevertheless, this is a normal part of any organization, it is here to stay, and it can provide positive benefits. He contends that the grapevine provides accurate information most of the time and that management can increase communication effectiveness by increasing its understanding and use of informal channels of communication.

In a certain college of education, the faculty became divided on a crucial issue. There were two groups that represented the opposing positions. Certain members of the faculty were clearly in one or the other group. Other members of the faculty tried to identify with both groups. In general, the "fence straddlers" were left out of real communication in both groups because they were not trusted. But they became "messengers" for both groups. When a group had a message that they wanted the other group to receive without knowing that it had been sent, the information would be "leaked" to the "messengers." This is using the informal channels of communication.

Receiver.   The receivers are the persons or groups that are the targets of the message. Their interpretations, understandings, feelings, and total reactions to the message are a function of many factors: their understandings of the symbols used, what they want and need to hear, their perception of the sender and his or her intent, what they want to conceal from themselves, and the limitation of the physical structure of the situation. Communication in organizations and among individuals is tremendously complex and difficult. Absolute congruence between what the sender wants to communicate and the understanding of the receiver is never achieved. Interaction may at times result in even greater misunderstanding of the situation; the feelings, purposes, and expectations of others; and the way people can help and support each other.

Skill in the area of communication is of utmost importance to the supervisor. Any supervisory action involves working with another person. If the interaction between supervisors and the others with whom they hope to relate is not real communication, neither the supervisors nor the other persons will be deeply affected.

NONVERBAL COMMUNICATION

Little attention is paid by many supervisors to the nonverbal situation, and this oversight constantly interferes with the effectiveness of supervisory communication. Physical arrangements affect communication. The way furniture is arranged, including positioning, and the symbolism involved make a difference. Most people are aware that to seat participants in a group in such a manner that they can see each other increases the possibility of better communication. Seating group members in such a way that certain individuals can get greater feedback gives those individuals greater control of the communication channels and restricts most of the ideas considered to those suggestions that the favored individual will sanction. Making it possible for each person to have equal feedback by the physical arrangement of the meeting increases the possibility that the group will have freer choice to determine the ideas that are important.

Color has an effect on communication. Harsh, bright colors cause a person to withhold true feelings and ideas. Soft, light colors contribute to the relaxation of individuals and encourages them to be more self-revealing.

Gestures communicate. Hall (1959), in *The Silent Language,* describes in detail how communication among people of different cultures is affected because of lack of mutual interpretation of gestures. Even within a single culture, people interpret gestures differently because of variation in past experiences. One graduate student becomes offended when a professor points a finger at him, while the person sitting in the adjoining seat sees no offense. Some policemen have come to believe, as a result of their experiences, that gestures, particularly unconscious ones, are more revealing of true feelings than actual words. They have become so accustomed to communication situations in which words are used to direct or maneuver, that they distrust verbal communication. They develop a skill in interpreting unplanned gestures.

The posture and the degree of hurriedness of gestures affect communication. If a supervisor wants a conference to be one in which the communication is open, it helps to have a relaxed posture, indicating lack of hurry. Any indication of tenseness or hurry conveys the impression that the situation is not one in which feelings or ideas are to be explored, but one in which a particular purpose or task is to be accomplished.

The slogans and symbols displayed also communicate. A supervisor needs to be aware of what the things in the office say to the person who enters. How many books are displayed? What topics do they deal with? How are the materials organized? What art objects are present? What do they show about the taste and sensitivity of the inhabitant? What do the pictures reveal? What does the prominence given certain items say? What does the type of furniture and its positioning say? Is it an office that looks hard and businesslike, or is it a place that seems to suggest that there is time and desire to explore ideas? The same type of questions can be asked about a conference room. The symbols and slogans that are present help to set the tone that fosters or inhibits communication.

Communication is affected also by the perceptions of roles held by the people involved and the ideas of authority that individuals associate with these roles. A professor commented to a former administrator, "You know, I can talk to you more openly and honestly this year." When asked why this was true, the professor replied, "You were in a position of authority last year." The stereotype that an individual carries about the role of the other person affects their communication. Also, a person's perception of self and role determines how free he or she is to communicate. If he or she sees himself or herself as inferior or superior, rather than playing a different but equal role, there is likely to be less open communication.

When one person sees another as having the power to affect his or her future, the communication is restricted. The person seen as having the authority to apply sanctions or give rewards may try as hard as possible to increase the depth and openness of the communication and make no progress. All verbal and nonverbal messages are disregarded or misinterpreted, because the other person is fearful of the consequences of self-disclosure. The subordinate may share only those facts and feelings he or she believes the power figure will approve. Supervisors who wish to communicate at a level that will affect teaching behavior should be aware of the possible effects of being a part of the chain of command.

Supervisors need to realize that all the nonverbal elements of the communication situation contribute to the effectiveness of their work with the people with whom they seek to communicate.

THE ROLE OF EMOTIONS
IN COMMUNICATION

The emotional element of a situation affects the quality of the communication. Emotional disturbances of individuals and lack of trust among members of the group restrict the communication. If people are deeply disturbed, only the facts that seem to them to bear upon the problem are important. They are unwilling to take the time to consider other ideas until their disturbance is decreased. Many research studies have tested the extent to which anxiety affects thinking, and the results always indicate that the greater the anxiety that exists, the less open an individual is to consider a range of alternatives or to engage in abstract thinking. If supervisors wish to have real communication in a conference, they will do all they can to decrease the anxiety of the other persons in the situation.

People hear what they want to hear. The human organism blocks out comments and actions that are destructive and seeks to preserve its own feeling of adequacy and competency. It is important to accentuate the positive during conversation with people. If they want help, they must trust the situation and reach for assistance, if they are to hear comments that will help them grow.

Nothing that a supervisor does will increase the communication if there is no trust between the people involved. The degree of trust determines the types of problems individuals are willing to examine. People do not reveal themselves to people they fear or people they do not trust. With people who are not trusted, a person will only share the thinking he or she wants the other person to hear. A supervisor who rates some people will not have the kind of relationship with these people that enables them to reveal their more serious problems, unless their past experiences with the supervisor prove that teachers are not adversely affected by the ratings.

The emotional element can be positive. If the persons attending a meeting have had many experiences together, trust and like each other, and enjoy their interaction, communication will be open and honest. If the participants expect to learn from each other, they share their fears, concerns, hopes, and insights. If previous conferences have been enjoyable, happy occasions, the members will anticipate repetition of the experiences and take the steps they think will make the coming meeting even more productive.

Emotions are either an asset to successful communication or they represent the primary problem with which a supervisor must be concerned.

SOCIAL ORGANIZATION
EFFECTS COMMUNICATION

Kelley (1951) found that the more rigid a social structure, the less honest the members will be in their communication. People who hold a low position in a rigid social structure engage in many extraneous and non–task-centered comments and actions. If a supervisor wants to have high-quality communication with others, he or she does everything that he or she can to decrease an emphasis on status and difference.

In situations in which the social status lines are evident, the persons in the more unpleasant positions in the hierarchy have task-irrelevant content in their communication, and the high-status persons tend to restrict the transmission of content that would lower their own status or that would make them appear incompetent. The existence of a heirarchy produces restricting forces against communicating criticisms of persons at another level, and hostility develops as a result of perceiving persons at another level as threats to one's own desirable position or as occupants of a coveted but unattainable position. People within faculties who are without status and can't find a way of rising, socially or professionally, are the people who aren't sincerely concerned about any kind of project that's undertaken as a faculty task.

If a supervisor hopes to facilitate communication, he or she will work to decrease status lines.

COMMUNICATION IN GROUPS

The most common attempt at communication in a school system is a meeting—committee, faculty, department, administrators, or teachers. If the meetings are successful, failure in other forms of communication is overlooked. If the meetings are unsatisfactory, it is difficult to develop cohesiveness and commitment within the staff.

Since many meetings are planned and conducted by supervisors, it is important that they know how a meeting can be conducted to facilitate communication. Skilled leaders can conduct discussions in such a way as to develop a quality of problem solving that surpasses that of groups working with less-skilled leaders, and they can obtain a higher degree of group acceptance than less-skilled persons. The most skilled leaders obtain agreement on the desired solution; their contributions consist of summarizing, encouraging analysis, supplying information, sharing ideas, and preventing hurt feelings. The amount of consensus and the change in consensus are positively correlated with the skill of the discussion leader (Hare, 1952).

The success of a group meeting depends to a great degree upon the skill with which the discussion is handled. If a group is unaccustomed to working together, it may be well for the supervisor who has skill in discussion leadership to preside at meetings. The discussion leader sets the mood of a meeting, and his or her skill determines the flow of the discussion.

The first function of discussion leaders is to create an atmosphere that is easy, yet businesslike. They must be friendly, exhibit a sincere welcome to all group members, and accept the comments and participation of all members. They must encourage all members to accept as worthy of consideration the comments of every other member. They help new members to become acquainted. They watch to see that the timid person who has an idea has the opportunity to bring it into the discussion. They prevent a few persons from dominating the meeting.

A second function is to guide the flow of discussion. It is the leaders' job to see that all who have comments or questions are recognized and to refer questions to the proper source in the group for an answer. To do this properly, leaders must keep the total flow of the discussion in mind and must remember the types of comments that each member of the group has made. With these points in mind, they are ready to shift a question to the proper person, or they can place two comments or two questions in opposition to each other or show their relatedness. They provide the transition from one question to another.

A third function of group leaders is to clarify questions. Many times, a question will be presented in such abstract form or will be so long or unwieldy that the discussion will be hampered by it. In such cases, the leaders must step in. They may ask the questioner to define certain words used or to state the question another way. Or the leaders may shorten the process and restate the question in a brief, direct form. In any case, as they finish clarifying the question, discussion leaders must get the acceptance of the questioner that the rephrasing has not changed the original meaning of the question.

A fourth function of the chairpersons is to keep the group on the topic. They must constantly watch to see whether comments and questions further illuminate the issue under discussion or whether they lead the group away from the point. Many times, leaders will be forced to make judgments concerning the degree of deviation from the issue that will be allowed. In bringing the group back to the issue, the leader must act in such a manner that even the person taking the group away is not made to feel that he or she is disrupting the discussion or making an unsatisfactory contribution to it. Ways of doing this include restating the issue after the participant has concluded his or her contribution; stating the points that have been made on both sides of the issue; pointing out how the last comment bears on the issue and ignoring the portions of the contribution that were leading the group away; and stating that the last comment opens up other issues or ramifications of the present issue that the group may wish to explore and asking the group whether they want to stay with the original issue or pursue these new possibilities further.

Summarizing the discussion is one of the most valuable functions that leaders can perform. Through this process, they give order to the discussion. They outline the flow of the discussion for the group at various times during the meeting. In situations in which a blackboard is not used to keep a running outline of the meeting, this function is essential.

The number of times that the leader summarizes depends upon the way in which the group is moving. If the discussion gets under way quickly, if the progress is rapid, and if all members of the group are keeping the issue clearly in mind, the leader can let the summarizing go for long periods of time. If the group does not have its purpose clearly in mind and is moving slowly, the frequent summaries will help to stimulate more rapid progress. It is especially important for the leader to summarize or to have some member of the group summarize as the meeting closes. Unless this is done, many people who are not too skilled in group discussion feel that nothing has been accomplished and that the period has been only a "bull" session. The morale of the group will be strengthened if the leader points out the specific accomplishments of the meeting.

Leaders have the responsibility for keeping order in the discussion. They must step in when several people attempt to speak at the same time. They must raise the type of questions that will pull back into the main group a small subgroup that starts a discussion within itself. They must watch for outside distracting influences, such as street noises, people walking in and out of the meeting, and scraping of chairs. They must take appropriate action to eliminate these disturbing factors as much as possible.

Leaders must watch all members of the discussion group they are leading. As they glance at the faces of participants, they can see whether or not they believe the meeting is moving satisfactorily; detect the glances that indicate that a person has a contribution to make; note the frowns that mean that a member of the group disagrees or questions what has been said; perceive indications of restlessness such as doodling, crossing of legs, and squirming in chairs; see which members of the group agree with other members of the group; obtain a picture of the development of consensus; and know when it is time to raise the question of whether or not the group is ready to make a decision. The signs are small, but they are the cues by which a leader of a discussion group must operate. Someone has aptly called leading a discussion group "playing by ear." And close observation of the group is the only way this playing by ear can be successful.

Participation in a discussion group depends upon the nature of the individual. Discussion leaders have responsibility for giving individualized attention. They must particularly watch the timid members of the group; when these members give the slightest indication that they have a contribution to make, leaders must call on them. Leaders must keep the overly talkative person from participating too much. They can do this by watching for overparticipation in the first part of the meeting; by not gazing directly at the offending participant as the meeting goes along; by referring specific questions to the less-aggressive members of the group; and, with groups in which the discussion leader has worked many times, by asking the talkative members to help bring out the less-articulate members.

The discussion leader must also watch for persons in the group who have leadership qualities. Such persons can be detected by watching the attention the group gives to various speakers. When these persons are recognized, they can be used in helping the meeting to progress. After these members have finished the statement of the point of view that they espouse, the discussion leader can ask the other members of the group whether that is the position they want to take.

Leaders in the group who disagree with each other can be used to help clarify a position. But a danger against which the discussion leader must be constantly on guard is the alignment of people in camps behind the opposing leaders, so that the discussion group becomes two groups instead of one. The discussion leader's responsibility after the issue has been made clear is to ask the type of questions that get members of the group to state the areas of agreement and then center the discussion on seeking more agreement in areas where it has not yet been achieved.

It is extremely helpful to discussion leaders in improving their techniques to have certain types of analyses made of the meeting and of their work. A common form of analysis is the use of a flow chart by which the flow of the discussion from one member to another within the group is charted. Such a chart shows whether the participation was widespread or was restricted to a few. The flow chart will also indicate the number of times the discussion leader stepped into the picture. The more skilled leaders become, the fewer times they will have to participate to keep the group on the issue, to summarize, and to maintain feelings of group unity. A flow chart will also tell whether or not the center of focus stayed within a certain part of the discussion group. If a flow chart of the first part of the meeting indicates that the leaders are all in one section of the group, some members of that section may be asked to shift positions before the next session starts. Or the flow chart may indicate that the seating plan of the whole group should be changed.

Another type of analysis that proves helpful to discussion leaders is to have someone make a verbatim listing of the comments they make. In this way, they can see whether their questions are the type that bring all members into the discussion or whether they encourage the discussion to become dialogues between the chairperson and a single member of the group. For example, one of the questions that stimulates dialogue is, "Don't you think our purpose should be to win community support, Bart?" Putting the name of the individual at the end of the question excludes all the other members of the group and makes that individual feel a responsibility for replying directly to the chair.

Some pertinent questions for the official leader to ask himself or herself in evaluating his or her discussion leadership are

> Do I listen more intently to some members of the staff than to others?
> Do I recognize certain persons more quickly than others, because their thinking is closer to mine?
> Do I tend to discredit thinking that is not in agreement with my own?
> Do I pass value judgments on contributions as they are made?
> Do I expect the staff to give me the floor before anyone else?
> Do I expect people to agree with me because of my status?

Probably the best form of in-service training for discussion leaders is to make a videotape recording of meetings that they conduct. The discussion leader can hear and see the mistakes that kept the group from making progress.

In summary, the discussion leader secures group agreement on the agenda, maintains an atmosphere that encourages full participation, is impartial toward ideas, helps the group establish its own rules of procedure, keeps discussion centered on the problem, summarizes as necessary, brings out issues and agreements, and makes or provides for final summary.

In the beginning of group work, it may be necessary to spend some time thinking about the various roles of members of the group. Definition of function through thinking together will relieve a sense of insecurity on the part of some staff members who have not participated in decision-making groups. Each participant has a responsibility to contribute ideas and suggestions, to listen to what others say and relate it to the problem, and to state points clearly and briefly without wrangling over details and technicalities.

As members of the group, all persons have, along with the discussion leader, a responsibility for the direction and speed of the meeting. They need to assume an active role. They may take action to change procedures when they think satisfactory progress is not being made. They may request clarification when it is needed. They may summarize and state what they believe the next steps should be. They may ask that certain persons be recognized. In short, they may assume any of the functions of the discussion leader with the understanding that they are attempting to assist the discussion leader to coordinate and move the group forward.

In some meetings, supervisors serve as consultants. Their role should be understood by them and by the group. They are brought to the meeting to help the group solve its problems. They are not there to express their concerns or to sell the faculty a bill of goods. During the meeting, their function is to participate as members of the group. They should not expect or be given preferential treatment. Like any other member of the group, they will supply special information that bears on the problem. This information may be volunteered when pertinent, or it may be requested by the discussion leader. As consultants, they will receive guidance from the discussion leader. The discussion leader is in charge of the meeting, and the consultant is there to assist in keeping the group on the topic and moving toward a solution.

On occasion, a supervisor will speak to the faculty. Such a situation should not be considered a group activity. It should be recognized and used as a straight lecture. It will help in the total group growth of the staff, however, if these talks grow out of problems that have emerged in group sessions and are looked upon as data-collecting activities. The information obtained should be taken back into the group for evaluation, rejection, or use.

Each meeting should have a central purpose that all participants recognize. Although a portion of the meeting may be used for announcements and the exploration of new ideas, most of the time should be devoted to seeking consensus on the central question. The chances of focusing attention and reaching agreement are greater if the meeting is used to consider a proposed solution to a school problem or a proposed improvement in policy or program. Meetings should be devoted in large part to discussion of the definition of a problem or to reports of study committees that are ready to make definite proposals. Meetings built around the consideration of proposals become definite and important. Members of the group know that time is being spent in making decisions that will affect them.

Meetings should not close without reaching conclusions. These conclusions may be decisions to accept proposals or to refer them back to a committee for further study of a specific nature. It should be pointed out that reaching conclusions involves clear indication of the responsibility of individual members for the execution of the decisions. Meetings that end without any feeling of accomplishment soon break the spirit of a group and their belief in the value of time spent in meetings.

During the meeting, the group needs all the assistance that can be provided to help it know its progress. It proves helpful in many meetings to have a person record on a blackboard or chart the issues being discussed, the points made, and the agreements reached. Some groups have found it helpful to use large sheets of paper that can be taped to the wall to record the progress of the meeting. Then there is no problem of running out of board space and having to erase, and the running account of the meeting preserved on these sheets serves as the basis for the minutes and as data for study by any persons interested in increasing the achievement in meetings. Time should be taken at the end of the meeting to check with the total group to see if the record that has been kept is an accurate account of the meeting.

A permanent record should be kept of every meeting. It should include the name of the group, date, meeting place, members present, members absent, problems discussed, suggestions made, problems referred, decisions reached, responsibilities accepted or assigned, and plans for the next meeting.

The record is essential for securing continuity of planning and avoiding waste of time through repetition. The record should be circulated to all who have participated in or are affected by actions taken or being considered. It keeps everyone in touch with the work of the group and serves to give a sense of direction and achievement.

Meetings can be improved by evaluation. One technique is the use of a process observer, whose function is to keep a record of the interaction among members of the group. He or she is an evidence collector. He or she is not an evaluator. On the basis of the evidence presented, an evaluation can be made of the process and progress of the meeting.

Guide sheets have been worked out to help process observers. Listed below are questions culled from many such forms.

Was the meeting slow in getting started?
Was the atmosphere easy, relaxed, and comfortable?
Was the tempo slow, hurried, or satisfactory?
Was the interest level high?
Was the purpose clear to all?
Were members cooperative?
Was information shared?
Were members sensitive to each other?
Were tensions brought out into the open?
Was there evidence of feelings of superiority?
Were ideas forced on the group?
Was the group able to accept differences?
Was the group able to discipline itself?
Was any decision reached?
Was there resistance to group decisions?
Was participation spread throughout the group?
Was discussion centered for a long period in one portion of the group?
Was the discussion initiated by group members?
Were there difficulties in communication?
Was there a feeling of give and take?
Were members eager to speak?
Were certain members taking more than their share of the time?
Were members showing aggression?
Was the discussion limited to the topic?

Were members assuming responsibility for the success of the meeting?
Were members attempting to draw out each other?
Did the leader help the group to establish a direction?
Did the leader give encouragement?
Did the leader attempt to include nonparticipating members?
Did the leader volunteer more help than was needed?
Did the leader recognize those who wished to speak?
Did the leader dominate the meeting?
Did the leader manifest feelings of superiority?
Did the leader keep things going?
Did the leader bring the specialized skills of members to bear on the problem?
Did the leader summarize as necessary?
Did the leader try to give answers for the group?
Did the leader get a consensus?

The study of a checklist for the process observer helps members of the group to become more effective participants in that group.

Out of the study of group dynamics has emerged the beginnings of a classification of certain types of participation in groups. Although the definitions of various roles—such as coordinator, clarifier, critic, protagonist, manager, arbitrator, reality tester, group conscience, encourager, and boss—are still hazy, discussion of these terms as related to the group operation serves to help supervisors mature in their thinking about effective group communication.

COMMUNICATION IN A
PERSON-TO-PERSON CONFERENCE

Much of a supervisor's work is done in person-to-person interviews. Planning a program, planning with teachers for the description and analysis of their teaching behavior, considering a proposal or request, and interpreting a policy are only samples of the constant use the supervisor makes of the interview. Much of the supervisor's success depends upon effectiveness in the person-to-person conference.

No pat formula can be established for an interview. If there is too-close adherence to a set pattern, the supervisor's interview is likely to be ineffective. A supervisor in one of the important school systems of the country had read books on the psychology of managing people. In conferences he used flattery, promised rewards, fear, and anger in the proper proportion and at just the right time to obtain his ends. With some personnel, this technique might have been successful. With the group he supervised it did not work. They had read the same books. They could predict the trend of the conference and block it if they wished.

The difficulty this man experienced was due to a false concept of the purpose of the conference. He felt a conference was the place to influence a subordinate to accept a decision he had made in advance. He conceived of supervision as making decisions and getting others to accept them.

Many of the difficulties and much of the dissatisfaction would have disappeared if he had learned that the supervisor's function in education is primarily to create situations in which planning can occur, not to make the plans. A conference between supervisor and supervised is designed to produce cooperative planning, not to impose a plan on the subordinate.

Using the conference for cooperative planning does not mean that the supervisor will not plan in advance. He or she will. But it will be a special kind of planning. During World War II, this writer had an opportunity to observe a consulting firm at work. Their business was to guide the planning of industrial concerns over which they had no control. Their most important technique was the individual conference. Before each conference, the consultants spent about half the total time to be used for the conference in getting ready. They reviewed all the information they had about the person with whom the conference was scheduled. They decided upon the pivotal questions for the talk. They determined additional information to be secured. They thought through possible solutions that might emerge from the conference. Under no circumstances would they allow themselves to be drawn into a conference without preplanning.

No conference was scheduled without a definite purpose. It might be an exploratory conference to establish facts, or a conference to reach a solution to a problem. In any case, the conference had a purpose. It should be emphasized again that the consulting firm did not conceive of the person-to-person conference as a selling proposition. The purpose was not to convince anyone of the rightness of the firm's thinking, but rather to reach answers through thinking together.

The purpose of an interview should be clear to all parties. Persons kept in the dark are afraid and insecure. They play their cards cautiously, until they know where the conference is going and what is expected of them. If supervisors do not want to waste time, they should state the purpose early in the conference or announce it beforehand. Of course, if the conference is requested by the teacher, the supervisor has an equal right to know the purpose. In either case, the person invited to the conference has a right to ask what it is to accomplish.

If the conference is to be successful, it helps to hold it in a quiet place where the participants will not be interrupted. A conference is an attempt to reach a union of minds and purposes. It is a delicate procedure. Most people maintain a front, composed of certain mannerisms, points of view, and positions that they believe their role in life demands of them. If the participants do not declare their positions openly, the conference becomes nothing more than a sparring session. They may win each other's respect for skill in offensive and defensive warfare, but they do little to win each other's confidence.

A quiet, uninterrupted atmosphere is necessary to facilitate the lowering of "fronts." As long as people feel they may regret letting the other person know what they are really like, they will not take the chance. They do not reveal the way they really feel if they do not trust the other person or if they fear that the information he or she offers may be used against them. No one tells his or her secret desires or plans on a street corner or at a party where all may hear. Nor will persons express themselves openly if the conference is being constantly interrupted by people entering the conference room or by the ringing of the telephone. No skilled psychiatrist or counselor holds a consultation where interruptions may occur that will break the trend of thought or that will destroy the atmosphere of mutual confidence. If the need for an interview arises in a crowded, noisy situation, the supervisor should suggest retiring to a quiet location for the discussion.

Interruptions do not matter, however, if rapport has not been established—neither does the conference! The building of rapport depends upon putting the other person at ease. If the supervisor has known the teacher for years, and if their work together has produced respect and trust, rapport has already been established, and this phase of the conference is taken care of automatically. If the supervisor has built a reputation for helpfulness, honesty, and trustworthiness, rapport is more easily established.

But even with the persons who trust him or her, certain actions can destroy a supervisor's effectiveness. Emphasizing superiority is fatal. Some supervisors arrange their offices in such a way that their chairs are in front of the window. Any person talking to them is at a disadvantage. Superiority feelings can be displayed by voice, by insisting on fitting the conference into the supervisor's schedule, and by not giving the teacher a part in determining the length of the interview. The surest way of guarding against such behavior is to remind oneself constantly that supervision is a service operation, and that supervisors exist only to help the teacher.

Barriers can be built in other ways. Always putting a desk between the supervisor and the supervised is one technique. Sticking to Mr., Miss, Mrs., or Dr. is another. When supervisors keep their shields high, they cannot expect teachers to lower theirs.

Informality is of great importance in a conference. Many supervisors fail to achieve it because they believe they must impress the persons with whom they work. They fail to realize that the only way people are impressed is by real value. If a supervisor has worth, it will make itself evident. Teachers will say, "He or she grows on you." Sham is equally easy for teachers to detect. A good show is recognized for what it is worth.

A successful conference cannot be rushed. When understandings are to be reached upon which future action will be based, both parties must have ample opportunity to clear up any hazy points. Neither must the conference lag. A sense of constant progress must exist. Progress, however, can be in the direction of establishing better relations, as well as in logical movement to a conclusion. Signs of impatience or dissatisfaction or confusion are an indication of a need for readjusting the speed of the conference.

It is not always possible to start a conference at a fast pace even with an old and trusted friend. He or she may be laboring under some emotional stress resulting from an immediate conflict with another teacher or with a member of his or her family. Financial problems or other personal matters may cause him or her to be less acute than usual. Paying attention to the emotional status of the teacher and adjusting to suit his or her mood will pay dividends in successful conferences.

A conference should end with a definite conclusion. It may be nothing more than the statement, "These are the facts we agreed on, aren't they?" Or it may be, "It is my understanding that we agree to try this solution." If the conference has not gone as far as the supervisor had hoped, he or she should try to plan with the teacher what steps should be taken next.

A conference should end with an outline of the next steps, and the teacher should be made to feel that he or she is capable of taking them. If he or she leaves with a fear of failure, the agreement will have been futile. Such a situation is worse than no agreement at all, because confidence in the supervisor will be lost when the procedure agreed upon fails, as it most certainly will if the participants lack confidence in it.

The supervisor has a responsibility for believing in a plan before it is accepted and for conveying his or her belief to the teacher. If doubts have not been eliminated in the minds of both persons, the planning period has not been adequate.

After the conference is over, the supervisor should make a record of the agreements. Failure to remember or to live up to agreements is a violation of the teacher's confidence and will result in the destruction of future effectiveness. Few people have memories good enough to keep all the agreements made in a busy schedule. Memories must be supplemented by written records.

Finally, it is helpful if both participants work hard for authenticity. This will facilitate credibility of agreements reached and attempts to carry out those agreements. It also helps to maintain and improve a relationship of trust, mutual understanding, and effectiveness.

INFORMAL COMMUNICATION
CENTERS

Not all communication takes place through official channels. In fact, the formal communication may not be the real communication. The bulletins and the discussions in faculty meetings are the overt and approved communication. But the communication that determines action is the covert and informal communication in the cafeteria or at the bowling alley after school.

Supervisors should not try to combat or ignore informal communication. Rather, the informal system should be recognized, understood, and used to improve the educational situation for children. It is important to work in such a way that the formal communication more closely approximates the message of the informal. If administration and supervision have created a permissive atmosphere in which diversity is valued and used, the covert communication will be more like the overt. For this condition to be obtained, it is essential to build trust and the freedom to differ.

The informal communication will exist whether the formal occurs or not. It will help determine the group's norms and its goals. Informal communication should be recognized and cultivated. If it is hoped the staff will become a cohesive group with common values, steps should be taken to foster informal interaction.

Social activities, attractive teacher lounges, and teacher work rooms are all efforts to provide situations for teachers to discuss problems informally. The ideas and agreements reached will be brought into the official channels if supervision operates in a manner that makes the informal interaction respectable. If the administration tries to repress the informal communication, it will find that it is unable to progress, because people listen to official statements and then act in terms of informal agreements.

The success of a school system is dependent upon the quality of communication in it. It is necessary to examine bulletins, meetings, conferences, and the social climate to determine whether they facilitate open and honest discussion and decisions by all or whether they lead to isolation, indifference, and covert resistance.

BARRIERS TO COMMUNICATION

Persons can be more effective in communication if they recognize some of the most common difficulties people encounter in seeking to understand each other.

1. *Use of symbols or words that have different meanings.* Persons interpret words in terms of their backgrounds, needs, and purposes. Words also differ in meaning in different contexts and situations. A friend may call another friend by a derogatory name if both interpret the situation as a humorous one. The same word used between the same people in a threatening situation could lead to combat.

2. *Different values within the group.* People may be so closely identified with their own values that they do not want to consider any others. They may not recognize that anyone could possibly hold another value. They want to hold to their own values and not have them threatened. They refuse to try to understand other people's viewpoints. Deep commitment on the part of individuals to a certain set of values that are in conflict with the values held by other people will interfere with communication in a group; so will ignorance that causes misinterpretation of the situation.

3. *Different perceptions of the problem.* If different interpretations of the problem exist, and no attempt is made to resolve them, people will propose and argue for a variety of solutions without reaching agreement. They will begin to belittle or mistrust their fellows, because they cannot see logic or reason in their disagreements and alternate proposals. They will cease to attempt to understand anyone who could possibly argue for such a stupid proposal.

4. *Emphasis on status.* If certain people have superior knowledge, official position, or experience, it can block communication if the superiority is emphasized. For example, if in a study group, the leader and resource people are sitting behind a table in the front of the room and the other people are sitting in a semicircle on the other side, communication is hindered. Communication is more valid and accurate if resource persons are dispersed throughout the group. Individuals hesitate to disagree with persons presumed to be authorities. They are less honest about what they believe, and may hesitate to present contradictory evidence.

5. *Conflict in interest.* When certain individuals are afraid that a decision will be made that will hurt their empire or take away some of the advantages they have, they may try to block communication. They often don't share all the facts. They

may even try to use parliamentary procedures or other tactics to divert attention from the real issues.

6. *Making decisions by the majority vote rather than seeking consensus.* Whenever a group seeks to make a decision by majority, the members attempt to convince, to win, and to score points, rather than to try to understand the other person or to find out what beliefs are held in common. When consensus is sought, it is necessary to try to find out what the other person believes, too, so areas of common agreement can be determined.

7. *Attempts to keep feelings out of the discussion.* Some people believe that if feelings come into a discussion, communication doesn't occur. Yet feelings are as important to communication as facts. To attempt to keep them out of a discussion is an attempt to limit the degree of communication. If group leaders view personal feelings as important data, then the expression of them by other people doesn't threaten them.

8. *Use of words to prevent thinking.* This practice is common. Advertisers use it. They are not trying to communicate but are trying to control action. It happens in many groups. Individuals use words and symbols that most members don't feel free to question. They seek to associate their argument or proposals with sacred symbols and shut off discussion. Some supervisors use this technique in an attempt to control action of teachers rather than explore the real issue. They attempt to get people to accept their ideas by the use of banner words—words that people line up behind.

9. *Lack of desire to understand the other person's point of view, feelings, values, or purposes.*

10. *Lack of acceptance of diversity.* Unless group members value their differences, they don't really attempt to use differences to grow. The tendency of individuals to defend themselves is a block to communication. When people attempt to protect their position and avoid being exposed as weak, they block any kind of attempt by other persons to understand their viewpoint. Whenever there is insistence on conformity, there is a distortion of communication. If a person of superior status refuses to allow differences in opinion among the members of a staff, persons without power or authority will reveal only the information they feel the high-status person will accept.

11. *A one-way concept of cooperation.* If persons with superior status believe that people cooperate by going along with their program or idea, other members of the group will not be honest in the messages they send. They will hunt ways of protecting themselves or of convincing the high-status person that they really understand and will do what is expected, even though they are engaging in a program of resistance. When receivers feel that resistance is necessary, they will break or distort the communication.

12. *Feelings of superiority.* Senders who have superior feelings do not communicate freely and openly with receivers. They feel it is unnecessary. The receivers who feel superior do not hear accurately, because they do not believe the words of the sender are important.

13. *Vested interests.* Persons who want to protect their special interest will not be completely open and honest in communication. The others constantly wonder what they are not revealing, and the message that is communicated is the receiver's perception of the nonspoken motives rather than an interpretation of the spoken words.

14. *Feelings of personal insecurity.* If senders have feelings of insecurity, they will

not reveal any type of information that will lower their status in the eyes of the receiver. They will not admit feelings of inadequacy. They will withhold the kind of comments that might reveal some of their reasons for being insecure. If receivers feel insecure, they will hear only those things that they want to hear. They will ignore comments that tend to accentuate their feelings of inadequacy or will interpret them as a personal attack. If they interpret them as an attack, they will immediately move to the defensive and hunt ways of further protecting themselves or launching a counterattack. In either case, the original message is lost, and the purpose of the conversation becomes clouded.

15. *An obvious attempt to sell.* When the sender attempts to convince or to convert the receiver, the receiver is forced to protect personal integrity by belittling the communication of the sender or by seeking ways of refuting the message.

16. *The concepts that the sender and the receiver have of their roles.* If the sender and receiver see themselves as coworkers and people with common purposes who play complementary and supplementary roles, they will communicate more accurately. If they see themselves as opponents or as persons with different degrees of responsibility for the successful outcome of the venture, the distortion will be increased.

17. *Negative feelings about the situation.* If people fear that the situation is one in which they are not respected or their contribution is not valued, they will not attempt to make a real contribution. If they feel that the other person cannot be trusted, they will send messages designed to deceive rather than be honest.

AN INDIVIDUAL CAN
IMPROVE COMMUNICATION

The perceptions people have of themselves as senders and receivers in a communication system determine their effectiveness as communicators. As senders, individuals should

1. *See themselves as sharing, not telling.* If they are there to tell and convince, they will not really hear the other group members. They will hear only things to refute. They will concentrate so much on what they have to get across that they will not understand what is happening.

2. *See themselves as seeking to relate to other people, not to control them.* If they see themselves as attempting to control, they hunt ways of blocking communication in order to increase their control. They also attempt to ignore messages from other members, which contradict their purposes. If they seek to relate, they will be constantly testing their own ideas and values against those of others. They will become more sensitive to others.

3. *See their task as seeking truth rather than convincing others.* If their purpose is to seek truth, they will increase the data base by becoming aware of the facts known and values held by others.

4. *Judge their own contribution by the feedback they get from others rather than by personal judgment.* If they depend on personal judgment, they cannot be sure what others hear, or what they are really saying; neither can they clarify their points for others. They do not know the areas in which they are not communicating effectively. If real communication is to occur, the feedback from the listeners is important to the sender.

5. *Look for agreement and any disagreement and seek the meaning the other*

person intends in the areas of difference. Senders should value disagreement as much as agreement, because it indicates the portions of topics that need further analysis.

6. *Seek to be empathetic.* An attempt to try to understand where the other person is coming from may provide completely new insights for the sender.

7. *Seek words with common meanings.* Use more than one word to explain a point to see if the other person makes a more accurate interpretation with one set of symbols than with another. Be willing to be questioned. Try to help the receiver raise questions about any point that is not clear or about words that are not understood. Value differences of interpretation and the exploration of meaning. If difference of interpretation is valued and seen as a way of increasing clarity, the receiver will not hesitate to make clear any lack of certainty about the intent of the other. He or she will recognize that each action affects the communication.

8. *Seek to eliminate from their behavior actions that threaten.* Senders will recognize that resistance is a part of communication. They will be listening with a "third ear" to discover what is not being said. They will attempt empathy to see how what they are saying sounds to the listener. They will use nonverbal cues consistent with the verbal statements they are making.

As receivers, the individuals should

1. *Seek to help senders clarify their meanings.* Receivers should even raise questions from time to time about meanings that appear perfectly clear to them, because they may be interpreting in a way that the sender did not intend. Much distortion in communication is produced by people thinking they are in agreement or disagreement when they are not. They will ask, "Is this another way of saying what you said?" They will understand that their experience determines what they can hear and will seek to discover the background of experience that causes senders to make the statements that they make. They will recognize that they are interpreting in terms of their own needs and purposes and seek clarification. They will try to eliminate stereotypes from their own thinking and ask for specifics.

2. *Seek understanding.* The first emphasis is on attempting to discover what the other person is saying, rather than evaluating it. Receivers can look for agreement in areas where it exists and seek to isolate the areas of difference that they will want to explore later. If they argue, they aren't attempting to hear, but, rather, they are trying to win the argument.

3. *Seek to identify what is not being said as much as trying to understand what is being said.* The ideas that are not expressed, perhaps deliberately withheld, are as important as the statements made. If the listener can react in such a way that it helps the sender move into areas that are not being verbalized, there is a better chance of achieving real communication with the sender. Individuals improve communication as they decrease emphasis upon status, remove fear and distrust as far as possible from the situation, remember that honesty begets honesty, avoid evaluating the other person's contributions, give attention to the same degree that it is demanded, avoid attacking or becoming defensive, and support persons who are venturing into areas where they are testing the situation to see how open they can be.

If there is effective communication, agreements will be understood, disagreements will be clearer, people will value each other more or less, and the open interpretations will be more nearly similar to private ones.

EXTRA COMMUNICATION TASKS
OF THE SUPERVISOR

As individuals with special responsibility for increasing communication, supervisors add another dimension to the communication system. They are senders and receivers, but they are also facilitators. They are developers and maintenance men or women for the communication system, as well as participants. As supervisors, they should

1. *Encourage people to know and value each other.* Supervisors provide opportunities for social interaction. They help people to become informed about the backgrounds and achievements of others.

2. *Provide the physical arrangements that contribute to better communication.* When conferences and meetings are planned, supervisors make sure that the location is the best available and that the furniture is arranged in a manner that encourages maximum interaction.

3. *Seek to develop a permissive atmosphere.* Permissiveness, as used by psychologists, means personal freedom to express a point of view or an idea, without fear of recrimination because it is in opposition to one held by someone with power or authority. If the atmosphere is really permissive, the members of the staff value the person who is different rather than attempting to force him or her to conform. The person who is different is encouraged to challenge, because out of this challenge comes more insight for all. Achieving this attitude is not easy. In some staffs, the person who is different threatens other people, and they hunt ways of quieting him or her.

4. *Seek to identify areas of agreement and areas of disagreement.* Areas of disagreement are just as important to a group as the areas of agreement. Good communication does not result in consensus. Consensus of all phases of a problem cannot usually be reached. The supervisor does what he or she can to help the group value areas of difference because they indicate the points that need to be explored further. Individuals grow to the extent to which the group is able to explore its differences without fear of coercion.

5. *Reflect to the group what they think the group has said.* Supervisors may say, "This is what I have heard you say," or, "Is this what you said?" This action helps the group summarize and move to the next point. By reflecting and asking if they are correct, supervisors also make it possible for the senders to clarify what they really meant or help the group understand a member who apparently differs. Many times an individual is not sure what the other person has said and begins to bristle. When supervisors reflect ideas, they help people understand each other and decrease conflict. If supervisors or other members of the group feel free to state a third person's position in other words and then ask if the interpretation is correct, the spokesperson has a chance to say, "No, I did not mean that. I meant to say . . ."

Another clarifying technique that can be used by supervisors or by other group members is to make an application of an idea and say, "Is this what you meant?" For example, if someone says the teacher should be permissive, another group member may ask, "Does this mean then that I should not question the little boy who said, 'Let's spend one-half of our time writing and the rest of the time playing.'?" As a listener states an implication of a remark and asks if the person meant to make such an implication, a chance is provided for the sender to clarify his or her remarks and to improve communication.

A supervisor has a better chance of being effective if he or she remembers that communication is a process in which people attempt to share personal feelings and ideas and to understand the other person's feelings and ideas; it is part self-disclosure and part seeking to understand the other; it is decreased by feelings of superiority and inferiority, by fear and anxiety, by rigid social organizations, by attempts to pressure or control, and by pressure to achieve, produce, or conform; it is increased as trust is developed, when people feel they have common values and goals, when diversity is valued, when the wish to explore differences is present, when each person is free to make his or her own interpretation and form his or her own values, when consensus is sought without coercion or manipulation, when individuals like and accept each other, and when people support each other in sharing emotion.

If the communication is good, agreements will be understood, disagreements will be clearer, people will value each other more or less, public comments and private comments will be more similar, and the formal and informal norms of a working group will be more alike.

This means that supervisors will work to build group acceptance and trust; that they will support the right of individuals to differ; that they will deemphasize social status; that they will provide time for group members to interact; that they will seek uncoerced consensus in decision making; and that they will utilize their formal and informal authority to develop a communication system that facilitates the release of the human potential of the organization.

6

SUPERVISION IS COORDINATING AND FACILITATING CHANGE

Instructional supervision exists to improve instruction which, in turn, will enhance the probability that the goals of student learning will be achieved. Since improvement implies change, it is our assumption that the coordination and facilitation of instructional and curricular changes are fundamental dimensions of instructional supervision. It is our understanding that there are many factors both within and outside the organization that affect the change process and make curricular and instructional changes inevitable. Is it possible for organizations to partly control these forces, to predict and to some extent control the change process, and thereby promote instructional improvement? We feel that this is indeed possible. Therefore, it is our intention to examine the nature of change, directions for change, and strategies for change, and finally to develop conclusions concerning constraints upon the change process. A specific attempt will be made to examine communication, leadership, and releasing human potential as critical dimensions of the change process.

THE NATURE OF CHANGE

What is change? What happens when it occurs? From where does the direction for change come. Are people as individuals or members of social groups or organizations able to predict, plan, and control their own change directions, processes, and consequences? Conversely, are people merely "straws in the wind" and victims of varied forces over which they have no understanding or control? The answers to these questions and many more that could be posed are critical for instructional supervisors since their very existence is predicated on the assumption that they can contribute to the processes of facilitating and coordinating educational improvement efforts that require individual, group, and organizational change.

Instructional supervisory behavior is thought of as an organizational behavior system that interacts with the teaching behavior system. Teaching behavior occurs within the context of a "social system," and so does instructional supervision. The interaction of these two systems is a possible source of improvement and change for both systems. In order to understand this process, it is necessary to have some understanding of the nature of social systems.

Social systems can be described in terms of boundary, tension, equilibration-disequilibration, and feedback (Chin, 1976, pp. 90-102). The boundary of the social system provides a special identity and is the way the system is differentiated from the outside environment. In the case of a supervisor working with a special group of teachers, the hoped-for behavioral changes in the teachers represent the goals of the system and the reason for its existence. In open systems the boundary is broken, and, therefore, there is the possibility of "input" from the outside into the system and "output" from the inside into the system's external environment. This factor makes it possible for the instructional supervisory behavior system to influence the teaching behavior system. It is possible to do this in at least two ways.

First, there can be direct participation in the teacher-student behavior system, such as planning activities, description and analysis of teaching, evaluation, and demonstrations. This process is an effort to help, support, and provide service to a particular teacher who is working with a particular group of students. The focus is on improving the direction, process, and consequences in that unique system. Thus, it is possible to gather and analyze data on a large number of variables that would be assumed to have significance for improving that system. Examples of relevant variables would be the needs and maturity level of students; needs, maturity level, and skill level of teacher; social climate of the classroom; equipment, materials, and physical conditions of the classroom; group interaction; and learning objectives. Data analysis can be used as feedback for the system, which could produce dissatisfaction or tension, which might result in the disequilibration of the system and provide a basis for system change and improvement. The function of the instructional supervisory behavior system is not only to facilitate the process of disequilibration, but also to provide service, help, and support as the system seeks a new level of equilibration, which will improve the effectiveness and efficiency of the system.

Second, there can be indirect intervention that focuses on influencing the teacher. It is assumed that the teacher is a significant factor in the teacher-student system and that if the teacher changes, the teacher-pupil system changes. Examples of indirect intervention would be supervisor-teacher conferences, special planning committees, workshops, summer school, general conferences, and curriculum planning.

What are some possible outcomes of the intervention process? As a result of input from the outside (supervisory behavior) as well as internal factors, tension develops in the system and it is thrown out of equilibration. The system must reach out for a new level of equilibration or risk collapse. It is for this reason that systems are often resistant to outside interference. Members of the system are often afraid that they cannot meet new demands; often they don't want to make the effort. Therefore, they set up barriers to change. For example, teachers often resist supervisory attempts to become involved by not inviting supervisors into their classrooms, by not doing anything or putting on a show when they come, or by not listening to suggestions or not trying new ideas.

At the same time, teacher-pupil systems are in a constant process of change. The system needs feedback that is a reflection of its output. It is a way of finding out whether goals are being achieved and if they aren't, why not. Such feedback can bring about tension in the system and produce disequilibration, which causes the system to seek a new level of equilibration. This is the change process that supervisors hope to set in motion in teacher-pupil systems.

What do we know about the change process in educational social systems? Is it possible to study the social system, identify weaknesses, and difficulties, and develop changes based on self-determined direction? Can supervisors and teachers work together to improve the learning situation for students? Can supervisors participate in teacher-pupil systems in such a way as to produce positive benefits for both students and teachers? It is our assumption that it is through the application of the principles of leadership, communication, release of human potential, cooperative problem solving, and cooperative evaluation that it is possible to produce dissatisfaction in systems, which can result in disequilibration, which can lead to reequilibration and system improvement.

A THEORY OF CHANGE

A concept of the change process is helpful to instructional supervisors, but there is also a need to understand how to change the system. Chin (1976, pp. 99–102) presents a model for changing systems that we believe has important implications for instructional supervision. His model assumes that it is possible for system members and change agents (supervisors) to work together to define current states of stability and change, as well as external and internal forces contributing to current levels of equilibration and disequilibration. He also believes that it is feasible and appropriate for system members and outside change agents to collaborate to set directions for change, stability, and improvement; identify and control to some extent external and internal forces affecting the system; and produce disequilibration and reequilibration that results in system change and improvement.

Some concepts, principles, and theories of leadership, communication, and release of human potential have been identified and discussed in some depth in previous chapters. It is through the application of these principles that it is possible for teachers and other professional personnel to become sensitive to discrepancies between the objectives, processes, and results that exist in their systems and the objectives, processes, and results to which they aspire. Such discrepancies are the basis for dissatisfaction and possible disequilibration that throw the system into a possible improvement effort. It is from participation in the processes of coordinating and facilitating change, improvement, and maintenance of the instructional program and process that supervision derives its unique function and behavioral characteristics.

Figure 6-1 helps to show how these ideas fit together.

Teacher A, student B, and student C constitute an example of a teacher-pupil system. The system members are held together by the assumption that they can achieve certain goals more effectively as a system than as individuals. It is this factor that provides the basis for the continuous striving of the system to achieve certain preferred outcomes. Thus, the system is involved in a continuous process of change, and this change is achieved through some sort of problem-solving activity.

There are both external and internal forces that affect the system's process

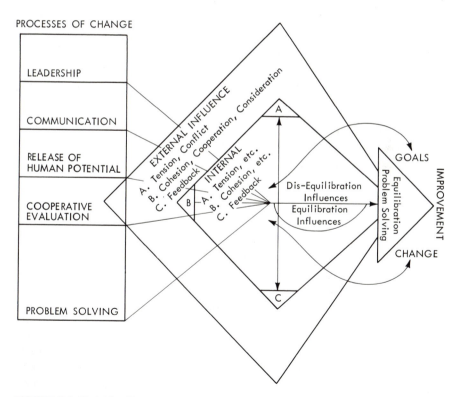

FIGURE 6-1 Model for Change

SOURCE: This figure is based on an earlier work by John T. Lovell (1967).

of change. Such factors as "feedback" from the external environment concerning the effect the system is having on external systems, new expectations, allocation of resources, rewards for system members, and threats from the supersystem are examples of external factors that can cause tension in the teacher-pupil system and create a state of disequilibration, which sets in motion the attempt by the system to achieve a new state of equilibration. Thus, change is achieved through the continuous process of disequilibration and reequilibration through problem-solving activities. Instructional supervisors attempt to facilitate this change process through leadership, communication, release of human potential, cooperative problem solving, and cooperative evaluation. It is through these processes that it is possible to create external and internal forces that will stimulate change and improvement in the teacher-pupil system.

Internal forces in the teacher-pupil system can also create tensions that set the change process in motion, that is, interpersonal conflicts, role conflicts, new system members, and new awareness or concern of system members. It is through "indirect" supervision that it is possible to help a teacher develop new insights or awareness that could result in changes in the teacher-pupil system. But it is through direct supervision that it is possible to provide the necessary support system to sustain the change. Leadership, communication, releasing human potential, cooperative problem solving, and cooperative evaluation are crucial processes in both direct and indirect supervisory activities.

From this perspective the instructional supervisor serves as a source of support, help, and service to many social systems that exist to maintain and improve instructional outcomes for students. Examples of social systems include a teacher working with a group of students in a regular class, a group of teachers working to improve reading instruction in a school, a principal working with a teacher, and a group of principals working on shared instructional problems. It is assumed that it is possible to improve the effectiveness and efficiency of these social systems through a process of planned change.

STRATEGIES OF CHANGE

Chin and Benne (1976, pp. 22-45) discussed three types of strategies for human and organizational change. Empirical-rational strategies were based on the importance of knowledge of the need for the change and the knowledge to implement the change. We agree that these are necessary conditions, but feel that in many cases they in themselves are not adequate. Patterson and Czajkowski (1979, pp. 204-206) reported that Zaltman, Florio, and Sikorski (1977) identified three necessary conditions for a reason strategy to be effective. First, the main reason that change has not occurred is a lack of knowledge. Second, the proposed direction for change is well understood and accepted. Third, the methods of implementation are both understood and feasible. Patterson and Czajkowski indicated that such conditions are not generally present in educational organizations. We agree and feel that empirical-rational strategies nearly always need to be used in conjunction with other strategies.

The second type of strategy for change discussed by Chin and Benne (1976) was normative reeducative. Under this strategy the rationality and intelligence of human beings are recognized, but it is also assumed that change will occur only as individuals change their values, attitudes, understandings, and skills.

The third group of strategies for change (Chin and Benne, 1976) were built around the concept of power. The use of this strategy requires the compliance of individuals with the wishes or directives of those assumed to be in a superior position of power. Strategies of physical coercion would rarely be used in educational organizations, but strategies involving material and symbolical rewards would often be used to gain acceptance of change efforts.

It is our contention that there is no one best strategy of change and that all strategies may have some relevance, depending on the circumstances. However, it is our belief that the normative-reeducative strategy, including the need for knowledge, is the most effective approach in instructional supervision under most circumstances.

Forced Field Analysis

In discussion of the change process, Lewin (1947, pp. 340–344) identified three phases of change: "Unfreezing, moving, and freezing of a level." He referred to systems being in a "quasi-stationary equilibrium" when driving forces for change and restraining forces for no change were equal.

The unfreezing process involves an attempt on the part of the system itself or outside agent to improve the system through processes of examination, analysis, diagnosis, and projection of an innovation. It is at the "unfreezing" stage that the system needs a definition of the current status of some phase of its program. This study would include a definition of the inputs such as money, personnel, facilities, and time; a definition of the processes of the program; and a definition of the program outputs. It would also be necessary to develop a definition of what inputs, processes, and outputs the system prefers. Discrepancies between the *real state of affairs* and the *ideal* state of affairs would represent problems.

The movement to a new state of being for the social system requires the strengthening of driving forces toward the change or a weakening of forces resisting the change. Force Field Analysis (Lewin, 1947) is a strategy for identifying, evaluating, and changing these forces. When the driving forces are stronger than the restraining forces, it is possible for the change to be implemented. Lewin made the important point that if the change agent just overcomes the restraining forces by increasing the driving forces, the process is likely to produce tensions that could interfere with the implementation process and the refreezing.

The processes of strengthening the driving forces and/or weakening the restraining forces are really what strategies for change are all about. It may be helpful to use a hypothetical case to clarify the process. The principal of an elementary school has become concerned about the utilization of room libraries rather than a central library. Talks with central office supervisors have indicated that they and the superintendent strongly favor central libraries. The supervisors also suggested a survey to get information about the utilization of materials. Talks with individual and groups of teachers showed that they felt they had worked hard to develop their room libraries and that they were meeting their needs for materials. They also said they were sharing with other teachers so they were already receiving the possible benefits of a central library.

Examination of parent attitudes revealed that there were strong "room-parent" groups that had worked hard with their teachers to build the room libraries. They were proud of their achievement and heavily favored room libraries. However a few parents were disgruntled when their children had to leave their own libraries when they were promoted. Some parents thought a central library would make more materials available to all the students and they favored changing. The principal tried to put it all together and came out with the chart shown in Figure 6-2.

It was apparent to the principal that the restraining forces were greater than the driving forces and, therefore, the change could not occur. She thought of various strategies for changing the forces in the field. First, she had information that materials utilization was not as great or as varied as it was in other schools with central libraries. She also had found out that teachers in the school were not sharing

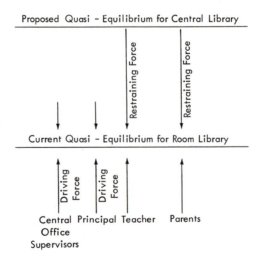

FIGURE 6-2 Conceptualization for Change in a School
SOURCE: The idea for this exhibit was borrowed from an exhibit used by Hersey and Blanchard, 1976, p. 279.

materials even though they claimed that they were. She provided this feedback to the teachers, and this produced tension. Some teachers became defensive and would not accept the data. Other teachers were concerned that their students were *not* getting the materials they needed and thought there might be a better way. Some teachers wanted to try a central library. They decided to meet with the central office supervisors. When this meeting occurred, the teacher restraining forces had already diminished and driving forces had increased. The meeting with the supervisors facilitated this process. During the meeting, the discussion centered around the advantages and disadvantages of room libraries and central libraries. The supervisors also brought word that the superintendent was very interested in their self-improvement effort and had released $10,000 to start the central library if the faculty chose to do it. The supervisors also agreed to provide needed help in the establishment of the library, including helping teachers develop needed new understandings and skills. Eventually, the teachers decided to try a central library, but with teachers having the option of keeping the materials in their room libraries that they had bought or acquired through the parent groups. The driving forces had become stronger and the restraining forces had weakened. The system changed to a new level of equilibration and hoped-for improvement. It is critical to provide a trial for the change with a rigorous system of evaluation. If the system is convinced that improvement has occurred, it is appropriate to make the decision to adopt.

Frey (1979, pp. 208–210) identified several principles of survival for an adopted program. He included the need for responsible direction and a continuous program to help staff members improve their competence. He also indicated a need for continuous change for improvement in the direction of goal achievement, completeness, and a better fit in the total program. Cost effectiveness was also mentioned as a contributor to program survival.

The example of the change from the room libraries to the school library describes the application of the empirical-rational strategy and the normative-reeducative strategy. There was clearly an attempt to broaden the knowledge base from which system members were operating. For example, teachers received new knowledge about the outcome of the room library system and how these results compared with the results other schools were getting by using school libraries. They were also sensitized to the lack of congruence between their actual behavior with respect to sharing materials and what they espoused they were doing. This process did create tension, but the facilitators of change did not stop with changing the knowledge base. Rather, they arranged for group discussions to iron out difficulties and provide further opportunities for communication, leadership, and attitude change. Specialists were brought in to participate in the discussion and provide support. Finally, the group made its own decision to participate in its own unique way with continuing opportunities for staff development and evaluation of the change. Thus, the change facilitators also utilized the normative-reeducative strategy for change. The superintendent's blessing and praise with strong economic support provided just a touch of the power strategy.

LEVELS
OF CHANGE
INTERVENTIONS

Hersey and Blanchard (1977, pp. 280-285) discuss levels of change, including knowledge change, attitudinal change, individual behavior change, and group behavior change. They contend, and we agree, that knowledge changes are the easiest. Attitudes are more difficult to change because they are supported by emotion. Hersey and Blanchard explain that individual behavior is more complicated because actual behavior may produce conflict with other behavior modes and attitude stances. For example, a person may have the knowledge that smoking is hazardous to health and may feel that he or she should quit. But, the actual behavior of stopping may be in conflict with the need to be accepted by peers or with his or her own self-concept. Change in group behavior is increasingly more complicated because of differences among group members in maturity level, past experiences, personal needs, and many other factors.

Blake and Mouton (1976, pp. 48-68) defined five types of interventions for change that could be used by supervisors in the change process. Acceptant intervention is a process of interacting with the client to support self-directed problem solving.

In the second type, catalytic intervention, the supervisor raises questions and makes contributions that help the teacher see the problem in a new light. Confrontation intervention, the third type, is an active intrusion into the situation of the teacher.

The prescriptive approach is an effort to diagnose the situation and prescribe an appropriate solution to the problem.

The fifth intervention strategy described by Blake and Mouton is an attempt to facilitate the process through which the individuals responsible for the outcomes utilize relevant principles, theories, and models to analyze the situation, test options, try solutions, and evaluate results.

We agree with Blake and Mouton that there is probably no one best approach for all situations. Rather, it is our assumption that all of these intervention models have some application in the supervisory effort to facilitate change. However, the use of principles and theories by the person doing the changing is a powerful and self-sustaining process that is consistent with the human resources approach to administration, which was discussed in depth in Chapter 3. It has special implications for clinical supervision since it equips the teacher to continue the program of change whether the supervisor is there or not. The utilization of the confrontation approach and especially the prescriptive approach could very well encourage teacher dependence on the supervisor. Unfortunately, there is some evidence that these approaches are widely used in the instructional supervisory process.

Harris (1975, pp. 32-34) identifed five options or combinations of options that could be used in planned change: (1) "physical changes, (2) rule changes, (3) organizational changes, (4) functional changes, and (5) personnel changes." Physical changes include such things as changes in the building and specially equipped classrooms, or new uses of computer technology. Such attempts are often doomed to failure when not used in conjunction with the other options. For example, the author recently visited a new and beautiful open-school that had been built "in the round." The building was divided into "pods" planned to house 120 pupils directed by a team of six teachers. The "pods" were built around and opened into a beautiful teaching and learning center. The six teachers in each pod had taken "their" twenty students to a "special" area marked off with filing cabinets and apple boxes and were continuing to teach much as they had taught in the "old" building.

Rule changes have to do with new policies, procedures, regulations, or programs that teachers must follow. Here again, if teachers have not changed their knowledge, attitudes, or skills in a direction consistent with the implementation process, the new program will likely be in trouble. Even if teachers have changed, but the organization has failed to establish an adequate support system including appropriate physical facilities, equipment, materials, technological support, and psychological support, the program will have difficulty.

Organizational changes and functional changes include such things as departmentalization, new systems of supervision, self-contained classrooms or team teaching, and the addition of new staff such as paraprofessionals to solve special problems. These changes are subject to the same difficulties described in the preceding paragraph.

Harris (1975, pp. 32-34) indicated that personnel changes, such as selection of new personnel, retraining, and reassignment, are the options that may have the greatest potential for change, but are the least used. We agree but would emphasize the difficulty of retraining and the necessity of using other change options in conjunction with personnel changes.

Rogers (1962, p. 18) has developed a conceptualization of the change process that has important implications for supervision. Rogers describes three interdependent parts of the change process: (1) Antecedents; (2) Process; (3) Results. The antecedents are defined as the psychological dynamics of the innovator and the innovator's perception of the situation. Such factors as anxiety or security, openness or defensiveness, mental ability, and skill development would be contributors to readiness for change.

The perception of the situation is important. Are the norms and rewards of the situation conducive to change?

The supervisor can be an important factor in the antecedents of change. He or she can support teachers' ideas for change, and provide needed security in failure. The supervisor can also communicate situational norms that support change and communicate recognition and deep concern for the teachers' change efforts.

The process of change is defined by Rogers as having five interdependent stages: awareness, interest, evaluation, trial, and adoption. The awareness stage is becoming aware of a new idea for change. The interest stage is developing a strong feeling that the idea is worthy of serious consideration for utilization. The evaluation stage is decision making on a trial or test. The trial stage is the period in which the idea is temporarily implemented with a strong commitment to a rigorous test of the consequences in order to determine the advantages or disadvantages of using the innovation. The adoption stage involves a strong consideration of the consequences of the trial in terms of preferred outcomes and a decision to adopt or not adopt.

These stages of change have important implications for supervisors who wish to facilitate instructional change. There is a need to create all kinds of situations in which professional workers can become "aware" of, develop "interest" in, "evaluate," and try out new ideas for change. Typical situations in which these stages of the change process could occur include clinical supervision, curriculum planning, evaluation of staff for personnel decisions, and professional staff development. Accordingly, these categories of change for instructional improvement will be considered in depth in following chapters.

There are a wide variety of sources of information to improve the change process. But it is clear that it is possible for the supervisory behavior system to serve as an important source of information. Feedback from student learning, new curriculum materials, and new approaches being used in other schools are examples of sources of information that could contribute to teacher awareness and interest in planning new approaches to teaching.

Guba (1968, pp. 292-295) defined the following diffusion techniques: telling, showing, helping, involving, training, and intervening. He suggested that the change agent will have to select from these six the appropriate techniques or combination of techniques. He explains that the appropriateness of a particular diffusion technique is a function of the assumptions that are made about the adopter, the hoped-for effect on the adopter, the innovator, and the substance of the intervention.

If the teacher is assumed to be a rational and competent professional, then the supervisor might first work to supply the necessary information. If the teacher is assumed to be inferior or subordinate to the supervisor, then it would be appropriate to sell or persuade, use politics, or reward or punish. It is the assumption of this book's authors that teachers and supervisors work together as colleagues and, therefore, share information, tell each other, and persuade each other, but that, in the final analysis, the teacher makes the decision and is held responsible for the consequences. It is hoped that the teacher will become increasingly independent of the supervisor and, therefore, more autonomous and self-supervising. The emphasis is on providing information systems, shared analysis, and shared decision making and problem solving.

BARRIERS TO CHANGE

Efforts to change can be handicapped, or even rendered unsuccessful, by either restraining forces that resist the change or inadequate driving forces to support the change. The following examples of barriers to changes illustrate both sets of conditions:

1. *Lack of commitment to system goals.* Sometimes individuals either do not accept or do not understand the goals of the system and, therefore, are not willing to seek new ways that may be more effective in goal achievement.

2. *Inadequate feedback.* When teachers do not have effective ways to determine the outcomes of their teaching efforts, there is no way to determine whether there is a lack of congruence between actual outcomes and preferred outcomes. Such a condition precludes the establishment of tension, dissatisfaction, disequilibration, and the acceptance of the need for change.

3. *Inadequate knowledge about the conditions of teaching and learning.* It is not enough just to have feedback about outcomes of teaching; it is also necessary to have objective and descriptive data about the conditions that contributed to those outcomes. This kind of knowledge provides a solid basis for making judgment about needed changes in the conditions of teaching and learning.

4. *Attitudes toward or values about the proposed change.* If teachers have negative attitudes about the change, or if they are expected to do things that violate their personal values, the change effort will have problems. Even if the driving forces overcome such restraints, there is a strong chance that alienation will develop, which will cause long-lasting problems in the change effort.

5. *Satisfaction with the status quo.* In some situations instructional personnel may just like the way they have been doing things and resent the idea of losing all those happy rewards.

6. *Inadequate skill development.* If personnel have not had an opportunity to develop the new skills and understandings needed to implement the new program, trouble probably lies ahead. They may feel threatened and insecure because of lack of skill, but may bomb the program on the basis of more "acceptable" reasons.

7. *Strong vested interests in the status quo.* Some individuals may feel that their personal interests are threatened by the proposed change. They may have developed the "current way of doing things" and may feel so strongly associated with those ideas that an effort toward change is almost a personal attack. It is also possible that individuals enjoy positions of formal or informal authority under current conditions, and that threat of their loss makes the status quo worth an all-out fight. Often the basis of the attack is on grounds other than the real reasons, and this clouds the issue.

8. *Lack of organizational support.* If the organization is unwilling to provide strong formal support at all stages of the change process, it is difficult for the change to occur. Almost all change efforts run into problems, and it is during these difficult times that organizational support may be needed. If the organizational support base does not provide personnel with rewards for change efforts, time for planning, needed human and material resources, and continuing support throughout all phases of the change, there is a good chance the effort will fail.

9. *Closedness rather than openness in the system.* If the system is characterized

by low-level communication both within the system and between the system and its external environment, then the chances for change toward improvement are much less. If individuals in the system do not share ideas with each other and with the external environment, they have little chance of developing awareness and interest in ideas for change. If they have to spend a great deal of energy to protect self because of personal anxieties and/or a hostile environment, the emphasis will be on maintaining boundaries and territorial rights rather than change toward improvement. All change involves risk and some threat to the participants. A supportive and open climate is needed to facilitate the processes of sharing and developing ideas, evaluating ideas, trying ideas, evaluating the trial, succeeding or failing, and moving on to new explorations.

10. *Lack of compatibility between the change proposal and other dimensions of the organization.* All parts of an organization are interdependent. A change in one part affects the other parts. If the consequences of the change effort to other parts of the organization are not anticipated and planned for, it is possible that these parts will resist the change.

11. *Threat to individuals.* The consequences of organizational change are often unknown to individual members. People are generally threatened by the unknown. Therefore, members often resist change without really being sure of the basis for their fear.

12. *Inadequate knowledge about restraints and possibilities in a situation.* Sometimes individuals misjudge a situation and feel restricted. They may assume that certain rules and regulations are less flexible than they are and therefore feel more bound to the status quo than is necessary. They may not be aware of the available resources for change, and, therefore, may underestimate their capacity for change.

13. *Static organizational role structure.* Sometimes the people occupying the official positions of leadership do not have the competence and/or personality to provide the needed leadership for change. Many times in such circumstances, there are people who could provide the needed leadership but are "cut off" because of threat to the official leadership, colleagues, or themselves.

14. *Inadequate expertise for solving problems.* In many organizations the needed competence for defining problems, deciding on solutions, implementing solutions, and evaluating results simply is not available within the organization or from sources external to the organization.

15. *Threat to officials of the organization.* It is not uncommon for officials in an organization to resist change for reasons such as the following: (1) fear that they do not have the ability to cope with the change, (2) fear that members of the organization cannot cope with the change, (3) fear that there are inadequate financial resources, (4) lack of motivation to make the necessary effort.

16. *Inadequate rewards for change efforts.* Many organizations "pay off" for conformity and passiveness. They do not reward individuals who raise questions, challenge the status quo, and try to facilitate change. In some situations such individuals may even be seen as "trouble makers" and be penalized for their efforts.

SOME CONCLUDING THOUGHTS

It is our assumption that it is possible and desirable to direct and control organizational change within certain limitations in such a way as to improve the probability of instructional improvement. Such a process involves setting the direction for change, identifying and controlling to some extent the driving and restraining forces of change, and producing system disequilibration and reequilibration that results in instructional improvement. The change process necessarily involves release of human potential, quality communication, and a broad base of effective leadership. It is through the application of these basic dimensions of human interaction that it is possible for the instructional supervisory behavior system to contribute to educational change and instructional improvement.

7

COLLABORATIVE SUPERVISION
A Delivery System for Supervision

The purpose of Chapter 7 is to identify and discuss emerging organizational needs and expectations for instructional supervision. Further, certain problems and concerns about the delivery of instructional supervisory services at the present time have been defined and elaborated. Finally, "Collaborative Supervision" has been developed and presented as a viable approach to the delivery of instructional supervisory services in the educational organization.

NEW ORGANIZATIONAL NEEDS AND EXPECTATIONS FOR SUPERVISION

Some educators have predicted that supervision will be eliminated from the educational organization. Perhaps they are right, if they are referring to a position labeled general supervisor. But if supervision is viewed as seeking improvement of curriculum and instruction, it will continue to grow in importance and in the number of personnel involved.

In many small school systems from the 1920s through the early 1950s, a person labeled "general supervisor" attempted to perform the entire supervisory function—instructional improvement, curriculum development, in-service education, media, remedial, and special service. Now, the number of people with the label "general supervisor" who have responsibility for all of these functions will probably decrease. School systems are being enlarged to make possible the provision of more services to the classroom teacher. It is being recognized that more specialized assistance is needed.

It is true that there is a need for more supervisors. But more importantly, the growing specialization of teaching and the rapidly developing knowledge base from which the content and process of teaching are derived require more highly specialized and accessible expert assistance to help teachers be sensitive to changes, develop new skills, and implement appropriate innovations.

Rapid changes in both the content and process of teaching generate greater psychological stress on teachers. The growing diversity of students, teachers, and supervisors indicates the growing difficulty of meeting certain basic requirements of a quality learning environment and points toward certain necessary tasks of instructional supervision:

1. Provision for psychological and technological support.
2. Helping people to communicate.
3. Helping people to help and be helped by each other.
4. Helping people to accept each other.
5. Coordination of the contributions of highly specialized people toward the needs of human beings in the learning environment.
6. Utilization of the total staff in the system of instructional supervisory behavior.
7. Leadership behavior to promote and facilitate change.
8. Release of human potential.
9. Curriculum development, coordination, and evaluation.
10. Continuous development and evaluation of educational goals.

The supervisory and teaching staff are more specialized and diverse than they have been in the past. The specialists in subject matter, learning disabilities, mental health, media, and research do not have a common background or depth of teaching experience. In fact, some may never have been teachers. They were added to the task force because they have a competency that can be used. They do not all know the curriculum design, or even quality teaching if they see it. Yet, each is able to make a contribution as a part of the overall effort coordinated by the head of the supervisory staff. Greater independence of learners, teachers, and supervisors and greater diversity and specialization of human learning resources require effective coordination in order to provide an internally consistent learning environment.

Since the background, training, and professional goals of all of the supervisory staff are not similar, the coordinating skill of the head of the staff is extremely important. All that this book contains about group development and leadership is critical for these persons. They need to develop common goals, mutual trust, cohesiveness, and a way of sharing decisions that gives the task force a plan and a strategy.

Even though all supervisors do not need to have the same knowledge or the same skills, all need to have understanding and competency in leadership, communication, and the ability to release human potential. More diversity in the supervisory staff must be accompanied by a common theory of change and common principles of working with people.

There is a need for a broadened base of participation in instructional supervision. The growing competence and specialization of teachers and administrators contribute to their capability to help each other. It is also true that students develop certain skills and understandings in the education process, and they need to be utilized in the instructional supervisory behavior system. It is also important that a broad range of resources outside particular school systems be provided and utilized. These outside agencies emanate from, among other sources, state and federal government, local and national industrial agencies, and private citizens. The proper coordination and utilization of these resources has become a major task for instructional supervision.

The growing need for instructional supervisory services is supported by the desire of teachers, supervisors, and administrators for more supervisory services. Numerous studies conducted by this author in East Tennessee support this contention. In a study reported by Lovell and Phelps (1977, pp. 7-8) it was found that 50 percent or more of the teachers indicated that the following services were not usually provided when needed and that they would desire an increase in the services:

1. Involving teachers in districtwide instructional programs.
2. Assisting in developing effective disciplinary techniques.
3. Planning in-service activities.
4. Providing teaching demonstrations.
5. Consulting with teachers on instructional problems.
6. Serving as a two-way communications link with the central office.
7. Helping describe and analyze instructional objectives.
8. Helping define instructional objectives.
9. Helping select appropriate instructional activities.
10. Helping choose methods for evaluating student progress.
11. Aiding in development of curricula.
12. Conducting or directing research.
13. Acting as a change agent.
14. Providing psychological support.
15. Suggesting new ideas and approaches for instruction.
16. Assisting in classroom organization and arrangement.

Even though organizations need and expect supervisory services, and though teachers desire more services, our review of the evidence indicates that teachers are not getting the services they need and desire, and are not satisfied with the services they are getting. For example, Carlton (1971) reported that teachers perceived that supervisors were mainly concerned with developing proposals for federal projects, staff development, administrative chores, policy development, and textbook selection. However, the teachers preferred supervisory assistance in the form of instructional conferences and observation to improve teaching, coordination for instruction, and provision of instructional materials and other activities more directly related to classroom teaching.

Lovell and Phelps (1977, pp. 6-7) reported that more than 83 percent of the teachers in Tennessee indicated that they had not been observed by a general or special supervisor during the 1974-75 school year. Also, 80 percent of the teachers said that they had not experienced an instructional conference with a general or special supervisor. More than two-thirds of the teachers perceived that observations were usually not preceded by a conference or scheduled in advance.

It is our contention that there is a growing need for instructional supervisory services in educational organizations. Teachers recognize that they need these services, feel they are not getting the services, and desire an increase in the services. What are some of the factors that have contributed to the current status of instructional supervision?

We feel that there are many reasons teachers are not getting the supervisory services they need and desire. First, supervisors are in short supply. In many organizations there are not enough supervisors with the appropriate competence to get the job done. In one large city system in which the author was recently working, a math supervisor said that he had the responsibility to work with all teachers who teach mathematics. This involved several hundred elementary and secondary teachers who were located in about sixty schools. This supervisor concentrated on several large meetings by grade level, tried to visit each school at least once each year, and concentrated on personal help for new teachers and teachers with serious problems. This situation is not unusual. Supervisors normally do not have the time to provide all the support, service, and help needed by teachers. There appears to be little chance of a move to employ large numbers of additional supervisors. As a matter of fact, the tendency is to cut back on supervisory personnel, especially during periods of economic difficulties.

In some situations supervisors are expected to give priority to administrative chores, political activities, writing federal project proposals, and developing in-service education programs. Thus, they have little time for providing direct support, service, and help to teachers at the local school and classroom level. Yet, the research evidence strongly indicated that teachers need and want feedback from their teaching, based on observation, demonstrations, instructional conferences to improve their teaching, and systematic evaluation.

It is also true that some supervisors do not have the conceptual, technical, or human skills to provide all the services and support that teachers need. This lack of skill may be because of a lack of training or experience, but it may also be a function of a delivery system that expects supervisors to know and be able to do all things for all teachers. This expectation is unreasonable and in many cases can be a cause of supervisors losing credibility and/or withdrawing from the delivery of supervisory services and retreating to safer activities such as administrative work, public relations, building maintenance, counting lunchroom money, or preparing federal project proposals.

In many situations the local school principal is either the primary or only source of supervisory help for teachers. But, principals often have to spend most of their time on other necessary activities such as pupil accounting, student discipline, public relations, and building maintenance. It is also true that principals are often called on to spend so much time on one phase of instructional supervision that other phases suffer. For example, in the last few years there has been so much emphasis on teacher evaluation for personnel decisions that principals have had little time to provide direct psychological and technological support to help teachers improve as professional persons and improve their professional performance.

It is not unusual for some of the conditions just described to contribute to a lack of trust and respect among supervisors and teachers. For example, if a supervisor has the position of local school principal and therefore has to give priority to administrative chores, student discipline, and teacher evaluation, leaving little time for helping and supporting teachers, then teachers may reach the conclusion that the supervisor does not really care that much about them, what they are doing, or the curriculum of the school. Also, if supervisors are expected to provide services for which they are not competent, they are likely not to be respected for their professional competence. It is also possible that principals who are forced to make evaluations for personnel decisions and also to provide help and support in a threat-free situation may lose the teacher trust that is so necessary in a helping situation.

We feel that one possible approach to alleviating some of the problems just identified is a new approach to the delivery of instructional supervisory services. This approach seeks to utilize in the instructional supervisory behavior system a broad base of human resources from personnel both within and outside the educational organization. It is our assumption that teachers, administrators, and students have the competence and willingness to participate in the delivery of supervisory services. We also believe that persons outside the organizations, such as college professors, local citizens, and state and federal personnel, provide a potential source of support for instructional improvement. What we believe is needed is an organizational structure and climate that supports flexibility and creative responses, together with personnel that have the competence and willingness to provide the leadership to identify and utilize a broad reservoir of human talent to improve the education process.

The opening up of the learning-teaching environment enhances the possibility for teachers, administrators, supervisors, and students to share engagement opportunities, describe each other's work, help each other analyze the learning environment, improve the curriculum, improve in-service education, and, in general, participate in self-supervision and the supervision of each other. A systematic approach for facilitating this process follows.

COLLABORATIVE SUPERVISION: A PROPOSED SYSTEM FOR THE DELIVERY OF SUPERVISION*

Collaborative supervision calls not only for the cooperation of professional workers in efforts to improve the instructional program, but also recognizes the reality and essentiality of differentiated roles of educational workers and the necessity for their collaboration in educational endeavors. An essential ingredient in the proposed model is the assumption of a broad base of competence and expertise among educational workers. The "need" is for the identification, analysis, and delivery of the reservoir of specialized competence to the appropriate problem-solving situations. It is recognized that individuals such as supervisors, coordinators, consultants, and principals who are formally assigned to the supervisory behavior system have specialized competence that should be utilized. But it is also assumed that they cannot be competent in all things or available in all situations. Therefore, it is proposed that the competence of organizational and nonorganizational members be utilized on an ad hoc basis. What is required is an organizational structure that facilitates this kind of flexibility.

The Assumptions of Collaborative Supervision

Collaboration supervision is necessarily based on a number of assumptions that need to be explicated at the outset:

Teachers in educational organizations are capable of providing leadership in curriculum development and policy formulation activities. Educational organizations are characterized by the fact that the basic worker, the teacher, normally has a very high level of preparation and specialization. As the educational enterprise has become more and more complex, the teacher has become better prepared, more specialized, and more competent. Growing specialization not only means that workers must achieve a greater expertise in certain areas, but it also precludes the possibility that certain workers, "supervisors," can be expert in all things. It, therefore, follows that it is logical for educational organizations to utilize the broad base of special skills and knowledges represented by teachers in the continuous effort to improve the learning environment for students. It is critical to get the person

---

*The idea for collaborative supervision was developed from many sources, most of which are unidentifiable. But, special credit is due Peter Husen, Amy Pace, Arthur Earp, Robert Simerly, Dewey Stollar, and Larry Hughes, all of The University of Tennessee. These colleagues discussed the idea, criticized the manuscript, and made suggestions. The human resources approach to organizational management discussed by Raymond Miles contributes significantly to the concept of collaborative supervision. Dr. Miles' contribution is discussed in depth in Chapter 3.

with the appropriate competence into the appropriate position with the necessary authority and time to "supervise" the achievement of a particular task. This requires a broad base of instructional supervisory behavior, rather than a narrow base.

Teachers in educational organizations are capable of giving help to and receiving help from each other. Teachers engage in similar kinds of activities with similar students. Sometimes they share students. Therefore, the special conceptual, human, and technical skills that a teacher has developed through the years could have relevance for other teachers. But it is not only help of a technical nature that can be shared; teachers also need psychological support. Teachers who are attempting innovations need the encouragement and support of fellow teachers. They need to know that someone cares—someone accepts the importance of their activities; and fellow teachers can be in the right place at the right time to provide this kind of "supervision."

Teachers and superordinates can and need to give help to and receive help from each other. Superordinates such as supervisors, coordinators, and principals are in a special position to provide support for the teaching behavior system. They can be highly specialized both in training and activities since they are not required to participate in the teaching behavior system. Thus, they can come with an expertise that is not generally available. They also have the time, and freedom to facilitate the process of teachers helping teachers. It is significant that teachers expect supervisors to participate in these kinds of activities, and this contributes to the potential effectiveness of the supervisor in facilitating teacher-teacher supervision.

Since teachers are involved in the direct process of actualizing engagement opportunities for students, they are in an excellent position to try out new content and methods and are therefore an excellent source of feedback on the effectiveness of ideas developed by "supervisors." Working directly with teachers in the teaching behavior system is also a way that "supervisors" can maintain close and direct contact with students.

It is also true that the process of teachers helping supervisors and supervisors helping teachers can be a psychologically rewarding experience. Either giving or receiving help can be a source of recognition. It is a way of saying, "I care about what you are doing and want to be a part of it." The opportunity to share successes in teaching with other adults can contribute to the feelings of satisfaction. Recognition and satisfactions from the work itself have been identified as important sources of teacher satisfaction in various research studies.

Effective supervisory behavior is not just a function of formal position, but rather is a function of many factors such as competence in area of group concern and level of esteem by fellow group members. Since organizational members have a broad base of expertise, esteem, and creativity, and since individuals have different strengths and weaknesses in different areas, it will be necessary for organizations to broaden the base of supervisory behavior throughout the organization on an ad hoc basis. This will make it possible to get the appropriate supervisory behavior where and when it is needed; and, thus, the organization will be able to utilize the special competence and esteem of a much larger number of organizational members.

Students have the competence to be effective participants in instructional supervision. Students have the opportunity to participate in a wide range of innovative activities. For example, a school system may start a nongraded program, open facility, open curriculum, or individualized program and self-directed learning. During the course of the students' participation in these activities, they have an opportunity to develop a "feel" for the innovation as well as certain "special" skills. If the school wanted to spread the innovation to other student groups in the same school or different schools, it is proposed that students with these special understandings and skills be assigned to the innovative groups on a temporary basis as teacher helpers. Thus, they would be participating in the supervisory support system on an ad hoc basis.

Many individuals outside the school system possess the competence and potential esteem to be effective participants in the supervisory behavior system. Faculty members from institutions of higher education are often willing to share their expertise at little or no cost to the school system. Teachers, supervisors, and administrators who have developed needed skills are willing and able to share in an effective way on a reciprocal basis. Members of the community, such as lawyers, medical doctors, business people, and public service workers, are often anxious to share their specialized knowledge and skills to improve the instructional program. The critical need is for the identification of these resources and the coordination of their utilization to improve the education process.

There is a need for authority in the educational organization, but it need not be static nor just "role" determined. When a task requires the coordination of human and material resources, there is a need for organizationally bestowed authority. Such authority can increase the probability of people working together and the availability of appropriate human and material resources. It is crucial that just enough authority for the particular task be provided, on the basis of an individual's expertise for this particular task. The difference between supervisor and supervisee is one of function in a particular task situation rather than a general assumption of superiority and inferiority. In fact, in the next task situation the roles might be reversed.

The supervisory behavior system should be a product of a scientific system for the allocation of human effort to improve the quality of learning for students. When supervisory behavior is thought of as organizational behavior provided to interact with teaching behavior in such a way as to improve the quality of learning for students, it is apparent that it can be a function of any person in the organization. A teacher who has been assigned to demonstrate a particular technique to fellow teachers is participating in instructional supervisory behavior. A supervisor who is observing for the purpose of describing a particular teaching procedure so as to make this "feedback" available to the teacher is participating in instructional supervision. The need is to allocate these functions on the basis of expertise, esteem by fellow teachers, needs of the situation, availability, and other factors, rather than to allocate such functions on the basis of role title.

It is impossible for the person occupying the offical role, "supervisor," to have the availability, esteem of fellow professionals, and expertise in all situations. The educational organization is highly complex; it requires organizational behavior of a sophisticated and specialized nature. It is also true that each learning environment is itself made up of unique individuals (both teachers and learners) in constant interaction. Effectiveness in the environment requires a depth of specialization unique to the environment. Therefore, supervisors could not possibly be expected to have the expertise to diagnose and prescribe for each learning environment.

New developments in the educational organization have contributed to the possibility of providing a broad base of instructional supervisory behavior. New developments such as open space, team teaching, differentiated staffing, media utilization, independent study, and large group instruction contribute to the possibility of teacher-teacher visibility, interaction, cooperation, and therefore availability for, and competence in, participating in collaborative supervision.

The supervisory behavior system should utilize resources from the teacher behavior system, the supervisory behavior system, and the internal administrative behavior system. Human competence that is needed to support the teaching behavior system will be broadly dispersed throughout the organization. What is needed is an organizational structure that is open and flexible enough to recognize, release, and utilize human resources when and where they are needed. The fact that a person is a principal of a school does not mean that person either has or does not have a certain expertise that is needed in the instructional supervisory behavior system. What is needed is a way of knowing who has the needed competence and a way of allocating that human resource where it can be helpful. The same could be said for a superintendent, teacher, or supervisor.

The Concept
of Collaborative Supervision

The foregoing set of propositions provides the framework for a proposed system of collaborative supervision. The concept, "collaboration," was chosen over possibilities such as collegial, peer, cooperative, and others for several reasons. First, the proposition that organizational members are specialized, competent, and interdependent workers leads to the need for a system of cooperation in curriculum and instruction, decision making, and problem solving. The lack of availability of a large enough group of people titled "supervisors" with a broad enough spectrum of expertise, and the availability of teachers and other professionals indicate a need to get the people with the expertise and esteem where they could collaborate with individuals needing psychological or technical support. But it is also recognized that organizational members achieve different levels of prestige and organizational authority. Therefore, it is assumed that organizational members will not always be collaborating from equal positions of influence. Rather, it is assumed that two or more people nearly always collaborate from positions of unequal influence.* Therefore, collaboration is cooperating, sharing ideas, solving problems, and providing feedback based on observation of teaching, with or for a person with greater or less influence.

It is proposed that a system of collaborative supervision will improve the probability of certain kinds of learning outcomes for students. It is hoped that the conceptual scheme in Figure 7-1 will clarify the major components of a model for collaborative supervision.

The first component of the model for collaborative supervision is the student behavior system. This system is the major consideration for educational organizations since students are in fact the basis of the existence of the educational organization. They are our client system and, therefore, their needs, interests, and level of development in concert with society's expectation for their development provide the basis for the development and actualization of the teaching behavior system. The second component is the teaching behavior system, which has the function of interacting with the student behavior system in order to improve the probability that the goals and objectives of the student behavior system will be realized. We believe that it is helpful to conceptualize teaching as having five interdependent dimensions: (1) planning, (2) actualizing, (3) describing, (4) analyzing, and (5) generalizing. These five dimensions of teaching are the critical point at which the instructional supervisory behavior system interacts with the teaching behavior system in order to contribute to the achievement of the goals and objectives of the teacher-student behavior system.

We believe that it is possible and appropriate to utilize human resources from the student behavior system, teaching behavior system, internal administrative behavior system, and external behavior system to strengthen the collaborative supervision behavior system. The arrows from each of these behavior systems point to the collaborative supervision system to indicate the use of these resources on an ad hoc basis. Instructional supervisors spend most or all of their time working in the instructional supervisory behavior system. Their role was defined in Chapter 1. Individuals in the other behavior systems serve on a temporary basis to provide service and help, according to their special competence, where and when it is needed. Instructional supervisors not only provide instructional supervision according to their expertise, but also have prime responsibility for identifying the people

*This idea was generated during a discussion with Dr. Peter Husen of The University of Tennessee.

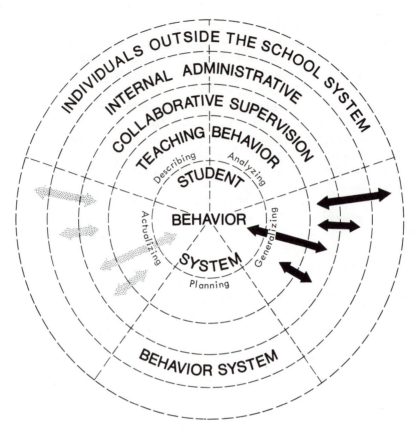

FIGURE 7-1 Collaborative Supervision

with a need and the people who can help, and facilitating the organizational structure through which these individuals can help and be helped.

THE APPLICATION
OF COLLABORATIVE
SUPERVISION

There are at least four operational areas of instructional supervisory behavior that are appropriate for the application of collaborative supervision. First, there is the operation of providing direct support and service to help particular teachers improve their performance as they work with a particular group of students. Such a support system involves establishing teacher-supervisor rapport, study of the client system, instructional conferences, observation and analysis of teaching, and application of findings and conclusions to future instructional activities. According to the collaborative model of instructional supervision, the delivery of these services is accomplished most effectively by the utilization of a broad base of human resources, including supervisors, administrators, teachers, students, and personnel external to the organization. Human resources are used according to the service needed and the competence and availability of the personnel, rather than the formal position occupied by a particular functionaire. One of the problems of clinical supervision has been the difficulty school systems have experienced in providing clinical supervisory services. It is our contention that the adequate utilization of human resources now available in organizations would help solve that problem.

The second operational area for the application of collaborative supervision is the process of evaluating the performance of individual staff members in order to make effective personnel decisions. This process involves the development of job specifications, continuous job analysis, personnel needs assessment, identification of strengths and weaknesses, improvement objectives, development and implementation of action plans, and continuous evaluation of outcomes. It is our position that it is not only desirable to use a broad base of personnel in this operation, but also that such a complex process actually requires such a broad spectrum of professional skills, that it is unreasonable to expect one individual or even a small group of individuals to deliver the service. The application of collaborative supervision facilitates the utilization of a broad base of teachers, supervisors, and administrators in the evaluation process.

Professional staff development is the third operational area for which collaborative supervision is an effective delivery system. Professional staff development is a program in which the organization seeks to develop and maintain a structure, climate, and work opportunities that contribute to the continuous growth and development of personnel. We contend that this process requires opportunities for broad communication, creative expression, exploration and implementation of new ideas, support for idea development, job enrichment, and broad opportunities to learn new skills. Such a program requires a utilization of appropriate human resources, and we feel the organization must work to deliver these services. This process is further discussed in Chapter 12.

Curriculum development, implementation, and evaluation comprise a fourth operational area that requires a broad staff of human resources. We feel that it is operationally unfeasible and, in fact, undesirable to employ enough curriculum specialists to get this job done. Rather, we feel it more effective to employ needed specialists, but also to use a broad base of human resources from within and outside the organization. This process is discussed in depth in Chapter 8.

STRATEGIES TO ACTUALIZE
COLLABORATIVE SUPERVISION

It is our assumption that the delivery of collaborative supervision will require a major organizational effort to develop and implement appropriate strategies. Descriptions of possible strategies follow:

The "Rifle Approach"

Supervisors often elaborate on the great difficulty of working with each teacher in each school in the system. They explain that there are just too many schools with too many teachers and not enough supervisors to go around.

The difficulty of being available at the right place at the right time with the necessary rapport and competence to be truly effective in their efforts to respond to the needs of teachers is often described. With so many teachers to see, it is difficult to establish a true basis of mutual trust and respect. When these same teachers are confronted with the idea of a system of "collaborative supervision" in which teachers are encouraged to participate in self-supervision and the supervision of each other, they like it but raise some serious questions. Do teachers have the necessary skills and understandings to supervise each other? Do they have the necessary training in group process, human relations skills, micro-teaching, and observation and description skills such as interaction analysis, videotaping and analysis, and evaluation. They also wonder if teachers "really" want to help each other and if they have the time. These are appropriate questions and certainly the answers are not all "in." But the "rifle approach" is suggested as one possible way to get started.

The rifle approach requires the identification of a school and some teachers in that school who have an authentic interest and readiness for "trying" collaborative supervision. Then a great effort would be made from the "central administration" to concentrate needed material and human resources in that school in order to get the program started on a limited and experimental basis. Supervisors could be assigned temporarily to work with the teachers in this school. Consultants could be employed to help teachers develop the necessary skills. The teachers could be released from part of their teaching responsibilities to develop needed skills and to help each other. The rifle approach provides a "multiplier effect." As the small group of teachers who are directly involved become more interested and secure, the idea will spread to other teachers in the school. Further, as the program becomes successful in one school, it will spread to other schools. The concentrated support system could be withdrawn and used in other situations since the teachers involved would have developed the necessary skills, interest, and understandings to maintain and extend the program.

The Cadre of "Floating Teachers"

The idea is to provide a group of "supervisor-teacher" professionals at the central office who are competent and willing to participate in either the teaching behavior or supervisory behavior system. Members of this cadre could be assigned teaching and/or supervisory responsibility. For example, if a "regular" teacher had the special expertise to help a fellow teacher, the floating teacher could be assigned to replace the regular teacher. It would also be possible, where appropriate, for the floating teacher to collaborate directly with teachers in a supervisory role or to work with teachers to help them develop needed supervisory skills. The cadre makes it possible to loosen up the availability of teachers and thus spread the potential for teacher participation in the collaborative supervision system.

Team Teaching

Team teaching is an organizational structure to facilitate the process through which teachers can cooperate in planning, teaching, and evaluating what has been done. This team approach provides for teacher-teacher visibility, interaction, and sharing, and thereby provides the potential for collaborative supervision. Teachers can share each other's plans, make suggestions, observe and describe the learning environment, provide feedback, and participate in cooperative evaluation. The potential exists for collaboration; all that is needed is desire, effort, and competence.

Open Space

Numerous school systems are beginning to use open space as a way of promoting cooperative teaching and learning, availability of specialized resources, differentiated staffing, independent study, and use of multimedia. The open space frees teachers to see each other work, to collaborate, to evaluate each other, and to describe each other. It also makes it possible to introduce "external" personnel with specialized expertise in "supervision" with less threat than might otherwise exist, since the situation is already open. The cooperative approach to teaching makes it more difficult to fix individual responsibility and thus provides more teacher openness to continuous study of the learning environment and student learning outcomes. These processes are collaborative supervision and can be nurtured and extended. But, it does not happen automatically with the development of open space. Professionals working in the open space need an opportunity to develop the skills and understandings of collaborative supervision and an internal system of administrative behavior that rewards and participates in that kind of action.

Microteaching

The Teacher Education Center of the University of Chicago has developed a model for microteaching that is consistent with the Stanford model but adds five stages (Guelcher, Jackson, and Necheles, 1970).

Microteaching makes it possible to participate in teaching situations with immediate feedback available. The teaching situation is "cut down to size" in terms of content, the number of students, and time.

The Stanford model consisted of an introduction to microteaching, through an opportunity to become acquainted with specific teaching skills and to participate in the teach-supervision-reteach cycles.

The Chicago model placed more emphasis on the content and procedures of the lesson. Reinforcement and questioning were logically related to the lesson. It was also found helpful to give prospective teachers a chance to practice on peers before encountering students. The practice of providing seminars to train students to supervise their peers was also tried and proved to be effective. Out of the micro-teaching cycle, the concept of the "nuclear lesson" was developed. It was found that a truly adequate lesson provides a "set" out of which numerous other "lessons" can emerge.

Microteaching is a procedure that provides an opportunity for supervisors and teachers to identify, define, try out, describe, analyze, and retry certain teaching skills without the risk of an actual teaching situation. Techniques such as films, videotapes, and interaction analysis can add greatly to the process but are not absolutely essential. In essence, microteaching provides an opportunity for school personnel to learn the skills of collaborative supervision through actual participation in providing instructional support for teachers.

COLLABORATIVE SUPERVISION
—SUMMARY

Collaborative supervision has been described as a systematic procedure for the release of a broad base of organizational personnel in the delivery of instructional supervisory services in the educational organization. It has been proposed as a systematic way to facilitate direct support, service, and help for the teacher behavior system; personnel evaluation; curriculum development, and in-service education. Finally, the "rifle" approach, the cadre of "floating teachers," and microteaching have been identified as strategies to facilitate and be facilitated by collaborative supervision.

8

SUPERVISION IS CURRICULUM DEVELOPMENT

The assumption that supervision is curriculum development demands not only a definition of curriculum, but a consideration of it as an important function of instructional supervisory behavior. Accordingly, in Chapter 7 a brief conceptualization of curriculum will be presented and followed by a discussion of the sources, forces, pressures, processes, decisions, and behaviors out of which the curriculum is wrought. The development and utilization of power, including both authority and persuasion, will be examined.

CONCEPT OF CURRICULUM

The curriculum has been defined in many ways. Beauchamp (1978, pp. 404-409) said that curriculum concepts range from "a set of specific objectives to something that seems to resemble a whole educational enterprise." He defined curriculum as a thoughtful answer to the question, "What shall be taught in schools?" The design of the curriculum is the form of your statement of the curriculum. Beauchamp (1978, pp. 404-409) carefully distinguished curriculum from instruction when he defined the primary instructional question, "How shall it (curriculum) be taught?"

Sergiovanni and Starratt (1979, p. 234) defined curriculum and instruction in a similar manner: "that which the student is supposed to encounter, study, practice, and master—in short the stuff of what the student learns." He goes on to define instruction as the "process by which the student is led to encounter the cirriculum."

Other writers have taken a more integrated view of curriculum. They defined the curriculum as engagement opportunities provided by the school. Gordon Mackenzie (1964, p. 402) defined the curriculum as follows:

> It appeared to be more fruitful, therefore, to define the curriculum as the learner's engagements with various aspects of the environment which have been planned under the direction of school. The assumption here is that engagements can be observed and to some extent controlled.

It is apparent that Mackenzie is moving toward a definition that shifts the emphasis from what is to be taught to the conditions with which the student interacts. Art Lewis and Alice Miel (1972, p. 27) have recently defined curriculum:

> The curriculum is taken to be a set of intentions about opportunities for engagement of persons-to-be-educated with other persons and with things (all bearers of information, processes, techniques, and values) in certain arrangements of time and space.

Lewis and Miel's definition is consistent with Mackenzie's except that it adds the concept of "intent." Mackenzie speaks of engagement opportunities with which the learner interacts, and Lewis and Miel are defining planned engagement opportunities with which it is anticipated that learners will engage.

Macdonald and others (1973, pp. 22-26) took a similar approach by defining curriculum as a part of the cultural environment selected and used to facilitate the educational process. This concept is more comprehensive and appears to move toward a synthesis of environment, curriculum, and instruction.

It is our position that it is possible and helpful to conceptualize the curriculum as the planned objective conditions of the interactions that it is anticipated will occur between the student and the school-selected and school-directed environment. There are numerous dimensions of these objective conditions. Fisher and Klein (1978, p. 393) identified the following components: "content, teaching techniques and strategies, learning opportunities, scheduling, curriculum materials/development, teaching–learning processes, objectives for the learner, facilities, and equipment." These components are comprehensive, but there are other aspects of the curriculum that are also important. For example, fellow students are an important part of the curriculum. Whether students are both black and white or only black or only white, handicapped and nonhandicapped or only handicapped or only nonhandicapped are important aspects of the curriculum. Others could be identified.

It is difficult and probably dysfunctional to separate curriculum and instruction. First, a crucial component of teaching is planning the proposed conditions with which students will interact. Therefore, curriculum planning is a part of instruction. On the other hand, the planned program can never be the ultimate conditions with which students interact, because of changing conditions caused by the introduction of students and other significant variables. Therefore, curriculum development continues during the instructional process.

A matter of grave concern is the possibility of the isolation of certain dimensions of curriculum development from the curriculum actualization process (instruction). For example, if curriculum developers and designers fail to take into consideration the needs, interests, and development of the students (clients) or teachers who are expected to implement the program, it is highly probable that the program will either not be implemented or be used in a distorted form. It is our contention that teachers and students need to be involved in appropriate curriculum development activities and that curriculum developers need to be involved with students and teachers in the process of actualizing the curriculum. Such a process would improve the quality of the curriculum through the utilization and release of a broad base of human resources.

It is our assumption that the process of curriculum development in school systems involves three interdependent processes: curriculum planning, curriculum actualization, and curriculum evaluation. Supervision has the responsibility for facilitating continuous curriculum improvement.

CURRICULUM DEVELOPMENT

Dr. Ralph Tyler (1950, pp. 1-2) has suggested four fundamental questions that need to be answered in order to develop a curriculum and plan of study:

1. What educational purposes should the school seek to attain?
2. What educational experiences can be provided that are likely to attain these purposes?
3. How can these educational experiences be effectively organized?
4. How can we determine whether these purposes are being attained?

It is not our purpose to attempt to answer these questions. This needs to be done at the teacher, school, system, state, and national level in terms of the demands of a particular situation. It is not even our purpose to discuss the study of these questions in great depth since this has been done by scholars who specialize in the study of curriculum planning. Rather, it is the purpose of this section to identify the questions, define the process of answering them, and discuss instructional supervisory behavior as it relates to this process.

Purposes of Education

The institution of public education is a subsystem of a larger society and, therefore, receives certain input from the society. Examples of input from the society include students (clients), professional personnel, financial resources, and specification of educational objectives. The society establishes and supports a number of subsystems on the assumption that these subsystems contribute to the well-being of the society. When the society perceives that a particular subsystem is not meeting its expectations, the support system is likely to be challenged. The system of education is no exception. Societal expectations are one important source of educational objectives. But our society is pluralistic; therefore, it is characterized by conflicting values, power thrusts, and expectations for education. It is also true that societal expectations are nebulous and general and, therefore, require constant study, definition, and interpretation by the educational institution at the school, system, state, and national levels.

The students constitute another important source of educational objectives (Tyler, 1950, p. 4). Student needs, hopes, aspirations, interests, achievement levels, and attitudes are important sources of data for developing educational goals and need to be studied on a comprehensive, intensive, and continuous basis. Such study needs to be done at the classroom, school, system, state, and national level and serves as input for the development of educational goals and behavioral objectives. Since students are a part of society, the study of students contributes to the understanding of societal expectations and the study of society contributes to the understanding of student needs.

The organized disciplines of study have been an important source of subject matter content and educational objectives (Tyler, 1950, p. 17). For many years the organized "learnings" of the disciplines were "translated" by subject matter specialists into subject matter for the school curriculum. But in recent years there has been a shift from this approach to an attempt to provide learning experiences for students that will help them develop a grasp of the structure and methodology of the discipline. In other words, the idea is to let the student experience the theoretical formulations, hypothesis testing, and synthesizing process as the scientist experiences it. There is little question that this is one of the important sources of educational objectives.

There are legally constituted bodies, such as school boards and state boards of education, that have the responsibility to study, define, and interpret from these sources the general goals of education. This is a continuous process that requires the services of professional educators, including teachers, supervisors, and administrators. It is necessary to develop general educational objectives from the statements of terminal goals. This is a professional job that demands the participation of administrators, supervisors, teachers, and students. Instructional supervisors not only participate in this operation, but also have special responsibility to facilitate both the process and the diffusion of the product at the next level of specification.

The general statement of objectives at the national, state, system, and school level provides a framework within which more specific objectives can be developed for specific students. It is necessary for teachers, students, and supervisors to work together in the development of teaching objectives in order to ensure some congruence among teacher, student, and system expectations.

Much has been said and written about the need for highly specified behavioral objectives. The rationale for behavior objectives is that they provide direction for learning, a basis for the establishment of the conditions with which students will interact to achieve the objectives, and criteria for the evaluation of learning outcomes. We support the use of behavioral objectives where they are appropriate, but also support the contention that it is impossible to establish all of the desirable learning outcomes on the "front end." Therefore, we think that the education process is not only an attempt to learn highly specified behavioral objectives, but also needs to be an attempt to explore the unknown, question the known, and develop objectives in the process. Such an approach demands flexibility both in the expression of objectives and the development of teaching strategies.

Eisner (1980, pp. 453-456) provided support for our position when he identified three goals for curriculum reform that we believe deserve serious consideration in any effort to improve the curriculum. He first discussed the need for meaning in learning activities. It was his contention that much of student activity involves going through the "motion" without a sense of intrinsic fulfillment for the learner. He emphasized the need for a curriculum that provides for opportunities to explore, judge, and reason. The need for quality living in the present with a concern for the immediate needs, interest, and resources of learners was discussed.

It is our assumption that some crucial educational objectives do not lend themselves to expression as behavioral objectives. Examples of other worthwhile learning outcomes would include attitudes, creativity, citizenship, learning to learn, values, and appreciation. The outcomes of learning are multiple, unpredictable, and in many cases long range. We need to develop a curriculum that provides for behavioral objectives and highly specified learning conditions, but we also need a curriculum that provides for exploration, free-lancing, developing new conditions and objectives, and releasing human potential and effort in new and unknown directions.

One of the basic sources of help for curriculum workers is the *Taxonomy of Educational Objectives* developed by Bloom and others (1956). They defined two basic categories of objectives in the cognitive domain as knowledge and intellectual abilities and skills. The knowledge category included knowledge of specific facts, ways and means of dealing with facts, and knowledge of universals and abstractions (Bloom and others, pp. 201-204). Such a classification provides a way of organizing objectives and sensitizing supervisors, teachers, and students to different levels of accomplishment in the knowledge domain.

The intellectual abilities and skills domain dealt with the student's ability to utilize knowledge in the process of defining and solving problems (Bloom and others, pp. 204-207). This domain was classified into comprehension, application, analysis, synthesis, and evaluation. Here again the classification system is helpful to supervisors and teachers by alerting them to specific dimensions of possible educational outcomes that can be sought in the learning process.

Bloom and others (1956, pp. 36-38) identified four curricular decisions that need to be made about knowledge objectives. These decisions are crucial to teachers and supervisors as they explicate educational objectives. The first decision has to do with what knowledge should be learned. Another decision is the degree of precision of knowledge the student should master. Is there a standard equally appropriate to all students or to similar students at different stages of development. A third decision relates to the organization of knowledge. The logical organization of content in a discipline is not necessarily the best organization to help a student learn the knowledge. The fourth decision relates to the importance of both the current and future interests and needs of students.

It is not our purpose to reach conclusions on these four decision areas. Rather, we want to define the questions and urge their serious consideration in the process of developing knowledge objectives. It is the consideration of such decisions that leads us to emphasize the central role of the teacher in curriculum development. The appropriateness of a particular objective is *contingent* on so many things, such as student needs and interests, teacher understandings and skills, and human and material resources for teaching, that we feel that such decisions must finally be made at the classroom level. However, it needs to be reiterated that such decisions are made within a reality structure of curriculum development at the school, school district, and state level. The supervisor is a key person in the total process: first, as a source of ideas; second, as a facilitator and coordinator of the process at various levels of decision; and finally, as an identifier and releaser of a broad base of human resources in the process.

Curriculum Actualization

The curriculum is developed in anticipation of the instructional process. The actualization of the curriculum is the process through which students interact with certain planned engagement opportunities under the coordination of a teacher or teachers in order to achieve certain educational objectives. This system of activities is instruction and is a function of the teaching behavior system. The selection and actualization of engagement opportunities are teacher responsibilities with special levels of support available as needed. The process of instruction and the function of supervision in this process will be discussed in Chapter 11 and Chapter 12.

Evaluation of Educational Outcomes

As a subsystem of the society, the institution of public education is accountable to the society for the achievement of educational goals and objectives. This fact necessitates a rigorous system, not only for evaluation of the extent to which objectives are being reached, but also for the adequacy of the objectives.

Evaluation is a process not only for determining the extent to which educational objectives are being achieved, but also for clarifying the conditions of learning and, therefore, possible relations between learning conditions and learning outcomes. It therefore provides the basis for a continuous program of curriculum and instructional improvement. Local schools can evaluate engagement opportunities being provided and actualized. Individual teachers can become sensitive to the outcomes of their own teaching efforts and develop new approaches based on continuous evaluation. An adequate system of evaluation requires that objectives (where appropriate) be stated in a form that defines the performance that it is hoped the student will achieve. This definition makes it possible to design a program to determine the extent to which students can demonstrate the appropriate behavior. These data provide feedback for teachers as they continue to develop and actualize engagement opportunities for learners.

SOURCES OF PRESSURE
FOR CURRICULUM CHANGE

Curriculum change is attempted by many people. The national government seeks to bring about curriculum change by making available federal funds for special projects. One example is the National Defense Education Act of 1958. The U.S. Congress decided that public schools should put greater emphasis on science, mathematics, foreign languages, and guidance. Funds were made available to support curriculum development and teacher education activities in these areas and to supply resource persons who would exert leadership in improving the curricula. Pressure for change resulted. In the mid-1960s, additional federal funds were supplied for other kinds of curriculum improvement, especially improvement of the program for the underprivileged. In the early 1970s, there has been support for career education. In the late 1970s, the emphasis has been on special education.

Curriculum change may also be initiated by foundations that make available funds to enable schools to undertake innovations in certain areas. For example, during the 1950s, the Ford Foundation made contributions to experimentation with education by television.

Community dissatisfaction with the existing program may lead to curriculum change. If a large segment of the community believes that reading can be more effectively taught, it can exert pressure on the board of education that results in efforts to change the program of teaching reading.

Associations of scholars that believe that more attention should be given to their discipline in the public schools can exert pressure to secure the addition of more courses in their field to a public school curriculum.

Persons who have access to the mass media can advocate a point of view that may influence boards of education to underwrite curriculum development in certain areas.

Accrediting associations may establish standards that must be met if schools are to be accredited, and these requirements lead to the initiation of curriculum change.

The impetus for curriculum change can also come from student dissatisfaction and frustration. In the early 1970s, students were pushing for relevance in the curriculum and a more meaningful role in curriculum decisions.

Curriculum change can come about as a result of study of students and educational outcomes by the professional staff. Data from this kind of study can create dissatisfaction among the professional staff and a motivation to change.

Finally, the board of education may decide that curriculum change is needed; the administration may recommend to the board of education that support be given to certain curriculum innovations; a curriculum council may decide to bring about a curriculum change; the faculty of a given school may decide that certain changes should be made; individual teachers may recommend changes and, if they are able to influence enough members of the staff, secure the change; or they may, within existing policies, carry on innovations within their own classrooms. The responsibility for the initiation of curriculum change has no preassigned location.

THE ROLE OF SUPERVISION
IN CURRICULUM DEVELOPMENT

When the first edition of *Supervision for Better Schools* was written, the major impetus for curriculum change lay in the supervisory staff. For the most part, the public, the national government, the mass media, and associations of scholars ignored the need for change in the curriculum of the public schools. Persons designated as curriculum directors, supervisors, and teachers with a professional dedication assumed the role of change agents. The point of view underlying the first two editions of *Supervision for Better Schools* was that the supervisor had to carry the major responsibility for the initiation of change.

By the mid 1960s, this condition had changed completely. Persons in the national government, foundations, scholars, students, and the general public had come to realize that the type of education provided determines the future of our society. Each group with its own vision of what the society should become had begun to exert effort to secure the kind of educational program that would realize its dreams. Public school administrators found themselves confronted by many different demands for curriculum change. The task had become that of deciding *which* change was to be made rather than *whether* or not problems existed; developing and implementing ideas for improvement; and evaluating results.

The supervisory staff in a school system found itself in a different role. Instead of devoting a major portion of its effort to the development of ideas for change, it found itself confronted with the task of assisting in the decision as to desirable changes, assisting in innovation, supplying the many types of resource help necessary in innovation, coordinating the incorporation of innovations into the program in such a way that student programs would have continuity, assisting in the evaluation of innovation, helping the staff become aware of the variety of alternatives being proposed, assisting in the choice of the alternative that seemed most appropriate in the system, and developing a plan and design that would determine the types of innovations to be supported financially.

TWO APPROACHES TO
CURRICULUM CHANGE

Many people during the late 1950s and early 1960s decided that the local school system could no longer serve as the unit for curriculum development. It was felt that curriculum development was so important that it could not be left to the kind of efforts that could be mounted with the monetary and personnel resources available to the local school level.

In many respects, it would seem that 1957, the year of Sputnik, was an important dividing line in proposals of strategy for curriculum change. During the previous three or four decades, when curriculum making was changing from textbook writing to program planning, most proposals were rooted to a philosophy of pragmatic evolution. Beginning in the early 1930s, it was believed that the best educational program would be produced by curriculum changes made by individual teachers, faculties of a given building, the staff of a system, and, in a few cases, by the state department of education. Since 1957, there has been a shift on the part of many to a belief in a strategy of directed change. Persons, often those outside of public education, assume that they know the change that is desirable and then use the best strategy they can devise to bring about the desired change.

Assumptions in the Pragmatic Approach

During the pragmatic period, there were certain assumptions that were made about the strategy of change. Some of these, stated perhaps in oversimplified terms, are the following:

Change in the curriculum is effected most efficiently at the local school building level. Koopman, Miel, and Misner (1943), among others, enunciated this assumption in *Democracy in School Administration.* It was their belief that if the curriculum is to change, the teachers must change, and the teachers must change through their involvement in curruculum development. Since it is almost impossible to involve all teachers in systemwide planning, the planning and involvement should be at the local building level.

Change in the curriculum occurs as people change through their participation in decision making related to the curriculum. With the emphasis on curriculum change at the local building level during the late 1940s and early 1950s, a number of persons (Koopman, 1943 and Spears, 1957) including many curriculum leaders, attempted to describe the process through which involvement could be deepened by participation in decision making.

Change in the curriculum is produced through in-service education that develops new teacher perceptions and skills. Spears (1957) in his book, *Curriculum Planning Through In-Service Programs,* described the ramifications of this assumption.

Change in the curriculum is effected by in-service education of the principal, which produces a change in his or her work style. Sugg (1955) found a vast difference in the amount and kind of curriculum changes in schools where principals followed one type of work style as opposed to curriculum changes in buildings with principals who followed a different work style. Grobman (1958) reported that in-service education can be effective in changing the work style of principals.

Change in the curriculum is effected by supplying teachers with consultants who assist them with innovation. From the time of the Eight-Year-Study through curriculum movements of the early 1950s, such as intergroup education and economic education, attempts were made to bring about change by using consultants to support those who were doing the experimenting.

Change in the curriculum is effected by providing workshop opportunities for key teachers in a building, who then become resource persons and leaders for other teachers on the staff. This assumption has guided the thinking of most of the organizations attempting to influence the curriculum from outside the regular administrative channel during the two decades prior to 1957. Workshops in economic education, family finance, intergroup education, and human relations are examples of the implementation of this assumption.

A RETHINKING
OF ASSUMPTIONS

Even before 1957, some observers of the process of curriculum change had reached the conclusion that some of the assumptions of the 1930s, 1940s, and 1950s needed rethinking. Teacher turnover during and after World War II was so great (from 10 to 50 percent a year), depending on the location of the school, that changes produced in teachers by in-service education failed to provide lasting curriculum changes. The in-service experiences provided modification in the perceptions of the teachers with regard to themselves, their role, and the situation; so the teachers made changes. But then they moved to another school system, and the residue left in the locality that had provided the in-service education was not as great as anticipated or as the situation demanded. With rapid teacher turnover, the process of changing curriculum design and structure needed to be modified if the changes made were to have any lasting effect.

Second, it was seen that changes in curriculum produced by the supplying of funds for a specific innovation were quickly dissipated when the funds were exhausted or when newer innovations received the extra financial support. An innovation that was not discarded or supplanted in a five- to ten-year period was unusual. In many schools, instead of innovation's being a sincere effort to produce major change in the program, it became a process of keeping up with the "Joneses," and there was no integration of the innovations into the curriculum structure.

Third, changes in the curriculum that were initiated by or identified by forceful leaders were modified when they were removed from the situation. If these leaders left the situation for a better job, the administrators who followed often lacked the same vision or had another vision and allowed the innovations of their predecessors to erode. If the forceful leaders were fired because they had created opposition, innovations that they had brought about were eradicated as quickly as possible. Such programs seemed to be closely related to the personality and values of the leader, and the quick turnover in school administrators made lasting impact unlikely.

Fourth, changes in the curriculum that aroused the opposition of the community power structure were soon curtailed or modified. Strategies for making major curriculum changes proved ineffective if school leaders had not directly or indirectly involved the community power structure leaders in thinking through what should be done.

Assumptions in Directed Change

In 1957, many persons were caused to rethink the question of who should make decisions concerning curriculum change. How free should professional teachers be to decide what they would teach and how they would teach it? Should they be free to ignore new knowledge if they so desired? Should they be free to use less effective instructional techniques? Is the faculty of a local school free to refuse to consider curriculum improvements or to ignore the necessity for promoting types of growth that may be needed in the community and in the nation?

Since the 1950s, some persons concerned with the national welfare have advocated directed change. They believe that change should not be equated with chance, but with development, and that innovation should be linked to long-term goals. The advocates of this position make the following assumptions:

Some persons in government, foundations, universities, public schools, or somewhere else must decide on the desired goals and plan innovations designed to promote them. How the decision makers will be selected is usually not discussed.

Basic research, program design, and field testing should be done by well-defined curriculum development projects. The best experts possible should be brought together to design a program based on the best available research, and it should be tested in many field situations to determine its quality and its adaptability. Huge sums of money and expert personnel are needed for the design and the testing, and the procedure is more expensive than a single system can underwrite.

Major instructional innovations should be introduced by the administration, because it can marshal the necessary authority and precipitate the decisions necessary for adoption. Each local school system should choose the prepackaged instructional systems that are appropriate for it. After a system has been developed, boards of education and staffs must be informed that such a system exists, must be convinced of its desirability, and must make the decision that it will be adopted.

The prepackaged instructional system can be introduced despite original opposition or apathy of the teachers. Although some may oppose it, they will soon begin to accept it. It is stated that faculty members begin to prefer new methods within four months to a year after their introduction. Faculty members develop a sense of commitment to the new methods, because these are the ones they are using.

The informal communication system determines whether formal presentations will be heard. It is important for the innovator to recognize that the formal organization is not necessarily the real power in the organization; he or she must seek to know and work through the informal system.

The earlier acceptors of the innovation, according to Barnett (1962), will be the dissident, the indifferent, the resentful, and the disaffected. They have nothing to lose and will readily accept the new. The later acceptors will be influenced by the prestige of those who sponsor and create.

Real or assumed knowledge of the innovator's identity is a major variable in the acceptance of a particular innovation. Teachers will be willing to try an innovation that is advocated by someone whose reputation they respect or who is associated with an organization or institution that they revere. To secure a change, many authorities must be ready to lend their prestige and their personalities to the cause of directed change.

The key to successful innovation is providing assistance to teachers as they begin to implement the adopted program. If attention is given to the teachers by the principals or other persons provided to assist them, it provides for the teachers an exhilarating effect that enables them to be more successful with and become more enthusiastic about the innovation.

The most persuasive experience that can be provided to convince staffs of the value of an innovation is to make provision for them to visit a successful new program and see it in action. No matter how much is said or written about a new program, it is not as effective in convincing teachers of its value as their seeing it in successful operation in a situation that they can identify as being similar to their own.

Because of teacher turnover, a continuous program of in-service education in the skills necessary to implement the innovation must be available for new teachers brought into the system. It is not possible to think of providing a program of in-service education on a one-shot basis. Each new teacher must be inducted into the instructional system.

The process of curriculum change contains three steps—innovation, diffusion, and integration. According to the advocates of directed change, innovation is developed on the outside, and the process described in the preceding paragraphs leads to diffusion and integration.

Changes in social systems are much more difficult than changes in individuals or groups. An individual changes in terms of his or her needs and purposes or his or her motivation. Groups change through interaction, but there is greater fear of a change in the organization, because of the results of structural alteration.

Some Second Thoughts

The period of the 1960s was a time of great effort for educational innovation. Proposals for change came from a variety of sources including foundations, federal government, scholars, and private enterprise. Examples of proposed changes included team teaching, nongraded program, informal education, computer-assisted instruction, curriculum changes proposed by the "scholars," programmed learning, and a wide variety of packaged materials. The "directed change" approach as well as other approaches were utilized, and the call and thrust for educational change was heard and seen around the nation. What has happened as a result of this great effort?

In a study by John Goodlad, Francis Klein, and others (1970), a major conclusion was that nothing much had changed in educational institutions. There was little evidence that teachers were guided by clear understanding of the behavioral outcomes for students that they taught. "Telling" and "questioning" were still the dominant "techniques" used by teachers. Students were not found to be discovering for themselves through inquiry. The textbook was still the prime medium of instruction, and the use of a variety of media was not observed. The organization and presentation of subject matter did not provide for individual differences. Teachers were in general unaware or unable to develop practices consistent with modern principles of learning. School buildings were still drab with egg-crate designs and self-contained classrooms. In short, schools and teaching were found not to have changed very much in spite of the innovations of the 1960s (Goodlad and Klein, 1970, pp. 77–94). More study and research are needed to determine the success and failure of attempts to change before and since 1957.

It is obvious that the contrast of the two approaches, *prior-* and *post-*1957, is sharply drawn to highlight the issues. Obviously, some innovations before 1957 were characterized by the second group of assumptions, and many current approaches to curriculum change still rely on pragmatic evolution.

It is also obvious that in the years ahead, there will be many sources of change in the curriculum. Many organizations and individuals will attempt to bring about the changes that they deem desirable. Each school system will be forced to make decisions from among conflicting proposals. Even if the board of education and the educators in charge of a system wanted to abdicate, they could not. The competing pressure groups from the outside will not allow it. Each system must devise a procedure for deciding the curriculum changes that it will make. It cannot simply abdicate and let others make the decision, because there are competing pressures from the outside to determine the curriculum. Decisions must be made ultimately by the local school system, the local school, and the teacher.

A Point of View

The legal decision concerning curriculum change is a decision by the board of education and the superintendent. How a system gets to the place where this decision is reached depends upon the theory of change that is being followed in that system.

One theory of change would postulate that the administrator can make a decision and then, by manipulation and influence, secure the adoption of that change by the members of the staff. The authority of the administrator will be used to insure that people follow the directives that originate from the administrative office. The supervisory staff will be used to make sure that teachers implement the change and to assist them in developing the skills to carry out the change.

The theory of change recommended here is based on the postulate that a lasting change occurs only as the people who must implement it are convinced of its worth. The strategy becomes a question of how to involve people in the process of making intelligent decisions.

It is recognized that each group develops some common goals and norms. These norms are the products of interaction and govern behavior of the members of the group. Any member of the group may advance the ideas that ultimately become the goals. But each idea stands in the open marketplace and is accepted or rejected in terms of its merits as judged by the purposes of individuals and the total group.

It is important to recognize that in a large school system there are many groups. One group will be the central office staff, and it will be composed of a number of small psychological groups. Each faculty also constitutes a group, and it is composed of small psychological groups. The school system staff is composed of many groups; and if the system is large, there is little development of groupness in the total staff. It is much more likely that departments and faculties will have goals than it is that the total system staff will have common goals. It is also more likely that the teachers of a given subject matter or given grade level will have common goals and norms than it is that the total system staff will have common goals and norms.

When anyone gets an idea for change that he or she hopes will occur, he or she faces the task of planning a strategy that will help various groups in the system staff have the opportunity to examine the idea and perhaps to adopt it.

There are at least three stages in the process from the idea to the adoption. First, there must be dissemination of the idea among all the groups that it is hoped will consider it. Second, when individuals or groups within the total staff become convinced of its worth, they will need to have the opportunity to demonstrate it. The demonstrations themselves become a part of the dissemination process because they give concrete illustrations of the idea. Persons who have been unaffected by the verbal description of the idea will have opportunity to see merit in it for themselves when they see the demonstration process. Seeing an idea in action increases the possibility that people will be able to examine it. The demonstrations provide a basis for discussion that enter into the forming of norms, which permit other people to experiment with the idea or lead to their rejection and elimination of it. If norms are developed that make possible individuals and schools joining in the demonstration, much of the process of adoption of the program into the system is already accomplished. The remaining step is merely sharing the skills that enable teachers to conduct their programs in the demonstrated manner.

Refereeing Curriculum Issues

When a proposal for curriculum change is brought to the school by an outside agency, the school staff must exercise its responsibility for decisions concerning the educational program that will be offered. A project is not more worthy because the preparation of instructional material was underwritten by some foundation rather than having been prepared with the backing of a publishing company. The authors in either case should have their wares evaluated in the open marketplace.

A project director has no more right to use classrooms of children for experimentation than any other author who wants a tryout of his or her materials. School people have the same responsibility for judging whether they should allow such an experimenter to use their pupils.

One curriculum project director of the early 1960s stated, "I get my directives from the world of mathematics. The hell with mental health." School officials have a responsibility to decide whether or not the products of a person who gets directives from a discipline are suitable materials for use in their schools; they must decide whether the materials produced will be more harmful than helpful to most children.

A curriculum project product must be judged by the contribution that it can make to a given school situation. Simply being the producer of something new does not mean that a person is entitled to have access to the facilities of a school system, or that the new product is better than existing ones. Also, the responsibility for attaining a sequence and a balance in the curriculum rests with the curriculum workers of a given school system. The curriculum innovators are working with only parts of the curriculum. They are producing segments, which can be inserted into the curriculum at appropriate places. To date, no adequate sequence has been developed in any field from kindergarten through twelfth grade. No producers of new curricula in subject matter fields seem to be thinking seriously of the pattern the total curriculum should have.

In a period in which many forces are attempting to bring about curriculum change, the assistant superintendent for curriculum and instruction, who represents the superintendent, must serve as the referee in many struggles for control of the curriculum. Representatives of curriculum projects or lay groups that become convinced of the importance of particular projects attempt to influence the board of education and the superintendent to install a particular instructional package in the school program. Although the proposed innovation may have merit, it may not be as desirable for a given community as some other alternatives.

The head of the supervisory staff must not be stampeded. While he or she should encourage desirable change, the decision to move in a given direction should not be made without consideration of a variety of alternatives evaluated in terms of the needs of the local situation. It should be insisted that there be a hearing for any proposal that is being considered. If there are other programs in the same field that have been developed by other groups, representatives of the competing projects should be asked to describe their products and their special features. Opportunities should be provided for members of the supervisory staff, interested principals, and teachers to study the various curriculum materials. Not only will much valuable in-service growth take place for the staff members who are involved in the consideration, but the choice can be made with full knowledge of all the staff and in terms of the needs of the particular population served by the system.

The important principle involved is that the administrator should not make the decision without thorough consideration by the people who will be involved in its implementation. If proponents know that any particular curriculum package will be evaluated by many people in the system before it is accepted, they will operate in a different manner. Their contacts will not be with boards of education or superintendents alone. They will want to discuss their program with the teachers, principals, and supervisors in the system.

Struggles for the adoption of particular curriculum projects will be decreased if the school system has an energetic curriculum development program in progress. In such a school, the members of the supervisory staff will be searching throughout the state, region, and nation for projects that seem to be preparing worthwhile materials. They will present these developments for study and consideration before anyone attempts to sell the board of education on a particular project. If members of the community and proponents of a particular project know that a school system conducts a regular and consistent program of study and development, their actions will be guided by this knowledge. They will know that this is a school system that does not buy a pig in a poke; that no particular pattern will be accepted without study, tryout, and evaluation; and that the system is applying criteria in its judgment of curriculum materials that prevent the adoption of an inappropriate product. With such an understanding of the situation, only the most foolhardy proponent would attempt to "sell" the superintendent or the board of education without submitting plans to the unit that is studying all the materials that are available.

The Curriculum Policy
Decision Makers

But who in the local system will make the decision? Should it be the superintendent? the board of education? the supervisory staff? the school faculty? the individual teacher?

Obviously, the board of education makes the official decision, but the board of education does not usually make the decision on its own. It turns to its professional staff for recommendations. Who in the professional staff will make the decision?

Ultimately, the decision must be implemented by the classroom teacher. If the perceptions and motivations of the classroom teacher are ignored, any decision will not be successfully implemented, either through ignorance on the part of the classroom teacher or through subtle resistance. In deciding upon who will be included in the decision-making process, the supervisory staff must decide whether it believes that it can influence and manipulate classroom teachers so that they will do what the supervisory staff decides, or whether it must bring the classroom teacher into the decision-making process.

The decision, in the opinion of this author, will depend primarily on the assumption that the central office staff makes regarding the professional nature of the classroom teacher. If it believes that the classroom teacher is a professional person operating in terms of principles and commitment, it will seek ways of involving the teacher in the decision. If it believes that the classroom teacher is a technician whose function is to carry out directives without professional integrity, the decision will be restricted to those persons who are designated as curriculum planners.

The decision about inclusion of teachers becomes more difficult when the staff of a system is one in which there is rapid turnover. If the tenure of a teacher in a system is of short duration, can that teacher be allowed to participate in the decisions? Should the assumption be made that any person who accepts a job in a given school system accepts the responsibility for carrying out the policies and program that were established before he or she came? Or should it be assumed that professional teachers have learned to make intelligent decisions in other systems and can in this one?

If the staff assumes that teachers should participate in the decision making with regard to curriculum change, the question becomes what types of decisions should be open to all members of the teaching staff? What types of decisions are appropriate for the faculty of a single school? What questions must be decided at the systemwide level? How can individual teachers participate in systemwide decisions?

Certain guidelines can be established. All teachers should have the right to identify the types of problems that they see in the curriculum of the school in which they teach. These teacher concerns should be fed into the decision-making channels. Teachers should have the opportunity to react to innovations that are being considered for systemwide adoption. It is also important that teachers be considered as critical human resources of ideas for curriculum change and strategies of change. Within these restrictions, the supervisory staff should feel free to move ahead to coordinate the change process.

Teachers should also know the limitations within which they are free to make decisions about change without consulting the faculties of which they are a member or the supervisory staff of the school system.

Principals should be informed of innovations that individual teachers are attempting, and if these innovations will affect the rest of the school, the principal should be consulted before they are undertaken. The principal should be a major force in the decisions concerning curriculum changes that will affect the entire school. If the local school has a curriculum committee, the principal will undoubtedly function as the executive secretary or as a very active member. Certainly, he or she should be aware of proposals being considered and should help the faculty examine them in the light of other alternatives. He or she also has the responsibility for implementing the decisions reached by the local faculty.

Beyond the local school, the principals should be represented in the curriculum decisions by a representative chosen by the principals' group. Principals as a group should have an opportunity to discuss changes that are contemplated in systemwide curriculum policy. The results of their deliberation should be fed into the curriculum council.

Some representative body of teachers, supervisors, and principals should have the final decision concerning the recommendations that will be made to the superintendent and board of education. This group may be called a curriculum council, a planning committee, or a program development committee, but it serves the function of being the official policy-recommending agency. Its membership should include a representative of each faculty, a representative of the principals, and a representative of the supervisory staff.

If these principles are followed, each member of the professional staff is represented in decisions related to curriculum policy.

THE ORGANIZATION
FOR CURRICULUM
DEVELOPMENT

The curriculum council should establish the framework within which local schools operate. It should recommend to the superintendent and the board of education those changes in policy that affect systemwide curriculum and instruction, including the development and evaluation of systemwide goals. It should have responsibility for recommending innovations that the council believes should be tried out in the schools. It should encourage the supervisory staff to establish and conduct the in-service program that will enable the system to implement the decisions that have been made with regard to systemwide change, be on the lookout for innovations that are proving effective in other systems and bring information about these innovations to the council for consideration and support, and assist individual teachers and schools with innovations that are being tried out on a demonstration basis.

The curriculum council serves as the nucleus for the formation of curriculum policy, but it will be relatively useless without an organization for initiating and implementing curriculum decisions at the building level. Each school in the system needs an extension of the curriculum council. It may be called what the system prefers, but there should be a curriculum committee in each building that is responsible for interpreting the system structure of goals and curriculum policies, and developing and evaluating the local school structure of educational goals and curriculum policies for consideration by the faculty. The curriculum committee in each building should be composed of representative selected teachers and the principal. It should identify problems it thinks the curriculum council should investigate and make decisions concerning the type of in-service opportunities needed by the faculty. Where possible, the chairperson of the curriculum committee should serve as the building representative on the curriculum council. The organization described can do much to coordinate the curriculum development program of the system.

The executive officer of the curriculum council should be the assistant superintendent for curriculum and instruction. All proposals for innovation from outside the system come to this person directly through the board of education or from the superintendent. The supervisory staff works with him or her and keeps him or her informed of new curriculum developments within and outside of the system. His or her relationship with principals provides sources of information. In addition to knowing what is going on, he or she is in a position to implement the decisions of the council. He or she can make recommendations to the superintendent and to the board. He or she has the staff to act. He or she can work with the principals to secure needed cooperation.

The supervisory staff carries the primary responsibility for the development and implementation of curriculum policy. Its members are a source of information and initiation. As individual supervisors become aware of demonstrations that are available in other school systems, they should visit them and bring back to the local system descriptions of practices that should be considered there. They should feel free to form study groups that will investigate new programs developed by massive curriculum projects or state groups, to secure ideas that individual teachers or individual schools within the system may wish to try. They should assume the responsibility of keeping fully informed about all experimental efforts in the local system and making available information about these to the total administrative and teaching staff. They are the executive officers assigned to implement a program recommended by curriculum council and approved by the board of education.

Executive action by a staff member may consist of locating teachers or schools that wish to experiment with a hypothesis, serving as consultant to the teachers and administrators who are experimenting, assisting in evaluating an innovation, conducting in-service education related to a project, and preparing a report of recommendations growing out of a specific demonstration.

The Organization and Operation
of the Central Office
Supervisory Staff

The central office supervisory staff has four kinds of responsibilities: to project a blueprint of what the curriculum in that school may look like five years in the future; to develop hypotheses that are important to explore either through research or demonstration; to support and assist in research and demonstration; and to facilitate the maintenance of the quality of the ongoing program.

These responsibilities require that the supervisory staff include persons with different competencies and responsibilities. In a school system of any size, a general supervisor is no longer sufficient. Specialists in subject matter, media, evaluation, research, and dissemination are also required. This need for specialists has led some people to assume that general supervisors are no longer needed. These people have failed to recognize the necessity of a supervisory team composed of both specialists and generalists, rather than a generalist who tries to be all things to all people.

Curriculum development for the supervisory staff consists of research, demonstration, and dissemination. The first responsibility of the staff is the collection and evaluation of existing research to insure that the system has available the data pertinent to the issue under consideration.

A wonderful period for supervisors has arrived. Much of the frustration many have felt with regard to collecting information about research has been alleviated. The U.S. Office of Education has set up ERIC, (Educational Resources Information Center), which makes it possible to secure existing research that relates to a given problem. Research and Development Centers have been established at various major universities throughout the country, which have a responsibility for doing research on a basic educational problem. Local school districts can turn to ERIC or a Research and Development Center and request information that will help them form hypotheses or make decisions. Regional Exchange is an example of a federal program that seeks to provide educational information to local school curriculum projects.*

The National Diffusion Network has become a major force for educational improvement by providing information and ideas for both in-service education and curriculum development. Allen, Achilles, and Owen (1978, pp. 14-15) describe the National Diffusion Network as follows:

> One major purpose of the National Diffusion Network (NDN) is to provide classroom teachers with proven educational practices that will help the teachers improve instruction. The NDN is primarily a dissemination link between developers of new programs and those who can benefit from using the new programs. The NDN often provides training functions.
>
> The National Diffusion Network emerged as the logical consequence of program development efforts funded by Congress. Over the years, Congress had funded thousands of program development efforts (and expended billions of dollars) in such programs as Title I, ESEA or the former Title III, ESEA (now Title IV-C). Many new programs or practices developed in local schools throughout the United States are of outstanding quality. The U.S. Office of Education (USOE) and the National Institute of Education (NIE) in concert now review these locally developed programs to determine if they are of high enough quality to merit wide-spread dissemination to potential users (or adopters).

Another factor that affects what supervisors do is the participation of the national government through various programs of education. When historians of the year 2000 look back to 1965, they will say that it was the year that the federal government said by legal action that it could no longer be content for any youngster to have less than a quality education. It was the beginning of major federal government support for program development.

*The authors wish to express appreciation to Dr. Charles Achilles, Professor, The University of Tennessee, Knoxville, for suggestions and information about federal participation in the provision of information and ideas for school improvement.

A basic function of the supervisory staff is carrying on curriculum-planning activities. There are very few supervisory staffs with a person who has a clear picture of the hypotheses being tried out and who knows how these relate to one another, or how experimental programs are being used to develop a new program for the future. This condition must be improved if satisfactory progress is to be made with the available resources. The supervisory staff must include persons who can state the present structure of the curriculum, project a blueprint for the future, and identify the hypotheses that need to be tested.

In addition to its responsibility for developing a curriculum design and for clarifying hypotheses to be tested, the supervisory staff is also responsible for developing proposals for desired research, for demonstration and dissemination activities, and for consultation and leadership in experimental activities.

The transition from the present to a blueprint for the future is accomplished by following a process that will involve approval by the curriculum council and implementation by the supervisory staff.

1. An ongoing needs assessment is used to determine strengths and weaknesses and to point direction for needed change and improvement. This process occurs at the central office level, the local school level, or the individual teacher level.

2. Certain hypotheses are formed concerning desirable practices or curriculum design, based on information secured from research or demonstration in another situation. Or the hypothesis might be formed by a member of the staff based on his or her experimentation and experience.

3. The promising hypotheses are investigated by research conducted in the system. This experimentation consists of finding someone or some staff that is willing to try out the hypothesis and have the results evaluated. The research personnel of the supervisory unit are made available to assist in the design and the execution of the experiment. Any school system that is seriously concerned with improving its program will have a number of experimental activities underway at all times. These activities are ways of collecting evidence concerning the value of hypotheses and determining which ones should be given further tryout.

4. When the research has been completed, the results should be presented to the total supervisory staff. If the results seem promising, the staff should secure permission from the curriculum council for experimentation with the idea in demonstration centers within the system, staffed by teachers and school staffs that are in agreement with the idea and are willing to try it. Announcements concerning these demonstration centers are made to the total staff, with invitations to staff members who are interested to visit the demonstrations. Opportunities should be provided for visitors to discuss what is being tried and to discuss results as they become available.

5. On the basis of the results of the demonstration and the sentiments for further expansion of the idea throughout the system, proposals for change in curriculum policies are made to the curriculum council.

6. Information concerning the proposal should be made available to the total staff, and local faculties should have opportunities to discuss ramifications of the proposed change. Through these discussions, pitfalls and needed modifications should be identified. Representatives of the faculty should carry back to the curriculum council the reactions of their staffs.

7. If the reaction of the various faculties is positive, the policy will be adopted

for the entire system. If it is not, further investigation and experimentation will be necessary. Perhaps options should be given to certain schools to move to the new policy while other schools retain present practices. A variation of this plan may be the establishment of a work group employed to spend a portion of the summer in revising and improving the programs that have been developed. The revision should then be resubmitted to the faculties for discussion and reaction.

The procedure outlined calls for continuous evaluation of current practices, securing new ideas, making them available to the total staff, providing demonstrations that enable people to evaluate the proposal more effectively, and thinking together, which leads to a consensus to adopt a new policy. The process depends on the principle of infection. As the central staff gives support and assistance to the teachers engaging in experimental effort, other teachers around them will look at what the experimental teachers are doing. Changes in other teachers come through their interactions with the teachers of classes involved in an experiment.

The process of curriculum development provides for initiation of innovation from many sources; establishment of an organization that provides for coordination and involvement; continuous experimentation based on the best hypotheses that can be formed from research and worldwide curriculum activities; multiple curricular innovations to permit many teachers to find curriculum improvement activities that they deem important; establishment of experiments and demonstrations in schools and classrooms, where the staff members involved believe in the hypotheses being tested; opportunities for other staff members to visit and discuss experiments and demonstrations; careful collection of evidence; and encouragement of continued questions and proposals for modification of the blueprint for the curriculum.

The supervisor's role is one of evaluation, studying new ideas, encouraging teachers to be creative, assisting teachers in their attempts to implement a hypothesis, conducting in-service activities organized around the study of a demonstration, and aiding in the collecting of evidence concerning the success of an experimental effort. It is the role of a student and coworker—not that of a proponent or advocate.

SCHOOL COMMUNITY COOPERATION AND CURRICULUM DEVELOPMENT

The school system has been described as a subsystem of a larger community system. As a subsystem, the school receives financial support, goal specification, and some control over activities. Therefore, the changes that may be made in a school program are limited by the beliefs and decisions of the community power structure. If the changes are small and will not adversely affect any vested interests that the power structure wants to protect, no interference will be felt. If, however, the change is major and will drastically modify the curriculum content or program organization, then consideration of the power structure may be needed.

All communities have a power structure which, according to Kimbrough's (1964) classification, may be monopolistic, competitive, or fragmented pluralistic. A monopolistic power structure is characterized by a unitary system of dominance over community decision making. A competitive power structure exists when two or more power groups engage in competition that transcends more than one election. A fragmented pluralistic structure exists when there are several fragmented centers of power. Each school district exists within a community power structure, and lack of knowledge about its existence or shape may lead to unexpected and unnecessary difficulties for educational leaders attempting curriculum improvement.

The knowledge that a community power structure exists and operates does not decrease the need for informing and involving the rest of the community. The power structure will be affected and influenced by the way the community sees and supports the school.

A school cannot move too far ahead of the community. If it does, its program will be criticized, and as soon as the community gathers its forces, action will be taken to eliminate the phases of the school program the community does not accept or understand.

It is essential that a school program include a public relations activity that keeps all community members informed of what is going on in the school. Keeping the community informed includes such customary activities as columns in the local newspapers, radio programs, annual reports to parents, open meetings of the board of education, open-house days or visits to classes, fathers' clubs, and P.T.A. meetings. It also includes supplying teachers and pupils to speak at service and women's club meetings. But these are not enough. New methods should be sought.

Student participation in thinking out problems of classroom operation, school policy, and program increases the possibility of effective relationships with the various community groups. As pupils understand the school purposes and programs by participating in the processes through which they are formed, the student body becomes a public relations unit. Pupils explain and interpret the school to the community.

But informing the community is not enough. School personnel must become involved in community activities if the work of the faculty is to be coordinated with community groups. One of the functions of the school group and the supervisor is to establish channels of communication with the community. These must not be one-way channels. If they are, the staff operates in a vacuum and does not know how well it is communicating or how well its ideas are being received. If the supervisor wants to bring about a receptive frame of mind for the constant improvement of the school program, he or she must establish a situation in which there is an exchange of ideas between community leaders and the members of the staff.

In some communities, one channel that exists for the exchange of ideas is the community coordinating council. In such a council, representatives of business, service clubs, unions, and welfare agencies discuss the problems of the community and ways of solving them. If the school is represented on the council, the school staff has a way of sharing its thinking with other community leaders. If the school is not represented on the council, it should take steps to join.

Other groups in the community are working on community problems. The school leaders should encourage the community to invite school representatives to join these groups and should encourage teachers to accept such invitations. In this way, the thinking of the school staff can be shared with various segments of the community. The greater the number of faculty members that can be involved in community activities, the easier it will be to maintain a two-way flow of communication.

A false assumption that prevents many school staffs from working effectively with their communities is their belief that the only problems that should receive school attention are school problems. A much sounder attitude for establishing communication with the community is that community problems are school problems, that the frontiers of development in the community are the most fruitful areas for the thinking and learning of children. Some of the more advanced school curriculum programs are built around the solution of community problems. Studies of effective ways of learning have indicated that children learn more adequate skills through the problem-solving approach than through other approaches. No school leader need be concerned that putting emphasis on the solving of community problems will decrease the effectiveness of the school as a learning situation.

It is important to recognize that coordination with community groups of the nature described here is hindered when school regulations prohibit participation in political affairs. An official leader must work for political freedom for teachers so that they can be first-class citizens of the community.

Another phase of coordination with community groups is to have the community participate in planning the school program. When community members have a part in determining policy and program, they become valuable supporters. When they are kept out, they become suspicious and potentially hostile. The community's participation in school planning must be continuous. If members of the community are asked to think with the school staff only when a bond issue is at stake, or when the administration is on the defensive, they realize they are being manipulated. But when they are regularly consulted before action affecting them and their children is taken, they recognize the good faith of the school staff, and cooperative responsibility results.

Specific ways the community can be brought into planning are

1. Having individual teachers meet with the parents of the children they teach to discuss the program and the growth parents want their children to make.
2. Establishment of a citizens' advisory council on education.
3. Formation of curriculum committees that include teachers, parents, and pupils.
4. Creation of lay advisory boards to provide consultation services for special phases of the curriculum.

5. Bringing community members into the discussion of the school budget or other special proposals before the proposals are submitted to the board.

Planning with the community does not in any way relieve the school staff of the responsibility of formulating policy for the school. In the final analysis, the school administration and staff must take responsibility for major curriculum changes. And the challenge again becomes one of working with the power structure.

It should not be assumed that the community does not want curriculum change. The members may want and support it. They may be pushing the educational leadership to get moving. They may not be informed about school problems or new possibilities. School personnel may not be informed about community expectations of the schools. The key is interaction and cooperation between school and community at the school system level, the local school level, the teacher level, and the student and parent level.

The preceding paragraphs should not be interpreted to mean that educational leaders should be pawns. They should not, in an effort to influence the power structure or to retain leadership in the staff, make statements or take actions contrary to their basic beliefs. If they do, their integrity will be so impaired that it will be only a matter of time before they are discovered, rejected, or ousted, and new leadership is sought.

It is necessary for educational leaders to be willing to be expendable. If they want a leadership role so much that they are willing to compromise on their basic values, they lose their leadership. They must, if necessary, be willing to relinquish a position and seek another in a community whose values more nearly coincide with their own. Being willing to be expendable makes them fearless, able to go beyond the present status and stand for unfulfilled hopes and desires, and thus increase the number of people on whose behalf they exert leadership.

9

CLINICAL SUPERVISION

It is our contention that the delivery of direct support, consultation, and service to help an individual teacher or a team of teachers improve their performance in working with a particular group of students should be a basic organizational expectation for the instructional supervisory behavior system. We have concluded that clinical supervision as developed by Cogan (1973), Goldhammer, Anderson, and Krajewski (1980), and others is an excellent approach for the delivery of these services. Accordingly, the purpose of this chapter will be to develop a concept of clinical supervision, and a description of its process and application, and finally, to evaluate clinical supervision as a dimension of instructional supervisory behavior.

A CONCEPT
OF CLINICAL SUPERVISION

It is possible and helpful to think of clinical supervision as an effort by the instructional supervisory behavior system to interact directly with a teacher or team of teachers to provide support, help, and service to those teachers in order to improve their performance as they work with a particular group of students. Cogan (1973, p. 9) defined clinical supervision as follows:

Clinical supervision may therefore be defined as the rationale and practice designed to improve the teacher's classroom performance. It takes its principal data from the events of the classroom. The analysis of these data and the relationship between teacher and supervisor form the basis of the program, procedures, and strategies designed to improve the student's learning by improving the teacher's classroom behavior.

Cogan's emphasis is on clinical supervision as a direct effort to help a particular teacher work more effectively with a certain group of students through the observation and analysis of the behavior of students and teachers in the teaching-learning process. Goldhammer, Anderson, and Krajewski (1980, p. 4) express a similar concept of clinical supervision as "the hands-on or eyes-on aspect of the supervisor who is attempting to intervene in a helpful way." Thus, the foci of clinical supervision include the needs of students, organizational needs, objectives of teaching, engagement opportunities for students, definition of learning outcomes, identification of problems, development and trying out of solutions, and evaluation of results. Since clinical supervision is consultation for a specific teaching-learning situation, it is possible to think of it as a problem-solving approach to instructional supervision. A critical component of the process is observation and analysis of teaching as a basis of feedback for teachers that can be used as a framework for change and improvement of performance. Emphasis is placed on objectivity in observation, analysis, and feedback for teachers, with both supervisors and teachers participating in the processes as colleagues. It is expected that teachers will have primary responsibility for evaluation and decisions on changes in teaching behavior, with supervisors playing a helping, supporting, suggesting, and servicing function.

Goldhammer, Anderson and Krajewski, (1980, pp. 3-6) developed a useful distinction between the concept of clinical supervision and the methods of clinical supervision. They took the position that it is possible, and even essential, to first develop a strong concept of clinical supervision from which a variety of methods could be derived. The nature of the method developed and used would be a function of the requirements of a particular situation. The point was made that an assumption that there is only one or a few appropriate methods of clinical supervision could, in fact, restrict its development. They emphasized that the method is important and, therefore, should be appropriate to the situation.

SOME ASSUMPTIONS
OF CLINICAL SUPERVISION

The purpose of clinical supervision should be a fundamental determinant of its nature. Cogan, (1973, p. 12) indicated that the central hoped-for outcome is professionally responsible teachers who are committed to self-improvement through help from others and self-correction. Goldhammer, Anderson, and Krajewski, (1980, p. 4) defined the purpose as the improvement of instruction and learning outcomes. We agree but also support the emphasis that Cogan placed on the development of the teacher as a self-directing and self-improving person. It is our assumption that this purpose indicates a process that not only provides outside help for the teacher, including observation and analysis of teaching, feedback for teachers, and development of improvement ideas and support for their implementation, but also demands a collegial relationship between the supervisor and teacher in which the teacher has full control of, and responsibility for, the teaching-learning situation. Since the teacher is in control of the supervisory situation, it is crucial that he or she has an opportunity to become knowledgeable about the concept of clinical supervision. It is also critical that teachers develop the conceptual, technical, and human skills needed in the delivery of clinical supervisory services, since it is hoped that teachers will become increasingly more self-directing, and self-sufficient. It is also our assumption that teachers should become increasingly able to provide clinical supervisory services to other teachers.

Our review of the literature, (Bellon, and others, 1976, pp. 20-21), (Sullivan, 1980, pp. 7-8), indicates that clinical supervision is based on the assumption that the teaching-learning situation is at least partly composed of behavior that can be observed and analyzed. At least part of this behavior occurs on a more or less regular basis and can be associated with learning outcomes. Therefore, the identification of certain patterns of behavior can result in improvement of instruction and learning outcomes for students. These are the assumptions that provide the rationale for the strong emphasis on the observation and analysis of behavior in the classroom that are characteristic of clinical supervision.

Authorities such as Cogan (1973) and Goldhammer, and others (1980) agree that there is a strong and compelling need for a teacher-supervisor relationship that is characterized by mutual trust and respect. Goldhammer, and others (1980, pp. 27-29) made the point that it is theoretically preferable for the supervisor to know more about instruction and learning than the teacher. It is our position that professional teachers and professional supervisors should work together on a collegial basis, and that it is highly unlikely that either will be superior in all things and have better answers at all times. Rather, we think it is more helpful to work toward a relationship of two professionals working for a common goal but from two different frames of reference. The reference of teachers is to become more effective teachers through both self-improvement and consultation from the supervisor, with the additional goals of helping the supervisor become a more effective supervisor. Conversely, the reference of the supervisor is to help the teacher become a more effective teacher and to become a more effective supervisor through self-improvement and consultation from the teacher. We prefer to work for a relationship in which each professional assumes that he or she can give or receive help, support, or service from the other.

Sergiovanni (1976, pp. 20-29) articulated the beginning stages of a theory of clinical supervision that we feel deserves special consideration since it provides not only direction for the development and implementation of clinical supervision, but also provides a rationale for clinical supervision. He started with the assumption that teaching behavior is a function of the teacher's assumptions, theories, and goals, which provide the basis for the teacher's educational platform. According to Sergiovanni (1976), the teacher's educational platform has an espoused dimension (what the teacher says it is) and a practical dimension, which is the basis for actual teaching behavior. Espoused platforms can either be congruent or incongruent with actual behavior in the classroom. When teachers become aware of a lack of congruence between their espoused behavior and actual behavior, it is assumed that disequilibration will occur and teachers will seek a new level of equilibration that would either change espoused behavior to match actual behavior or change practiced behavior to match espoused behavior. Since espoused behavior is assumed to be closely linked with self-expectations and expectations of significant others, it was predicted that the change would be in the direction of the practiced behavior.

From the Sergiovanni frame of reference, it is our conclusion that clinical supervision should provide an opportunity for teachers to

1. Examine, discuss, and explicate their espoused educational platforms.
2. Receive objective feedback on their practiced platforms.
3. Examine the relationship between their anticipated and actual behavior in the classroom.
4. Examine the relationship between the desired consequences of their behavior and the actual consequences of their behavior.
5. Examine the relationship between their espoused platform and other assumptions, theories, and research about effective teaching.
6. Develop, implement, and receive support for appropriate changes in both their espoused and practiced educational platforms.

THE PROCESS
OF CLINICAL SUPERVISION

Clinical supervision is often thought of as a structured model with certain stages or as a cycle of phases. Goldhammer, and others, 1980, pp. 31-44, identified five stages of clinical supervision.

> The prototype of a sequence of clinical supervision consists of the following five stages: (1) preobservation conference; (2) observation; (3) analysis and strategy; (4) supervision conference; and (5) postconference analysis.

Cogan (1973, pp. 10-13) defined eight phases of clinical supervision which constitute the cycle of supervision:

Phase 1. Establishing the teacher-supervisor relationship
Phase 2. Planning with the teacher
Phase 3. Planning the strategy of observation
Phase 4. Observing instruction

Phase 5. Analyzing the teaching-learning processes
Phase 6. Planning the strategy of the conference
Phase 7. The conference.
Phase 8. Renewed planning.

The reader is referred to both of these structured models of clinical supervision for excellent descriptions of the clinical supervisory process. However, we feel that it is more helpful and certainly less restrictive to think of clinical supervision as an instructional supervisory behavior system with three interdependent dimensions: 1. Preobservation behavior, 2. Observation behavior, 3. Postobservation behavior. Though we believe that clinical supervision requires behavior in all three of these dimensions, it is not our assumption that a rigid structure, including both the order and nature of events, is required. Rather, it is our belief that the order and nature of events should be a function of the requirements of a particular situation. Some of the factors that deserve special consideration include the needs and expectations of both the teacher and supervisor, the teacher's and supervisor's prior experience together, the needs of children, and the organizational climate and expectations. In essence, we are recommending a contingency approach to both the order and nature of the clinical supervisory process. Therefore, the process of clinical supervision will be discussed under preobservation behavior, observation behavior, and postobservation behavior.

Preobservation Behavior

The preobservation behavior system provides an opportunity for the supervisor and teacher to establish a relationship of mutual trust and respect. Trust means that the supervisor and teacher see each other as individuals who care about the other's well being. Teachers need to see supervisors as persons who are not only committed to improving the learning situation for children, but who are also dedicated to helping teachers improve performance and become more fully functioning individuals. Supervisors need to perceive teachers as persons who want to improve, who want to help and support supervisors, who are willing to share their professional behavior in a "give and take" situation. These are the conditions of mutual trust.

But, trust alone is not enough. Supervisors and teachers must also respect each other as competent professionals who are not only eager to improve their professional behavior, but are also eager and able to help and be helped by each other. What are some of the factors that contribute to the establishment of a supervisor-teacher relationship characterized by mutual trust and respect?

We believe it is important to operate from the assumption that teachers are professionally competent individuals who should be held responsible for the outcomes of their professional performance. Therefore, it is necessary for teachers to have control of the teaching situation and the clinical supervision process. We recommend that clinical supervisors and teachers operate as colleagues, with authority based on competence and esteem. It is also felt that a system of "privileged information" between the supervisor and teacher contributes to the establishment of trust and respect. Such a system means that the teacher has control of the utilization of the information coming from the supervisory process. This control means that teachers could determine whether or not data generated in the clinical supervisory process could be used by the organization in the process of making personnel decisions. It also means that teachers would have the final determination for the utilization of analysis data for the improvement of their performance.

It is during preobservation behavior that teachers and supervisors get to know each other as fellow professionals. Supervisors need to get a feel for teachers and where the teachers are coming from. Cogan (1973) discusses working with teachers in the planning process where educational philosophies, objectives for teaching, engagement opportunities for students, and evaluation strategies are explored in depth. Educational assumptions can be explicated, explored, evaluated and changed. Teachers have an opportunity to try out their ideas on fellow professionals and get honest reactions, including positive support, questions, and suggestions. Supervisors have an opportunity to develop understanding of the frustrations and needs of teachers. Supervisors also have a chance to help, suggest, support and share themselves, including their ideas, frustrations, and insecurities. This is the stuff out of which professional colleagues can establish trust and respect. It is essential to the establishment of the foundation for the observation and analysis of teaching.

Supervisors should develop a knowledge base and sensitivity to the situations in which the teachers work. Some of the factors that deserve special study include the nature and needs of students, the community of the school, the school climate, the teacher's relation with other teachers and the administration, and the physical setting in which the teacher performs. The study of these factors could help supervisors gain a feel for teachers and where they are coming from. It is necessary to the establishment of trust and respect.

Preobservation behavior occurs in both the formal and informal setting. Teachers and, or supervisors need to arrange for a variety of formal situations in which they have an opportunity to interact on matters of mutual concern. One supervisor planned a conference with each teacher just to talk about the needs and concerns of that teacher and to make plans for future work together. Some teachers request visits from supervisors. Some teachers like to have lunch with supervisors before they get into more formal professional conferences. Some supervisors like to study student records and the teacher's classroom before they arrange for a conference. The possibilities are inexhaustible. But, it is crucial that a wide variety of opportunities for preobservation behavior be arranged and that supervisors and teachers have an opportunity to work together in significant ways such as planning lessons, developing engagement ideas for students, trying out plans for teaching, and evaluating teaching. These activities provide the basis for mutual trust and respect and lead to the observation and analysis of teaching that should be preceded by a preobservation conference.

The preobservation conference was discussed in depth by Cogan (1973) and Goldhammer and others (1980). It is such an important dimension of preobservation behavior that it deserves special consideration in our discussion. It is a special conference in the clinical supervision process that sets the stage for observation behavior. Normally, it comes about as a result of work done in other preobservation behavior. For example, the teacher may be discussing with the supervisor a specific activity that she or he plans to use with a group of students. She or he invites the supervisor to observe the activity and provide feedback. In other situations, teachers may invite supervisors to observe and analyze their teaching. In any case, we feel that observation and analysis of teaching in clinical supervision should be mutually agreed on by both the teacher and the supervisor.

The preobservation conference should be held prior to, and as close to, the observation as possible. It should occur at a time and place mutually agreed to by teacher and supervisor. It is possible to hold the conference in the morning before school starts, in the afternoon when the school day is over, during a teacher's "free" period, or at a time when the teacher can be released from normal duties. It is important to be in a quiet place relatively free from distractions. It is also helpful to meet, if possible, in the room where the observation will occur. This contributes to the need to get a feel for the teaching that is to take place.

The purpose of preobservation behavior is to set the stage for clinical supervision, and the purpose of the preobservation conference is to establish the framework for a specific observation. Naturally, the time and place for the observation should be set. But, more importantly, the supervisor needs to set the tone for the observation. The purpose of the observation should be reaffirmed with specific emphasis on the idea that the teacher is in control of the situation, and that data will be collected in terms of the teacher's needs and within the framework of "privileged information." The process will be service, support, and help for the teacher. It is hoped that these assurances will help relieve any feelings of threat or anxiety that the teacher might have.

One of the first steps in the conference is to find out as much as possible about the purpose of the lesson to be observed, the instructional plans of the teacher, and the teacher's plans for evaluation. There is a strong need to encourage discussion about these important matters by careful listening and enthusiastic response, including questions, suggestions, support, and clarification. The supervisor *must* have more than a superficial understanding of the teacher's plans.

The supervisor also needs to explore any specific *concerns* the teacher may have about this particular lesson or group of students. The plans and concerns of the teacher provide the basis for the observation. It is our contention that the behavioral data that are collected should be based on the *needs* and *concerns* of the teacher. If these needs and concerns can be explicated, than it is possible to define fairly specifically what behavioral data will be collected. At that point, the supervisor and teacher need to agree both on what data will be collected and how they will be collected. This agreement makes it possible for the teacher to know what procedures will be used, how they will be used, and what to expect from the observation. The observation is an exciting opportunity for teachers to find out some things about their teaching behavior. The preobservation conference should clarify the teacher's needs and concerns, the observational data that is needed, the method for collecting the data, and the way it will be used.

Our experience has been that in many situations in the initial preobservation conference, the teacher is just not ready to pinpoint specific concerns and needs and will often ask the supervisor to "just come in and observe and let me know what you think." In such situations, it is possible to use a more general and exploratory approach. But, it is still necessary to focus the observation on certain dimensions of student or teacher verbal or nonverbal behavior. It is impossible to describe everything that is going on. The teaching situation is just too complex. But, it is possible to explore certain general dimensions of behavior that can be agreed on during the preobservation conference. Examples of dimensions of the teaching-learning situations include student or teacher questioning behavior, teacher reinforcing behavior, and the physical environment. Agreement between the teacher and supervisor on the category of behavior to be observed could provide a focus for even a general exploratory approach.

Observation Behavior

Observation of a particular teaching-learning situation is the process through which a supervisor attempts to develop an objective description of the behavior of students and teachers in interaction, within the context of a physical and social environment. During observation, the emphasis is on objectivity, which involves faithfully recording perceptions of behavior and physical surroundings, rather than generalizations about the motives of the actors and the value of their behavior.

The importance of a strong and valid data base that can be used as feedback for teachers to examine their "actual behavior" in contrast to what they hoped to achieve cannot be overstressed. If the data base is fuzzy, distorted, not relevant to teacher concerns, or not presented in an adequate way, the supervisory process is likely to be worthless or, worse, alienating to the teacher. So the effort to be objective is fundamental. However, it is well to remember that supervisors can only perceive what they "think" they see, and this is affected by their own past experience, needs, values, selective stimuli to which they react, and many other factors. The field of observation is so complex and filled with stimuli that it is impossible to observe everything. Therefore, we feel there is a need to recognize the difficulties in observation and take appropriate precautions.

Since it is impossible to observe everything, it is necessary to restrict observations to a particular category of behavior, such as student or teacher responses, teacher positive reinforcements, or interaction flow. The selection of the specific behaviors to be observed should be a function of the needs and concerns of the teacher that have been revealed in various dimensions of preobservational behavior. The behavior to be observed and the method of observation and recording should be agreed upon by both teachers and supervisors as appropriate and valid procedures before the observation. Such agreements should contribute to teacher understanding and teacher acceptance of the credibility of the results.

The decisions about the method of observing and recording during observation is a function of what is to be observed; the understandings, needs, and skills of the supervisor and teacher; and the availability of materials and equipment. Various approaches are available. One approach is for supervisors and teachers to design general instruments or procedures that can be adapted to particular situations. These instruments can take the form of providing general categories of behavior, with specific behaviors of students or teachers listed under each category and with spaces provided for recording incidents of specific behavior. Such a system provides a frequency tabulation of the occurrence of certain specific behaviors within a certain timeframe. Various well-developed and well-known interaction analysis systems can be used if desired.

Another form of observation instrument that teachers and supervisors can develop together provides behavior categories such as teacher questions, student responses, and student questions that observers can record by hand during an observation. In place of a checklist, this approach could take the form of a narrative account. Some supervisors develop their own system of "shorthand" and achieve great effectiveness in recording observed behavior.

The use of audiotape recorders is an effective technique for recording the exact verbal behavior that occurs in a classroom or a small group. It can be used during postobservation conferences to play back pieces of classroom interaction as feedback for teachers. It is an excellent device for validating other observational techniques.

Videotaping is an excellent technique for recording both verbal and nonverbal behavior. Classroom behavior is recorded on the tape and is available for playback by both teachers and supervisors. This kind of feedback can be extremely effective. The following example illustrates the point.

> An elementary teacher had been videotaped while teaching a reading lesson to a first grade group of students. During the course of the lesson, one child was having difficulty with a particular word and the teacher had helped him repeatedly. During the playback the teacher observed herself move forward toward the child and with a certain tenseness say, "The word is "if," "I.F.," and I hope you have it now." The child was cringing behind his book. The teacher exclaimed, "Oh my goodness, I did not mean to do that."

The nonverbal and verbal behavior that threatened the child came through clearly on the tape. It made a deep impression on the teacher.

Videotapes make it possible to examine and discuss various kinds of behavior occurring simultaneously, as well as sequential behavior. The total picture is there for repeated examination. It is true that the camera cannot record everything. Therefore, it is still a selective procedure. Another difficulty is that cameras, wires, and microphones can be factors in the learning situation and can make a difference in the behavior of students and teachers. Our experience has been that teachers and students soon adapt to the intrusion, and the initial confusion subsides in much the same way that teachers and students adjust to an observer.

The most prevalent method of recording teaching and learning behavior is the individual supervisor sitting in the classroom, making mental notes or written notes, or tabulating the frequency of certain well-defined behavior. Though it is impossible to be completely objective, it is possible to describe behavior. It is impossible to observe and record all behavior, but it is possible to select certain categories of behavior to observe and to attain fairly comprehensive and valid data. It is a professional service that requires training, practice, and constant evaluation and improvement. It is possible to use a narrative account to describe behavior, flow charts of interaction, frequency tabulations, audiotaping, videotaping, standardized systems, and other methods. Any of them can be appropriate or inappropriate, depending on the situation. We feel that teachers and supervisors must work together to determine what to observe, how to observe it, and how to record it. They both must understand the approach and accept it as a valid procedure for getting the job done. For a more in-depth discussion of observation behavior, including the purpose of observation, categories of behavior to be observed, systematic data collection instrument, and general approaches to observation and recording of behavior, students are referred to the work of Cogan (1973) and Goldhammer, Anderson, and Krajewski (1980), among others.

Postobservation Behavior

Postobservation behavior includes the analysis of the data collected during observation of instruction, the evaluation of teaching and learning behavior, the process of providing feedback for teachers, and the final stages of the evaluation of the clinical supervisory process. Observation and recording of data in the classroom situation are efforts to describe, as objectively as possible, what is occurring in the situation. The analysis of the data is an effort to try to understand and make sense out of the data.

The effort to make sense out of the raw data collected during the observation can be facilitated by organizing the data in appropriate categories. Examples of possible categories that might surface from initial study of the data include teacher behavior while introducing the lesson, student nonverbal behavior while teacher introduces the lesson, teacher questioning behavior, and student response behavior, to name only a few. Consideration of the agreements reached during the preobservation conference about what should be observed should be helpful in establishing categories but not sufficient unto themselves since unanticipated categories may emerge. Ordering the data into categories should help in identifying patterns of behavior. Patterns of behavior are behaviors that repeat with great frequency over time. Since the behavior often occurs, it has the potential for being an important factor in the learning. Whether or not certain teacher or student behavior is important, is at least partly a function of whether or not it contributes to or detracts from the achievement of the goals of the learning environment.

Recurring behavior can be either verbal or nonverbal and can be either teacher or student behavior. Examples of teacher and student behavior patterns are

1. The teacher repeatedly calls the name of a student before asking a question.
2. The teacher often uses "OK?" after a statement to a child.
3. The teacher rattles change in pocket before responding to student questions.
4. The teacher provides positive reinforcement when a student answers correctly.
5. The teacher becomes irritated when a student disagrees.
6. The teacher normally interacts with the same six students.
7. The teacher stands on the right side of the room when leading a discussion.

Examples of possible teacher or student habits of behavior are inexhaustible. It is well to remember that in order for it to be a habit, each generalization must be based on specific behavior that recurred over time. All generalizations, such as positive reinforcement, must be supported by specific behaviors that add up to reinforcing behavior. A crucial decision for the supervisor and teacher during analysis is whether or not the habit is a significant factor in the learning environment. If it is significant, it should be encouraged or discouraged, depending on whether it is facilitating or inhibiting the achievement of learning goals. Goldhammer, and others (1980, pp. 97-112) identified three criteria for deciding on patterns that should be included as feedback for teachers: 1. Saliency, 2. Treatability, 3. Finesse. The criterion of saliency included significance in effect on student learning, frequency of occurrence of behavior, and relationship to other patterns. By treatability they referred to the conditions of the environment such as teacher readiness for consideration of the pattern. The criterion of finesse was recognition that only a limited number of patterns can be considered.

Identification of patterns of behaviors and decisions about their relevance to the supervisory process are essential to analysis. Individuals develop consistent ways of behaving to meet certain needs. These patterns and/or needs may be conscious or subconscious. The importance of a particular pattern is a function of the way the behavior relates to other variables in the teaching-learning situation. If the pattern is a significant factor in whether or not students learn, and if it is subject to change without too much emotional turmoil, then the data should be used as feedback for the teacher. For example, a teacher may be concerned about lack of student response in discussion. Analysis of observational data could reveal that the teacher has a pattern of taking over discussions and, in fact, dominating and outperforming students. Each time the teacher did this, the students were observed to withdraw from the discussion. The teacher's pattern of behavior needed to be considered in relationship to the student's patterns of behavior.

Analysis of observational data is dependent on a strong data base that is understood and accepted by teachers. Teachers need to understand the categories of observation, and they need to see and accept the specific observations that support the patterns of behavior. We like the idea of teachers and supervisors collaborating in analysis, discovering categories together that help order data, finding patterns of behaviors, and deciding together on their significance. We think this helps establish credibility, implements the collegial approach, and facilitates mutual trust and respect.

The postobservation conference is an important part of postobservation behavior. After the analysis of the data, it is essential that teachers and supervisors get together to

1. Compare anticipated teacher and student behavior and actual teacher and student behavior.
2. Identify discrepancies between anticipated teacher and student behavior and actual student and teacher behavior.
3. Make decisions about what should be done about discrepancies and congruencies between anticipated and actual behavior.
4. Compare projected use of subject content, materials, equipment, physical space, and social environment with their actual use, with emphasis on the identification of congruencies and discrepancies, and plans for their future use.
5. Compare hoped-for learning outcomes with actual learning outcomes within the context of other appropriate factors in the situation, as described by the observation.

It is obvious that it is impossible to achieve all of these objectives in any particular postobservation session. Rather, these objectives define the parameters of the objectives of the clinical supervisory process and give direction to things to accomplish in the postobservation conference.

Any time individuals are getting feedback on their behavior and possible effects of their behavior, the possibility of tenseness, or even anxiety, is great. However, it is our belief that a solid base of trust and respect, colleagiality, valid observational data agreed on by teacher and supervisor, teacher-supervisor collaboration in analysis and evaluation of patterns of teaching, and teacher-supervisor cooperation in generalizing to future behavior will ameliorate tension and produce improvement.

It is absolutely essential to explore the data that are related to the expressed concerns and needs of the teacher, and to reaffirm that there is still agreement on the results of the analysis before discrepancies and congruencies are evaluated. In the consideration of the worth or value of certain practices or results, it is well to emphasize the positive, but it is crucial to deal also with the negative. The positive elements in the situation need to be maintained and supported. The negative elements need to be considered for change. Decisions about what is positive and negative, and what needs to be changed rest with the teacher. The supervisor and teacher can provide and organize data; make suggestions; be supportive; introduce assumptions, theories, and research about teaching; and evaluate behavior; but the teacher generalizes to future practice.

One of the problem areas in clinical supervision has been the effort to evaluate behavior patterns and other characteristics of the classroom situation that have been described. Some research efforts on characteristics of effective teaching (Bloom, 1956), (Hunter, 1979, pp. 62-67), (Levin and Long, 1981) are beginning to become available for use in the evaluation of educational practices. For example, Hunter reported that effective teachers make and implement decisions that are based on what is now known about human learning, and decisions that are appropriate to the environment and current needs of the learner. Based on the concept of teaching as decision making, three categories of decision were identified as "content, style of the learner, and behavior of the teacher." It is crucial for the teacher to understand the "incremental nature of learning" and to be able to make on-the-spot decisions based on the diagnosis of what students know and do not know, and what they need to know to proceed with learning.

Hunter emphasized the need to recognize that students have different learning styles and, therefore, teachers need to help students broaden their repertoire of learning options. Teachers also need to vary teaching styles according to the needs of learners.

Levin and Long (1981) discussed in depth "active learning time," "feedback corrective procedures," and "instructional cues" as significant variables that contribute to effective learning. Their discussion was based on a solid foundation of scientific research. Active learning time was conceptualized as student involvement in the learning process and was projected as a function of certain student characteristics and learning processes. Feedback corrective procedures involve the definition of standards, evidence of achievement, and feedback and corrective procedures. The use of instructional cues is the process through which teachers use a variety of stimuli to communicate to students what is to be learned and possible paths that can be used for reaching learning goals.

The postobservation conference is a kind of culminating experience in which supervisor and teacher have an opportunity to examine observational data, evaluate findings, and make plans for the future, in an open, supportive, and psychologically rewarding climate. The supervisor should be a consultant working from a strong base of expertise recognized by the teacher. The situation should be relaxed, with teacher and supervisor working as colleagues within the framework of privileged information. Sources of data that support generalizations should be available for easy reference by either supervisor or teacher. Finally, lines of communication for future work together should be kept open.

The clinical supervisory process should be evaluated from beginning to end, with appropriate changes as needed. Both teachers and supervisors must participate in the process. The evaluation should consider supervisor-teacher rapport, relevance and validity of observation data, analysis of observation data, effectiveness of the process of providing feedback for teachers as well as the quality of the feedback, the process of evaluating findings, and the support for change of practices. The end of the process is an excellent time to take stock, but evaluation and changes should be made continuously as the process unfolds.

PITFALLS IN THE DELIVERY
OF CLINICAL SUPERVISION

We strongly believe in clinical supervision as a system for the delivery of help, support, and service to the teaching behavior system. However, we also believe that there are certain obstacles or pitfalls that have interfered with efforts to implement the idea in educational organizations. It is hoped that the explication and discussion of some of these barriers will make some contribution to their future solution:

1. Some organizations like the "sound" and "glamour" of clinical supervision but do not have the conviction and/or the ability to provide the human and material resources. To implement clinical supervision, it is essential that supervisors and teachers have *time* to participate in various kinds of activities on a continuing basis. Time is needed for preobservation conferences, observation and analysis of teaching, and postobservation feedback and corrective procedures. Clinical supervision requires in-depth thinking and working together over an extended period of time. If it is going to work, the organization must provide the necessary personnel, arrangements, rewards, equipment, leadership, and support.

2. Some organizations make the assumption that all teachers should have clinical supervision continuously. This is impossible, given the restraints in most situations, so the supervisors say, "I'd like to do clinical supervision, but I just don't have the time." It is our position that organizations must search for new arrangements, such as collaborative supervision, providing services for a smaller number of teachers less often, group clinical supervision, self-supervision with the use of audiotapes and audio-visual tapes, cadres of floating teachers, and the rifle approach, to name only a few.

3. In some organizations, the instructional supervisors do not have the understanding and skills of clinical supervision. This can result in an ineffective approach that never gets off the ground, or it can cause covert resistance to the idea so early that it is never tried. Systems need to recruit and select supervisors who already have the necessary understandings and skills, or they need an educational program for the supervisors they have.

4. In clinical supervision, it takes "two to tango." Teachers need certain understandings and skills, which they may not have. They may have had experiences with supervisors that were threatening and alienating. They may feel dependent on, and even inferior to, the supervisor, and these factors could make it difficult to accept joint responsibility for the process. Some teachers need an opportunity to gradually develop the needed understandings and skills.

5. Some organizations have yielded to the temptation to use "clinical supervision" as a system for evaluating teachers for personnel decisions. Such a decision precludes the use of privileged information, can be threatening and can limit willingness to share problems and concerns, can put teachers in a role of dependency and inferiority, and can limit the hoped-for outcome of teachers' becoming better-functioning and self-improving professionals.

6. Sometimes clinical supervision is delivered in a rigorous and inflexible series of steps, which may not take into consideration the needs and concerns of a teacher, or his or her readiness to participate in things like observation and analysis of his or her teaching, feedback, and corrective procedures. This practice could be a

"turnoff" for some teachers and downright "shattering" for others. Supervisors need to be sensitive to the *individual* differences among teachers.

7. Sometimes supervisors are not willing to take the time, or do not have the ability, to establish a basis of mutual trust. Such a condition is essential. However, there is also a need for mutual respect for professional competence. Without these two conditions, it is impossible to have effective clinical supervision.

8. Sometimes supervisors think that the way they observe a situation is the way it is. It is impossible ever to see things as they are. We can only see them the way we think they are. It is necessary for supervisors to share their observations with teachers and get teacher feedback, with the hope of reshaping data toward agreement. The teaching situation is too complex and filled with stimuli to see everything. We need to remember that observational data are rough and incomplete at best, and we need to keep working to improve it.

9. The possibility of tenseness and fear are present when teachers are getting feedback about their behavior. Supervisors must take appropriate steps to ease these situations.

CLINICAL SUPERVISION: WHERE DO WE GO FROM HERE?

According to Goldhammer, Anderson, and Krajewski (1980, p. 186), the practice of clinical supervision is more of a goal sought than a goal achieved. We agree but also feel that it is an approach to instructional improvement that must be pursued now and with vigor because it is so desperately needed and because it is possible to achieve. It is needed because any professional has the basic need to constantly change and improve his or her practice. This improvement is required because the context of the practice is constantly changing. For example, theories and research findings on teaching effectiveness, learning, teaching models, and learning models are constantly changing. The content of what is being taught also changes. New equipment, materials, and physical spaces are constantly being changed. Such changes require the professional to develop new understandings, skills, and practices. We believe that clinical supervision is one of the keys for accomplishing this. Clinical supervision is an effective and possible approach for providing consultation, support, and service to help teachers improve their professional performance. There is a strong body of prescriptive theory and demonstrated practice that gives direction to its implementation (Cogan, 1973), (Goldhammer, Anderson, and Krajewski, 1980). There are the beginnings of a base of descriptive theory that could provide a unity of purpose and a framework for practice (Sergiovanni, 1976), (Cogan, 1976), (Seager, 1979), (Flanders, 1976), (Anderson and Krajewski, 1980). There is also a broad base of change theory, leadership theory, motivation theory, organization theory, and communication theory that provides a framework for the development and practice of clinical supervision. We believe that the processes of clinical supervision that were defined in this chapter are consistent with the theoretical context defined in the chapters on communication, leadership, change, and motivation presented in this book.

10

SUPERVISION IS FACILITATING HUMAN DEVELOPMENT

Staff development is a continuous and comprehensive process that utilizes human development in-service, selection of additional staff members with appropriate competence, reassignment of staff members, and replacement of staff members. The purpose of Chapter 10 is to discuss the process of human development in educational organizations. The processes of staff recruitment and selection, assignment of staff members, and replacement of staff members will be considered in Chapters 11 and 12.

THE NATURE AND PURPOSE
OF HUMAN DEVELOPMENT
IN-SERVICE

Educational organizations are necessarily concerned about the continuous growth of members of the professional staff. Tyler (1978, p. 142) developed his concept of preservice education for teachers. He said that "the primary function of preservice education is to help the individual develop a rough cognitive map of the phenomena of learning, teaching, and professional ethics and to give him or her some practice in using the map so that they can get the feel of professionalism." The cognitive map and, therefore, the practice in using the map would be somewhat different for administrators and supervisors, but the same idea applies. Preservice education is more of a starting point than a finishing point. We feel that it is beneficial to think of in-service education as a process in which professional educators change and improve both the professional base from which they operate and the practical application of that base to their professional performance. We agree with Tyler (1978) that critical dimensions of that professional base should include knowledge of relevant concepts, theoretical formulations, research findings, and information coming from the study of learning, teaching, and professional ethics. However, it is our assumption that there are other fields of study that are critical to the base of professional educators: communication, leadership, human relations, complex organizations, change, and human motivation. We also feel there is an affective dimension of the base from which professional educators operate. Such factors as emotions, feelings, satisfaction, zeal, warmth, despair, and happiness can be important factors in professional performance. Values are also a critical part of the base. Examples of critical areas of values include

1. standards for personal and student performance
2. human life
3. students
4. education
5. professional ethics.

Values help determine both the direction and method of professional performance.

The central task of educational institutions is the learning of students, and the behavior system for achieving this task is teaching behavior. The quality and effectiveness of teaching behavior is partly a function of the professional base from which teachers operate and the application of that base to their professional performance. From the perspective of professional educators, the purpose of professional growth in-service is to change and improve their professional base and the application of that base to their professional performance. The organization should seek to provide a climate and structure, including expectations for performance and results, psychological and technological support, open communication, rewards for creative performance and change, and time for growth, that facilitates the process through which professional educators plan, implement, evaluate, and accept responsibility for their professional growth in-service. The direction and method of professional growth for staff members should be a reflection of the needs, past experience, and aspirations of the educators; the needs and expectations of the organization; new developments in fields of study that have implications for their professional base and performance; and new societal expectations for the educational organization. The critical question is the interplay of these factors as they relate to individual growth objectives and programs. It is our assumption that individual development programs should originate from the needs of those particular individuals. Professionals should be expected to accept responsibility for the direction and nature of their own program for growth. They should also be held accountable for their professional performance. An adequate program of professional growth should be reflected in the performance of the staff members.

Organizations should facilitate the process through which staff members become aware of organizational needs and expectations. It is through this process that organizational needs and expectations can be reflected in growth programs of staff members. Since individual staff members and organizations are subsystems of the larger society, the needs and special problems of the larger society should be expressed through the organization and individual staff members. Even though staff member growth is predicated on the needs, concerns, interests, and problems of the staff members, we feel that these growth programs should reflect organizational and societal needs and problems.

THE IMPORTANCE
OF HUMAN LEARNING
AND GROWTH IN-SERVICE

There are strong and compelling reasons why educational organizations must assume responsibility for facilitating the process through which members of the organization can continue to grow in-service. Professional educators do not emerge from preservice programs as finished products. Rather, they have a partially defined professional base and some practice in delivering services primarily developed from an inadequate student teaching experience. More importantly, they have a readiness for professional growth that should be recognized, utilized, and—it is hoped—maintained throughout professional practice.

Educational organizations are subsystems of a larger society and are, therefore, subject to societal expectations. Societies change and develop new problems and concerns, which translate into new expectations for the schools. The organizational response often requires new objectives and programs whose development and implementation are dependent on the professional growth of staff members. A primary reason for the failure of new programs is the organization's failure to provide adequate opportunities for the professional staff to develop needed new attitudes, understandings, knowledges, and skills, coupled with opportunities for practice.

The constant development of new concepts, theoretical formulations, and research findings that have important implications for the knowledge base from which educators operate is another important basis for the continuous growth of staff members. Knowledge developed from the study of learning and instruction, communication, leadership, change, organization, and human motivation are examples of fields of study that are active in theory development and research and that have special application in the field of education. New organizational structures, such as team teaching, nongrading, schools within a school, and open education, need to be evaluated. Other technological developments, such as computer-assisted instruction, electronic equipment, new curriculum materials, and styles of teaching, are only examples of developments that have possible implications for educational change and the corresponding need for staff member development.

Educational organizations need a constant flow of new ideas, new skills, and new enthusiasm that can form the basis for improvement. Until recently the growth of student enrollments and the corresponding need for additional educational workers provided an opportunity to attract new staff members with needed new ideas, skills, enthusiasm, and leadership. In recent years educational organizations have faced declining enrollments, declining opportunities to hire new staff members, and the possibility of a stagnant, sluggish, and lethargic staff with a low level of enthusiasm for change and improvement or even for maintaining current standards. The need is for a program of continuing staff renewal.

GUIDES
TO PROGRAM
DEVELOPMENT

Recognition of the uniqueness of each participant is essential in effective programs to facilitate the growth of educators. Teachers operate from their own professional base with unique strengths and weaknesses, different client systems, and, therefore, unique improvement objectives. Improvement programs must be built around the improvement objectives of a particular teacher in order to have meaning for that teacher. This does not mean that several teachers cannot get meaning from a common learning experience. They can. But it does mean that each teacher must be able to relate the learning experience to his or her own improvement objectives.

Attempts to promote staff growth should correspond to the principles that underlie all good learning situations. There should be recognition that

1. learning is occurring all the time;
2. the learning that an individual does in a situation is determined by his or her purposes, needs, and past experiences;
3. when force is applied, the learning that occurs may be the opposite of what is desired;
4. all individuals in the situation, including coordinators, consultants, and the teachers, are learning simultaneously;
5. teacher growth is promoted when teachers exchange ideas and when they are encouraged to test the hypotheses they establish;
6. "active learning time," "feedback corrective procedures," and "instructional cues" promote learning (Levin and Long, 1981);
7. continuous decision making about learners and other learning conditions contribute to learning outcomes (Hunter, 1979, pp. 62-67).

The study of in-service education is beginning to produce some important considerations for the planning of human growth activities. Joyce and Showers (1980, pp. 379-385) made a careful study of the research on in-service education and concluded that teachers are great learners with the capacity to sharpen current skills and develop new skills. However, they also found that certain known conditions, which are *not* normally provided, are necessary to this improvement.

It would appear that the opportunity for teacher improvement in-service is here if educational organizations would develop programs consistent with research findings.

They (Joyce and Showers, 1980, pp. 379–385) examined the "levels of impact" of certain training components on "fine tuning current skills" and "learning new ways of teaching." Presentation of the "rationale, theoretical base and verbal description" of an approach improves awareness and control of knowledge. However, for most teachers this instructional component does *not* contribute to the development of skills or their application in teaching.

The demonstration component was effective for helping teachers develop awareness and mastery of knowledge. It does help teachers improve their already existing skills, but generally, unless demonstrations are used in concert with other components, they are most effective in helping teachers develop new skills and/or apply them in teaching.

Simulation is an excellent way to help teachers learn new skills and sharpen old skills.

"Structured feedback" can help produce awareness of teaching strengths and weaknesses and can provide incentive for self-initiated and other-initiated development and application of new skills.

The most effective approaches to in-service education utilize more than one instructional component and probably all of the components (Joyce and Showers, 1980, pp. 379–385).

Zulette Melnick (1981, pp. 137–139) reported the following findings from a comprehensive review of the literature to determine factors associated with in-service education effectiveness.

It is important for significant participants (teachers, administrators, and consultants) to collaborate on important decisions, such as purpose, methods, and evaluation, within an atmosphere of mutual trust and respect. An effective method of in-service education was found to be individualization according to participant needs, interest, and concerns.

In general, fellow teachers were preferable to administrators or external experts as consultants. However, in some situations outside consultants were preferred, depending on the purposes of the training. Melnick (1981, p. 138) indicated that "instructional techniques that utilized any combination of theory, modeling, practice, feedback, and coaching for application also achieved maximum effectiveness."

The following dimensions of effective in-service education were identified: "ongoing extended training held at the local school site; the provision of skills and the time necessary to focus on the school site problems; and choices related to on-the-job needs" (Melnick, 1981, p. 138). Melnick concluded:

"The literature did not recommend top-down, administratively controlled planning; large group formats which provided little or no individualization;

outside consultants used on a short-term or one-shot basis; instructional methods which were not experimental; scheduling which did not provide release time on a regular basis; diverse locations and disjointed time allotments which did not allow for continuity; and sporadic evaluation with little feedback."

It is interesting that it is not unusual to observe in-service education programs with a heavy emphasis on the components not recommended in the literature.

Effective in-service programs provide for the meaningful *involvement* of *all* participants in establishing objectives and programs, and evaluating results. The establishment of objectives should be based on careful needs assessments so that objectives and programs can be closely related to areas of recognized strengths and weaknesses of all participants.

It is important to utilize a broad base of human resources according to appropriate knowledge, competence, and human relations skills. These personnel should be recruited and selected both from within and outside the organization. Emphasis needs to be placed on colleagues helping and being helped by sharing information, ideas, skills, and psychological support.

The emphasis on the utilization of teachers, supervisors, and administrators as helpers in human growth programs provides the basis for a strong effort to provide an opportunity for all personnel to develop their leadership and helping skills.

It is essential to provide for a broad variety of opportunities for members of the organization to continue their own development. Individuals have different needs, interests, incentives, and problems. Programs must have enough variability to provide for individual differences.

Opportunity for creative teaching, creative supervision, and creative administration are important conditions for facilitating staff growth. When staff members are supported in their efforts to assess needs, define problems, develop improvement objectives, create and actualize improvement programs, and evaluate results, they are engaged in effective staff development.

Programs of curriculum improvement constitute in-service training. Too frequently, it has been assumed that in-service education and curriculum development are separate functions. As teachers work on identifying inadequacies in the present program, on preparing changes in policy or curriculum content, or on devising operational procedures, they are growing in insight and in teaching skill. They themselves improve as they work to improve the program.

Underlying any program of improvement is a belief in people. If staff development is to be successful, the supervisor must believe that the faculty can grow. Lack of such faith makes the staff development program a meaningless ritual.

Staff development training is not something that is provided by the official leader for other members of the staff. Many leaders have made the mistake of assuming that it is their job to provide staff development training for others. Such an assumption makes clear to staffs that leaders consider themselves better than they. If, on the other hand, the leaders share the staff development opportunities with the staff, they will grow with the leaders in ability and in a sense of working together. They will be accepted as one of the group, rather than as an outsider who is trying to do something to the group.

Staff development training must not be haphazard. The first task of the official leader is to learn what type is needed. Some clues come from evaluation. As a staff evaluates itself and the school program, the areas of weakness indicate the experiences that should be made available. A second source of guidance is the direction the school program is taking. If the faculty has agreed to institute certain changes in the curriculum, and if a practical approach toward the transition is being taken, an investigation must be undertaken to see if the faculty members possess the skills necessary to follow through. If they do not, the function of staff development training is obvious. Curriculum programs have often failed because this step was not taken.

Changes in the nature of the community are clues to the human development needed. If teachers are not prepared to deal with the educational problems that arise from desegregation, the greater numbers of socially disadvantaged people, and the increased demand for technically skilled people, and if these are the changes occurring in the school's community, then the education needed should be apparent to those planning the staff development program. Opportunities to build new skills are necessary in any situation where a new program is being evolved or where the nature of the community is undergoing rapid change.

Staff education is more profitable when it is centered on improving the school program. It is purposeful learning. Areas that have proved fruitful in many situations are

> Examination of the recent developments in theories of learning and child growth, and adapting the program to meet them.
> Preparation of more adequate materials of instruction.
> Reorganization of courses, marking schemes, promotion policies, and reporting systems.
> Study of individual children, and the planning of experiences for them.

Staff development should not be confined to experiences that promote only academic growth. Many times, a faculty will be further advanced in its academic learning than in other abilities that make the success of the school program possible. Growth in ability to work with others, improved skill in democratic processes, the development of social skills, and the rounding out of the individual as a social being may all be areas in which teachers need more help than they do with methods of teaching or with content.

A faculty may have emotional problems that create such a strain among members of the group that no cooperation can occur. In such a situation, a staff development program must provide, as its first step, experiences that will enable people to relieve themselves of the emotional tensions that hinder constructive work. For this purpose, the program may include recreation, dramatics, and arts and crafts, as well as more formalized education.

Staff development needs to contribute to a growing together of the faculty.

Any faculty needs to feel that it is a unit, that it is a team working for a common purpose. Some phase of the staff development program should be held at a place where the members of the group are away from distracting influences and have a chance to really learn to know each other in many different ways. Retreats or workshops held at camps or resorts enable the staff to play together, work together, and think together. Through such experiences, friendships and feelings of oneness emerge and make possible really cooperative solutions of the problems facing a school staff.

Development programs may take many forms. It is not always getting together for common experiences. Reading, attending conferences, or other types of individual experiences can be growth experiences. Some official leaders find that the best contribution they can make to teacher growth is to take the place of a teacher who is attending conferences or visiting some other school. Others have found that their most helpful contribution consists of making readily accessible to teachers, professional material that contains suggestions and ideas. A strong professional library is a basic element of a good program.

Activities may take the form of study committees; workshops; clinics; participation in the evaluation of the school program; forums in which teachers, parents, and pupils exchange ideas; or study of learning problems based on direct classroom experience and on interschool studies of curriculum development and programs.

One of the most important kinds of experience is participation in an experimental program. An examination of the history of staffs in schools that have participated in experimental programs leads to the conclusion that such participation produces people who are stronger and more capable. People grow as they have a chance to try something new and come to look upon their jobs as a chance to explore better ways of teaching. To put it briefly, people grow as they try new things. When supervisors can make a teacher's day-by-day experiences an experimental attack on a problem, real professional development is being provided.

APPROACHES
TO PROFESSIONAL GROWTH

There are at least two interdependent contexts in which members of the staff grow professionally. First, and most important, is the individual context. As independent practitioners with unique needs, goals, interests, concerns, and problems, it is important for staff members to plan, control, actualize, and evaluate their own programs of self-improvement. Naturally, they need support, help, service, and time to pursue their professional improvement goals, and it is crucial that the organization facilitate this process.

Second, even though members of the staff are independent practitioners, they are also members of various formal and informal groups that are characterized by group goals and activities, member specialization, and member interdependence. For example, a member of an elementary school faculty may be expected to behave in certain well-defined ways to contribute to the achievement of certain goals. Faculty decisions could have been made to change either the curriculum or instructional process that would require that faculty members "as part of the team" develop new knowledge or new skills. Certainly, this situation is an important context in which professional development occurs. However, to be effective, it is essential that individual goals and group goals are integrated so that when the individual is working to develop certain skills to facilitate the achievement of group goals, he or she also sees this as consistent with personal needs for professional growth. In the discussion that follows, various approaches to human growth programs as they relate to the individual context and the group context will be discussed.

In-Service Education— Promotion of Creative Thinking

Supervisors are coming to realize that human growth programs must have the individual teacher as their basis. If a better school program is desired, an environment in which classroom teachers can be creative and can improve their teaching must be established. Unless supervisors see their task as encouraging creativity in teachers, their function becomes restrictive. They see their work as an attempt to discover what is going on and to bring about conformity to the existing instructional pattern. Emphasis on creativity is the threshold to improvement; stressing conformity means, at best, preserving the status quo.

In instructional improvement, final decisions must be in the hands of the teacher. Although certain common principles operate in all good learning situations, it is impossible to say what good teaching will be, except in a particular situation. Judgment concerning that situation must be made by someone who knows all the factors and has the ability and freedom to take the action that will meet the specific requirements of the situation. No one has as much knowledge about a particular classroom as the teacher in that situation.

Creative thinking involves being dissatisfied with the results obtained from present procedures, feeling that perfection is something never quite attained but constantly sought, having new ideas, and being willing to try the new ideas and evaluate the results produced. Creativeness is really a constant state of experimentation. This experimentation has three phases: planning, testing, and revising.

Courage is needed to try new procedures, and many teachers will not depart from the methods with which they feel at home unless the supervisor helps them. For the supervisor, promoting creativeness in teachers involves solving three problems:

How can teachers be helped to obtain a clear sense of direction?
How can the willingness of teachers to try new procedures be increased?
How can the teachers be given greater security during the process of change?

If teachers have a part in the establishment of the purposes of the school program, their sense of direction becomes clear. Therefore, a primary step in helping teachers to become more creative, just as in encouraging teachers to assume responsibility, is to spend time with the staff to examine the purposes of the school and revise these purposes in terms of the basic values that the staff holds. Time is not wasted if it is spent in arriving at the common philosophy. This step is essential.

Once agreement has been reached on the purposes of the program, the next responsibility of the supervisor is to increase willingness to try new procedures by providing a permissive atmosphere and a secure relationship with the supervisor, plus removing the factors in the situation that encourage conformity to a pattern.

Teachers cannot be expected to be creative if the supervisor believes that there is one best method of teaching. If such is the case, teachers bend their efforts to discover new approaches and follow the method the supervisor accepts. But creativeness is encouraged by the supervisor's frank admission that the best procedure for any given group must be developed by that group, in terms of its personnel and the limiting factors of the situation. The best method for any individual teacher will be an adaptation of the basic laws of learning to the personality and skills of a particular teacher. Much has been learned from research and experience, but teachers must continue to experiment to increase their effectiveness.

An essential step in promoting creativeness in teachers is to remove as many citywide or schoolwide restrictions as possible.

> In a California city, a typing teacher returned from a summer of graduate work with the idea that his method could be improved by putting the markings on the keys of the typewriters. Before he could make this change, he had to submit a written request to the city curriculum committee for permission to deviate from the method used in other typing classes. When the committee did not act on the request within a reasonable time, the principal of the school sent through a purchase order for the necessary key caps. But the curriculum committee, which had worked out a relationship with the purchasing department whereby it passed on all orders relating to materials of instruction, stopped the purchase order. The teacher was thus unable to try out a method of whose value he had become convinced after much study. It is easy to imagine the lack of enthusiasm of that typing teacher for his job and his school system.

If teachers are to show creativeness, they must be accepted as people who have ability, understanding, and sufficient knowledge to prepare the best type of learning experience for their students. If teachers are not so accepted, creativity is easily stifled.

A way of increasing the teacher's willingness to advance new ideas and procedures is by supervisors' being receptive to new ideas about teaching. If supervisors insist that their own answers are the only correct ones, teachers will turn from attempts to create for themselves, to efforts to learn what the supervisor's answers are. By keeping personal answers in the background, the supervisor encourages teachers to think, try, and evaluate for themselves. Discussions in which teachers' opinions are accepted on equal terms with those of the supervisor promote self-reliance, which is basic to creativeness.

One of the most effective ways to promote creativeness is to shift the emphasis on proof. Too many times, proof of the value of a new method is required before it can be tried. Too many supervisors feel that their chief function is to raise questions about teacher proposals in order to compel teachers to think through their ideas carefully and to leave out those ideas that are not worthwhile. Although this function is a valuable and important one, it can be carried to such an extreme that teachers find it easier to follow customary procedures than to attempt to convince the supervisor that something new is worth doing. If supervisors put as much emphasis on proof that new procedures should not be tried as on proof they they should, creativeness will be greatly encouraged, and many more new methods will be tried. In either case, the supervisor should not feel that the teacher's job is to give answers or proof that satisfy the supervisor. The supervisor's questions are only for the purpose of helping teachers evaluate their own work.

One concept that has held back the development of creative teaching has been the idea that there is a model that should be emulated. Teachers should be encouraged to develop rooms that reflect the character of their work, the personality of their group, and their own best thinking. Not only does this practice add variety and color to the experience provided for children in school, but it also leads to the emergence of more effective techniques of classroom organization.

Promoting a willingness to try new things is only the first step in developing creativeness in teachers. When this willingness is put into action, the supervisor must then give the security that makes any venture into new types of work satisfying.

A further way of promoting creativeness in the teaching staff is by giving recognition to those people who are trying new procedures. This recognition may consist of nothing more than having the people who are doing the experimental work tell the staff about what they are trying to achieve and the results they are getting.

Experimentation should not be limited to a few members of the staff. All should be encouraged to experiment when they have ideas they want to test. If creative activity is limited to a few members of the staff, the status of those who are denied the privilege will be jeopardized; interstaff jealously and diminution of creative endeavor will develop.

A second form of recognition is the commissioning of certain staff members to attend summer workshops on scholarships, to develop new ways of working and of using materials in a given area. The choosing of the teachers to receive the scholarships should be made on the basis of expressed desire to attend, the extent to which the teachers involved have demonstrated willingness to try new procedures, and the need for spreading such experiences throughout the entire faculty.

Another way of giving the creative teachers recognition is by encouraging them to discuss new procedures with parent groups and by having the parents plan with them ways of making the procedures more worthwhile. Monthly planning meetings of parents and teachers, a practice that is becoming more widespread, make this type of recognition possible.

One of the big handicaps that many teachers feel as they attempt new procedures is the difficulty in obtaining evidence of results. School officials and teachers have become accustomed to determining pupil progress by the amount of subject matter acquired. Tests of subject matter information are seldom questioned by supervisors, parents, or pupils. On the other hand, attempts to measure other types of growth have been so infrequent in the past that they are viewed with suspicion by parents and students. A supervisor can help teachers feel more secure by working with them to develop types of evaluation procedures that will measure a wider variety of types of pupil growth. As teachers learn how to evaluate additional types of pupil growth and to see the results of the procedures used, they become freer in their attempts to develop newer methods of teaching that promote the so-called "intangible" types of pupil growth.

Creativeness in teaching is not something that can be bought or commanded. It can only be encouraged. It is encouraged by the attitude of the supervisor, by the removal of unnecessary restrictions, by demonstrations of belief in the ability of teachers to make intelligent decisions, by providing a wide range of materials and the financial means of securing those materials not available, and by placing emphasis on proving why improvement should not be attempted rather than on proving why any new procedure should be tried.

The task of working with beginning teachers is easier, because neophytes expect to receive help and are not ashamed. They feel a need for support and for a source of assistance in time of trouble. They know their range of techniques is limited, and they want more information. But even in the case of first-year teachers, the length of time they maintain freedom within themselves to utilize available resources will depend upon the extent to which the general climate is one that permits questioning, admission of difference, and independence of action.

In-Service Education—
Intervisitation Programs

Opportunities for professional educators to visit with fellow professionals are an excellent approach to sensitizing staff to new ideas and approaches that may have relevance for their own operations. The stimulation of observing and interacting with fellow professionals can be an exciting and challenging experience. Questions can be raised about old ways of doing things, and new ideas can be examined and weighed as possible innovations. The process of growth also requires the implementation and evaluation of the innovation, and the intervisitation program can provide for opportunities for continuing observation and interaction during the entire change process.

The following paragraphs describe how one South Carolina county system conducted an observation program in which every elementary teacher participated:

> As soon as the day of observation had been placed on the school calendar, the supervisors began working with other school staff personnel to study possible plans of conducting an organized observation program. Following their discussions, they adopted some general procedures for operating:

1. Observations were to be arranged for small groups of teachers, rather than for individuals.

2. If possible, teachers were to visit within their own administrative areas in order to encourage respect for power within their own group. In other words, teachers were to be encouraged to feel that each had a worthwhile contribution to make in the development of the school program, and therefore, that it would not be necessary to go outside the area to find good teaching situations.

3. As far as possible, the interests and special skill needs of teachers were to be considered in arranging for the day.

4. Because the major purpose in conducting the program was to provide situations and experiences in which teachers might continue to grow professionally and find better ways of meeting needs of individual children, as preparation for the day of observation, the supervisor would plan with and assist, wherever possible, the teacher who was to be observed.

5. Schedules were to be arranged to meet the needs of observers and the teacher who was to be observed.

6. A conference for readiness was to be held on the day of observation just prior to the classroom visitations.

7. A conference for evaluation and sharing of ideas was to be held in the afternoon of the day of observation.

The supervisor worked closely with the teacher who was to be observed. Help in planning the day's schedule was given; the teacher's general and specific plans of procedure for the various teaching situations were discussed; and any other help that the teacher requested or which the supervisor could suggest was provided.

Occasionally in setting up plans for the day of observation a teacher said to her supervisor, "If you will help me, I should like to attempt some work in an area where I am not good at all. With this day as an incentive, perhaps I can improve the quality of my own teaching." As a result, the teacher and the supervisor planned together some experiences with the requested topic. After a number of days with the two working in this manner, the teacher provided a period on the schedule for observers that was most valuable and satisfying to the visitors and also to the teacher herself.

Teachers who are to be observed desire help from the supervisor before they teach. They do not want to feel that they have failed to carry forward the program on which agreement has been made. Teachers, like children, have needs that should be met. Teachers who are engaged in one of these observation-teaching experiences have the need for a feeling of security— of warm acceptance by the supervisor; they have the need for a feeling of recognition for a valuable contribution from their fellow teachers who are their guests for the day; and they have the need for a feeling of belonging in the group.

While teacher and supervisor always planned very carefully each period for a day of observation, in no instance was the work rehearsed with children. The observation day was as natural as the teacher could make it. The teachers were concerned about doing as good a teaching job as possible, and therefore, some may not have been as relaxed as they would have been if the visitors had not been present. But every effort was made to provide the students with a normal day of work.

Between the middle of October and the last of March, every elementary teacher in the county experienced a day of observation. One hundred and thirteen teachers taught for the groups, and eight schools were visited in the tour pattern, with members of the group observing in classrooms from first through seventh grades.

A department in a large city high school made a less elaborate approach to intervisitation:

It was decided to make Mondays a film day for all social studies students. All classes of social studies meeting during the same period on that day would assemble in a large visual aids room. Because there were six periods during the day, six different instructors on any Monday would assume responsibility for the discussions accompanying the films. Because many teachers would be present each period, every member of the department would get a chance to see, over a period of time, every other member of the department handle a teaching situation. Because there was no pressure of any kind to imitate anyone or to follow any set procedure, individual teachers experimented in various ways, from traditional question and answer lessons to panels of students and committee work. The result was a stimulating experience for all members of the department to share experiences, observe each other informally, confront similar problems, and gain from each other's efforts.

Although the possibility of all classes being ready for a film at the same time might be questioned, the approach described above made it easy for teachers to begin to share ways of improving teaching-learning situations.

In a large city system a group of middle school principals developed an intervisitation program for themselves. They decided that they had much to learn and that each principal was an important source of learning for the other principals. It was decided to meet one Monday each month in the building of a particular principal. The group was to serve in a consultative role to the principal of the school where the meeting was to be held. The principal being visited had the responsibility of sharing the operation of his or her school with the other principals. Ideas were discussed, questions were raised, suggestions were made, and changes were designed and implemented. These principals learned from each other first, and finally began to use outside consultants as well.

It would be possible for a school system to exchange principals, assistant principals, and supervisors in order to expose them to new ideas, problems, and responsibilities. For example, an elementary school could be interested in an innovation being implemented in another elementary school. The principal of the former school could be assigned as an assistant principal in the innovative school. The assistant principal in the noninnovative school could become principal on a temporary basis, and the assistant principal of the innovative school could be assigned to the noninnovative school. All of the involved supervisors would have an opportunity to work in a *new* environment with *new* challenges and *new* opportunities for professional growth.

We feel that it is appropriate for supervisors to go back to classroom teaching on a full-time basis periodically. Such an experience can sharpen old skills and provide an opportunity to develop new skills. More importantly, it can help the supervisor maintain a "feel" for the teacher's world of problems, frustrations, and achievements. Finally, the experience can contribute to the supervisor's credibility as a helper and supporter of teachers.

It is also important for teachers to have opportunities to serve in various supervisory roles, such as consultant for teachers, chairperson for curriculum committees, and even as full-time supervisor on a temporary basis. We think these kinds of experiences not only contribute to the professional growth of teachers, but also to their receptivity to utilize supervisory services.

In-Service Education–School– University Cooperation

It is essential for school systems and institutions of higher education to cooperate in their efforts to facilitate the professional growth of their staff members. Faculty members need an opportunity to work in school systems because this is where the action is. It is an opportunity to develop, try out, and evaluate ideas. New technical and human skills can be practiced and shared with fellow practitioners. These are the basic ingredients of professional growth.

The opportunities are equally great for professional educators in school systems. Faculty members in higher education can be an important source of ideas, technical skills, psychological support, and technical services, such as needs assessments, computer technology, and surveys. A few examples of university-school system cooperation may help clarify the concept.

A small city system made an approach to staff development that utilized university services:

> A decision had been made to organize the elementary school faculties into teams consisting of a team leader, teachers, and teacher aides. The junior high school and high school faculty had been organized into departmental teams consisting of a team leader, teachers and teacher aides. The new arrangements had created some questions and even anxiety about the role of the team leader, the principal, teacher, teacher aide, and the ways these roles fit together.
>
> A planning committee was formed and the problems and concerns were identified and discussed. They included such things as the need for role descriptions, communication development, improving group and leadership skills. Arrangements were made with a university to work cooperatively on these problems.
>
> Role descriptions were first developed by team leaders and principals. Then, they were taken to teams for discussion and revision. When consensus was achieved the team leaders began to implement their new roles on an experimental basis and with feedback from team members. The continuing education meetings were used for principals and team leaders to share successes and failures and to continue to work for improvement.

The program just described is an example of the way school improvement, continuing education, and college credit can be woven together to improve the quality of education for students.

A county school system became concerned about the quantity and quality of its supervisory services. Contact was made with a university, and a consultant worked with the school system. Group thinking involving representatives from the school system and the university determined that the first need was a definition of the problem. In order to define the problem, the school system developed a statement of the way they would ideally prefer for their supervisory services to be. Next, a study was done to describe as objectively as possible the supervisory program as it was perceived by teachers, administrators, and supervisors. The local school staff and university consultants analyzed the relationship between the "ideal model" and the actual situation as perceived by the professional staff. Discrepancies between "ideal" and "real" were identified as the problem, and a program of staff development was initiated that included both the recruitment and selection of two new supervisors and the educational development of current staff members. The total effort was an attempt by a school system not only to define and solve a problem through a program of staff development, but also to help staff members grow in their ability to define and solve future problems, thus, grow professionally through in-service education.

Yarbrough (1975, pp. 335–338) discussed the "Field Services Cluster" as an idea for facilitating university, school system, and community cooperation to achieve the goals of "improving teacher competencies, identifying educational needs of children, testing innovative programs and approaches, and utilizing community resources in instruction." The Field Services Cluster operates in various communities, according to the needs of each community. It is composed of three teams including a University Team, Community Team, and School Team. An effort is made to facilitate the use of financial and human resources through the use of the three teams to promote local school improvement.

In-Service Education—
Teachers Center

The development and implementation of the concept of the teachers center is a significant effort to improve opportunities for teachers to continue their professional growth in-service. The idea had its early beginnings in England and many American approaches were based on the English idea. David Burrell (1976, pp. 422–427) described the functions of the Centres in England as curriculum development and in-service education, information dissemination, educational services, and social activities. Though the purposes included teacher consideration of externally developed curriculum materials, emphasis was on local needs and concerns. Therefore, decisions for utilization, adaptation of curriculum, and local development of curriculum were points of major focus.

Kathleen Devaney, (1976, pp. 413–416) discussed the idea of teachers centers in contrast with the notion of the teaching center. The teachers center was described as a warm and inviting place where teachers could pursue their self-defined goals based on their personal needs and interests. Opportunities were available to work on curriculum materials, communicate with fellow teachers, try out ideas, participate in workshops if desired, study in the professional library, and engage in many other activities. The emphasis was on self-directed learning with needed support, help, service, materials, and equipment available. Human beings in the centers worked as equals on neutral ground without the need to be competitive or self-protective.

We like this approach and think it is consistent with the assumptions that should give direction to in-service education. However, we do not believe that teachers centers can or should take the place of other approaches to facilitating teacher growth. We feel that the *teaching center* is also a worthy approach and compatible with the teachers center approach.

The teaching center was described by Devaney, (1976, pp. 413–416) as an attempt by the organization to sponsor a structure in which members of the organization could develop new understandings, skills, and attitudes that were consistent with the goals and needs of the organization. Such an approach does not rule out goals based on individual needs and interests. But, it does place high priority on organizational goals and, therefore, organizational input in the determination of center goals and activities. Organizational control should be accompanied by organizational responsibility for financial, technological, and psychological support and a strong sense of concern for the needs, interest, problems, and goals of organizational members.

Devaney (1976, p. 413) mentioned that organizations often develop teaching centers that coordinate the services of other agencies, such as institutions of higher education and state departments of education. This approach requires consideration of the goals of these agencies as well as the goals of the organization and organizational members. Such an arrangement complicates the process and opens up the possibilities of objectives and programs that do not meet the needs of participants and that cause resistance and even alienation. However, it is our position that the utilization of these agencies broadens the possibilities for the quantity and quality of effective services and that potential problems can be overcome by effective planning and implementation.

We agree with Rogers, (1976, p. 412) and Rubin, (1978, p. 16) that the teachers center is a promising idea for facilitating teacher growth in-service. We also agree that there are still many unanswered questions and that the movement is in the early stages of development. Though it has not been adequately researched, we feel it deserves serious consideration by organizations that wish to improve their staff development program. The form of the teachers center or the teaching center has not been standardized and we do not think it should be. Rather, we feel that school systems should examine the experience of the many forms that have been tried and develop their own form based on local needs, goals, and resources. Basic consideration should be given to assumptions about such things as goals and human learning. Our own assumptions were explicated earlier in this chapter.

In-Service Education—Self-Directed
Improvement Approaches

A fundamental part of any staff development program is the effort of each staff member to direct, implement, and evaluate his or her program of self-improvement. The individual must accept responsibility for the outcomes of the program. The organization must provide the opportunity that includes time, technical support, and psychological encouragement.

We agree with the statement of purpose for the continuing education of professional educators expressed by Rogers, (1976, p. 412):

> Allow for the total personal development of the individual as a human being and as a professional. There is more to becoming a good teacher than the accumulation of a set of skills. Teachers need to express-to feel-to write-to dance-to move-to create-in nonthreatening, unpressured situations. Teachers need to rid themselves of the idea that "I cannot do therefore I teach." Good teaching is doing in a hundred different ways. This clearly is tied up with the almost desperate need for teachers to develop self-trust, self-respect, and confidence in themselves as teachers and as people.

Rogers's statement emphasizes the total development of the individual with the implication that personal development and professional development are inextricably tied together. It is our assumption that approaches to human learning programs that focus on self-initiative, self-direction, and self-implementation will be more consistent with the needs and interests of the individual and, therefore, more motivating, relevant, and effective.

Some school systems have attempted to individualize and promote self-direction in in-service education by encouraging teachers to develop their own program objectives and activities. In some cases, where there are a certain number of days allocated for in-service, elaborate "point systems" have been developed in which certain activities are classified according to their worth in points. Teachers are obligated to earn a minimum number of points for a given year. In some cases, teachers have the option of planning the entire program according to their own interests. In other situations, teachers plan part of the program but are required to participate in certain activities to meet organizational requirements. Yeats, (1976, pp. 417-421) reported a version of the "point system" used by the Campbell County Public Schools, Rustburgh, Virginia. Shelby County, Tennessee; Memphis, Tennessee; and Loudon County, Tennessee, are examples of other systems that have used the "point system."

Systems using a "point system" need to provide a broad range of activities from which teachers can select in order to achieve their points. Otherwise, the activities for earning points may not provide enough range to provide for individual differences. It is also possible that placing a point value on each activity can stifle and restrict teacher initiative and creativity. The "point system" is an important step in the direction of individualization, but we prefer more flexible approaches.

One approach that we have recommended involves placing responsibility on all members of the professional staff to design their own program of improvement. The design should include a needs assessment by the individuals of the life space in which they practice their profession. The focus of the needs assessment is for each professional to define his or her own strengths and weaknesses in professional practice. Statements of strengths and weaknesses become the sources of improvement objectives. It is important to emphasize that strengths should also be a source of improvement objectives. Individuals are motivated to do things they do well, and they receive satisfaction from strong achievements.

After the improvement objectives are well defined, there is a need to design an action program to achieve the objectives. The professional implements the action program, evaluates the results, and shares the outcomes with the organization.

The organization has a responsibility to provide support during all phases of the program. We believe the establishment of support teams of peers facilitates the exchange of ideas, formulation of creative ideas, support for actions, and evaluation of results. Support teams should be selected by the staff member and should serve on a voluntary basis during all phases of the process.

Olivero, (1976, p. 197) indicated: "The most powerful staff development, in my opinion, is a development program prescribed by the individual educator, a growth plan unique to personal needs." He helped design, and presents in the article, a tool for individual growth plans. The tool is called the *Self-Performance Achievement Record.** The following seven parts of the tool are illustrated in the article: "I. What is your institutional or personal goal statement? II. What are the activities? III. What are the objectives? IV. What are evidences of success? V. Individualized continuing education program. VI. What are the starting and completion dates? VII. Log of Progress Reports."

Clinical supervision is a powerful structure that organizations can use to facilitate self-directed professional improvement of staff. This process is discussed in depth in Chapter 9.

Seminars built around problems identified by teachers or the organization can be used to facilitate self-improvement. If some very significant research has been found, for example, on education of the disadvantaged in language arts, a seminar on the topic is announced, and the people who are interested have an opportunity to become a part of the study group and to examine the findings. Only those who are interested enough to apply are in the seminar. If the study group is successful, some ideas for implementation will be formed as the people in this group look at the evidence.

Certain teachers who participate in the seminar will develop ideas that they wish to try. These experiments may be with content or instructional procedures. Money will be made available to cover any additional expense. Members of the supervisory staff, perhaps the leader of the seminar, and a research worker will be made available to assist. The research worker's function will be to aid in the collection and interpretation of evidence.

*Information about SPAR can be obtained from Nueva Learning Center, 6565 Skyline Boulevard, Hillsborough, CA 94010.

Seminars are held to consider the evidence obtained from the experiments. The members of the seminar will include the experimenters, supervisors who are interested, researchers, and other teachers who have become excited about the experimentation. On the basis of study, the seminar group may make a proposal to the curriculum council.

Open hearings are held on proposals. The purpose of the open hearings is to inform as many teachers as are interested about the experiment and the results. In large systems, this open hearing can be presented by television and include samples of the classroom operation.

If the council believes there is merit to the proposal, demonstration centers will be established in as many schools as possible. Teachers who are in sympathy with the proposal will be selected, brought together for training, and then identified as demonstration teachers. Supervisors will be assigned to support and work with the demonstration teachers.

Opportunity will be provided for interested teachers to study the demonstrations through clinics. Each clinic will operate on a schedule that includes observation and discussion throughout several weeks. The plan will enable the observers to see progress and perhaps to do some tryouts on their own. The discussions will include the demonstration teacher, who will profit by the chance to get feedback from fellow leaders; the supervisor; and the observers. The supervisor must help the group think through the concept that the improvement of the profession comes from people who are professionals questioning each other's assumption.

When persons or committees prepare a project, they bring to it all the data they have been able to collect and the data of their past experience. They do not bring to it the data that the total group looking at a project is able to provide. This is the kind of data that might produce an improvement. A supervisor gets assurance from questions because he or she knows that the real in-service growth takes place as people redefine the problem together, look at the differences in interpretation of the problem, and anticipate the consequences of various alternatives. If a staff doesn't disagree with each other, doesn't look at different interpretations of the problem or the data or the anticipated consequences, no large faculty discussion is needed, and no new insight will be attained.

After demonstrations have been held throughout the system, the results may be so satisfactory that the curriculum council will legitimatize the procedure and recommend it or make it systemwide curriculum policy. In this case, opportunities will need to be established in which other teachers have the opportunity to develop the skills and concepts needed to implement the policy.

BARRIERS TO EFFECTIVE
IN-SERVICE EDUCATION

We believe it is possible to improve in-service education in educational organizations if teachers and supervisors recognize some of the most important barriers to effective in-service education.

1. *Lack of organizational support.* Organizations often have failed to provide adequate human and material resources that are essential for effective in-service education. Released time to pursue professional growth has not been provided by some. In some cases, when it has been provided, it was used for other purposes. The reward system has not always recognized outstanding professional improvement. The provision of a climate conducive to and supportive of the development and implementation of ideas for change and improvement has often been spotty and inadequate. When organizations are not aware of the importance of in-service education and fail to support it, it is difficult for teachers and supervisors to continue to develop professionally.

2. *Lack of consistency with principles of human learning.* When organizations fail to provide for factors such as individual differences, positive reinforcement, multiple learning climates, adequate learning time, and feedback on performance, the chance of effective in-service education is greatly diminished.

3. *Failure to utilize a broad base of human resources.* When organizations fail to utilize the competence, creativeness, and leadership of both internal and external personnel to help individuals in the organization improve, the program suffers.

4. *Failure to follow what is known about instruction.* When in-service education programs do not utilize a variety of recognized instructional techniques in concert, the chance of an effective program is reduced.

5. *Lack of focus on individual teacher needs and problems and local school concerns and problems.*

6. *Lack of a program that considers the total development of organizational members.* The professional and personal development of teachers and supervisors are interdependent. It is inappropriate to try to pull them apart and deal with them separately.

7. *Failure to utilize teachers and supervisors in the planning, implementation, and evaluation of in-service education.* It is our contention that collaborative planning will not only result in greater participant satisfaction and support, but that it will also actually result in a better program.

8. *Failure to recognize that experimental teaching and participation in curriculum development constitute opportunities for in-service education.*

9. *Failure to recognize community needs in planning in-service programs.* The schools are a subsystem of the community and, therefore, community expectations for the schools are important. If schools are to serve the changing needs of the community, teachers need to develop needed skills and understandings to provide these services.

Continuing professional growth in a school system is to a large extent the intellectual atmosphere of the system. If many in the staff are excited about making improvements, individual teachers will become more professional and creative. They will be infected by the belief that the educational process can become better, and they can make a contribution.

When the administration is committed to experimentation, development, and diffusion; when financial and supervisory support is given to innovators; when opportunities are provided for all to explore and experiment; then serving as a member of the staff is an in-service experience. When courses and workshops brought to the system are organized as a way of implementing the ideas people have accepted, the courses are meaningful. When persons seeking admission to in-service activities must make application and be accepted, then the efforts are being expended to help those who are ready to hear.

11

THE SUPERVISORY TEAM AT THE SCHOOL DISTRICT LEVEL
Its Organization and Functions

A basic assumption of this book is that the purpose of instructional supervision is to improve the quality of learning for students. This purpose is achieved through the instructional supervisory behavior system, which has the following functions: (1) goal development and evaluation, (2) program development, actualization, coordination, and evaluation, (3) psychological and technological support, help, and service for teachers, (4) evaluation of personnel performance, (5) professional staff development, (6) evaluation of educational outcomes. These functions have been identified and discussed in Chapter 1. They are repeated here because they give direction to the organization and operation of the instructional supervisory team at the school district level.

The activation of activities that have such a broad range of functions requires careful selection, allocation, organization, and deployment of essential human resources. In the educational organization, instructional supervision personnel are deployed at both the district level and local school level. Utilization of such personnel at the school district level necessarily requires a consideration of their function, allocation, organizational structure (including interdependence with structures at the local school level), roles, authority, needed specialization, and channels of communication. The purpose of Chapter 11 is to develop a discussion of these factors. No attempt will be made to prescribe specific organizational structures, formulas for allocation of personnel, specific role descriptions, or exact descriptions for district-level functions. We assume such decisions are best made within the framework of the needs of a particular system. Rather the discussion will focus on development of appropriate concepts and generalizations, the identification of crucial issues, and descriptions of representative examples.

THE FUNCTIONS

The central office instructional supervisory behavior system has many functions. If the staff is fulfilling its mission, it will have a definite program in the following areas:

Goal Development and Evaluation

It is a function of the central office curriculum and instruction team to develop a continuous process of goal determination and evaluation for the total system. In order to accomplish this, community expectations must be studied, interpreted, and translated into educational goals for the total system. It is necessary to involve local schools and their communities in this process. The overall system goals provide the framework for the development of objectives at the system, local school, and individual teacher level. The goals and objectives at these various levels provide the rationale for the overall design and coordination of the curriculum. An organizational structure is required to make sure that the necessary operations are accomplished. Specialized personnel operating from the appropriate authority structure must be provided and deployed. Human resources from the organization and community must be organized and utilized. Two-way communications must be open between local schools and communities and the school district level. Communication among local communities, local schools, and teachers must also be facilitated. Decisions must be made and implemented. The organization needs to be structured according to these functional needs.

Program Development, Actualization, Coordination, and Evaluation

The curriculum design function is an essential one that many school systems have neglected, and so have state departments of education and the U.S. Office of Education. Individual schools or individual teachers have been encouraged to move ahead on their own in experimentation and innovation without much effort to develop a scope and sequence that gives coherence and continuity to the program. It has been assumed that a design will emerge.

It is essential that someone be responsible for coordinating the total curriculum offering. Some of the things that this coordinating effort should include are listed as follows:

1. Objective description of patterns of curriculums followed in the school system.

2. Agreements on the types of developments that are needed and an outlined strategy to achieve the desired goals.
3. Identification of resources that are available for curriculum development, such as developments in other schools or curriculum packages developed by foundations or the government.
4. The development of a strategy for change that includes identification of needs, development of interest, evaluation of possible innovations, field testing, and a pattern of research that will collect data about the effectiveness of current programs and innovative efforts.

In recent years, one of the functions of the supervisory staff in some school systems has been to become informed about governmental programs that make federal funds available to schools, and to develop the proposals that will secure the funds to enable the system to engage in innovation. Too frequently, school systems have moved in all directions without any coordination of efforts. Because funds were available, requests were made and projects were funded that had little relationship to the pressing curriculum needs of the system. In other school systems, a fund-seeking staff is not related to the supervisory staff, and no attempt is made to coordinate federal programs with the rest of the curriculum.

Any satisfactory supervisory program includes a projection of curriculum development that makes it possible to know whether an action being considered is one that is progress or simply a diversion. A blueprint of curriculum development needs to be drawn. Although experience may reveal that revision is desirable, the original plan is essential. If money and effort are to be spent wisely, a plan and a strategy must be conceived. In a small system, the entire central office supervisory staff may develop the plan with the advice and consultation of teachers and principals. In a large system or a state department, it is important to have a designated curriculum planning group that assumes the responsibility of developing the master plan. Curriculum coordination is a difficult task. It is important not to demand such strict adherence to a curriculum framework or a curriculum development plan that an individual school or teacher is not free to innovate. It is also necessary to have sufficient detail in mind that intelligent decisions can be made concerning the establishment of study groups, innovative undertakings, curricular materials, development groups, and diffusion activities. The coordination activities should include the development of goals for the system, the description of existing plans, the establishment of the organizational machinery that enables people to be kept fully informed about the present status of the program, the opportunities for innovation, the innovations and demonstrations that are being tried throughout the system, the collection of data concerning the results obtained by innovations, and the method for agreeing upon change in curriculum policies and programs. In addition, the coordinating unit must have the authority to encourage deviation from existing plans and the funds to support the implementation of promising ideas.

An effective coordinating effort will also include the bringing together of individuals and faculties that have common concerns and that want to engage in similar innovative efforts. Members of the central office supervisory staff can assist the innovative groups by providing support, consultation, and opportunities to exchange ideas and results.

In some systems, the coordination will be carried on through curriculum councils. In others, the central office supervisory staff itself provides the coordination. One of the tests of a given pattern of work will be the extent to which the teaching staff of the system feels that the coordination is their effort rather than a control imposed by the central office staff. The creation of an apparatus that encourages participation and facilitates communication is an essential part of the coordination effort.

Coordination can be fostered by the development of curriculum bulletins and descriptions of desirable curriculum procedures. These bulletins describe the program as it exists and in terms of its ideal form. They serve as a description of the status quo from which individuals should be able to depart through innovation. The supervisory staff, including media specialists, has a responsibility for locating and making available the materials of instruction that are appropriate. Publishing companies, curriculum projects, and other school systems are constantly making available new materials. Teachers do not have time to become informed about them. The supervisory staff must survey what is available and recommend the desirable new materials.

A part of the selection of instruction materials is choosing the correct textbooks. They may be chosen by the central office staff, but one of the best ways of acquainting teachers with the new instruction materials is to make provision for their participation in the selection of new texts. Committees of teachers in each of the subject matter fields can work with the resource people on the supervisory staff to choose from among the available texts, three or four that seem most satisfactory for the instructional program of the system. As teachers participate in establishing the criteria for use in the selection of texts and survey the texts that are on the market, they not only become better informed with regard to what is available, but they also become more intelligent users of textbooks.

An important part of providing materials of instruction is arranging a distribution system that enables teachers to secure supplementary materials quickly. Whether the materials are films or pamphlets or photographs or illustrative materials, they should be quickly supplied to the schools and to the teachers upon their requests. Well-organized programs of supervision have developed a system that supplies materials from the central depository to the teachers after a few days' notice. This function of selecting materials, storing and maintaining materials, and supplying them to classrooms in which they are requested is part of the supervisory function.

A neglected function of supervision has been the conducting of research into instructional procedures and curriculum design. In too many systems, the development of new content and procedures has been left to other school systems, to publishers, or to individual teachers. Little money has been spent in research and development. As systems increase in size and more money is made available to produce quality education, individual systems must assume responsibility for investigation of the educative process and the development of more effective practices. A well-developed supervisory staff will include research workers who are able to design and conduct research projects. Each system needs to determine its frontiers and organize appropriate research projects. In a given system, the research may consist entirely of investigations of new instructional practices. In other systems, different content and curriculum designs may be tested. Research is frequently being conducted at the universities and by the major curriculum projects, but local research efforts are also desirable.

The supervisory staff has a responsibility for securing and supplementing information concerning research results in other locations. They should also investigate appropriateness of practices and instructional procedures, in the local situation. Information can be quickly secured from various sources of research information on which local school systems can base their planning efforts. If the research already available supplies the answer the system needs, the local system will be able to make its decision on the basis of this evidence. But when additional evidence is required, the local supervisory unit must take the leadership in securing it.

Another function of the central office supervisory staff is the dissemination of research information. Appropriate methods of conducting this activity have not yet been developed. Research bulletins in their present form are not widely read. Research reports, for the most part, have been rather meaningless to teachers. Someone must engage in the process of translating and interpreting research results, and this responsibility falls to the supervisory staff. Once the translation has been made, the method of providing it to the teachers who need the data must be developed. Experimentation with presentation of materials by educational television, by bulletins, and by conferences must be conducted. The supervisory staff is faced with the task of determining which procedures work and which make a difference in the way that teachers practice.

One method of dissemination that is being investigated is the development of demonstrations. Each school system needs to have demonstration centers that are a regular part of the curriculum program of the school. It is the hypothesis of the authors that the same result will be obtained through demonstrations in education. Upon this basis, it is recommended that supervisory staffs seek to establish demonstrations in each of the schools in a system. These demonstrations may be teachers in given classrooms who are demonstrating certain new practices. They may also be a single school demonstrating a new type of curriculum design that can be observed by teams of teachers from other schools in the system. Much experimentation needs to be conducted with the ways that the demonstrations can be used as a basis of clinics in which principals and teachers analyze what they observe in a given demonstration.

It is also crucial to improve dissemination of ideas that are developed at the local school level. This approach can be encouraged by a program of teacher-teacher visitation, groups of principals who visit in different schools, workshops, and curriculum planning activities.

Psychological and Technological
Assistance to Principals and Teachers

Historically the most important function served by the supervisory staff has been to provide resource help to teachers and principals; this function must continue. The administrative relationships between principals and the teachers on their faculties prevent the principals from being of service to certain teachers. The principal's requirement to make judgments concerning tenure and increases in salary prevents the kind of openness and honesty that is necessary for in-depth analysis of the teaching practices of teachers who are labeled less-than-satisfactory by the principal. Such teachers need the help that can be supplied by a consultant who does not engage in the rating practice. Each school system needs a reservoir of resource people who can be called upon by the principal or by a teacher to assist in a given instructional situation. These supervisors may work with a teacher who is having difficulty or may assist the teacher who is experimenting with new practices.

Further, no matter how adequate the principal may be, he or she will not have all the special competencies that given members of the staff may require. By having a number of supervisors with different competencies, it is possible to make available assistance of the specific type needed by a given teacher. And the principal needs resource people to call upon for advice and consultation about specific instructional and curriculum problems. A school system strengthens its administrative staff as it makes available to the principal the kind of support and assistance that is needed.

All staff members in a school system, whatever its size, need support and stimulation if their vision is to be enlarged and their growth nourished. In each system, there is a necessity for resource people who are not administrators. These people may be curriculum workers, supervisors, research workers, instructional material workers, and others who provide services designed to support and enrich the learning experiences of children.

In no sense is this statement a criticism of the competency of teachers or administrators. Instead, it is a recognition that school programs must be constantly improved if they are to meet the demand for an adequate educational program. In a period when knowledge is multiplying, when society is changing at an almost inconceivable rate, when new tools for teaching and learning are being developed, and the schools are attempting to serve an ever-increasing range of pupil needs, teachers and administrators need encouragement, support, and assistance in developing new competencies required by the added dimensions of their role.

A critical question for a school system is whether to assign these instructional resource persons at the school district level or the local school level. We believe that such resources should be available to teachers from both the local school and the school district. Consultants provided at the local school level have the advantage of being on the scene and available when needed. They can be a part of the faculty and gain both acceptance by the teachers and an understanding of the teachers and their needs. This makes it possible to deliver services on a continuing basis and with less "waste" of time moving from location to location. The local school is where the action is, and technical consultants, in addition to administrators, need to be assigned at that level.

Teachers have a broad base of needs, concerns, and interests. Therefore, there is a need for consultants with a broad base of competencies and interests. Resource persons with special competence need to be available to all the teachers in the system, and, therefore, need to be assigned at the school district level. We also believe that there is a broad base of human resources available to provide support and help to teachers, from teachers and administrators in the organization and from other human resources outside the school system, such as people in the community with special competence, university personnel, and state department workers. What is needed is an organizational structure that will facilitate the process of making people with the appropriate competence available to support and help organizational members with needs.

A prime function of the curriculum and instruction staff at the central office level is to know the special competencies and skills of the professional staff. A knowledge base of this sort is the starting point in the process of utilizing the special expertise of teachers, administrators, and supervisors in activities such as curriculum development, support for teachers, demonstrations, research, and dissemination. The challenge to the central staff is to get the person with the appropriate expertise in the right place at the right time.

Evaluation of Personnel Performance

An essential characteristic of any organization is a competent staff that is motivated to work toward the achievement of organizational goals. Naturally, organizations attempt to recruit and select members of the organization who are competent and motivated. But, it is also essential to evaluate personnel performance. Selection procedures are not perfect. Organizations and organizational expectations change. Professional personnel often change and lose their competence or fail to change and lose their competence. Therefore, it is necessary for organizations to have a special structure for the evaluation of the performance of professional staff members.

It is our assumption that personnel evaluation should be decentralized and, therefore, accomplished as close to the work as possible. This would indicate that teachers should be evaluated at the local school level with the school principal coordinating the process. However, we also believe that the central office supervision team should be actively involved. They need to coordinate the effort to develop a design for the evaluation process for all professional personnel, with strong emphasis on input from teachers and administrators. They must make certain that all personnel understand the process and have the necessary skills and attitudes to participate effectively in the process, either as an evaluator or an evaluatee, depending on job responsibilities. They also need to monitor the process to ensure quality control and should provide for systematic evaluation and change as needed. The training process for all personnel should be comprehensive and continuous to provide for new personnel, changes in the system, and dysfunctions in the process. An organizational structure must be provided at both the school district level and local level to achieve an adequate process of personnel evaluation.

Professional Staff Development

Professional staff development is an effort by the organization to improve staff effectiveness by human development in-service, recruitment and selection of new staff members with appropriate competence and motivation, evaluation of personnel, and reassignment of staff members. When these personnel functions involve teachers and instructional administrators, they are so relevant to the learning outcomes for students that we feel they should be a part of the instructional supervisory system. Further, it is our contention that much of the work of in-service education and personnel decisions for local schools should be done at the local school level, since the personnel decisions and professional growth needs of these personnel are so closely related to their performance in the local school. The tendency to centralize professional staff development at the central office level without adequate involvement at the local school level has been a grave dysfunction in educational organizations.

The central office supervisory behavior system should coordinate the effort to maintain a system of in-service education for professional personnel. But, actual plans of human learning should be primarily developed by individual staff members, and local school teams, departments, and committees. Central office personnel should support these efforts; provide quality control; support evaluation and change efforts; conduct needs assessments; provide teacher centers; serve as a clearinghouse for interschool coordination; and plan, actualize, and evaluate programs for groups of teachers with compatible needs.

Personnel recruitment should be planned, organized, and coordinated at the central office level. However, there is a need for strong local school input, not only to communicate needs, but also to participate in the identification and recruitment activities. But the central office staff should take responsibility for the development of an adequate pool of recruits to meet the needs of the system.

The selection of personnel is the process through which an organization makes the decision to employ. The central office staff should have responsibility for the overall design and coordination of the program. But, the local school, including the administrators and teachers, should be deeply involved in the process and, normally, no local school personnel should be employed without the recommendation of the local school.

Reassignment of personnel is a powerful but little used process for staff improvement. A new environment, new colleagues, new job requirements, different grade level, and new instructional support are some of the factors that can make a critical difference in the performance of a staff member. Reassignment can occur within the same school, among schools in the same system, or among systems. There is a need for an organizational structure at the central office level and the local school level to facilitate this process.

The central office staff is concerned with evaluation from two important perspectives: first, the school system needs data on the effectiveness of local schools and individual teachers in the achievement of educational goals. It is essential that the central office instructional team develop and implement a design for getting and making available this kind of information. It is recommended that the development of the design should be a function of broad participation of teachers and administrators. The process should be comprehensive and continuous and represent the best thinking of the system.

The evaluation should focus on the outcomes of instruction and learning, rather than the instructional process itself. The system needs to know the effectiveness of each school and each professional person in the system in order to make appropriate decisions about the future operation of the system.

Second, there is a need to facilitate the process of self-evaluation of both individuals and school units. This process involves the technological and psychological support system and has the function of helping teachers explicate their objectives and program conditions, describe what happened, analyze what happened, and generalize for future planning.

THE ORGANIZATION

The supervisory staff, regardless of the size of the system, is the task force organized for curriculum development and instructional improvement. Its membership must supply the resources and leadership that are needed by teachers and administrators for continuous evaluation and innovation.

No adequate formula has been developed for the number of supporting people that should be provided to assist teachers. The kinds of resources and resource people that should be made available in a school system will vary from community to community and from school system to school system. Each has its own needs and priorities. Each must define the type of supervisory unit that it needs in terms of its own priorities and available financial support. Each board of education should have a plan for adding resources that take into account the state requirements, the community needs, the staff needs, financial resources, and, most important, the needs of students.

The Allocation of Human Resources

The rational allocation of personnel for the central office team requires consideration of the needed activities, the function of such activities in the achievement of the goals of the school, the specialized competence that is needed to conduct the activities, the size of the school system, and the organization of the school system.

As school systems have grown, become more complicated, and extended instructional services as well as other services for students, the need for central office personnel has expanded rapidly. The Educational Research Services of the American Association of School Administrators made a survey of three hundred school systems (AASA, 1971). A general trend was determined in the direction of increasing size of central office staff. It was reported that it was rare to find a central office staff that had decreased in size in the last five years. Chief causes for the increases in central staffs were identified by school systems as

1. Increase in educational services for all pupils
2. Development of compensatory programs (financed by federal funds)
3. Growing school enrollments
4. Change in organizational structure.

During the 1970s, increases in instructional supervision personnel have continued. Emphasis on vocational and technical education and, later, the expansion of special education programs emphasized at both the federal government and state government levels have contributed to the growing number of supervisors, directors, and coordinators, among others.

There may be a change in the 1980s. There has been a decline in school enrollments. We are entering a period of economic constraints. There is a growing wave of public sentiment to cut the cost of government at all levels, but with emphasis on the federal government. The executive branch of government is leading this movement, and at this time it appears that the Congress will follow. The effect of these developments on central office personnel at this time is not known. However, there are strong reasons to believe that there will be temporary cutbacks in educational services for students and the development of new programs. These factors, together with declining enrollments, will probably produce a temporary decline in central office curriculum and instruction personnel. But, we believe that for the long range, the need for instructional supervision personnel will grow as a result of changing societal needs, expanding student needs, organizational changes and growing complexity, technological developments, new developments in both the methods and content of teaching, and the growing needs for teachers and administrators to continue to change and improve.

Certainly, it is true that central office personnel in curriculum and instruction have increased and will continue to do so. Unfortunately, it is also true that such positions have often been added without careful consideration of the rationale for the position, description of the position, or the way the position would relate to other parts of the program. Positions have often been added to bring prestige or to get federal monies, and not necessarily after careful consideration of school objectives, necessary activities to achieve those objectives, and the personnel and organizational structure needed to activate the activities.

The proposed list of functions for the supervisory staff requires a broad base of human specialization to carry on the necessary activities. The continuing development of knowledge and methodology in such content fields as mathematics, science, foreign language, social studies, language arts, reading, physical education, and fine arts (to name a few) requires specialists to help keep teachers abreast of new developments. The schools have expanded programs in vocational and technical education, and this development requires specialized coordination at the central office level.

The supervisory team must also coordinate curriculum design; program evaluation; professional growth programs; and initiation, development, and support for innovative programs. Educational media resources have expanded dramatically in the last few years, and it is up to the central office teams to make the ideas available to teachers as well as to provide teachers with an opportunity to develop necessary new skills.

To allocate human resources for the central office team requires not only a careful definition of each required specialization, but also the establishment of priorities within the framework of economic reality.

It is always difficult to decide whether or not a specialized service should be provided at the central office level or the local school level, or brought in on a temporary basis from a cooperative of which the school system is a member, from a university, or from various kinds of local community resources.

Activities that involve and require the support of the total organization need to be provided at the central office level. Curriculum development and design; overall planning for the continuing education of staff; procurement and organization of the staff; dissemination of certain materials and other resources of teaching; experimentation, demonstration, and development and application of educational innovations are other examples. Certain highly specialized subject matter consultants need to be stationed at the central office level. Naturally, needed expertise can often be provided from throughout the system on an ad hoc basis. For example: there may be a principal with special competence in early childhood education. Such a person could be temporarily assigned to head up a study of the needs, needed resources, and personnel to establish a kindergarten program in the school system. A person from the central office staff could be used to fill in for the principal while he or she is on special assignment.

The possibility of school systems joining together in educational cooperatives so as to make it possible to provide certain services that could not be provided otherwise is an idea that merits careful consideration. For example, a group of school systems in Tennessee felt that they needed the services of an "educational planner." However, it was economically unfeasible for each system to employ such a person. Therefore, they considered hiring the person through the "cooperative" in order to provide services to all the systems.

There are also untapped community resources that can be studied, analyzed, and made available to the teaching behavior system. Professional and technical persons such as lawyers, medical doctors, physicists, geologists, and social workers are examples of people in the community who can provide support for teachers and supervisors.

It is also crucial that the opportunities for student educational activities be extended to the community, and this extension needs to be coordinated at the central office level. Otherwise, there could be confusion among teachers, local schools, and the community that could lead to problems for the program.

We assume that the local school is the basic action agency for school improvement. Therefore, the central office team exists primarily as a support system and change agent for the local school. Appropriate specialists from the central office team, local schools, or outside agencies can be assigned to local schools on a temporary basis in order to achieve a change, develop an idea, help teachers develop new skills, or give needed support to a new curriculum development. It is the function of the central office team not only to provide a considerable amount of expertise from its own ranks, but also to be sensitive to, and able to deliver, appropriate expertise from throughout the school system and community.

The size of the school system is an important factor in the allocation of central office personnel. In large school systems, it is economically feasible to allocate more specialists with a broader range of specializations to the central office team. Smaller systems need to utilize "outside" resources, such as educational cooperatives, nearby universities, nearby school systems, or community resources. The assignment of an instructional supervisor to a particular school has a tendency to limit his or her services to that school. But, it is also true that an instructional supervisor who is assigned to a particular school has a greater chance to become an effective worker in that school. Certainly, there is a need for instructional supervisors at the local school level. Principals, assistant principals, and department heads often help to provide the needed support. The size of the school system, the size of the local schools, the physical proximity of local schools, and the organizational structure of the system are important factors in the allocation of human instructional resources at the system and local school levels.

The Organizational Structure

The central office curriculum and instruction team is a subsystem of the organization. Organizations exist because certain human beings feel that certain objectives can be achieved more effectively through the organization than through individual effort. The central office team exists because it is assumed that as a unit, it can achieve certain objectives, which will contribute to the achievement of overall organizational goals. Therefore, the organization has certain expectations for the curriculum and instruction team and is willing to allocate material and human resources to it. But, it also holds the team accountable. The curriculum and instruction team must not only produce the desired ends but must be able to demonstrate the achievement of objectives.

If the curriculum and instruction team is to be an effective unit in the organization, there are certain factors that should be given careful consideration:

1. *The need for overall coordination and authority.* (Van Miller, 1965, p. 507). There is a need for a single executive officer for the central office curriculum and instruction unit. He or she should be responsible and accountable for the effective-

ness of the unit and, therefore, needs the appropriate authority to coordinate the activities of the unit toward the achievement of the unit's overall goals. Certain specialized individuals and subunits are necessarily concerned about their own special goals and might, in the heat of operation, fail to consider the overall goals and the way the subsystems fit together. A central system of authority provides for the coordination and control of the subsystems in the unit.

The official leader for curriculum and instruction also provides the formal connecting link between the team and the rest of the organization. He or she is directly responsible to the next echelon of authority and is probably a member of the superintendent of schools' executive team. This communication and influence link makes it possible for curriculum and instruction to hear and be heard, and influence and be influenced by the rest of the organization.

2. *The need for organizational members to participate in decision making and policy development according to expertise and achieved prestige, and not just formal position in the organization.* It is essential for the organizational structure to provide enough flexibility, communication linkages, and cooperative endeavors so that human beings can assume certain leadership roles on an ad hoc basis and with responsibility and authority as needed. Historically, this has been difficult to do. People assigned to a unit worked in that unit. Not to do so could lead to disfavor by the leadership of the unit. It could also be threatening to the official leadership. Organizations need temporary systems, with temporary leadership with temporary authority. Organizational members need to recognize and accept this.

3. *The need for specialization and generalization.* The broad range of functions of the curriculum and instruction team underlines the need for specialization. There is a need for people with highly specialized skills and understandings. This specialization makes it possible to work on tasks and assignments where they have the greatest interest and competence. They can perfect their work and thus enhance their potential contribution to the goals of the organization.

But specialization can also narrow the interest and competence of an individual so that there may be more difficulty in seeing the relationship between the specialized work and other segments of the organization. He or she may even have difficulty in understanding and appreciating the contributions of other specialists. The specialists may have a contribution to make but may not have the human skills necessary to put it into effect.

Therefore, there is also a need for generalists who are sensitive to the total situation, so they can see how the parts fit together to form a totality. It is also necessary to facilitate the process through which the specialized expertise can be delivered where and when it is needed. Human and technical skills are fundamental in this process.

4. *The need for communication.* The communication process has been discussed in depth in Chapter 5. Suffice it to say that it is crucial that the organizational structure facilitate communication in the supervisory team. Included is the need for communication between the instructional component and other central office teams such as planning, personnel, and business; the need for communication with local schools, including both teachers and administrators; the need for communication with the superintendent and board of education; and the need for communication within the curriculum and instruction team. It is important that teachers and administrators in one school know and understand what is going on in other schools, and members of the central staff can facilitate this process.

Effective communication requires not only that people can be heard, but that they are also crucially involved. The organizational structure must provide for a deliberate plan of broad-based involvement in such areas as curriculum planning,

planning for continuing education, and planning the teacher support system. People need to get involved in crucial decision making and policy development in matters of curriculum and instruction. The organizational structure should provide for this need on both a formal and informal basis. The formal communication structure should provide for both permanent and temporary systems of decision making and implementation. The informal channels should be supported by providing time, physical space, and human participation.

5. *The need for control and conformity.* Organizations need a certain level of predictable behavior by organizational members. Certain people need to be at certain places at certain times, prepared to do certain things. Various segments of the curriculum and instruction teams are dependent on other sections for their proper functioning. For a "line of cooperation" to work effectively between the central office curriculum and instruction team and the local schools requires reciprocal and predictable behavior from both. The organizational structure must provide for a line of authority that can ensure this kind of interaction and cooperation.

6. *The need for flexibility, creative response, and nonthreatening interpersonal influence.* It is true that there is a need for control, but it is equally true that there is a need for freedom of movement so that organizational members can exercise their expertise and creativeness in organizational work. Societal expectations for the educational organization change, and organizations must also change. Members need new understandings, new skills, and new attitudes. Too much control and too much conformity can lead to complacency and inability to change. Creative ideas for improvement can get smothered by complacency, defensiveness, and "put downism." The need is for a structure that not only provides, but also seeks out, the release of the creativeness of organizational members. The reward system must recognize both creativeness and those who support it.

7. *The need for human consideration.* The most important part of any organization is the human membership. People have physiological, psychological, and sociological needs; and organizational structures should contribute to the satisfaction of these needs. The need for close and positive identification and acceptance in certain groups is well known. The structure of the organization can provide the setting and time in which organizational members can carry on a dialogue, come to know each other, share ideas, recognize each other, help each other gain esteem and affection, and become an important, fully functioning part of the total operation.

8. *The need for a broad base of leadership.* Leadership can be thought of as the effort of one or more individuals to influence the behavior of other individuals. The assumption is that the capacity for creativeness, innovative ideas, intelligence, and influence is widely dispersed throughout the organization. The need is for an organizational structure that provides for the release of this potential leadership behavior. It would be possible to seek the leadership wherever it is found in the organization and apply it where the problem or decision situation exists. An important function of the permanent members of the curriculum and instruction team would be to seek out problems, places where help is needed, places seeking new ideas, and places trying new ideas, and bring the needs and resources together. Potential leadership people could be released on a temporary basis and provided with the appropriate authority for that particular task.

9. *The need for change.* Societal expectations for the educational organization change. The needs of students change. Teaching methods and content change, and the educational program and process must change. The organizational structure should facilitate change through activities such as needs assessment, creating dissatisfaction, initiating and implementing change attempts, evaluating results, and facilitating decisions to adopt or not to adopt. But, change can be threatening to

organization members, and can create conflict, alienation, and poor performance. So organizations must monitor change efforts, including watching for dysfunctional developments and providing needed support, service, help, and rewards.

10. *The need for motivation.* Chapter 3 provides an in-depth discussion of motivation in organizations. There is a need for a structure that makes it possible for organizational members to participate in a broad base of activities that help satisfy their needs for esteem and their needs for being an important part of a relevant task. Such activities should promote satisfaction and motivation.

ROLES AND RESPONSIBILITIES
FOR INSTRUCTIONAL SUPERVISORS

Organizations develop positions through continuous analysis of the jobs needed to achieve the objectives of the central office curriculum and instructional team. In a sense, position descriptions are formal expectations that the organization has for the responsibilities, behavior, and achievement of the person occupying the position. We believe that it is important for organizations to carefully define the jobs in the central office instructional supervisory team in terms of overall objectives, or subprogram objectives. It is true that positions change constantly and, therefore, position definitions need to change. But, it is also true that organizations need to have a current position definition to use as a basis for recruitment and selection and for evaluation of performance, and to help members of the organization understand not only their own jobs, but also how their jobs relate to other jobs in the organization.

The professional occupants of the positions develop roles in the organization according to organizational expectations, personal expectations, and expectations of other workers. The role organizational members play determines to a considerable extent what they can or cannot do, their influence potential, and of course, their overall effectiveness. The roles that members of the curriculum and instruction team play are of crucial importance to the overall influence of the team in the organization. We refer to power in broad policy decisions that can affect the overall support for the instructional program.

Griffiths and others (Griffiths, Clark, Wynn, and Iannaccone, 1962) have defined two kinds of positions that appear appropriate for the supervisory staff. The position of coordinator is recommended where there is a need for the coordination of certain programs at the central office level. Examples of such programs would include vocational and technical, early childhood, middle school, elementary, secondary, special education, science, and languages. The position involves the specification of objectives, program conditions, and evaluation of the outcomes for the program. The coordinator is also responsible for planning manpower needs and the recruitment, selection, coordination, and evaluation of specialized personnel. Naturally, he or she performs the activities in cooperation with other segments of the organization.

A program requires overall coordination since normally there are certain specialized services and consultants that have to be shared by different local schools. In some situations, various parts of the program have to be provided in different schools but need to be available to all students. For example, in a vocational and technical education program, "School A" might offer automotive mechanics, cosmetology, and other subjects, while "School B" offers electronics, building masonry, carpentry, and other subjects. Students from "School A" may need to take electronics at "School B" and vice versa. The sharing of resources, facilities, and students among local schools requires careful and continuous coordination at the central office level.

The coordinators of programs would normally be specialists in their own right and would provide appropriate service and consultation to local schools and other segments of the school system within the limitations imposed by the overall demands of the position.

The position of consultant is provided to deliver specialized services and consultations to the teaching behavior systems and others such as local school administrators, personnel services, business, and school board. The service dimension indicates the provision of something that is used. For example, media consultants may provide certain films, books, and audio-visual equipment. They may even make videotapes of teaching situations so that teachers can see themselves in action. Other services could include psychological and physiological examination of children, teaching certain specialized subjects, providing workshops, or developing educational programs for the professional staff.

Consultants also participate in the psychological and technological support system for teachers. They consult with teachers. They react. They make suggestions. They provide descriptive feedback. It is hoped that consultants can participate in this kind of work with teachers on a nonthreatening basis since they are not on the authority line and serve only on a cooperative basis. It is not recommended that they participate in the process of evaluating teachers for personnel purposes such as tenure and merit pay. Rather, the assumption is that teachers need a source of nonthreatening help and support.

Esposito, Smith, and Burbach (1975, pp. 63–67) defined the supervisory role as a result of their research. They reviewed the literature and identified a population of supervisory tasks that they developed into a Likert-type scale, which was used to study the frequency of performance of these tasks by supervisors. The analysis of their results showed that it is possible to categorize supervisory roles under two basic umbrella concepts: helping role and administrative role. Some of the tasks under the "helping role" included

1. "plan and arrange in-service education programs"
2. "visit and observe in the classroom"
3. "hold individual conferences with teachers"
4. "develop curriculum designs and coordinate curriculum improvement efforts"
5. "develop and prepare new instructional media"

Some of the tasks that were classified under the "administrative role" are

1. "coordinate instructional programs"
2. "assist in the evaluation and appraisal of school programs"
3. "routine administrative duties"

We think it is possible and helpful to think of the work in the instructional supervisory team at the central office level as being consultative and administrative. Job descriptions and the role of the position holder would normally be instructional supervisor-consultant, or instructional supervisor-administrator, or some combination of the two. Figure 11-1 may help clarify the concept.

The line of the large circle is the boundary of the instructional supervisory behavior system at the school district level. The system is a subsystem of the education organization. The behavior system is made up of two kinds of behavior: 1. Consultative, 2. Administrative. Some roles are "pure" consultative or "pure" administrative. But most are a combination of administrative and consultative.

The consultative part of the supervisory behavior includes direct service to teachers, such as help in planning, preobservation conferences, observation and

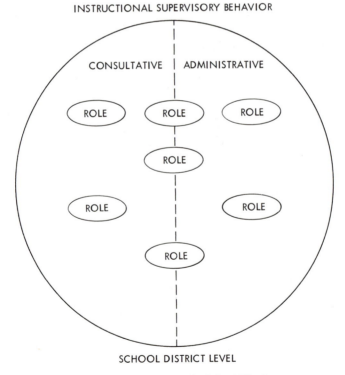

FIGURE 11-1 Supervisory Roles at the School District

analysis of teaching, postobservation conferences, suggesting ideas for improvement, and help with implementation of ideas for improvement. It also includes indirect service to teachers, such as helping with planning and implementing in-service education programs and helping with curriculum development and evaluation.

The administrative part of the school district supervisory team includes managing, coordinating, providing quality control, and evaluating programs. It also involves policy development and decision making, planning for personnel needs, recruiting and selecting personnel, placement and reassignment of personnel, and evaluation of personnel.

THE AUTHORITY FOR
INSTRUCTIONAL SUPERVISORS

The authority that an instructional supervisor has is the right to influence the behavior of other organizational members. We agree with Blau (1956, pp. 397-401) that this right is granted by the persons to be influenced. So the authority that instructional supervisors have to influence teachers and administrators is in reality what teachers and administrators are willing to give them. One crucial question is the basis on which authority is granted.

After a careful review of the literature, Peabody (1962, pp. 463-482) derived four sources of authority for organizational members: 1. legitimacy; 2. position; 3. competence; 4. person. Authority granted on the basis of legitimacy means that teachers would accept the influence attempts of supervisors because of certain laws, rules, or regulations that indicate compliance behavior. Positional authority would be a factor when teachers grant supervisors the right to influence them because the teachers accept the authority of the supervisors' positions. The supervisor could even be empowered to impose sanctions. Competence of a supervisor is another source of authority. In this case, the teacher is willing to follow the supervisor's authority because the teacher assumes that the supervisor has the knowledge, professional skills, or experience to be helpful. Finally, teachers follow supervisors just because they are attracted to them as people. This could be a function of social skills, moral values, or even common interest.

It is our position that the authority structure for instructional supervisors' consultative functions should be different from the authority structure for instructional supervisors' administrative functions. The school district needs coordination in the curriculum and instruction program. There is a need to select and evaluate personnel, provide quality control, coordinate the efforts of personnel, and execute many other management activities. We believe that instructional supervisors' administrative function needs legitimacy authority and position authority. But, we also believe they need competence authority and person authority. Without competence and an adequate personality, position authority will be shallow and will likely result in member alienation, noncompliance behavior, negative feelings, low satisfaction, and ineffectiveness. There is a need to emphasize reliance on competence and personality authority, with reliance on formal authority only when needed. Hornstein and others (1968, p. 389) reported that when teachers perceived that their superordinates' influence was based on expertise and mutual influence, they reported greatest satisfaction. They also reported that teacher perception of high-influence superordinates was positively related to person and expert power and negatively related toward coercive and legitimate influence.

Instructional supervisors–consultative should normally operate on a basis of mutual respect and cooperation, with almost total reliance on competence and person authority. We recognize that there is a need for the consultative supervisor to have some legitimacy and position authority. For example, they need to have the right to plan with teachers, observe and analyze teaching, and provide feedback for teachers. They should not have the right to prescribe or dictate to teachers what or how they should teach. Certainly they should have the right to suggest, but the action decision is left with the teacher.

Consultative supervisors from the central office need the formal authority to visit schools and confer with administrators. But their influence should be based on their competence and personality.

THE ASSISTANT SUPERINTENDENT
FOR CURRICULUM
AND INSTRUCTION

The paramount responsibility of the assistant superintendent for curriculum and instruction is to develop and implement decisions about what should be taught and how it should be taught. More and more, these decisions must be based on the changing needs of students and the changing expectations that society has for the schools. This requires close and continuing communication with the students, the local schools, the community, and other segments of the superintendent's central office team. The assistant superintendent for instruction is the hub of this communication network, has the responsibility for communication, and must have the authority and resources to effectuate the process.

The facts of changing curriculum, differentiated staffing, open facilities, open curriculum, cooperative teaching, new roles, and needed new skills and understanding for teachers complicate the responsibility of the position. The growth of schools, federal programs, and new services for pupils demand more specialized services from the central office team.

Someone must be responsible for charting the work of the supervisory staff and for developing a plan of action to implement the curriculum development goals of the school system. Someone must secure the personnel and the financial resources to conduct the activities listed. This person is usually designated as an assistant superintendent in charge of curriculum and instruction or as the director of instruction.

It is important in the organization of a supervisory unit that assistant superintendents in charge of curriculum and instruction be responsible for the work of all the specialists within the unit. They must see that the unit works as a team without competitive and divisive programs being sponsored. They must ensure that there is clear and free communication within the division so that there is sufficient opportunity to resolve issues that may arise among the various specialists. The supervisory staff serves the total system. It is not fulfilling its function when it makes conflicting demands upon administrators and teachers within the system. The assistant superintendents must ensure that the decisions, relationships, and activities affecting curriculum or instruction are in accordance with the established policy of the system. They must also see that any recommendations for policy change are formulated after consultation with persons who will be affected by any such decision. If conflicts of personality or interpretation arise within the staff or between resource people and teachers or administrators, they should be settled directly by the assistant superintendent or in consultation with the appropriate administrative authority. It should be clear, however, that the supervisory staff does not function as a separate entity within the system. It provides the apparatus through which the system works to formulate policy with regard to curriculum and instruction.

THE CURRICULUM AND
SUPERVISION PLANNING COUNCIL

As stated in preceding chapters, each school system needs some continuing body with responsibility for making recommendations and decisions concerning curriculum and supervision, within the framework of the overall policy of the system. In some school systems, this group is called a curriculum and supervision planning council. It may have other names, such as planning committee, development committee, or curriculum policy committee. In any case, it should be representative of students, classroom teachers, administrators, and curriculum specialists.

In a small school system, all teachers might participate in it directly. In a large system, it will be necessary to have representation. This body initiates, and is a clearing house for, studies, experiments, and innovations; it makes decisions; it formulates recommendations; and it advises the administration with regard to all curriculum and instruction policies and problems.

It is important to recognize that curriculum and instruction decisions are made at many levels. Pupils decide what their curriculum really is. The teacher makes certain choices about content and procedures that are within the framework of a given school. The principal and the faculty of the school make certain curriculum decisions within the policies of the total system. On the systemwide level, the curriculum council is the body in which are formulated the decisions that will be implemented by the supervisory staff.

The important principle to keep in mind is that a decision should be made as near the level of implementation as possible. If it is a decision that will not interfere with the sequence of pupils from year to year, or with the working relationship with other pupils in the building, the teacher should be able to make it. If it is a decision that can be implemented in one school without affecting the other schools in the system, the faculty of that school should be able to make it. If it does involve systemwide operation, the decision with regard to policy should be made at the curriculum council level. Throughout the entire process of policy development, groups and individuals should be guided by the principles of keeping available as much freedom of choice as possible. The place where a decision should be made and the people who should be involved in the study on which it is to be based are determined by the kind of policy or policy change that is proposed and by the nature and extent of its anticipated effects.

It is also important to keep open the channels through which requests for initiation or review of policy can be made. Any teacher, principal, faculty member, or resource person, as well as any board of education member or administrator, should be able to get consideration of a problem that may call for new policy or a redefinition of existing policy. If staff members can secure consideration of problems that are important to them, they feel that the system is responsive to their feelings and their needs. This belief is basic to good morale and to the assumption of responsibility by all individuals.

It is our assumption that the curriculum and supervision planning council has three interdependent areas of responsibility: (1) curriculum development, maintenance, evaluation and change; (2) direct support service, and help for instruction; (3) professional staff development. Therefore, we see a need for three subcommittees of the curriculum and supervision planning council that have responsibilities in these three areas. Each of the three subcommittees should have a representative on the curriculum and supervision council and on each of the other subcommittees. This procedure should facilitate the effort to coordinate the activities of the four committees and the planning council. All of the subcommittees need a formal leader with the appropriate authority to coordinate the work of the staff. The interface between the work of the committees and local schools is crucial.

A POSSIBLE ORGANIZATIONAL STRUCTURE

It has been previously stated that each system is unique. Each has its own goals, priorities, human resources, and problems. Certainly, the organizational chart should reflect the individuality of the system. Therefore, Figure 11-2 is presented only as a possible structure and certainly not as a model.

It is assumed that the system is a medium-sized county system with about 25,000 students. Approximately one-third of the students are in early childhood education (kindergarten through grade 4), one-third are in middle school (grades 5–8), and one-third are in high school (grades 9–12). The chart in Figure 11-2 represents the organizational structure of the superintendent's team and the way it relates to the board of education, the community, the rest of the professional staff, and the students. The reader is referred to Griffiths, Clark, Wynn, and Iannaccone,

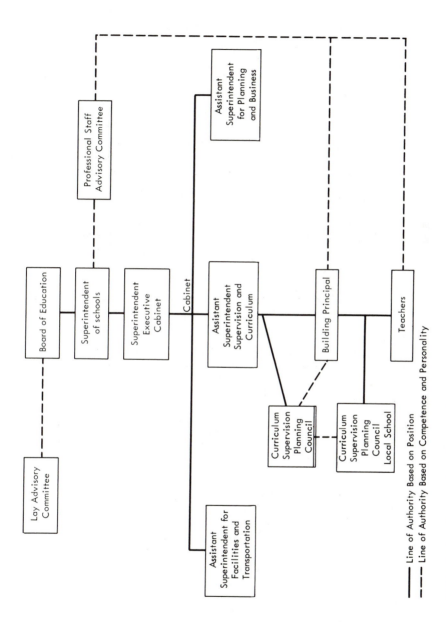

FIGURE 11-2 Organizational Chart for School System

Lay Advisory Committee

Board of Education

Professional Staff Advisory Committee

Superintendent of schools

Superintendent Executive Cabinet

Cabinet

Assistant Superintendent for Planning and Business

Assistant Superintendent Supervision and Curriculum

Assistant Superintendent for Facilities and Transportation

Building Principal

Curriculum Supervision Planning Council

Curriculum Supervision Planning Council Local School

Teachers

——— Line of Authority Based on Position

– – – Line of Authority Based on Competence and Personality

Organizing Schools for Effective Education, for excellent representative charts on various-sized school districts.

The organizational chart clearly shows the board of education as the basic source of formal authority in the organization. The superintendent acts on the authority of the board of education. The superintendent's executive committee, composed of the assistant superintendents, is an important policy-developing structure within the organization. The board of education has a lay advisory board that can be representative of the community and therefore could help keep the board sensitive to changing community educational expectations.

The superintendent has a professional staff advisory board that provides direct contact with teachers and local administrators on a line of cooperation.

The assistant superintendent for instruction is on the direct line of authority with the superintendent, the principal, and the curriculum and supervision planning committee. This authority makes it possible for the assistant superintendent for instruction to provide for the necessary cooperation among members of the central office supervision team and the local school, and for cooperation among local schools. The assistant superintendent is also in a position to communicate needs and expectations of local schools and the central office curriculum and instruction team to the superintendent's executive cabinet and, conversely, to communicate and coordinate central office expectations for local schools. Thus, the foundation is provided for communication and coordination of all the elements of the program of instruction.

The areas of responsibility of the curriculum and supervision planning council have already been discussed. Figure 11-2 shows a corresponding council for each local school. The central office council is on the formal line of authority from the assistant superintendent and has a formal line of cooperation with each school.

Figure 11-3 illustrates the organization of the central office curriculum and instruction team. The assistant superintendent is on a formal line of authority to the curriculum coordinator, staff development coordinator, and teacher services coordinator. These three coordinators plus representatives from the principals and teachers make up the curriculum and instruction planning committee. It is through this planning that the assistant superintendent can coordinate the planning, implementation, and evaluation of the total program of instructional supervision. Goals can be formulated. New programs can be designed and implemented. Needs from local schools can be gathered and assessed. Recommendations for human and material resources can be developed and communicated to the superintendent and board. Programs of support for local schools originating at either the central office level or school level can be evaluated and changed if appropriate. This council is basically a policy-formulating and managing group. It has the power of implementation through the curriculum committee, staff development committee, and direct services for teachers committee. These three subcommittees are composed of a coordinator; staff specialists from early childhood education, middle school education, and high school education; appropriate specialists in the subject fields; and a specialist in the particular area of responsibility. It is felt that at least one member from each subcommittee should serve on each of the other committees to facilitate communication and coordination of effort. These committees not only provide

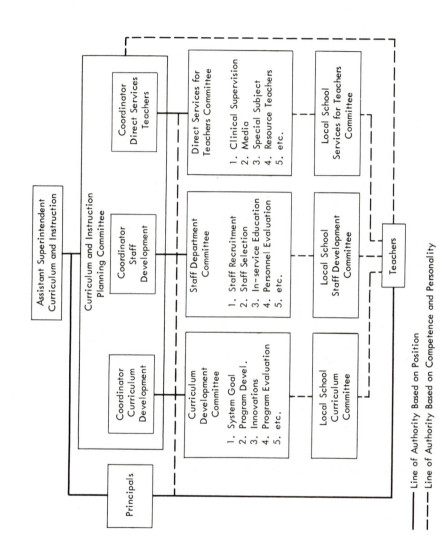

Line of Authority Based on Position

Line of Authority Based on Competence and Personality

FIGURE 11-3 Central Office Curriculum and Instruction Team

technical services to teachers, but also provide technical assistance for the efforts to provide instructional services at the local school level.

The staff development committee would not only coordinate the effort to design and implement the school system's in-service education program; the program of staff planning, recruitment, and selection; and the program of teacher evaluation; but would also be expected to maintain quality in all aspects of the program.

The curriculum committee would not only coordinate the effort to design, implement, and evaluate the curriculum system wide, but would also be responsible for providing technical assistance and monitoring curriculum development at the local school level and individual teacher level. It is important for the organization to know that curriculum development is moving in an effective manner.

The services for teachers committee would provide some services but, in a more important sense, would provide technical assistance toward the delivery of services at the local school level. It is our position that supervisory consultants should be stationed as close to the teachers they serve as possible. However, the effort to use a broad base for personnel in the delivery of supervisory services requires a strong educational program for teachers and others who participate in the program. Supervisors from the central office could be assigned to local schools on a temporary basis to help start new programs such as clinical supervision. Clinical supervisory service could be provided, and local personnel could develop the skills and understandings they need to deliver these services.

The responsibilities of the coordinators have already been defined. Each coordinator has a staff of specialized consultants who are on the authority line to the coordinator, but also on the line of cooperation to the local school planning committees, the principals, and the teachers. Each local school has a curriculum and instruction planning committee that is represented on the systemwide curriculum and instruction planning committee. Local schools also have subcommittees of the curriculum and instruction planning committee that correspond to the three subcommittees in the central office. These subcommittees work closely with the central office subcommittees in order to utilize all resources in the development, implementation, and evaluation of programs in curriculum development; in staff development; and in providing direct services for teachers. The work of these committees will be discussed in depth in Chapter 12. The crucial part of the system has to be the way the teachers, principals, supervisors, and assistant superintendent work together.

THE PRINCIPAL AND THE
CENTRAL OFFICE
SUPERVISORY STAFF

Sometimes lack of harmony in a faculty exists because supervisors and principals do not have their working relationships clearly defined. Teachers are caught in the struggle for control. The functions of all official leaders should be known to the staff. Where there is conflicting authority, the program and the morale of those involved will suffer.

The principals are responsible for the program in their buildings and must abide by the goals that have been established for the system. Supervisors, general and special, are available as consultants and helpers, but they cannot direct the work of individual teachers in a manner contrary to the wishes of the principal. If they do, the principal cannot be held responsible for the program.

If a superintendent told principals how to operate their building or told teachers how to teach, he or she would be depriving them of their responsibilities. Instead, principals should be held responsible for developing programs in their buildings that produce the kinds of pupil growth sought.

To assist principals, the superintendent may make available supervisors with special skills and knowledge. The principal may draw on these supervisors for advice or ask them to assist teachers who are facing difficult problems. But the supervisors should not be made responsible for the program itself. If the program in a building is not getting desirable results, the superintendent should hold the principal accountable and should require him or her to demonstrate that steps to improve the situation have been taken, including the use of available resources.

Supervisors should be present at the planning sessions of the superintendent and the principals. Otherwise, they will not feel that they have a vital part in the program and they will lack the information they need to be of assistance to the principals. If supervisors are to perform most effectively in improving instruction, they must be fully informed and included in the planning.

> A major city of the United States employed forty supervisors. During a ten-year period, the superintendent did not hold a meeting with the supervisors. They were not included in the principal's meetings. At one time during the period, they were told to direct the programs in their areas. Again, they were told to serve as consultants and to stay in their offices until called. Difficulties arose with various principals, and personality and friendship determined the use made of the supervisors in each school. The supervisory positions became dead-end jobs in which people lost hope and faith.

The relationship between principals and supervisors needs careful examination and discussion. Supervisors are not errand boys for principals, nor are they the bosses of principals. Supervisors and principals are persons of comparable professional ability and skill performing different functions. Supervisors are consultants to be called in to help analyze problem situations, to try out remedial measures, and to assist in evaluation of results. They can be called upon for advice and suggestions, but they abandon their intended function when they try to sell or convince. The responsibility for decisions rests with the principal and his or her staff. When principals are responsible for the programs in their schools, the general or subject-matter supervisor serves as a resource person for the principal and teachers.

> The principal of a high school in a southern city was concerned with the quality of the intramural program in the school. He asked the physical education specialist to come to his office to discuss intramural sports. During the conversation, he requested a set of criteria by which to judge a high-school intramural program, and the physical education supervisor agreed to prepare and send it.

A week later, the principal called a meeting of the physical education staff and representatives of the student council and invited the physical education supervisor to be present. He submitted the proposed criteria to the meeting for analysis. Some objection was raised to some of the criteria. In the course of the meeting, some students and teachers began to apply the criteria to the intramural program in the school, and the head of the physical education department asked the supervisor to join a future department meeting in which an evaluation of the intramural program would be started.

The physical education supervisor revised the proposed criteria for intramural programs and placed it in the system-wide curriculum bulletin in the hope that other principals or departments would be sufficiently challenged to request a meeting to discuss them.

The special subject supervisors' success depends upon their competency in their fields and their way of working with people. If they do not show insight in their discussions with principals and staff, they will be ignored. They cannot succeed simply because they bear the label, supervisor. If they do not present their ideas in a friendly, relaxed manner, they will not be taken seriously or called upon again. We build defenses against people who threaten us by their manner or by their use of knowledge. The supervisors' participation must convince others that their knowledge is a tool at their service rather than a club to force conformity to a pattern they cannot understand or accept.

Sometimes supervisors have a delicate consultative function to perform. They may feel it necessary to call shortcomings of the school to the attention of the principal. Whatever their relationship with the principal, their task is dangerous. If they make generalizations about the situation and then attempt to document them with specifics, they almost always fail. If they approach the problem by proposing joint examination and evaluation, they have a better chance of succeeding. If they can make the study of the situation a part of action research designed to improve the program, they are less likely to fail than if they collect data to use in making a judgment about another's work.

There may be times when special subject supervisors are not used in a school. The principal may lack vision or may be antagonistic to the individuals serving as supervisors. In these situations, the supervisor must depend upon the superintendent, who is ultimately responsible and to whom the principal is accountable. If the supervisor is not able to report progress in a certain school, the superintendent is the individual who can and must open the door to improvement. He or she is the one to ask the principal for evidence of progress and for an accounting of how the available resources are being used. If the principal develops confidence in a supervisor, the supervisor feels free to help individual teachers.

A Kentucky supervisor spent fifty hours his first semester on the job talking with one principal who had some doubts and who apparently liked to talk. But as a result of this exploration of ideas and the mutual respect that resulted, the supervisor was able to work effectively in this school. The reputation he established for helping teachers in this school spread throughout the county and opened doors and invitations to help in other schools.

Supervisors find it hard to be effective in working with teachers when the principal resents their efforts. In the day-to-day contact in the school, the principal's casual belittling or slighting remarks about the supervisor's assumed importance can breed in teachers a feeling of insecurity and doubt, if not downright suspicion and hostility.

It is the supervisor's responsibility to work with teachers and administrators. They need the authority and should be expected to establish and maintain contact with teachers. If the principal believes in the supervisor, if the teacher's contacts with the supervisor in group meetings have been easy and nonthreatening, and if other teachers have testified to the supervisor's worth and friendliness, the chances are good that teachers will request assistance. But if the supervisors show aggression, a desire for power, feelings of superiority, or insecurity, teachers will hesitate to establish working relationships with them.

Occasions may arise when it is necessary for the supervisor to ask to visit a teacher. If the principal believes that an unsatisfactory teacher needs help, or if complaints of parents or pupils indicate that an inquiry is warranted, the supervisor may request permission to observe. The teacher has no choice but to issue an invitation. To refuse is to admit that something is not able to withstand scrutiny. What happens after the supervisor enters the classroom depends upon the supervisor's skill in communication and analysis of the situation.

If the working relationship between principals and supervisors is not satisfactory, the superintendent must assume responsibility and take leadership in improving the situation. The superintendent is the only individual with the authority to make decisions in this area. When the superintendent uses this authority and is willing to share the decision-making process, a control exists that holds the group together until agreement is reached. When it is not clear that the superintendent is assuming responsibility for reaching a decision, persons without authority can only hope that cooperative impulses will prevail.

12

THE SUPERVISORY TEAM AT THE LOCAL SCHOOL

The local school is the basic action agency for the development and activation of learning opportunities for students. Certainly, teachers are the primary agents in this process. But, it has been a major thesis of this book that there is a need for a support system that interacts with the teaching behavior system for the purpose of improving learning opportunities for students. The local school instructional supervisory team is an important part of that process. The purpose of Chapter 12 is to discuss in some detail the work of this team, the allocation of personnel for the team, and the organization of the team.

THE WORK
OF THE SUPERVISORY TEAM

The tasks of the local school instructional supervisory team are quite similar to those of the central office team. For example, participation in and coordination of the continuous development and evaluation of educational goals at the local school level; provision for the psychological and technological support system for teachers; experimentation, development, and supervision of new programs; inter-sharing of educational ideas with other schools in the district; continuing education for the professional staff; curriculum design, coordination of various specialized subsystems in the local school so as to maintain balance and common direction in the program; selection, procurement, allocation, and deployment of materials and equipment of instruction; educational planning; and manpower planning, selection, induction, and utilization are all proposed as tasks of the local school instructional supervisory team.

Goal Development and Evaluation

It is essential that each local school provide a means for the continuous specification of projected outcomes of the instructional program. Such a projection is necessarily developed within the framework of system objectives, community expectations, teacher concerns, and the interest and needs of students in the school. One key to effectiveness in this task area is to provide a broad base of participation. In this way it is possible to increase the probability of having a program that reflects the needs, interests, and aspirations of students, teachers, administrators, and members of the community. Broad participation also contributes to the level of understanding of, and support for, the program. Faculty awareness of overall school goals is an essential ingredient for motivation to achieve these goals.

Psychological and Technological Support

Teachers need technological support. They need specialized service in the procurement and utilization of materials and equipment. They need expert consultation in specialized subject fields. They also need assistance in the development and activation of learning opportunities for students. There is a need for teachers to have a continuous source of feedback on the effectiveness of their own teaching efforts. They need sensitive and knowledgeable people who are nonthreatening and who are available for interactions about instructional plans, observation, analysis of instruction, and cooperative evaluation.

Obviously, some of this service and consultation can come from the central office. But there is also a need for support at the local school level. Such support has the advantage of constant visibility and availability. A teacher can get to know, like, and respect a local media specialist, helping teacher, department chairperson, or curriculum specialist. These people eat, play, take duty, and drink coffee with teachers. They provide service and consultation for teachers when it is needed. Thus, the potential for an effective working relationship is there.

The local school instructional team not only has the advantage in providing services and consultations, but also has the advantage in developing sensitivity to the needs of teachers. Since these local instructional leaders are in close contact with members of the local school faculty and instructional personnel at the central office level, they are in an excellent position to facilitate the process of bringing together personnel with needs and personnel with special competence to provide service. A crucial function of the local school supervisory team is to broaden the base of participation in the delivery of technological and psychological support for teachers. Certainly, it is important to use human resources from the supervisory teams at the central office level and the local school level. However, it is our assumption that there are other equally important sources of support, help, and service. Teachers and administrators from the same school and/or other schools represent a source of largely untapped human resources. There are also resources outside the school system, such as medical doctors, psychologists, nurses, and social workers, that may be available. Resources are often available from universities and other school systems. It is an important function of the local school supervisory team to identify these resources and facilitate their utilization in the delivery of supervisory services.

Psychological support is a crucial need of teachers. When things are not going well, when a new idea failed to work, when there is insecurity in trying a new idea—there are times when members of the faculty need special support. The principal is the chief executive officer of the school; therefore, he or she is in an excellent position to provide needed support. Since the principal has a formal position and some formal authority, it helps teachers to know that he or she understands, wants to help, and will stand behind them in failure as well as success. Other members of the instructional team can also provide the right kind of support at the right time. The need is for behavior that communicates sensitivity, understanding, and caring. Members of the local school instructional team are in the right place at the right time; they should have the competence to deliver this kind of support.

In a recent meeting of a group of principals, one principal told of an experience in which he had visited a teacher's class. During the course of the visit, he and the teacher chatted about several things that were going on. As the principal was leaving, the teacher began to tell him how much the visit had meant to her. He was curious and asked about it. She indicated that he was the first adult in six years who had visited her class, and that it was just wonderful to know that someone cared about what she was doing.

Teachers need to feel that what they are doing is important. Getting this feeling is at least partly a function of the recognition and support that they receive from others who are important to them. The instructional leadership team at the local school is not only in an excellent position to provide this kind of support, but can also facilitate the process through which teachers can receive support from their fellow teachers, parents, and students.

Curriculum Design, Implementation, and Evaluation

Development of, experimentation with, diffusion of, and evaluation of new programs are crucial tasks of local school leadership teams. Naturally, this experimentation is an essential part of the ongoing process of curriculum design. The local school is the place where the students interact with program conditions. It is necessary for the various segments of the program to have a common direction. They need to be interdependent parts, and this condition requires overall design and coordination. It is not only necessary to design engagement opportunities for students in terms of overall objectives, but it is also necessary to examine the way they fit together in the total program. This is curriculum design and it is a crucial function of the local school supervisory team.

Some members of the supervisory team need special competence in curriculum development. They can be given the time to devote to curriculum planning and the opportunity to be aware of expectations from the central office. This fact does not mean that teachers do not participate in curriculum planning. They do. But it does mean that local school instructional leaders have a special part to play. One aspect of the role is to make sure that teachers are heavily involved.

Educational objectives change. The expectations of people in the community change. The needs of students change. There is constant development of knowledge out of which flow ideas for new programs. Programs must constantly change, and this requires the development of new ideas, evaluation of the ideas in terms of the overall curriculum design, trying out appropriate ideas, and evaluating the trial. The local school supervisory staff must provide the leadership for this process. When a decision is made to adopt, then leadership must be provided for the diffusion of the new program.

Materials and Equipment

Teachers need a broad base of instructional materials and equipment. Such materials and equipment are in constant production and change. Programs change and require new materials and equipment; new knowledge and technology provide the basis for new media for education. New packaged programs, computer-assisted programs, tapes, videotaping equipment, overhead projectors, and films are examples of new materials and equipment that are becoming available. Teachers need to keep abreast of these developments. But their teaching responsibilities limit their opportunities to do so. Therefore, it is proposed that the local school instructional leadership team provide these needed expert services and consultations. The teachers not only need to be made aware of the new developments, but also need an opportunity to develop the understandings and skills that will ensure their use in the activation of learning activities for students.

The local school instructional team is in a strategic position to provide these services. Since they are in constant interaction with teachers, they know their needs. They are also constantly available to give assistance and provide for follow-up activities. Certainly, some things need to be provided at the central office level. But, it is the function of local school specialists to stay informed of such services and facilitate their effective utilization at the local school level.

Educational Planning

Effective educational planning at the local school level requires a definition of goals to be reached in each program, an operational definition of the goals, projected target dates, and a clear statement of needs, including new personnel, equipment, materials, and facilities. The process is continuous; it needs to be carried out on a long-range basis.

Planning is a comprehensive process and requires the participation of all personnel. But the supervisory team should be expected to provide much of the leadership and hard work required to get the job done.

Staff Development

Staff development includes recruitment and selection of staff members, facilitating continuous professional growth on the job, evaluation of personnel for staff decisions, and assignment of personnel. There is probably no function of the local school instructional supervisory team that affects the quality of education for children as much as staff development. The educational program must constantly change to meet the changing needs of students. Teachers need new conceptual, technical, and human skills. Current staff must be provided an opportunity to develop these skills or new staff members who already have them must be employed. Both approaches must be used.

The opportunity to select a new staff member at the local school level represents an important way to improve the delivery of educational services. It is crucial for the local school to do a needs assessment to determine what weaknesses and strengths exist and to establish priorities of technical skills, human skills, and conceptual skills needed by the person to be selected for the new position. The local school faculty should have a central part in this process. Their involvement not only provides for the utilization of their knowledge and skills but also provides an opportunity for their own professional growth in the needs assessment process. It is also recognized that their investment in the selection process should contribute to their willingness to help the new faculty member succeed on the job. The local school organizational structure should facilitate the process of the involvement of local school professional personnel in recruitment and selection activities.

In-service education for the professional staff at the local school is a crucial function of the local school supervision team. Since the local school is where students and teachers are and where instruction and learning occur, it is our contention that the local school should be the primary place where in-service education is planned, implemented, and evaluated. Chapter 10 was devoted to human learning in educational organizations as a supervisory process. The ideas, principles, and activities discussed in Chapter 10 have implications for the organization and implementation of in-service education at the local school level.

The work of educational organizations is done by the instructional faculty. Administrators and supervisors play a supporting role. But, whether or not educational organizations succeed in achieving their goals (effective learning for students) is largely a function of the effectiveness of the performance of supervisors and teachers. Therefore, educational organizations need a reliable and valid method for the evaluation of teachers, supervisors, and administrators in order to make appropriate personnel decisions. It is our position that this process is an appropriate function of the local school supervisory team. The overall process for the school system should be planned at the central office level, but the evaluation of instructional staff should be planned, implemented and evaluated at the local school level within the framework of the school system plan. The process of instructional staff evaluation for personnel decisions is a major function of the local school supervisory team.

Reassignment of professional personnel is a well-known but little used process of improving performance. When the process of personnel evaluation indicates that teachers are having difficulties, are dissatisfied with their work, and/or are performing below normal expectations, they should not only be provided an opportunity to improve within that job, but consideration should also be given to current job enrichment or reassignment to a similar or different position, either within the school or in a new environment. A new school environment, new students and parents, new supervisory support, and new responsibility are examples of factors that can make a difference in performance. Certainly, it is important to guard against stereotyping teachers as failures or losers and just passing "problems" from school to school. This procedure represents a denial of responsibility and is self-defeating for both the school system and the individual. But, it is important to provide a new chance, a new opportunity in a supportive environment for teachers with performance difficulties. If the problems persist, other possibilities should be considered, including termination of employment.

THE ALLOCATION OF PERSONNEL

The allocation of personnel for the supervisory team requires a consideration of the size of the school, the organizational structure, needed activities, and the specialized competence needed to conduct the activities. The size of the school is a crucial factor in decisions concerning whether to provide a needed service or consultative resources on a permanent basis or an "on call" basis from the central office. The larger the school, the easier it is to justify permanent assignments.

The size of the school is also a factor in determining the needs for coordination. For example, relatively large elementary schools may have as many as two or three teams of teachers who conduct learning activities for students in early childhood education. Such teams require official leadership to coordinate the activities of the team and the team's interaction with other teams within the school. Department heads and program coordinators might serve similar functions in middle schools and secondary schools.

There is also a need for a broad range of specialized services. Teachers need help in the selection, procurement, and utilization of materials and equipment. They need technological and psychological support, and it needs to be available when it is needed. Certainly, every effort should be made to provide a team of specialists at the local school level who can give the broad range of services and consultations required. But economic realities make this impossible. Therefore, it is proposed that such services also be utilized from the central office level, fellow teachers, and members of the community at large.

The assumption is that teachers have not only a broad range of needs, but also a broad range of specialized competence that can be utilized in providing needed services and consultations to other teachers. An important part of the job of the supervisory team is to locate available resources and develop procedures for their utilization. Therefore, it is proposed that in the allocation of human resources, provision be made for the release of teachers on an ad hoc basis to participate in instructional supervision. This release of personnel could be facilitated through the allocation of personnel who participate both as teachers and instructional leaders. They could fill in for teachers who are needed to provide supervisory services.

A broad range of specialized people is normally available in the community. Social workers, scientists, counselors, medical doctors, and business executives are examples of individuals who could be called on to provide needed services for teachers.

Specialized services and resource people are also available from the state and federal governments. Funds are constantly becoming available that can be used to support special programs and provide specialized services to teachers. Schools that are aware of such programs and can also attract that funding can improve the quantity and quality of support for teachers.

It is obvious that there is no single rule that can be used to allocate personnel for the supervisory team. Rational allocation requires study of the way the school operates; the need for services; resources available from the central office, community, and local instructional staff; and the particular activities of a school at a given time. For example, if the school is giving serious consideration to the development of a new program, certain resources may be needed. If a program has been adopted and teachers need to develop certain skills, other resources may be needed.

If the school operates according to a formal bureaucratic model, the need for supervisory services might be different than if the school is trying to get a broader base of involvement in decision making and problem solving. If the school is highly dynamic with a high thrust for improvement, the needs would be different than in a relatively stable situation. The need for study is apparent, and so is the need to provide for the uniqueness of each school.

THE ORGANIZATIONAL STRUCTURE

In Chapter 11 the following needs of organizations were identified and discussed as they applied to organizational structure at the central office level:

1. The need for overall coordination and authority
2. The need for organizational members to participate in decision making and policy development, according to expertise and achieved prestige and not just formal position in the organization

3. The need for specialization and generalization
4. The need for communication
5. The need for control and conformity
6. The need for flexibility, creative response, and nonthreatening interpersonal influence
7. The need for human consideration
8. The need for a broad base of leadership

The reader is referred to Chapter 11 for a more detailed discussion of these factors. The assumption is made that they are equally appropriate as needs of the local school organization as they are for the organization of the school district.

In essence, what is being recommended is an organizational structure that is characterized by "openness." Such an organization is responsive to external influences. It can evaluate the meaning of such "input" and develop decisions for future direction and action. It is willing to constantly evaluate ends and means in terms of constantly changing internal and external conditions.

The need for specialization and differentiated staffing is recognized and provided for, but so is the need for sharing, learning from each other, and recognizing and utilizing expertise wherever it exists. The need for constituted authority is assumed, but the source of that authority is the human being who must be guided in order to provide for the coordination of specialized parts to ensure the achievement of overall goals. Organizational members who understand and respect each other can provide enough conformity to facilitate interdependence of parts and can provide enough individual uniqueness to ensure creative responses.

The emphasis is on a broad base of organizational member participation in goal setting, program developing, problem solving, evaluation, and planning. Formal position is utilized to facilitate these processes. The identification and release of faculty intelligence and creativeness are recommended as functions of the local school supervisory team. The delivery of service and consultation, wherever it is found and whenever it is needed to improve the quality of education for students, is central to the work of the instructional team.

The Principal as Instructional Leader

Principals of local schools are designated by boards of education as the primary formal leaders. As instructional supervisors-administrative, they have a primary responsibility to coordinate the efforts to define and evaluate local school goals; plan, implement, and evaluate instructional programs to achieve those goals; attract, select, support, and facilitate the professional growth of staff members; evaluate and coordinate the work of professional personnel; and see that adequate and appropriate instructional materials, equipment, and facilities are provided. Such a broad range of responsibilities requires both consultative and management services. Therefore, we believe that principals need all sources of authority including legitimate, position, competence, and personality. For example, a principal not only needs formal authority from the organization to evaluate personnel, but also must have the competence and personal skills to do the job without creating faculty alienation, poor motivation, and inferior performance. The same is true for other management and consultative responsibilities.

The principal is one official leader at the local school level who is primarily concerned with the overall goals of the school. The local school organization is a dynamic web of interdependent parts that are assumed to contribute to the realization of the overall goals. But the parts are subsystems of the suprasystem; they have their own goals, which may or may not be congruent with local school goals. For example, a school may have a football team with a winning tradition that has become a powerful factor in the school. The need to win may precipitate certain practices that are detrimental to other parts of the school. The power of the subsystem (the football program) may make such practices possible. The need for coaches and assistant coaches may influence personnel selection in such a way that coaches are hired with the hope that they are competent teachers. Students may be pulled out of classes for football practice to the disadvantage of academic objectives. A "part" has gotten out of balance in terms of overall system goals. A major function of the principal is to weave these parts into a balanced, coordinated, and fully functioning whole that can maintain optimum goal achievement.

The principal is a central factor in the communication network. He or she has direct contact with the central office and, thus, responsibility to interpret and communicate central office expectations to the local school. He or she is also the chief communicator of local school needs and expectations to the central office. The local school internal network of communication is a major concern. It is crucial that local school curriculum specialists and resource people work as a team among themselves and with teachers. Teacher-teacher, teacher–curriculum worker, and teacher-administrator communications are paramount in the planning and actualization of learning activities for students. Communication with other schools in which new ideas, materials, equipment, and human resources are shared is largely dependent on the effectiveness of the principal.

The principal not only provides leadership to identify and utilize appropriate personnel to provide an adequate system of psychological and technological support for teachers, but must also participate in the process.

The goals and means for achieving goals are constantly changing. Open facilities, open curriculum, differentiated staffing, new programs, and cooperative teaching all demand new understandings and new skills for organizational members. Schools must change and people must change. But, there is also a need for stability. The forces of change must be understood, utilized, and controlled. The principal is the chief instructional leader of the school; he or she is responsible for maintaining this delicate balance.

Principals are leaders of the supervisory team at the local school level. It is our position that supervisory competence and the need for supervision are widely dispersed throughout the faculty. Therefore, all members of the faculty, including those officially designated as instructional supervisors, are expected to provide supervisory services. Principals should coordinate this effort.

The Supervisory Staff

Even though all members of the faculty are expected to participate in the delivery of supervisory services, we assume that there is a need for personnel at the local school level who are formally designated as instructional supervisors.

The positions of coordinator and consultant were recommended as appropriate positions for the supervisory staff at the district level. These same positions are recommended for members of the curriculum and instruction team at the local school level.

The position of coordinator is called for where there is a program with definable interdependent parts that need to be pulled together toward the achievement of certain goals. The position of coordinator could be used to designate a team leader of a group of kindergarten teachers, aides, technicians, and student teachers. One school system developed the following definition of the team coordinator's role:

1. To involve the team in the development of goals and behavioral objectives for students that are consistent with the expectations of the local school and school district.
2. To involve the team in designing and developing plans for the actualization of engagement opportunities for students in order to achieve the goals and operational objectives.
3. To involve the team in developing a plan for the evaluation of the achievement of student goals, together with the actualization of the plan.
4. To involve the team in the planning and implementation of a design for staff selection and evaluation that is consistent with personnel policies in the organization.
5. To facilitate the provision of the psychological and technological support system for the team.
6. To facilitate the communication and actualization of team expectations of the system and system expectations of the team.
7. To participate in the process of helping and being helped by team members and to facilitate the process of team members helping each other.

The preceding role definition is not presented as a model, but rather as an example of a possible role definition. The role definition of a particular team leader would be a function of the organizational expectations, team member expectations, team leader expectations, and the way the team leader relates to these expectations.

Other examples of how coordinators are needed and utilized at the local school level would include principal of the school; coordinators of content departments, athletics, guidance services, teaching resource centers, and laboratories such as science, language, and drama. Coordinators exist to design, implement, and evaluate programs in cooperation with other specialists.

Consultants are used to render certain services or help through active participation in the teaching behavior system. Examples of the behavior of consultants would be helping a teacher use videotaping equipment, helping a teacher use some system of interaction analysis to describe student-student interaction, listening to a teacher talk about plans for actualizing certain engagement opportunities for students, making a suggestion to a group of teachers about using microteaching; demonstrating the use of microteaching; and helping a group of teachers reach consensus on an approach to the teaching of reading.

It is important to recognize that coordinators participate in consultative behavior and that consultants often become coordinators on an ad hoc basis. This practice is also true of teachers, teacher aides, technicians, and administrators.

POSSIBLE STRUCTURES
FOR INSTRUCTIONAL SUPERVISION

The effectiveness of any system of instructional supervision is at least partly a function of the organizational structure. It has already been explained that each school has its own identity, needs, priorities, and human capabilities. Therefore, the possible structures described in this section are not necessarily recommended for a particular local school. Rather, it is hoped that various elements might be appropriate for a particular school, but, more importantly, that the use of actual models may help clarify the implications of assumptions, concepts, and principles discussed in this chapter.

The following example was developed for an early childhood school (kindergarten through grade 3). There are 150 children in the kindergarten program and 900 children about equally divided among first, second, and third grade children. The school operates on a nongraded basis, and an attempt is made to provide all children with an opportunity to develop and explore interests, intellectual skills, human skills, and creativeness in their own way and according to their special capacities. There is an assumption that children develop at different rates and have different interests in, and capacities for, learning and also that children need to interact with other children of different ages, interests, and capacities.

It is assumed that all the people in the school, including children, teachers, consultants, coordinators, custodians, aides, and administrators, are important and, therefore, their needs are important. Needs for belonging, affection, stability of structure, change, recognition, and achievement are recognized, and an effort is made to provide a working environment in which those needs can be satisfied.

All the people in the school have a potential for making a contribution to school improvement and are therefore considered as important human resources. Every effort is made to provide a broad base of human involvement in problem solving and decision-making activities. Administrators, teachers, consultants, and coordinators can help and be helped by each other. There is also a broad base of human competence with focus on utilization of the competence in school improvement.

The need for coordination and control is recognized and utilized, but organizational members have a say in the development and continuous evaluation of that control system.

The system of instructional supervision is built on the notion that it is an organizationally sponsored behavior system that interacts with teaching behavior for the purpose of improving the quality of learning for students. Since teachers are assumed to be professionally competent and to represent a broad spectrum of specialization, it is recognized that teachers need to help and support each other. Therefore, an important task of administrators, coordinators, and consultants is to study the competence of the staff and to facilitate its utilization in the program of supervision.

It is known that the content, methodology, and materials and resources of teaching must constantly change along with the changing needs of students and new developments in knowledge and technology. A broad technological and psychological support system is provided for the teaching behavior system. Coordinators and consultants with special skills and knowledge are available to teachers at the local school level. Other specialists are utilized from the school district instructional team, institutions of higher education, local community, and other local schools.

In summary, supervision in this elementary school is perceived as a dynamic web of interpersonal influence, help, support, and collaboration that is wrought out of communication based on human openness, competence, trust, and authenticity. Figure 12-1 is a conceptual scheme for visualizing instructional supervision in this school.

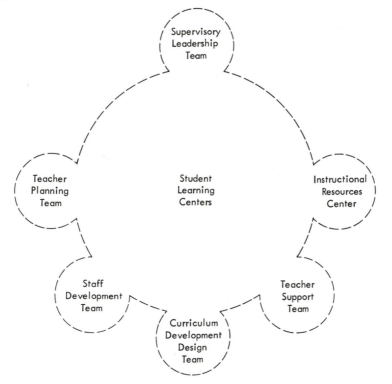

FIGURE 12-1 Supervision in a Local School

Student Learning Centers

The conceptual scheme clearly shows the student learning centers as the focus of the instructional supervisory behavior system. The six support systems are identified as the teacher planning team, supervisory leadership team, instructional resources center, curriculum development and design team, staff development team, and teacher support team. Each of these subsystems is shown to have its own identity (reason for being) but is also shown to be interdependent with the student learning center, with each other, and as a subsystem of the local school system.

The student learning centers are where the action is; that is, engagement opportunities for students are actualized there. Programmed learning, computer-based instruction, packaged materials, taped cassettes, large group instruction, and small discussion groups are examples of instructional techniques and ways of grouping children that might be utilized.

In the example school, there is one student learning center for 150 kindergarten children. There are six learning centers for the children from grade 1 through grade 3. Each unit is made up of 150 children who vary in age, interest, physical development, social development, and intellectual development.

The Teacher Planning Team

The teacher planning team for each learning center is composed of a teacher-team leader, two general teachers, two special teachers, a media technician, and three aides. The situation is open in both social structure and physical facilities. Students and teachers have easy access to each other so that helping, providing feedback, and demonstrating come easily and naturally. The team leader has the responsibility for involving the team in cooperative planning, teaching, and evaluation. Objectives of learning are defined; programs are designed, implemented, and evaluated on a cooperative basis. Quality control is explicit in the total process of goal development, program implementation, and evaluation. The team leader is the crucial factor in facilitating the processes of teachers: planning together, observing each other, analyzing each other, and generalizing from the analysis.

As a subsystem of the school district, the student learning centers also have special consultants and services available from the central office instructional team. This service is used, and the team leader is in an excellent position to help in this endeavor. The doors remain open to other agencies such as special community resources, including institutions of higher education.

The Supervisory Leadership Team

The supervisory leadership team is made up of the principal, student learning center team leaders, coordinators, and special consultants. The instructional leadership responsibilities of the principal have already been defined. It is through the instructional leadership team that the principal can implement his or her role. Objectives for the school can be hammered out. The various specialized parts of the school can be studied, analyzed, and evaluated according to their contribution to the achievement of overall goals. Long-term and short-term planning can be implemented, including a consideration of long-term goals, programs, personnel needs, and facility needs. Such planning needs to be coordinated with district-level planning. Therefore, a member of the supervisory leadership team serves as a member of the district supervisory leadership team. This type of interlocking membership facilitates the process through which local schools can become aware of the needs, expectations, human and material resources, priorities, and economic constraints of the school district. Even more important, the school district can become aware of local school problems, concerns, needs, expectations, and resources. Thus, the structure is provided for school district and local schools to share in the development of mutually beneficial policy formulation, decision making, and problem solving at both the local school level and the school district level.

Each teacher planning team, and each of the supervisory support teams—staff development, curriculum development, instructional resources center, and teacher support—are also represented on the instructional leadership team. Such an arrangement should facilitate the coordination of these subsystems as well as the flow of information between these subsystems and the leadership team and among the subsystems. With such a braod base of involvement, the possibility exists to utilize the potential of available human resources in policy formation, problem solving, clinical supervision, in-service education, and many other functions. It is our contention that the utilization of the human potential at the local school level will improve the quality and quantity of supervisory services, teacher performance, and educational outcomes for students.

The Curriculum Development and Design Team

Curriculum development and design are primarily a function of the teacher planning teams. However, we believe there is also a need to coordinate and facilitate this process. There is a need to examine and interpret school goals, describe and evaluate current curriculum, develop new curriculum designs, help teacher planning teams develop, implement and evaluate curriculum, and constantly examine the interdependence of various aspects of the instructional program. These tasks are the work of the curriculum development and design center. Each learning center is represented along with the various other subsystems in the school. There is also a representative to the school district curriculum development and design center. The interlinkage of these centers facilitates curriculum coordination at both the local school and school district levels.

The Instructional Resources Center

The instructional resources center is primarily a service center to the student learning centers. Materials and equipment are developed, collected, and made available according to the needs of the learning centers. The function of the center is not just to make materials and equipment available, but rather to involve students and teachers in the process of development, procurement, and use. Examples of such involvement would include student-made movies, slides, and photographs to share certain ideas; teacher-developed instructional techniques; and commercially developed programs. In a fundamental way the instructional resources center can contribute to the sharing of instructional materials, equipment, and know-how among the student learning centers.

The Staff Development Team

The tasks of the staff development team in this school include coordination of recruitment and selection of personnel, in-service education, and staff evaluation. The assistant principal for supervision and curriculum development serves as co-ordinator of the team, and the principal serves on the committee. The committee has representatives from each of the teacher planning teams, curriculum development team, and the instructional leadership team. One member of the team serves as a member of the school district staff development team in order to ensure effective communication and cooperation between the school district and the local school.

In this school system the central office has primary responsibility for staff recruitment and the development of a pool of qualified applicants that can be used in the selection process. However, the local school staff development team helps by defining personnel needs, identifying qualified applicants, and facilitating their applying through the central office. The local school is the primary agency for the selection of personnel, and the local school staff development team coordinates the effort to define personnel needs, establish selection committees, and make final recommendations to the central office. Local school involvement in staff selection contributes to school improvement in a number of ways. First, utilization of local school personnel in defining personnel needs will help ensure that the particular technical skills, human skills, knowledge base, and attitudes needed by the local school will be given prime consideration in the selection process. Second, staff involvement in a consideration of professional expectations for new staff members will facilitate staff involvement in an evaluation of their own qualifications as members of the staff and should point to areas of needed improvement. Third, involvement in staff selection and acceptance of responsibility of the results should contribute to the willingness of staff members to support, help, and provide service to new staff members.

The staff development team also coordinates the effort to provide an organizational climate that promotes the continuous professional growth of staff members. The team coordinates the planning, implementation, and evaluation of in-service education activities. Growth needs at the local school level are communicated to the school district, and growth opportunities at the school district level are communicated to the local school.

The principal of the school has primary responsibility for staff evaluation and personnel decisions and uses the staff development team in an advising and recommending capacity. The responsibilities of the team include evaluating current practices, obtaining feedback from teachers, recommending changes at both the local school level and system level, serving as a sounding board for the principal and other faculty members, and hearing grievances from faculty members.

The Teacher Support Team

The teacher support team coordinates the effort to provide help, support, and services to teachers as they attempt to improve their performance in the student learning centers. This process involves person-to-person, person-to-team and team-to-team supervision within the school. A major task is identifying special human competence, and identifying teachers with needs or problems, and bringing them together in a helping situation. Teachers are often released on a temporary basis to be helped or to share certain ideas or skills with other teachers or teams. Coordinators or consultants often fill in for teachers on such occasions.

The team also coordinates the use of consultants from the school district and other external sources such as institutions of higher education.

The school in this example uses clinical supervision to help teachers improve their performance in working with a particular group of students. The team coordinates the effort in such a way as to insure that all teachers have clinical supervisory support; that all human resources available to the school are utilized; that the clinical supervision process is continuously evaluated, including feedback from supervisors and supervisees; and that needed changes are designed and implemented.

The local school is a dynamic system of interacting parts that fit together to achieve certain common goals. The instructional supervisory behavior system interacts with the teaching behavior system to improve the probability that these goals will be realized.

13

ORGANIZATION
AND OPERATION
OF THE FACULTY

A faculty cannot exist without organization. It may be an informal working arrangement, or it may be a carefully charted plan in which the functions of each participant are enumerated. The plan of organization may be dictated by the principal or it may be developed by the group. But some structuring of the group, some organization of communication channels and coordination of effort are necessary. This chapter discusses how coordination can be achieved, how the organization should be developed, what control is necessary, and how relationships should be established and maintained with other groups.

THE DEVELOPMENT
OF THE FACULTY
ORGANIZATION

If principals start with the basic premise that they want to use all the intelligence of all the faculty members, they will apply it to the establishment of faculty structure as well as to the solution of problems. They will make provision for the faculty to participate in the establishment of its own organization. Let's look at two situations where that practice was followed.

In a faculty of 200 members, a committee was appointed by the principal to draw up a plan of faculty organization. This committee consulted with other faculty members and formulated a proposed organization that was submitted to the entire faculty for revision. After the revisions had been made, the plan was voted on by the faculty and became the official organizational structure. Under the plan, the final authority and decision in areas in which the school is autonomous rest with the total faculty. All committees, in the final analysis, report to the faculty, and no major change can be made in the program without the approval of the faculty.

Any member of the faculty can bring an issue before the total faculty at any meeting, but it is customary for policy changes to be presented to the faculty through regular committee channels. This right of faculty members to expedite committee procedures is maintained to provide for emergency measures and to ensure that any faculty member has the opportunity to make minority proposals in spite of opposition within the committees.

An elected group, the faculty council, serves as a screening body to keep faculty meetings from becoming overburdened with business items. In addition to the faculty council, the plan of organization calls for the establishment of committees to be responsible for development in various phases of the program. All members of the faculty are asked to choose one of the committees on which they would like to serve. As far as possible, all faculty members are given their first preference. Under the plan, each committee meets and elects its chairperson and decides upon the subcommittees that will be necessary to carry on its work.

Each subcommittee works on the problems in the areas assigned to it. From the subcommittees come recommendations for policy upon which the major committee is asked to act. If the committee accepts the recommendation of its subcommittee, the proposal is sent to the faculty council. All the general committees feed their proposals to the faculty council for acceptance or rejection. If a proposal is accepted by the faculty council, it is submitted to the faculty at the next faculty meeting. If a proposal is rejected by the faculty council, it is returned to the committee in which it originated. The plan for organization, however, provides that any faculty member can bring any proposal to the floor of the faculty meeting.

An important part of the plan is a committee on committees that constantly reviews the success of the organizational structure and makes recommendations to the faculty for changes that the committee feels will make the organization more effective. No changes can be made by the committee on committees itself. It can only recommend; the faculty approves or rejects any proposals.

This plan is cumbersome and designed to serve a large faculty, but several important principles are involved.

First, the structure of faculty organization is established by the faculty. No special committee responsible only to the administration has formed the plan. The procedure leaves no feeling that any group or individual is establishing a plan by which faculty thinking and action can be controlled.

Second, the plan calls for a structure built around the solution of current problems. It is functional. The major committees are working in areas in which many specific problems arise and in which rethinking of existing policy is needed.

Third, the organization is flexible. It can be changed as desired. When the focus of problems shifts, one committee can be abolished, and a new one can be formed. The procedures for constant study are defined in the description of the organization.

Fourth, faculty members are given an opportunity to work on the phases of the program in which they have the greatest interest and competence. Under this procedure, it is possible for faculty members to relate their committee work on policy with their teaching problems and special research. Their participation and policy formation are not something apart from their customary thinking and activity. Also, members of the organization participate in solving problems and developing policies in areas of their greatest competence. This process improves the quality of problem solving, the quality of the organization, and the performance of members of the organization.

Fifth, the plan makes use of an executive group to relieve the faculty of the responsibility for debating all the policy issues that arise. At the same time, it makes possible a review of the faculty council's actions, ensuring that no faculty member will be denied the right to question and promote revision of any policies.

Sixth, all members of the faculty have representation. This representation is indirect in the faculty council, whose members were elected by the total faculty, and direct through participation in the committee the faculty member selects.

Seventh, all matters of policy are referred to the faculty. No single, small group can gain control of faculty policy. No action becomes faculty policy without total faculty approval.

The faculty of a small-town school system put into practice the same principles. The administrator and two teachers of the system attended a workshop. At the workshop, they decided to work for more democratic practices in their faculty operation. Upon their return, the superintendent appointed a committee to get the faculty program under way. This committee, consisting of the superintendent, the principal of the high school, the principal of the elementary school, a teacher from the elementary school, and a teacher from the high school, called the faculty together and explained its desire for more democratic determination of policy. The faculty was asked to state what they thought should be done. Three faculty meetings were devoted to the discussion of the problems of the school and of the ways the faculty might organize to solve them.

At the fourth meeting, the committee appointed by the superintendent resigned, recommending to the faculty that it elect committee members who would more nearly represent the faculty and administration. A supplementary recommendation of the superintendent's committee was that the new committee, to be called a steering committee, be comprised of the superintendent, the two principals, three teachers from the elementary school, three teachers from the high school, two members of the community, and a member of the board of education. This recommendation was accepted by the faculty by secret ballot, and an election was held to determine the membership of the steering committee.

The steering committee conducted a survey of the faculty to determine the problems around which they felt the faculty should be organized for study. On the basis of this survey, seven choices were offered to the faculty and each faculty member selected a committee on which he or she desired to work.

As the year progressed, committees explored their assigned problems until they were ready to make recommendations. Faculty meetings were then called for a consideration of the reports of each committee. These reports consisted of recommendations for changes in the program of the school. Those that were accepted became school policy. If the recommendations were rejected, the committee was asked to study the situation further and to make revised recommendations or to drop the matter.

One aspect of the plan was a shifting of personnel in the steering committee. Each member, with the exception of the three representatives of the administration, was elected for a six-month term. In this way the faculty had a close control over the membership of the steering committee.

The primary function of the steering committee was to serve as a clearinghouse for the work of the general committees and to plan the faculty meetings. Members of the steering committee also advised the administration on ways in which the policies adopted by the faculty could be implemented.

It is important to point out that in both the plans described, the administration is a constant factor in all committees. In the large faculty, the official leader serves as chairperson of the faculty council and faculty business meetings, and members of the staff are designated as ex officio members on each of the major committees. In the small school, the three members of the administration are continuing members of the steering committee and have the responsibility for executing the policy arrived at through faculty deliberation.

A very simple type of faculty organization is that adopted by an elementary school in Colorado:

> At school this year, the teachers appointed a committee of three teachers to act with the principal in determining instructional problems. One committee member was chosen to represent the kindergarten, first- and second-grade teachers; one to represent the third- and fourth-grade teachers; and one to represent fifth- and sixth-grade teachers. It is the job of this committee to interview other teachers and to decide on problems that need to be considered for the improvement of instruction. One committee member presides at each faculty meeting.

PITFALLS TO BE AVOIDED
IN A FACULTY ORGANIZATION

Any faculty considering a plan of organization should be aware of certain dangers inherent in the committee system. First, committee work is time-consuming, and provision must be made for meeting time as a part of the regular schedule; otherwise the work may be considered as extra and unimportant by some faculty members. Second, certain faculty members may become overloaded with committee work. Faculties have a tendency to turn to certain members for leadership on any problem that arises. Unless some regulation is established that will keep any one faculty member from serving on too many committees, certain members may become so overloaded that their teaching will suffer.

Third, the official leadership must learn to work through existing committees. It is easy to feel that none of the existing committees covers the particular problem facing the staff and to appoint a new committee to discharge the new function. Such a practice leads to many committee memberships for faculty members and to confusion about the way new committees fit into the existing committee structure.

Fourth, the functions of the committees should be carefully defined. Unless they are, overlapping of committee activities occurs, and the sense of order is lost. In setting up a new organizational structure, the functions of each group or individual must be stated. Such a practice does not stifle creativeness. It frees it. When energy does not have to be spent in wondering about function, full attention can be given to performing the role creatively. In planning, lack of restrictions are desirable. In execution, a planned framework gives guideposts and security that enable the person or work group to give full attention to the job.

Fifth, a way must be formulated to insure implementation of the policies established by the faculty. If the administration is not directly responsible to the faculty for such implementation, and if the policies are not put into practice, faculty members acquire a feeling of frustration and develop the opinion that committee work is a waste of time.

If the committee-work dangers are avoided, and if the faculty can see that the time spent in policy formulation really results in program change, faculty members assume real responsibility for the program and mature through their broader understanding of the overall program.

Any plan that is developed will be satisfactory if the faculty keeps in mind the desirability of widespread participation and the need for a functional organization that makes possible small groups working on problems that are their concern, for continuity of problem solving and program development through standing committees with a responsibility for a portion of the program, and for flexibility that permits necessary revision and necessary coordination under the authority of the total group. The productivity of a group depends upon the integration of a number of diversified abilities, interests, and needs into a unified endeavor.

DECISION MAKING
IN THE FACULTY

As the faculty moves into more use of group decisions and group responsibility, some insecurity may develop. Any change brings some tension. Supervisors can do certain things to help the group feel more secure during the transition.

In reaching a decision, much time must be spent on the what, the how, the when, and the who. The procedure to be followed will be definite, even though the results may be in doubt. Those staff members who gain responsibility from knowing what their specific jobs are will have security.

Do something. If too much time is spent discussing before any action is taken, the group will conclude that discussion is useless, a waste of time. As soon as possible, one of the hypotheses agreed upon by the group should be selected and put into action on an experimental basis. All members of the staff should be encouraged to watch the results and participate in an evaluation of its worth. By the process of taking action, the group will develop more faith in group work.

The leader must help the members of the group become aware of the process of interaction. Group efficiency must become a joint responsibility. Unless a group has control over its own actions and a responsibility for making them efficient, it has not really become a group; it is still directed and operated by the official leaders. Checklists of good group procedures against which the members of the group can check their own participation and group operation help group members to accept responsibility for the group operation. Asking some member of the group to keep a flow chart of the discussion, which can be presented to the group for their consideration at the end of the meeting, is another way of encouraging the group to examine itself.

Some teachers fear change. It adds to their insecurity. The techniques they already know may not work under the new conditions, and they are not sure they can acquire new ones that are as effective. In a changing situation, the only way a staff can achieve security is through the development of a method for the control of change.

As the group grows more mature, the principal will want to place greater personal emphasis on coordination and less on setting the stage. Other leadership will emerge in the group, and it must be used if the group is to develop. Other members of the group who show skill may be brought into service as chairpersons of discussion meetings. A planning committee may be organized to take the lead in initiating ideas and establishing the agenda for meetings. Subcommittees may be formed under the leadership of various staff members to assume responsibility for portions of the program.

Although as a result of group procedure, the entire staff will have an overall view of the program and the way the pieces fit together, someone must be alert for places where segmentation is developing, must call the staff's attention to the hazard, and must suggest ways of overcoming it. Someone must collect information about, and coordinate, the group's activities. That person is the principal. Someone must watch for places where leadership is beginning to falter and must be ready to serve as a resource person in group work procedures. That person, too, is the principal.

To make coordination of the program easier, the principal will avoid sole jurisdiction by any individual or group over any phase of the program. *All sub-groups, departments, and committees should be responsible to the total faculty.* All members of the staff should have a sense of responsibility for the total program if the faculty is to remain a group.

The decision-making process is the most important phase of successful democratic leadership, because sharing decisions is the only control democratic leaders have. If they cannot get group members to participate in decision making, if they cannot help them to gain satisfaction from the process and believe in the soundness of the decisions, they must resort to authoritarian procedures.

When a problem has been identified, the next step is to define it and to explore its ramifications. This step involves analyzing the conditions of the school, making explicit the maladjustments of the situation, and advancing tentative solutions.

The official leader should recognize that the first attempts to reach joint decisions in a group are tests of the leader. As a result of past experience, various members of the group have different feelings about the sincerity of the principal in introducing the process. Leaders should expect doubts and should welcome tests of their integrity.

A basis for decisions should be sought. Are there any common values that the group seeks to promote? In school faculties it is usually easy to secure verbal agreement that all staff members want to improve the welfare of children. Of course, the decision-making process may reveal that other values are more important to some staff members, but verbal agreement serves as a working basis at the start.

The issues should be clearly defined. Time should be spent in examining the problem before study is undertaken. Individuals may be asked to cite specific examples. Opportunity must be provided for members of the group to state the issues as they see them.

More than one possible solution should be examined. Ask the committee to propose several solutions, and provide time for the group to discuss the pros and cons of each. Other members of the group should be free to make other proposals. Expression of all opinions should be sought. Opinions cannot be repressed. If they are not stated in the meeting, they will be expressed elsewhere. The leader should watch for unspoken disagreements and should encourage the members to express them.

Examination of the problem should be started early. Most issues can be resolved if there is sufficient time. Rushed decisions do not permit everyone concerned to study issues and solutions and to talk through differences. One of the leader's functions is to help the group develop machinery for determining problems far enough in advance so that there is time for study and discussion.

Principals will want to encourage the group to seek consensus. If they allow decisions to be made on a simple majority basis, the group will not arrive at agreement on the problems they should investigate or on the ways of solving them. One way the leader can promote consensus is by taking straw votes with the definite understanding that members of the group see voting in terms of the way they see the solution of the problem at the moment and are not in any way committing themselves to a final decision on the issue. Straw votes serve two purposes: they reveal how nearly the group has arrived at consensus, and they isolate differences that are still unresolved. When leaders find that disagreements exist, they can call for those who have voted against the proposal to state their reasons and then give the persons who have voted for it an opportunity to explain theirs. In this way, a straw vote is a means of setting the stage for further analysis of the issue. Sometimes consensus on the total solution will be impossible. In such a case, it is better to proceed with the portions of the proposal on which agreement has been reached.

The areas of disagreement should not be forgotten, however. They are not liabilities. They constitute the problems on which further study is needed. By examining the unresolved differences, the faculty has an opportunity to gain new insight through mutual endeavor. If, however, the minority is forced to accept a program that it disapproves, wholehearted support of the program's implementation will be lacking.

Any innovation on which there is not consensus should be undertaken as an experiment. It is a trial run from which evidence is collected to be used as the basis for a more intelligent decision. Whether or not the leader recognizes this condition, it does exist. The proponents and opponents will be looking for data to support their positions. If the group officially recognizes the experimental nature of the situation, an evaluation can be undertaken to collect more comprehensive data to be used in subsequent decisions.

In the majority of cases, principals will want to focus their attention on the process of reaching a decision rather than on getting any one solution accepted. If they are firmly convinced that one solution is essential, they should surrender the chair and work for it openly. Such action is additional proof to the staff of the principal's honesty.

Throughout his or her work with the faculty, the principal should continually put emphasis on *what* is right rather than on *who* is right. As the group is encouraged to center upon what is right, personalities and vested interests fade into the background.

In studying possible solutions, the principal should also suggest possibilities. Until the faculty has learned to trust, there is a need to emphasize that these are only possibilities and not necessarily the course of action that should be accepted by the group.

LEADERSHIP
IN THE LOCAL SCHOOL

If it is recognized that leadership is any contribution to the establishment and achievement of goals by a group, it is easy to see that official leadership must be concerned with the fullest possible cultivation of the leadership potential of each member of the group. Merely apprenticing one member of the faculty for future status leadership is too limited a concept of the responsibility for developing leadership. It restricts the possible accomplishments of the group.

The development of leadership in group members involves getting them to assume responsibility for the planning and development of a program; it also involves creating the type of atmosphere in which they are encouraged and stimulated to exert their full native ability. Through helping staff members achieve leadership, the full power of the group is released. Members make their maximum contribution as they have the opportunity to lead, and they grow in strength and ability through the experience.

In a school faculty, leadership is fostered by creating a permissive atmosphere in which individuals feel secure enough to make their unique contribution; providing positive support for faculty members who attempt leadership; rewarding successful leadership attempts and providing psychological support and technical help for unsuccessful leadership attempts; offering individuals an opportunity to participate in decision-making and problem-solving activities according to their interests and expertise; and providing an opportunity for faculty members to assume responsibility with appropriate authority in program development, human development, staff selection, goal development, and other activities on a temporary basis.

DEVELOPMENT OF LEADERSHIP
IN OTHERS

Why aren't teachers willing to exert their full leadership? In light of what has been already said about people wanting recognition and the feeling that they are making a contribution, it would seem that everyone would want to lead. Some group members are willing to lead; others are not. Much of the difference lies in the type of supervision they have had. If their official leaders have been reluctant to delegate authority and have attempted to control all member actions, only the unusual people will volunteer to assume responsibility. After teachers have been dominated and directed for years, they cannot be expected to rush to assume leadership. Any new formal leader will have to work with them a long time before they will lose their suspicions, feel that the program is theirs as well as the leader's, and become willing to exert initiative. If, however, teachers have experienced stimulating official supervision that has worked for teacher leadership, they exert leadership.

Official leaders must begin with people where they are. Members of the instructional leadership team must accept teachers for what they are, without condemning them for behavior that is the result of their past experiences, and attempt to create the type of environment that makes it possible and desirable for people to assume leadership.

Leadership involves pioneering. As people venture into the unknown, the chance of making errors is greatly increased. If supervisors want to encourage leadership, they must support teachers as they work out solutions to new problems. If principals have a faculty that has never taken a field trip and they want to begin to utilize community resources, they must make clear their backing of field trips, help arrange schedules and transportation that make trips possible, and then give teachers freedom to experiment.

The first prerequisite for increasing a teacher's willingness to risk making a mistake is the establishment of an atmosphere in which mistakes during innovation are not penalized. Supervisors must recognize that teachers incur some insecurity through creative efforts, that some mistakes will occur, that advances and new learning come about as the result of mistakes as well as successes, and that some sense of order may appear to be lost while new methods are being tested. They must understand that teachers who are attempting creative work need greater support from their supervisors. People are less willing to take chances when there is a possibility of being punished for mistakes made. Principals must let the staff know they understand that a teacher may make mistakes in attempting procedures for which no pattern has been set.

If team leaders want to foster leadership, they must recognize and respect the need of staff members for security. They must eliminate, as far as they can, the possibility of reprisals for unsuccessful innovations. Because formal leaders exert power over promotion and salary, some teachers will hesitate to place their ideas on an equal basis. Some schools have attempted to eliminate fear of supervision by creating consultants or resource teachers who assist but do not rate, by involving teachers in the coordination of supervision, and by holding workshops and camps where teachers and supervisors work together as equal members of a work team. All such efforts should be judged by their effect on the creation of a school environment in which teachers feel secure enough to risk making an error in judgment or to differ in opinion with the formal leadership.

The principal must avoid stereotypes of what constitutes worthwhile contributions and good teaching. Otherwise, teachers learn not to assume leadership, because the person who does assume responsibility and carries it out in a way that differs from the principal's original idea is reprimanded. Teachers in such a situation quickly become afraid to "stick out their necks." They avoid any type of work that leads them beyond their customary routine into activities in which they are unsure of the principal's desires or their ability to meet them. As teachers find that the easiest way to be happy and safe from criticism is to stick to the regular job, it becomes more and more difficult to get them to assume leadership. A principal may repress growth without realizing it.

After twenty years of teaching, a junior-high-school English teacher had decided that teaching grammar for the full period each day was not the most effective teaching procedure or the most enjoyable. She searched and found a magazine published in London for British adolescents. She subscribed to the magazine, using money from her salary. The pupils enjoyed it. They took copies home and their parents approved and commented favorably to the teacher.

One day the principal came by and saw it. Reacting in light of public opinion that opposed UNESCO, he commented, without any attempt to discover the facts, "I'd get rid of those magazines. Someone might think we are teaching UNESCO." The teacher, who had begun to venture after twenty years of conforming put the magazines back in the closet.

Opposition to the ideas of principals, team leaders, department heads, and other members of the official leadership team must be accepted and recognized as a contribution to group growth and program improvement if leadership is not to be confined to areas the official leader has already explored and described. It is easier to accept the philosophic concept of valuing opposition than it is to practice. It is difficult for administrators to keep from ascribing unworthy motives to the persons who oppose them. It is easy to believe that the opposition is seeking power or protecting a vested interest. It is more difficult to assume that they are intellectually honest or that they are acting because of a deep commitment to fundamental values.

It is especially hard to give due credit to the opposition when it adopts tactics that seem unfair. Occasions that test supervisors are when certain groups always oppose change, when it is obvious that there has been a decision before the meeting and that a plan has been developed for blocking consideration of an idea or for railroading one through, or when an argument descends to name calling and appeals to emotion. At such times, principals are torn between the desire to utilize everyone's contribution and their responsibility to conduct the business of the school in such a manner that a unified, consistent program is developed. If unjustified and unfair opposition continues, principals may have to discuss the decision-making process with the leaders of the opposition, but they should recognize such procedures as an act of desperation to be used after all other techniques for achieving group integration have been exhausted. If discussion does not secure positive results, principals will be forced to use their authority to make sure that consideration is given to issues and possible solutions.

THE USE OF AUTHORITY

Group leaders who are seeking to develop more effective ways of using their authority can share it. As they give others a part in determining how authority shall be used and who shall use it, they are sharing their authority and their responsibility. They do not relinquish either authority or responsibility, but the group acquires them both by accepting the invitation to participate in decision making. Of course, they are responsible to those who delegated authority to them for the way it is used.

But so are the other members of the staff after they have shared it. They become coadvocates and defenders, if necessary, of the steps taken. Principals are never alone against the board or the community if they have shared their authority.

Sharing authority is not as familiar a concept as delegating authority. The right and necessity for an official leader to delegate authority are never questioned, but principals have not been equally clear about the possible results of sharing authority.

From the point of view of those who have granted the authority, official leaders are responsible. They cannot escape this responsibility. If they delegate authority, they are performing an administrative action. If they share authority, they are using an administrative procedure. As far as the persons previously mentioned are concerned, the principals have full authority and responsibility. They can exercise the authority as they see best. They are free to share authority if they feel it will get better results.

From the point of view of the staff working beneath the principal in the line of authority, there is a vast difference between delegated and shared authority. Persons to whom authority is delegated assume responsibility for its use but not for the decision about how it will be used. They are responsible to their official leader but not to anyone else. The arguments of the lesser Nazis in the trials following World War II illustrate the refusal to accept responsibility for decisions concerning the use of authority. On the other hand, persons with whom authority is shared assume responsibility for decisions concerning its use as well as for the execution of decisions. All persons who accept a share in deciding how authority will be used become responsible to each other and to persons outside the group for the utilization of the authority.

The official leader's decision about whether to delegate certain authority to certain staff members or to share authority with the total staff must be made on the basis of how the work of the staff will be affected. Autocratic leaders can secure cooperation in carrying out their goals by using threats and rewards. If people are afraid or if they wish to obtain what the leader has to offer, they will surrender their will and cooperate in doing what the leader wants. If leaders choose to operate democratically, their major source of control is sharing their authority to make decisions. They cannot force people to join in making decisions. If they are not willing to share voluntarily the decision making, they will be forced to use the same techniques of control that the authoritarian leader uses. If, however, the members of the group see value in sharing decisions and understand that in the process their purposes will be considered and utilized, their participation is voluntary, and it results in their assuming responsibility in the execution of the decisions. Cooperation is voluntary because the individual's purposes are included in the determination of the action to be undertaken.

The basic way nonauthoritarian leaders have of receiving cooperation is to give group members a share in deciding how the authority allocated to the group and its official leader will be used. As members of a group make decisions about how authority is to be used, they inescapably acquire a sense of responsibility for the success of their decision. If they are willing to live by the agreements reached, the decision-making process becomes the control, and authority is spread throughout the group. All become responsible for the decision and its enforcement.

Shared authority is contingent on the good faith of the members of the group. Unless individuals are willing to live up to an agreement, the principal has the responsibility to enforce the decisions of the group.

Members of a staff have many ways of resisting an activity in which they do not believe. Passive resistance, such as forgetting, missing the point, coming late, getting simple arrangements confused, postponing, overemphasizing details, and being oversubmissive to and glorifying the past, are not always recognized by official leaders as means of resistance. Active resistance, such as disagreement, a counterproposal, or a refusal, is sometimes considered insubordination.

If supervisors are to be real leaders, they must recognize manifestations of resistance; be able to facilitate and tolerate expressions of resentment, disappointment, and antagonism without becoming defensive; hear valid criticism; be sensitive to cues concerning the real dissatisfaction underlying negative expression; be willing to discard practices that do not contribute to group purposes; and be able to help groups find common purposes. In brief, they must be willing to accept the fact that another person's purposes and ways of reacting are as natural and valid as their own.

But official leaders cannot allow programs to disintegrate. They are hired to accomplish a mission. If they can move forward by using a procedure that enables members of the staff to grow by assuming more and more responsibility, they are exerting leadership. If the level of staff morale is low, of if a portion of the staff is bitter and antagonistic as the result of previous experiences, it may be necessary for official leaders to use their authority to control the organization and to keep it functioning. When forced to use authoritarian measures, the principals should recognize that such measures may prevent them from ever becoming a successful leader in the situation. But they cannot with any conscience allow the program to disintegrate.

For effective group operation, official leaders must take steps that make clear their willingness to share authority and keep the lines of communications open so that all who wish to participate in the formulation of policies may do so. But the group leader must also assume the responsibility for exercising the authority that forces individual members to live up to group agreements and systemwide policies. In any case, they must continue to believe in people and work for shared responsibility.

Acceptance of official responsibility by staff members means accepting and executing assignments. In the context of shared leadership, this acceptance is enlarged to include responsibility for contributing ideas, helping the group to reach cooperative agreements, joining in the establishment of plans, and accepting and executing assignments that grow out of group planning.

NO VETO WHEN
AUTHORITY IS SHARED

It is impossible to share authority and use the veto. It is a contradiction of terms. The use of shared authority means that the official leader is willing to share the power of decision making with the group. The use of a veto verifies that the authority was not shared in the first place. Many formal leaders have felt that they could not eliminate the veto from their work with the group, but it really becomes an impossible instrument in a group that is operating cooperatively. Leaders who start with the idea that they are going to share authority with the faculty, and then apply a veto will find that they cannot use it. If they have been unable to justify their point of view in faculty discussions, they will not be able to make their veto stick. As one principal stated it,

> I have a vote, and an important one, but only one. I suggest. I recommend. I try to persuade. I vigorously defend. But if my faculty doesn't understand, doesn't believe in, doesn't agree with my ideas, regardless of merit, then my ideas haven't much chance of being carried out effectively—and so I wait. I continue to work vigorously for those things that I believe, those things that seem to me to be best for the young people with whom I work.

This statement illustrates why group leaders who share authority must state to their groups that they will not use the veto. If they work as this principal does, really thinking with their faculty, a veto is as ineffective as it is unnecessary. Holding it as an official club destroys most of the possibilities for sincere group work. If a group attacks a problem enthusiastically and arrives at an answer that is vetoed, it knows that the group study was a fake, a way of manipulating people. The result is the same if the leader holds the group together until it accepts his or her hypothesis.

> A New Jersey junior high school faculty was assigned a new principal. The former principal had used good group process and teachers were accustomed to real participation in policy-making and planning. The new principal gave verbal allegiance to the procedure, but disagreement with him was a personal matter; he refused to let the group make a decision with which he disagreed even though the straw vote was as much as twenty to one against him. One of the faculty members finally said:
> "It is no longer any use to participate in faculty planning sessions. We see they are used to manipulate us. The only thing to do is go back into our classrooms and teach and let the school program go hang. Yesterday after the faculty council meeting the principal stopped me in the auditorium and asked 'You are going along with my ideas, aren't you?' "

This statement from a strong, idealistic teacher is added evidence that the principal must believe in group work and group thinking if group decision making is to succeed. If principals do not want or understand group thinking and action, teachers will have to stage a revolution to get it, and most teachers find it easier to submit or to change positions than to declare war on the principal.

THE CONTROL NECESSARY

The efforts of any organization must be coordinated if the organization is to achieve its goals. A group cannot expect to be successful unless it carefully plans its goals and devises ways of achieving them. It must also establish effective control over the activities of its members. Anarchy has no program. Laissez-faire does not lead to group accomplishment. Disciplinary control of group members by each other is a necessity.

A group is more than the total of the individuals who compose it. Individuals may be self-disciplined and able to control their own behavior, but as a group, they may still display anarchy. The purposes for which individuals control their own decisions may be at such wide variance that no group control exists, and coordination and progress are impossible. Self-discipline by individuals is not enough. To be successful, groups must have ways to bring individual action into line with the goals of the group.

As group leaders face the responsibility of coordinating group activities, they are confronted with the task of securing and maintaining discipline. If the group is to exist, it must have discipline. It may be discipline that the group establishes to carry out its purposes, or it may be discipline forced on the group by the official leader. Or, it may be developed by the group itself and administered by the leader.

Authoritarian discipline is control of the action of others by an individual with greater power. Persons with power over others decide what they want done, how they want it done, and when they want it done, and then force others to carry out their purposes and plans. As they become sure of the willingness and ability of others to execute what they want done, they give them greater freedom to plan and act within the framework of their purposes. A disciplined member of the authoritarian group is one who has accepted the leader's wishes and is guided by them. The leader's control is imposed. He or she regulates the action of others through the power of fear or respect.

Group self-discipline comes from within. As the members of the group accept common purposes, they develop a basis for coordination. As these purposes become sufficiently strong to guide the group actions, group self-discipline is achieved. Leaders do not impose the control; they help the group form it. Official leaders administer the control the group imposes on itself.

Let's examine these concepts in terms of the operation of a school faculty. Members join the faculty of their own free will on a contract basis. They have accepted the official leadership of the principal, department head, or supervisors. They have agreed to provide their services to the school for a certain number of hours per day for a definite number of days per year. The school is to be operated within the regulations laid down by the state department of education, the local board of education, and accrediting agencies, and within the budget provided by the local board. Within this framework, any course of action may be taken by official leaders. They may tell teachers what to teach and how to teach, and they may present the school's purposes and the rules by which teachers must abide. If they have enough power over the staff, they can enforce their decrees and have authoritarian discipline. If they do not have enough power, there will be no discipline. On the other hand, the official leader may seek to develop self-discipline within the framework of the faculty group by bringing teachers into the decisions regarding purposes, implementation, and execution.

The effectiveness of the authoritarian approach is denied by available research on the ways to release group potential. The principal should seek ways of helping a group establish self-discipline.

Some official leaders have found it hard to make the transition. They have moved from authoritarianism to anarchy. Group members are left to make their own decisions; the group disintegrates, and no progress is made in developing a school program. Such conditions are worse than authoritarian discipline.

Group self-discipline exists when a group has common purposes sufficiently strong to control the actions of individual members. A basketball team trying to win a tournament may develop such strong purpose that its members will abide by training rules and will help each other abide by them. Faculty members agreeing on the desire for a salary increase may be willing to levy a tax on themselves to underwrite a publicity campaign. In each case, personal plans and actions are subordinated to the group purpose that the individual has helped to establish.

As was described earlier, a part of the process of leadership is to help the staff evolve its purposes and plans. It is also the first step toward group self-discipline. Group leaders must meet with their staff to think out together common purposes that all accept. When groups become committed to certain purposes, members of the staff are able to measure their actions by a yardstick they helped to develop. A disciplined teacher, then, is a teacher with a clear understanding of the goals of the school and a compelling drive to reach them by working with, in, and for the group.

A second part of the achievement of common purposes is the development of group feeling. The members of the group must like and respect each other. They must trust each other and believe that each will assume his or her full share of responsibility. Otherwise, they will not be willing to undertake a common enterprise.

A third basis for group self-discipline is the clear definition of function and responsibility. Otherwise, there can be no wholehearted acceptance of purposes. Group members must see what the purposes involve in terms of time and energy before they are willing to accept responsibility. Without voluntary acceptance of responsibility, there is no basis for group self-discipline.

Fourth, the members of the group must know that changes in group purposes and procedures can be initiated. Without this assurance, individuals are afraid to submit to group discipline. They fear that group control may be unfair. They may be allocated more than their share of work. As long as it is possible to initiate change, there is no reason to resist group authority.

Fifth, the group must agree on the rules necessary for attaining its purposes. If rules are related to purposes, they will be logical and acceptable and they will coordinate activities. If they are established for the group without reference to the implementation of the common purposes that comprise the basic element of unit for the group, the group has no reason to accept them. They come from outside the group and can be enforced only by pressure from outside.

Sixth, the rules for the group must not involve unrelated activities. Teachers resent rules that affect personal living, apart from the school program. Rules that emerge in group self-discipline are related to the coordination of the school program.

To make group discipline work, it is essential for group leaders to be disciplined by the group purposes. If leaders take advantage of their position, the staff can see that they are not really accepting its purposes. If, however, leaders accept the purposes sufficiently to come to work before the other members of the staff and work longer than other members of the staff, many of the petty problems that exist in some schools will disappear during the time the staff participates in policy formation. A high correlation exists between clock watchers on the staff and a clock-watching principal.

Group purposes will not be equally accepted by all members of the staff; some will deviate and will not carry their responsibilities. Some teachers may not even live up to their contract agreement. What then?

THE DISCIPLINING PROCESS

A clear distinction must be made between *discipline* and *disciplining.* Where discipline exists, no disciplining is necessary. Where an individual is not controlled by the group self-discipline, disciplinary action must be taken. It is polite in some circles to pretend that disciplining is never necessary. Such would be the case if leaders were perfect in their work with groups, but no one is. Formal leaders, even though they are striving for group self-discipline, will find it necessary to take disciplinary action on behalf of the group. Group morale cannot be allowed to suffer because an individual refuses to be controlled by the self-imposed discipline of the group. Under the authoritarian type of administration a breach of discipline occurs when a teacher violates one of the rules set up by a principal. Under group self-discipline, undisciplined action on the part of a member of the group is activity that hinders the accomplishment of the purposes set up by all. If teachers frequently fail to meet deadlines, the discipline problem is not that they are breaking a ruling of the principal, but that they are hindering the accomplishment of the purposes of the staff; and the discussion between principal and teacher should be on that basis.

How should disciplining be done? This topic is unpleasant, but certain procedures for treating persons who have broken the discipline of the group have been developed, which give better results in helping individuals return to a voluntary acceptance of their responsibilities to the group.

The leader should, first of all, try to get all the pertinent facts. It is well to begin the discussion of the problem with a question designed to get the group member's side of the story. As the teacher talks, all the facts should be brought out into the open to see whether or not there is complete agreement on them. Until agreement on facts has been established, the decision as to whether disciplinary action is necessary is on an unsound basis.

After facts have been ascertained and the breach of discipline is clear, an attempt should be made to discover the reason for the unsatisfactory behavior. Was it due to disagreement with group purposes? Was it the result of conflict with individuals in the group? Was it caused by distractions from the job? Was it prompted by lack of recognition for contributions to the group? Was it due to resentment of some act by the formal leader?

In dealing with teachers, principals should study their own behavior to eliminate anything that may be causing a breakdown of discipline in the group. They must attempt to be as objective concerning their own actions as they are concerning the teacher's actions. At no time during the discussion should there be an unnecessary display of authority. If the teacher agrees that he or she has violated the purposes, or rules, the principal will seek to work out a mutually satisfactory solution, which may mean bringing in other members of the staff to help think the problem through.

If the teacher refuses to accept the solution, it may be necessary to suspend, transfer, or terminate the person. These measures are a last resort; they are not to be taken to maintain the authority of the official leader but, instead, to enable the group to continue to be a self-disciplining group. Final decisions should be made in terms of the course of action that will do most to promote the purposes of the school. If there is agreement on facts, but disagreement on whether an action has been undisciplined, other members of the group should be brought in to help make the final decision. The situation should never be allowed to become an issue between the teacher and the principal.

At no time during the analysis of the situation and the attempt to reach a solution should principals allow their emotions to come to the surface. They should maintain a calm, objective attitude and constantly seek facts and solutions, rather than attempting to overpower the teacher through emotional pressure. Always the paramount question should be: What is best for the pupils? What is best for the group? What is best for the teacher? It must be kept in mind, too, that every personal contact with a member of the group must be thought of in terms of its possible group implications.

The meetings involved in working out the problem should end pleasantly. The principal should seek to help the teacher regain self-confidence and a place in the group. In this situation, a principal's responsibilities are twofold: to help the group maintain self-discipline and to help individuals to grow. Mistakes and lack of discipline should be looked upon as an opportunity to help the individual get new insight rather than as an occasion to punish.

These suggestions should not be interpreted to mean that principals do not exert authority. They are empowered to act, and they must act to keep the staff members working together and making their full contributions to the success of the school program. They use their power to implement the best thinking of all, including the ones who violate group discipline.

GETTING OTHERS
TO ASSUME RESPONSIBILITY

As staff members assume responsibility, deadlines should be agreed upon for the completion of the work. Members of the group who are assigned responsibility, or who volunteer to accept responsibility, should do so in terms of a date set by the group's production schedule. If deadlines are agreed upon, they serve as the control factors in the situation. They become the impersonal taskmasters. When teachers agree to a deadline, they commit themselves and establish their schedule without pressure from superior authority. If the official leader uses his or her personality or force to control a situation, antagonism and personal antipathy may easily develop.

If group leaders want others to assume responsibility more than once, they must ensure that the persons allocated the responsibility have the necessary authority for carrying out the task they have assumed. Frustration often results when authority does not go with responsibility, and the acceptance of future responsibility is avoided. Persons cannot do their best when they do not know how soon they will come to the limit of their authority or when they do not have the necessary authority to take action. Teachers must be secure in the knowledge that the immediate decisions they make in carrying out the responsibility will be accepted and upheld by the group and the supervisor.

Supervisors must not grab control again when they think a teacher or a staff is making mistakes. When they retract the authority that they have shared, they are telling all the staff members that they did not share authority at all; that the person responsible for carrying out the action was really acting without authority, because no authority was actually shared. Whenever authority is revoked, it is apparent to teachers that they have not had responsibility and that they will not have to assume responsibility in the future. They know that if they get into a difficult spot, they will be saved. The supervisor has continued to assume full responsibility and has indicated no real confidence in the ability of the staff members. After a few experiences of this type, the teacher will refuse to accept new responsibility.

The supervisor must keep the channels of communication open if teachers are to discharge the responsibilities they have accepted. People are willing to work together when they are fully informed. They lose the desire to work toward the achievement of goals they may have helped establish if they are not kept acquainted with the progress that is being made. Channels must be kept open both ways. If the people who are carrying out the program have no means of pointing out their difficulties, the difficulties may assume such importance in the minds of the teachers that progress will stop. If, however, those who are expending the energy necessary to make the program succeed have a way of getting the attention of the total group focused on the difficulties encountered, they feel that they are not working alone, and that their obstacles are the concern of the group. When workers feel that their problems are being considered by the group, their sense of belonging to the group and their sense of responsibility to the group increase in spite of the difficulties.

In a group situation, the supervisor should constantly encourage a group to recognize members who have made exceptional contributions toward the completion of a program. As official leaders give praise, or encourage the group to give praise, for work well done, they are providing an additional stimulus for the assumption of further responsibility.

Formal leaders invite trouble if they give the impression that they are out to make a record for themselves. If the members of the group receive this impression, it will be recognized that the participation in policy formation that the principal is suggesting is simply a device for manipulating the group. The techniques of principals are judged in terms of the motives that the group attributes to them. If principals take all the credit when the program receives praise, the teachers will let them carry full responsibility for "their" program. They have made it clear to the community and to the teachers that the program is theirs and the teachers will let them have both the program and the responsibility for it.

Some teachers feel that principals use them as steppingstones to better positions. They say a principal comes to their building, institutes a new program, and is promoted to a higher rank on the basis of the results of their efforts. They develop a feeling of resentment and are determined that they will not be further exploited by a person who stands to gain through their efforts.

When teachers see inequality in the workload, they develop resentment that keeps them from assuming new responsibilities. This inequality may be among teachers, as when some are asked to assume many extra duties or to carry a heavy pupil load while others have less responsibility, or it may exist between the teacher's load and the principal's load. When teachers see a principal taking life easy, they have a good reason for refusing to increase their own burden.

Another reason many people do not assume more responsibility is that they are already overburdened. It is common practice in some schools to exploit the willing worker. If supervisors want people to assume responsibility, they must not overload the members of the staff who are quick to accept extra work. If people see that those who are willing to work hard are not protected from acquiring too much of a load, they become very reticent about assuming responsibility. One of the functions of a principal is to see that no member of the staff is overloaded. If the principal protects staff members from assuming too many responsibilities, the hesitancy to volunteer disappears. Teachers then know that the leader wishes to protect, not overload, them.

A great number of insignificant chores may lead teachers to feel that they are being overworked. When they are asked to perform clerical duties that could be better performed elsewhere, they find a reason for not accepting more responsibility for the formation of policy, for participation in the community, or for doing the other things that lead to more effective teaching. If the school does not have a policy of substituting new responsibilities for old ones when the load becomes too heavy, it is only natural for teachers to fight against assuming new responsibilities. Individuals cannot be expected to assume more than their share of responsibility. If a teaching staff is already overburdened by a heavy pupil-teacher load, or by a large number of community activities, new responsibilities will not be accepted willingly.

In working with people and getting them to assume responsibility, team leaders should assume that they are going to say yes. They can make this assumption only when they have thought the proposition over and have no doubts in their minds that it is fair. If they don't think it is fair, they certainly question whether the other person is going to say yes, and they are reduced to the status of seeking ways of overcoming the other person's objections; they rely on arguments in which they cannot have much faith. Asking an individual to assume a new responsibility for the group should not become a situation in which the team leader sells staff members on assuming a new assignment. It should be, instead, a conference to plan the work ahead and to discuss how the responsibility will be divided. It is looking at the facts together and seeking agreement on the next steps to be taken. On this basis, a conference may actually result in reduced or reassigned responsibilities!

It is evident that getting people to assume responsibility involves helping the staff have a part in deciding upon the work to be done, giving the staff an opportunity to plan and think through problems together, letting the staff assign the responsibilities to its members, making possible constant communication among all members of the working team, and building within the staff a habit of looking at the job distribution and making reassignments when any inequalities exist.

14

THE BEGINNING SUPERVISOR

The first ten months are critical to the long-range effectiveness of supervisors in the school systems where they work. Whether they are supervisors-consultative or supervisors-administrative; whether they are general supervisors, special supervisors, resource teachers, principals, or assistant superintendents, they will create an image with their beginning efforts that will facilitate or hinder their work as supervisors. Therefore, it is desirable that they think about the way they will attempt to work, formulate the theory that will guide their actions, and establish some criteria by which they will judge their progress.

THE FIRST STEPS

The new supervisors may be employed either as supervisors-administrative or supervisors-consultative. Supervisors-administrative would normally have formal responsibility for coordinating programs and, therefore, would have formal authority granted by the organization to facilitate the control of personnel, materials, equipment, and facilities. The use of this authority is critical to the long-range success of new supervisors and is filled with possibilities for facilitating or hindering success.

Part of the problem is that the program must move forward, decisions must be made, and authority must be used; but supervisors may not be ready. They may not know their personnel or organizational needs well enough to take the actions that must be taken. Yet, they will be judged by the outcomes. If early decisions, actions, and use of authority prove to be rewarding to the organization and to members of the organization, then the next attempts at leadership will be more likely to be successful. If, however, early attempts to influence are successful, but fail to produce positive benefits to the organization and/or the members of the organization, the new official leader could lose the esteem of fellow workers, and become less influential in the organization and more dependent on formal sources of power (Bass, 1960). The amount of prestige lost would be related to how critical the decision is to the well-being of the group. Early decisions of great importance to group members that turn out badly could create so much loss of confidence in the leader, or even alienation, that future attempts at leadership could be unsuccessful, or, if forced, could fail from lack of cooperation or even positive resistance.

The new supervisor-administrative may wish to consider the "power with" approach to leadership to solve early problems. This approach requires the sharing of authority and responsibility with the group and has the advantage of the utilization of the talent, creativeness, and experience of group members. It is our position that this approach increases the probability of making decisions that will be rewarding to the group. However, there are dangers involved. The informal group leadership might have vested interest that could be detrimental to the group. But, a broad base of group participation in problem solving should minimize this possible negative outcome.

If new supervisors decide to share leadership and authority, they must be willing to accept the consequences of group decisions and solutions. Their credibility is on the line. The nature of group decisions would have serious consequences for their future efficiency and effectiveness as group leaders. Consultative supervisors are in a different situation. They do not have programs to coordinate and, therefore, they have limited formal authority. But, they must help, support, and provide service for their professional colleagues, which requires informal authority based on their ability and personality characteristics as perceived by the people they wish to help. It is our assumption that the first few months of consultative supervisors are critical to their effectiveness in future years. It is during this time that teachers and other professionals decide whether or not these supervisors have the ability to be helpful and whether they can be trusted as people who care about the teachers with whom they work. How is this relationship achieved?

First, there is no substitute for ability. Supervisors must have ability in the area of group or individual concerns. If they do not have the ability, they must locate sources of help. They must also be willing to make every effort to acquire needed abilities. Teachers can be a great resource for learning new skills and understandings. Interestingly, learning from teachers on a give-and-take basis is an excellent way to establish relationships and credibility. However, trying to fake ability practically never works and can be a disaster to future relationships.

When supervisors have the appropriate ability to help teachers, and when it is used in an effective way, the basis is being developed for future relationships. This kind of work extends beyond the teacher being helped to other teachers in the situation. Conversely, a poor performance with a teacher gets around to other teachers and cuts off opportunities to help.

Second, there is a need for supervisors to be recognized as persons who are trustworthy. This can only be achieved by the supervisor's *work*. Supervisors need to reach out. They need to be around in both a formal and informal sense and on both social and professional occasions. A chance to help is an opportunity to build relationships and demonstrate competence, credibility, and the meaning of interpersonal trust.

Supervisors can reach their positions by two routes. Either they can be promoted from the ranks, or they can be brought into the situation from an outside position. Both routes have their advantages and possible pitfalls.

If official leaders are promoted from the ranks, the staff knows their strengths and weaknesses before they start exercising official leadership. They are members of the group. They must not allow that relationship to change. Their chief problem will be their own behavior. They will have to choose their words much more carefully. They will have to guard against actions that will be mistaken for assumptions of superiority. They will find that exercising leadership from the supervisor's spot requires different procedures from exercising leadership without official status within the group.

When a supervisor is brought in from the outside, first impressions can do much to win acceptance or to build up enormous hurdles that must be overcome.

Out of the first meeting with the staff should develop a feeling that a new official leader is friendly, has a sense of direction, and is willing to learn. Actions that tend to create feelings of antagonism, suspicion, distrust, or the impression that the official leader knows all the answers should be avoided.

Nor should supervisors give the staff the impression that they are out to make a name for themselves. The following excerpt from the letter of a beginning supervisor shows awareness of this pitfall:

> The work here becomes increasingly exciting. Slowly and gradually, teachers are beginning to extend their confidence and enlarge their hopes. What's especially pleasing is that they are not pinning their hopes on me, but on themselves. In spite of this, however, I'm centering most of my activities in the system.
>
> The state executive committee proposed me to represent them on the national council. I asked them to reconsider the nomination. I have the feeling that as much as I'd like the growth that might come from this work, it might seriously impair my work here. I've had to overcome a certain amount of wariness in the teachers. They are afraid of the possibility of my using them and their work in the system as a stepping-stone of some sort. Nothing personal—just the result of sad experience. While I think few, if any, feel that way now, I don't want to give any reason for believing there is a possible element of opportunism in my work.

One way to get staff members to work for group goals is to let them know that their help is needed. One of the first duties of supervisors is to make clear that the program is not theirs, but rather that of the staff; that any progress that will be made will be progress of the staff. Supervisors are there to help staff members develop the program, and they can help only if staff members indicate to them ways in which they can make a contribution. They need to recognize that they will make mistakes because they are new, but that these mistakes will be fewer if they have the guidance of the staff.

Many young supervisors experience difficulty because they fail to win the support of older, more experienced members of the staff who look upon the younger person as inexperienced and immature. Unless supervisors go out of their way to let the older members know that they intend to make use of their experience and knowledge, the chances are great that the older members will not give their full support to the program. One of the surest ways to secure their assistance is to seek out information and help from them and let them know that they have great responsibility for giving clear interpretations of the values of the present program; and to let them know that the staff needs their ideas, by utilizing these ideas.

One of the sources of help for a new supervisor is his or her predecessor. Even though the person who was in the position before is being relieved of responsibility and feels bitterness toward those responsible, he or she will have much helpful information for the new supervisor. The newcomer will want to secure the former leader's analysis of the situation. Although this information may be biased, it should be evaluated to see what guidance may be obtained from it. Particularly helpful would be the outgoing supervisor's estimate of the strengths and weaknesses of various staff members, description of the plan of operation of the program underway, and statements concerning the pitfalls and problems involved.

It is important to put the staff at ease. It is just as important to take this step as it is to devote the first part of an interview to making the other person feel at ease. Although the need for putting the other person at ease in an interview is widely recognized, the need for spending the first phase of work together in getting acquainted and making persons feel secure in their relationships with each other is not as well understood.

To put the staff at ease, one of the first things an official leader will want to do is to meet as many of the staff as possible on a social basis. This process will give the staff members a chance to learn that the new supervisor is accessible and easy to know. It will give the official leader a chance to observe the personal qualities that will hinder or promote the socialization of the staff. Staff members will be glad to know that the offical leader likes people and wants their friendship. They will try to discover whether they can respect him or her as a person as well as a professional leader. Professional leadership is not enough. Staff members need the type of relaxed, tension-free social relationships that enable them to accept, understand, and work with one another. The staff watches to see whether the official leader contributes to this type of emotional environment.

Another aspect of putting the staff at ease is to start with the assumption that all members of the staff can contribute to the group. The supervisor will want to start by looking for the good qualities that can be utilized. As recognition is given to the positive side of the existing program, the confidence of staff members will grow in their relationship with the new supervisor. An analysis of weak points at the beginning of working together will alienate some members of the staff who would otherwise be willing to give the new official leader a chance. Starting out with an accent on the positive serves the same purpose as discussing common interests in the beginning of an interview.

If official leaders stress their roles as coordinators rather than as dictators of policy, they will help put people at ease. Teachers will then feel certain that no one is going to come into the situation and institute change more rapidly than they can accept it. Emphasis on the coordinator role makes it clear that the supervisor conceives of the job as a service function rather than as a directing function.

The initiation of change is a critical problem for new supervisors. They may not know the situation as well as they should. Staff members may be insecure and lack confidence in the new leader. Change is difficult in the most favorable of circumstances for leaders and followers, but problems will probably be multiplied and intensified in situations where the supervisor is new. The next section discusses the change process in depth.

APPROACH TO CHANGE

Any change should be made on the basis of evaluation. New supervisors will want to approach the program from an evaluation point of view. They will want to collect the facts, pass judgment with the staff on these facts, and make plans for revision in terms of the judgments made. Through this approach, they will show that they are not making the changes just to be different. They will emphasize their respect for evidence. They will demonstrate their respect for the members of the staff by recognizing the effort and work that the staff has put into the existing program. They must remember that the program they find represents the best thinking and effort that the staff has been able to achieve. Any negative judgment by the new supervisor without evidence that the staff has helped develop that judgment could be perceived as destructive criticism of the staff members as persons. It could result in antagonism and alienation.

By following the cooperative evaluation approach, the new supervisor is making clear to the staff that the program is the staff's program and its responsibility. This approach keeps the staff from feeling that programs belong to official leaders and that they change completely as official leaders are changed.

New supervisors should listen more than they talk. Persons going into a new situation will make mistakes based on lack of information about the job. The more experienced members of the staff will know many details of the methods of operation that the supervisor cannot hope to know. Foolish statements based on this lack of information will put new supervisors in the unfavorable position of having to correct or revise any mistakes that they have made.

An industrial engineer was placed in charge of the sales department of a large concern. One of the members of the department who had hoped to be appointed supervisor came to the engineer and asked how he should conduct the mailing campaign that was then in progress. The new supervisor wisely recommended that the older employee go ahead with the program the way it had been planned until the new supervisor had become thoroughly acquainted with the department and its operation.

Another supervisor in the same organization proceeded on an entirely different basis. When he met his staff for the first time, he stated publicly that he did not like the way the program was being conducted and from now on everything would be done differently. He put his declaration into effect immediately. Although his staff went along with his program, they did not thoroughly accept it, and as soon as the man moved to a new job, they began working for the return of the practices that had been used in the department before he came. This man never thoroughly sóld his staff on his program and his procedure, because he had discarded without a fair evaluation a system to which they had contributed and to which they felt loyalty.

Supervisors should become acquainted with the program in which they are to work. If they do most of the talking, their chances of becoming acquainted with it are decreased.

If supervisors conceive of their job as one of helping the staff, they will want to start with the problems that the members of the staff have. This approach will be a way of demonstrating both a desire to help and their acceptance of the value of the program that the staff has developed. New supervisors have difficulty when they tell the staff which problems are important in the school. They can best create a situation in which the staff will bring its important problems into the open, and in which the supervisor may be of assistance in helping the staff solve those problems.

One technique for bringing the problems of a school to the surface was followed by a new superintendent. He wrote to all the teachers in the system and asked them to list the problems on which they felt the staff should be working. Using the statements of the teachers, he compiled a list of the twenty-five problems mentioned most frequently. He requested the staff to select those problems from the list thus created to serve as the basis for an in-service training program that was to be instituted in the school system that year.

A new supervisor was starting his first job and decided to begin by visiting each school and talking with each principal and teacher on an individual basis. The purpose of the contact was not just to get acquainted but also, more importantly, to listen to the concerns and needs of teachers. The supervisor attempted to develop understanding of the hopes and aspirations of the teachers and their plans for achieving their goals. This interaction became the basis for establishing specific ways that the supervisor could be helpful.

In talking with the staff to learn about the program and the personnel involved, the new supervisor must be careful not to build up a caste system in the faculty. All persons should have equal access to the door of a new supervisor. If it becomes apparent that the supervisor is depending upon certain members of the staff for information and guidance, the teachers not included in this inner circle will begin to form resistance groups to the program being evolved by the unofficial cabinet. This condition is particularly likely to arise if the stated functions of the persons to whom the new official leader turns for advice do not include leadership in portions of the program about which decisions are made.

One way to avoid the development of feeling that the advice of only a portion of the staff is sought is to make many decisions in an open conference. Thereby, the staff will have the opportunity to see how the supervisor brings out all the evidence, encourages everyone to listen to all data and opinions, considers with the staff all the possible solutions suggested, and seeks consensus before a decision is reached. Even though such conferences are time-consuming, they will ultimately pay dividends and will be effective in building morale and saving time. The staff will acquire confidence in the way the official leader works and will develop a trust in the fairness of decisions that are made when they are not present.

Another important task of new supervisors is to persuade teachers that they know that it is their job to release the talents of those with whom they work. They must let teachers know that they want suggestions on steps they can take to remove hindrances to creative thinking.

The official leader helps set the pattern of work in the organization. If new supervisors want members of the staff to be on the job on time and to work efficiently, they must set that pattern from the moment they begin their new job. If the leader is prompt, hard working, and thorough; if he or she sets an example of coming to work early and not leaving before the day is over, the staff will more likely assume the same responsibility. A new executive director was appointed in an organization in which tardiness and leaving the job early were a consistent pattern. The new official leader made it a habit to get to work half an hour earlier than anyone else and to stay half an hour after the last person left. Without a word being spoken, the staff began to work a full day. The example was more forceful than anything the supervisor could have said.

As they enter a new job, supervisors must avoid any change in their personalities. New responsibility must not be allowed to interfere with friendliness and a relaxed manner. It is so easy to become overwhelmed by new duties and responsibilities, so that new formality, hurriedness, and hardness may begin to appear in the supervisor's actions.

One exception to being natural is being more careful about chance remarks. Comments of supervisors have much wider implication than remarks made by other members of the staff. Much humor in ordinary situations is at the expense of others. Belittling remarks by staff members are accompanied by a smile and are usually accepted in the same spirit in which they are given. When such remarks are made by a supervisor, they have a far different implication. As persons step into a supervisory role, they have a much greater effect on the future of their coworkers. Remarks made by a supervisor may be misunderstood. Remarks that are made in jest may be taken seriously. Statements that are understood perfectly by everyone present in a given situation may cause much misunderstanding when they are told to persons who were not present. Care must be exercised to avoid the type of statement that will be misunderstood if it is repeated out of the context in which it was spoken. A remark made in good faith may be twisted by repeated tellings until it becomes a barbed threat by the time it reaches the person concerned. Persons in positions of responsibility must be constantly on their guard to be sure they say what they mean and do not depend upon inflection of the voice or upon gestures to convey the impressions they intend.

The effectiveness of new supervisors is at least partly a function of the organizational climate in which they work. Organizational climate refers to the way members of the organization "fit" together and fit with organizational goals. An important task of the new supervisor is to work toward a climate in which curriculum development, instruction, and student learning can continue to improve. What are the qualities of a school situation in which a supervisor can hope to contribute to instructional improvement?

THE NEW SUPERVISOR'S ASSUMPTIONS ABOUT CHANGE

It is our position that supervisors who operate from an explicit set of assumptions about change enhance their effectiveness as coordinators and facilitators of change. Such a set of assumptions not only provides direction and consistency for the behavior of new supervisors in the change process, but it also provides a basis for evaluation of that change in their behavior. The statement of assumptions should help answer certain questions about change. What is change? How does change occur? What can a new supervisor do to bring about change? What strategies of change should be used? We feel that the following assumptions about change are worthy of consideration by new supervisors.

First, it is possible to think of organizational change occurring in social systems. Therefore, all that we know about social systems including their origin, growth, change and improvement can be applied to the improvement of instruction. It is the facilitation and coordination of this process that gives direction to the change behavior of the new supervisor.

Second, change occurs in programs and institutions as people change. What people believe, how they think, and the skill that they develop all determine what happens as they live and operate. A change in policy statement or in an organizational chart will mean nothing unless the people who operate in terms of it believe that the change has occurred and that it makes a difference. People are what they believe. Their beliefs govern their behavior.

Third, people change as they change their perception of themselves, their role, or the situation. People do what they do because of the way they see themselves in the situation. As their picture of themselves in the situation changes, they operate differently. And the situation changes because they have changed. If persons feel that they are more adequate, they begin to behave differently. If they see that their role has not been what they thought, they tend to live up to their new expectations in the situation. If they gain greater understanding of the realities of the situation, or become less sure of this reality, their behavior changes. Therefore, if a person hopes to bring about change, he or she places effort on helping people change their perception of themselves, of their roles, or of the situation.

Fourth, people change as they interact with each other on matters that concern them. People do not change because someone else wishes they would, or because someone tells them they must. People change themselves as they become involved in matters that are important to them. They are affected by the comments or the actions of a person in a situation that is important to them; the way others behave toward them affects their perception of themselves or their roles. The additional facts that others bring to them about the situation change their perception of the situation. If a change agent hopes to bring about change in people, he or she seeks to create the kind of situation where they will interact with others.

Fifth, desirable change occurs when people intelligently examine the issues that divide them. Individuals do not see the situation, themselves, or their role in the same way as other people see them. Each person approaches and interprets a given situation uniquely. Out of this uniqueness of perception comes the difference that leads to conflict. Whether people grow as a result of differences, or whether they regress and withdraw depends upon the way the situation develops. If people can be helped to objectively examine and thoroughly explore the data and the alternate courses of action, desirable change will occur. If, on the other hand, people make emotional, hasty attempts to resolve their differences, or they are not brought into contact with a wide variety of data and courses of action, the change that occurs will probably not be desirable because it will be unintelligent.

Sixth, the place of the supervisor is to develop an organization, a structure, and a procedure through which the next steps for any given group can be intelligently considered. This is the major function of official leaders who hope to bring about intelligent change. They cannot produce lasting change by coercion, or bribery, or threat. People will live with this kind of force only until they are able to extricate themselves from the situation. But if a change agent wants the change to be lasting, he or she will bring it about by creating the kind of situation where people can interact in an intelligent manner about problems that concern them. Attention will be given to the kind of structure that enables such interaction, and to guiding the procedure that frees intelligence to collect data concerning a variety of alternatives and to make choices in terms of consequences.

In Chapter 6 of this book, the authors assumed that supervisors and the systems members with whom they worked could

1. define, evaluate, change, and improve system goals;
2. define, evaluate, change, and induce internal and external forces that produce tensions that either maintain or disrupt system equilibrium;
3. utilize scientific problem solving to help the system achieve a new level of equilibration or change that will improve the system's current state of being and its ability to continue to improve; and

4. utilize concepts, theories, and principles of communication, leadership, releasing human potential, and change process to improve system change and stability.

The supervisor, in applying these assumptions in his or her attempt to create change in the public school program, will recognize that there are internal and external forces that work for change in a public institution. Pressure groups in the world, nation, and community seek to bring about change in school programs. The government at the local, the state, and the national levels attempts to influence the direction of education. Boards of education attempt to establish policy and to give direction. Administrators pressure for change. Teachers are making their purposes and needs felt. Students are a real force working for change. There is no question that change will occur. The question is really whether or not the change will be intelligent and in a desired direction. Haphazard change will not produce the most desirable change. Decisions in such situations will be made by power rather than by intelligence. Where power is the determining factor, the change may be in the direction of advantage for a few at the expense of the many.

An institutional structure must be created that makes possible free and open consideration of the alternatives, and choice based on evidence and the prevailing values. This kind of structure means that all who will be involved should have the opportunity to suggest items for consideration, to supply data, to advance alternatives, and to ask that the course of action taken be an implementation of the prevailing values.

Of course, it is recognized that if the values are wrong, the direction of change will be wrong. Those who hold different values will see the direction of change as regression rather than progress. If, however, those who will be affected have an opportunity to participate in the decision making, and if ideas and values are brought into the open for evaluation and are tested by all concerned, the choices made about values will be the most intelligent that people in the situation can make.

One of the real problems is deciding which people shall be involved in which decision. It is important to define the areas of decisions and the degrees of freedom of choice to be allocated to each decision-making element of the organization. The safest criterion that the writers know is that those who will be affected by a decision should be involved. In a school situation, this is obviously an impossible criterion to apply in all cases. The school system must fall back on representative participation in decision making. This means that the official leader must be concerned with the structure that determines the method of choice and the kind of communication channels that exist between those represented and their representative. If the communication is not good and not two-way, participation in the decision making by all will fail.

Implicit in what is being said is that the structure that is created must allow people to be deeply involved in decision making through their representatives. If the supervisory staff hopes to bring about lasting change in the program, the primary concern must be with the degree of involvement. If people change only to the extent that they are involved, the change agent must put his or her primary focus in examining the structure or the degree to which people have an opportunity to participate and feel a responsibility for the decision taken. The supervisor's assumptions about change serve as a frame of reference against which all decisions, actions, and the change process can be evaluated.

LOYALTY TO IDEAS

The new official leader must win acceptance and respect. He or she cannot demand loyalty to himself or herself. A former college professor went into a job as the head of a department in a national organization. On the first day, he called the staff together and opened the meeting with the remark, "I expect all of you to be loyal to me." One of the members of the staff spoke up immediately, "I do not know whether or not I can be loyal to you." The college professor, taken aback by the response, asked why; the staff member replied that he would develop loyalty if he found the supervisor deserved it.

An industrial relations director, in discussing the problem of winning the support of a staff, put it in another way: "Loyalty is a two-way proposition, and a supervisor must be the one to demonstrate it first. Workers are loyal when the supervisor earns their loyalty by being loyal to them."

In the cooperative approach, loyalty to an individual official leader is not the quality desired. Teachers must develop loyalty to the values that they accept, and loyalty to the program that emerges through the implementation of these values. Formal leaders should not be concerned about whether people develop a personal loyalty to them. Staff members should be unfettered by personal loyalties that keep them from taking issue with leaders when the leaders violate the values of the group. Leaders should seek, instead of loyalty, acceptance as worthwhile contributors to the development of a good program, and respect for their abilities and skills that make the school more effective. Acceptance and respect are built through the way the leader works. It is a longtime proposition.

ASSUMPTIONS THAT CAUSE
DIFFICULTY FOR SUPERVISORS

A new supervisor should know that persons in positions of official leadership have found themselves in difficulty in the past because they have operated on the basis of false assumptions about the nature of human beings, human groups, communication, and learning. Some of these trouble-causing assumptions will now be examined.

1. *Appointment to a status position gives one leadership.* A principal in a midwestern city was appointed to the position of assistant superintendent in charge of instruction. In one of his first meetings with a large group of teachers, he began

to tell them what he wanted them to do. Several teachers raised objections. The man lost his temper and told the group in angry words that he was the assistant superintendent and that they would do what he said.

This man assumed that teachers should and would follow him because of his appointment. He did not realize that leadership is earned and does not come automatically with the title. Two years later, the assistant superintendent was replaced.

2. *Communication follows the organizational chart.* An organizational chart is a picture of someone's wishes. It may be drawn to coincide with the flow of communication, but it does not always reflect the true organization or the true flow of communication. Unless supervisors recognize that decisions are made in both formal and informal situations and unless they discover the real channels of communication, chances are they will be ineffective.

3. *Loyalty is to persons rather than ideas.* Many official leaders become unhappy and begin to distrust the members of the staff because they make this assumption. They become insecure because they cannot understand why persons who are their friends, persons they have helped, persons who have stood shoulder-to-shoulder with them in previous battles, do not support them in the present situation. They feel that their colleagues are being treacherous and disloyal when actually the colleagues are being moral and are living up to their values. A concept of loyalty that requires a person to agree with the official leader and support him or her on all issues weakens the leader's self-confidence and leads to disruption of the group.

4. *Staff members should adjust to the official leader.* When supervisors assume that they can be moody, nagging, and inconsiderate, and that others must still work with them, the rocks of failure are immediately ahead. They may retain their position, but they will lose their leadership. Leadership is bestowed by a group upon an individual who is sensitive to the feelings of its members.

5. *Feelings are not important.* It is easy to say that staff members should be adult and not become disturbed over an action. But saying what should be does not make it true. The way a staff member feels about an action by the supervisor is more important than the action itself. If a teacher interprets an action as a reprimand or a recrimination, his or her future behavior is governed by that interpretation, not by the leader's intention. Unless supervisors constantly attempt to place themselves in the other person's position and to see how actions look from there, their leadership is in jeopardy.

6. *Formal leadership is decision making.* A principal from an eastern state objected vigorously to the idea of sharing decisions. He said, "My job is making decisions. If you take that function away, I have no function." His point of view is one that is held by many.

The concept of "power over" has been a part of human culture for many years. It is only as supervisors begin to discover that sharing decisions is a more effective way to release the power of a group, that they see a different function for the leader. Conceiving of the leader's role as that of decision maker is only possible in situations where teachers are willing to surrender their professional judgment.

7. *The status quo can be maintained.* When people try to keep the program as it is, they are attempting the impossible. People change day by day, and the program continues to be dynamic. When leaders fail to recognize this fact and do not plan for growth, they are left with the choice of either repressing change or withdrawing from active leadership.

8. *People can be told what their problems are.* A high school principal wanted

the staff to work on the student-activity problem. The teachers felt they would profit more by studying techniques of pupil-teacher planning. For four days of a preschool planning conference, the struggle continued. At last the principal capitulated.

Even if he had won, the work would not have been productive. People must believe there is a real problem before they are willing to give their full energy to a project. When supervisors attempt to tell people what the problems are on which they should work, they encounter resistance.

9. *People grow by being told.* In one inquiry, when teachers were asked where they secured the new ideas they put into practice, they placed the suggestions of supervisors twenty-seventh on the list. This discouraging condition is not the result of lack of ideas among supervisors. It is a reflection of how we learn. Teachers learn when they are ready. When they want help on a problem, and when they discover a solution by reading or by talking with someone of their choosing, they learn.

10. *People can be forced to be democratic.* Unless a staff wants to participate in policy formation, going through the process is fruitless. Democracy cannot be achieved in a staff by autocratic means. Frequently a staff rebels and accuses the official leader of asking it to do his or her work and to assume his or her responsibilities. Securing staff participation is a gradual process in which the official leader continues to offer to share the decisions he or she has the authority to make.

11. *Actions between an official leader and a staff member are individual.* A Texas principal spent many hours attempting to help a beginning teacher become a successful one. Because the teacher was an attractive woman and the principal was a man, other teachers began to talk. Although this supervisor was making a professional effort to help an individual teacher, it adversely affected the work of the entire school.

The assumptions just listed conflict with the implications of existing research. They constitute stumbling blocks to supervisors who continue to accept them.

WORKING CONDITIONS
PROMOTED

The effectiveness of new supervisors is at least partly a function of the organizational climate in which they work. Organizational climate refers to the way members of the organization "fit" together and with organizational goals. An important task of the new supervisor is to work for a climate in which curriculum development, instruction, and student learning can continue to improve. What are the qualities of a school situation in which a supervisor can hope to contribute to instructional improvement?

1. *Each member values himself or herself and others.* When individuals dislike themselves or feel inadequate, they attempt to hurt themselves or to find solace in proving themselves superior to others. Either type of action decreases the power of a group. The productivity of a staff is increased when its members take steps to enhance the sense of self-worth felt by other staff members, by recognizing their contributions and supporting their efforts.

2. *A deep concern for the welfare and feeling of each individual exists.* A superintendent in a western school system faced a problem that was serious enough to

cost him his job. As he sat in his office trying to decide what to do, he put his head in his hands for five full minutes. An observer might have guessed that he was worried about losing his position. When he raised his head, his questions were: "What will this do to John? How will Sally feel about this action?" His constant concern was how the individuals involved would feel. The success of his solution was to be measured in terms of people's emotions as well as other factors.

Such concern for the feeling and welfare of each individual has its effect on the group. In such a situation, teachers feel more secure and are more concerned with the feelings of their students and the improvement of the school program.

3. *Members of the staff feel that they belong to the group.* When individuals do not feel that the other members of the group accept them or want to be associated with them, the chances are great that they will not be able to make much of a contribution to the school. They will be so involved in discovering ways to become accepted that they will not be able to concentrate on staff projects or on improving the quality of their work. Or they may reverse the procedure. They may be so resentful about being excluded that they will engage in harmful and aggressive activity toward other group members. Supervisors will want to do the things that help each person feel "free to come and safe to go." They will strive to help each staff member to feel that he or she may enter any formal group without a sense of intruding and that he or she may leave without fear of being talked about in a derogatory manner.

4. *People trust each other.* When there is no trust, individuals must be on the defensive and more concerned about protecting themselves and their status than with seeking more effective and productive ways of working. Trust is the foundation of communication. Unless we trust other persons, we resist their ideas and refuse to share with them our deep convictions. Unless trust is established, persons in the situation will deal only with superficial topics or attempt to outmaneuver others.

Trust cannot be achieved by official leaders stating that they want to be trusted. Trust is something that is earned, and each action of the individual affects it. It works two ways. If we hope to see it prevail in the staff with which we work, we must be the first to demonstrate it.

The way in which official leaders work with group members demonstrates their faith or their lack of faith; it determines whether group members will trust them or trust each other. One of the best tests we can apply to our own actions is to ask these questions: Does the step that we are about to take make future working together possible? Will the action increase the possibility of honest communication? If an action fails to meet these tests, it probably is not a good supervisory procedure.

5. *The administration shares responsibility for making the decisions within its authority.* The simple process of sharing decisions is the most powerful tool a leader has. It is the key to the securing of leadership, the assumption of responsibility, the acceptance of assignments, and the development of high morale.

Any decision within the authority of the official leader may be shared, but care should be exercised to distinguish between those decisions that the official leader can make and those that are made by a higher authority, such as the board of education. Failure to make the boundaries of authority clear may cause frustration and may lead the group to reject further participation in decision making.

If there are certain decisions within the authority of official leaders that they wish to retain, they should make these clear to the staffs with which they work. Such action will be more acceptable than pretending to share all decisions and then vetoing decisions in areas in which the leader feels the staff to be incompetent.

6. *Each person can maintain his or her integrity.* Permissiveness is the foundation of self-respect. Unless persons are free to express their disagreement, the situation

is one in which they cannot behave morally; they cannot work in terms of the values they hold. Persons who must forfeit their integrity to hold their job cannot value themselves or those who force them to debase themselves. Growth and increased contributions come only when individuals value both themselves and their colleagues.

7. *Increased self-direction and self-improvement by each staff member is sought.* Although it seems contradictory, a group grows in strength as its members become increasingly self-directing. As staff members define together what they hope to accomplish, and plan the procedures by which these goals will be achieved, each individual becomes better able to make valid decisions. As he or she has access to more information and becomes more familiar with the thinking of the group, an individual develops the security that enables him or her to make judgments without turning to someone else. Confusion and indecision are diminished.

8. *Information is available to all.* A staff cannot be expected to make wise decisions if it does not have access to relevant information. Inaccessibility of information, caused by the administration's refusal to share it or by clogged channels of communication, may cause the group to make a poor decision. And a poor decision results in loss of faith in its own ability or in its leadership.

Because of the position of official leaders, bulletins and other documents come to them. They attend meetings in which information is shared by the administration. It is difficult for them to know which information to share. They do not want to burden or bore staff members with unnecessary and unimportant details. But screening is dangerous. Sometimes the information they consider unimportant will be important to certain members of the staff.

9. *Ideas are considered the property of the group.* When ideas are identified with people, decisions are too often made on the basis of the proponent's status rather than on the inherent value of the ideas. If ideas are considered a resource of the group, teachers share them freely. But if proposals and practices are constantly related to the individual who originates them, selfishness begins to operate. For example, at one major teaching-training institution, the staff members are careful to keep the new materials they develop away from other staff members. Materials are hidden in filing cabinets and desk drawers. Each person wants to be sure that he or she keeps control of the innovation until it is recognized by the total staff as his or her contribution. In another teacher-training institution, great emphasis is placed on joint planning, and staff members frequently share the materials they develop. Very infrequently is any material labeled with the name of an individual staff member. In the first situation, suspicion and jealousy prevail. In the second, a spirit of cooperation and shared creativity dominate.

10. *Loyalty is to ideas and values, not to persons.* This condition is closely related to the one just stated. If disagreement with the official leader is considered disloyalty, the only type of creativity that can exist within the staff is improvement within the areas in which the official leader has interest.

11. *Teachers speak out, and the administration capitalizes on their ideas.* In some situations, the persons with ideas that differ from those of the official leader are considered troublemakers. They find themselves unwanted in the school. They are ignored in faculty meetings, and if they persist, attempts are made to belittle them and their ideas. The easy path for them is to remain quiet and to accept the policies of the administration.

If the supervisor wants to release the full potential of the staff, this procedure cannot be accepted. Insight comes as differences are examined. If all members of the faculty believe the same thing, progress is unlikely, because of the complacency that develops as a result of the uniformity of ideas. If morale and a sense of group

unity have been developed to the point where the staff feels that it belongs together, disagreement is not dangerous; it will not destroy the group; it is a source of
creativeness.

12. *Decision by consensus is sought.* A decision leads to action when the group
members are convinced of its value. If only a majority is in favor of the proposed
course of action, the full power of the group will not support it. Decision by
majority is only second best. When time and the skill of the group permit, achieving
consensus insures the group's total commitment to the enterprise.

13. *Teachers and administrators have the opportunity to tell each other frankly
what they expect of each other and what kind of help they would like to receive
from each other.* At a principal's conference in a midwestern city, each principal
brought one member of his or her teaching staff. Small groups of teachers and
principals were formed, with no teacher in the same group with his or her principal.
For the major portion of the week, the members of each small group considered
what they expected and the help they wanted. New understandings, more common
perception of roles, and more satisfying ways of working resulted.

14. *The staff accepts responsibility for the decisions made and is willing to live
with the consequences.* Participation in decision making has little meaning if it is
divorced from the responsibility of living up to the decision. If it is not expected
that all will be bound by the decision, behavior will be irresponsible. Every staff
member should expect that the official leader will hold every member of the group,
including himself or herself, accountable for fulfilling the obligation imposed by
the decision reached.

15. *Creativeness in teaching and coordinating is encouraged, supported, and
rewarded.* In light of present knowledge, the conditions that have been listed here
should increase the probability of staff productivity. They are recommended for
consideration by new supervisors.

When teachers have assurance of their own worth and of their jobs' importance,
a sense of belonging to the group, and a trust in the official leadership, they are
ready to attempt to improve instruction. The official leader can assist in improving
the teaching-learning situation in many ways, such as

seeking agreement of purposes.

making provision for sharing of ideas.

stimulating and assisting the staff to prepare self-evaluation checklists.

keeping all teachers well supplied with up-to-date materials.

asking for proof of why a new method should not be tried as frequently as
for reasons why it should.

encouraging teachers to develop distinctive classrooms that reflect the work
and activities of their classes.

recognizing persons who are trying new procedures.

establishing a petty-cash fund for the purchase of expendable materials.

providing in-service training experience in self-expression in a variety of
media.

helping teachers develop techniques for evaluating a variety of types of
pupil growth.

organizing staff meetings around the study of teacher problems and the
improvement of the school program.

using workshops as a procedure for program change.

assisting with the experimentation that grows out of a workshop.

encouraging pupil-teacher planning.

encouraging teachers to meet and plan the curriculum with parents.

encouraging self-evaluation of teachers and their classes.

using faculty meetings to discuss evaluation techniques that individual teachers have found helpful.

stimulating intervisitation as a method of providing more data on which to base judgments.

providing feedback for teachers, based on observation and analysis of their teaching situations.

providing a source of new ideas for the improvement of instruction.

helping, supporting, and servicing teachers who are attempting to implement new ideas.

recognizing outstanding teacher achievement.

facilitating the processes through which teachers help each other.

SELF-EVALUATION PROCEDURES
FOR SUPERVISORS

Self-evaluation is ongoing. A man takes a furtive glance at the toes of his shoes as he goes by the shoeshine person. A woman takes out her compact to see whether her lipstick is still as it should be. Persons judge themselves against unstated standards.

People do not, however, take stock as frequently of the way they do their jobs. They are more inclined to let others judge them. They feel that they can tell how well they are doing if they get a satisfactory number of promotions and raises and if the people working with them are happy and fond of them. Many of them will even refuse to evaluate their work when they are not pleasing their superiors or coworkers. They escape by blaming the other person for their inadequacies.

Few people do the type of work they are capable of doing. They work at less-than-full efficiency because they have not analyzed their position and evaluated their work in terms of the requirements.

Supervisors need evaluation for both personal and professional reasons. To preserve their own self-respect, they need to seek ways of increasing their strengths and decreasing their weaknesses. To grow professionally and to be sure that they are doing an adequate job, they need to establish goals or criteria and evaluate their actions by them.

What are the ways they can judge their work? At least two phases should be examined constantly: How well do they manage their activities? What are the results they achieve? Let's first examine the way they work. The following questions have significance:

1. *Do I set up a schedule of activities for each week?* Supervisory work will control supervisors unless they make some attempt to organize it. No one can do

a hundred tasks at once, and supervisors constantly have that many ahead of them. The tasks seem overwhelming unless supervisors list one-by-one the things they are going to do and eliminate the others from their mind until the immediate task is finished. Setting up a schedule of work is a way of freeing themselves from the burden of a workload, because it enables them to carry only a portion of it at one time.

2. *Am I flexible in my schedule without becoming disturbed?* Schedules are made to be broken. They constitute the best organizational hypothesis at the start of the day. They give stability and form to the day. But they are not sacred. As the day progresses, the supervisor gets more information, and new situations arise that render unwise the schedule he or she had originally planned.

3. *Do I get upset when my plans do not go as I hoped?* When people plan cooperatively, the plans developed are rarely the ones they initially brought to the situation. Plans are often revised as more people participate in studying and executing them. It is to be expected that plans will be changed in the light of other people's thinking and in the light of inaccuracy in predicting the outcomes of action. If supervisors are disturbed by the failure of their plans to develop exactly as they had devised them, they probably are more concerned with controlling people than they want to admit.

4. *Do I check off the things I have accomplished?* Everyone needs a sense of achievement. Records that show the completion of tasks a person has established give this satisfaction. Failure to record the things done continues the burden. Each task finished remains a part of the mental load he or she must carry unless there is a way of recording its accomplishment and forgetting it.

5. *Do I allow my feelings to be hurt?* When supervisors are suspicious of others and their actions, when they spend a large portion of their time trying to guess the hidden motives that underlie the actions of others, when they view actions of others as threats, they are displaying insecurity. To exert leadership, a supervisor must be the type of person in whom others can place confidence. If they are insecure, afraid, or suspicious, they decrease the strength of the group of which they are a part.

6. *Am I able to take criticism?* This criterion is related to the preceding one. A weak, insecure person is threatened by criticism from others. Instead of using criticism as information that helps him or her grow, he or she tries to avoid it and fights against those who offer it.

Some persons are able to take criticism from their superiors, but not from individuals they consider to have less rank or importance. Two factors may account for this condition. The first is their expectation. Their stereotype of a superior may be a person who tells them what to do, how to do it, and how well it has been done. When criticism comes from a superior, it is the expected thing and not a threat. The person with less status, on the other hand, may be stereotyped as an individual who takes orders and is in no position to criticize. Second, they may have feelings of superiority toward persons of less status. They may believe that they hold their present position because of superior intelligence and ability. Either of these feelings deprives them of access to the intelligence of a large percentage of those with whom they work and of the opportunity to provide real leadership for them.

7. *Am I able to put myself in the other person's position?* In supervision, persons work through the efforts of others. They succeed or fail according to the success or failure of those with whom they work. To be effective necessitates that they empathize with others. They need to be able to see the way in which difficulties,

purposes, surprises, and actions look to others. As they approximate the way others feel about the events of the day, they enhance their ability to plan and work with them. If they are not able to put themselves in the other person's shoes, their actions may be a constant threat to others without their knowing it.

8. *Am I making a sincere effort to learn more about the staff?* Much of a supervisor's success in placing himself or herself in the other person's position depends upon knowing a lot about the other person. If supervisors do not want to know about their colleagues, they probably will not have much empathy for them. It is difficult for a supervisor to understand a teacher's reaction to the lack of a salary increase, if the supervisor does not know that the teacher has five children and a mother and father whom he or she helps to support. If supervisors are not taking the steps that will help them learn how they can help the people around them, the probability that they will be successful supervisors is decreased.

9. *Do I consult those who will be affected by an action before I take it?* Action that is taken without consultation is frequently misunderstood. If supervisors want to be sure that those who will be affected by a step that they take will accept it, they need to provide an opportunity for them to have it explained and for them to react to the proposal. By telling the supervisor how they feel about it, the teachers suggest revisions that should be made in the proposed procedure. Furthermore, individuals who will be affected will have a greater sense of commitment to the change, because they have had a chance to express their opinions about it and to propose revisions that would make it more acceptable to them. Even though supervisors are not able to adapt the action to the interests of all, they know the risks and are then in a better position to make a decision about whether the gamble is a good one.

10. *Do I live up to commitments?* If supervisors want people to have faith in them, it is necessary for those people to be able to rely on the supervisor's word. When a decision has been reached in a group of which they are a part, staff members have a right to expect that the commitment will be honored. If staff time is spent reaching a decision, and then the supervisor does not put into action the agreements reached, he or she breeds disillusionment and dissatisfaction.

Now let's turn to the ways of evaluating what we accomplish. The measure of a supervisor's success lies in the worthwhile change he or she is able to effect. The supervisor's contribution should be evaluated in terms of the desired outcomes of his or her work. The following questions are examples of outcomes. We feel supervisors should develop their own criteria based on their own values.

1. *How many more teachers are experimenting?* Teachers grow as they try new procedures and measure the results. If supervisors are effective, teachers are trying more new things than they were a year ago. If a supervisor is not effective, more teachers will have discontinued their search for better ways of teaching and will be following lesson plans and procedures that they developed last year or several years before. As supervisors look around in the schools in which they work, they should find more faculty groups attempting to develop better evaluation procedures, seeking to improve the living in the community, and searching for better ways of meeting the emotional needs of youngsters. They should see more faculties seriously attempting to measure the results of their innovations, rather than carrying out hunches without any attempt to collect evidence concerning the results. If a supervisor's work has been effective, a greater number of teachers will be basing their

decisions on the scientific approach and will be spending time seeking evidence and basing conclusions on it.

2. *Has there been an increase in the calls for help in thinking through problems?* This does not mean an increase in calls for answers, because if people are coming more and more for answers, they are increasing their dependence and not developing their leadership. Calls that indicate that people value our thinking as they look at a problem, want our help as they analyze the various facets of a problem, and value our ideas as they plan possible courses of action and make selections are the kinds of evidence for which we want to look.

3. *Has there been a change in the nature of the problems presented?* For example, are people bringing fewer problems that deal with how to do something and fewer questions that deal with interpretation of policy? Are they moving toward types of problems that call for thinking together about the application of values and principles held? If people are asking the supervisor more and more questions about how he or she interprets policy, then he or she is not getting anywhere in this matter of spreading leadership and encouraging the emergence of other leadership; if they are asking specifically how to do something, this behavior is not the kind of growth the supervisor should try to achieve for professional people. Supervision should develop people who are able to supply their own creative ways of applying the principles and values to which they are committed.

4. *Is there an increased demand in the staff for professional materials?* Are more people asking for professional materials on certain topics? Is there more pressure within the staff for an adequate professional library? Are people sharing their magazines and books? Although reading professional books is not an end in itself, the number of teachers who are interested enough to sample what is being published in their field is an index to the extent of professional alertness in the staff. Are more new professional books available? Has the circulation increased? Are more teachers telling other teachers about books and recommending them? Is a greater proportion of the staff searching for suggestions on ways to improve its work?

5. *Is there more sharing of materials among members of the staff?* When a teacher gets a book or some teaching material, is it shared with the other staff members? Is there less hiding in cupboards and closets of the materials that are especially valuable? Is there more experimentation by the faculty? Do more teachers say, "I'm dissatisfied with this phase of my work. What's the best hunch I have? How can I try it out? What kind of help can I get? How do I collect evidence as to whether the new procedure is any better than the present one?"

6. *Is the faculty identifying the problems it has to face, further ᵕhead, so that it is not confronted with so many emergencies?* Does it say, "Here's a problem that is coming up. We'd better get on it."

7. *Is there a greater use of evidence in deciding issues?* Is the faculty moving away from saying, "How do we feel about it?" to "What is the evidence?" or, "On the evidence, what is the best course of action to take?"

8. *Is there within the faculty a greater acceptance of difference?* Are there fewer derogatory remarks by teachers about other teachers? Are there more questions about how we can get into a more effective working relationship with people with whom we disagree? When a conflict arises, do we ask, "How can we work together?" or, "How can we isolate this person who is on the other side of the fence?"

9. *How many more parents are involved in the school?* Teachers alone cannot improve the school. Adults of the community are needed to help the program and to serve as resource persons for classes and activity groups. In schools without an

adequate staff, they may assist with the service functions of the school. If a supervisor has been effective in increasing the vision of the staff concerning the potential contribution of community members to education, more parents will be involved in school activities.

10. *How many rooms are attractive?* If pupils and teachers are to spend six hours a day in a room, it should be attractive—a place in which a person likes to be. It is becoming widely recognized that barren, empty, harsh classrooms do not stimulate the kind of learning the teacher desires. How many more rooms have color, pictures, drapes, displays, and other devices that reflect and support the quality of teaching that is sought?

11. *How many more teachers are active in professional organizations?* Although activity in a professional organization does not guarantee classroom competency, participation in local, state, and national organizations is another indication of the professional spirit of the staff. A supervisor's behavior and attitudes should motivate teachers to exert leadership in improving education through professional organizations.

12. *How many more teachers are seeking in-service experience?* Some school systems require that staff members take awareness courses every few years, as a minimum insurance of curriculum improvement. Teachers should be looking for opportunities to improve. Has the system made available the types of workshops and resource people that the teachers consider helpful? Have staff members requested the supervisor to provide a seminar or workshop on some problem facing them? When a volunteer workshop or meeting is announced, does a greater percentage of the staff attend? Are more teachers working in the teachers centers? Are more teachers developing individual designs for their own self-improvement?

13. *How many more teachers are planning with other teachers?* Teachers grow through interaction. Teachers grow through teachers planning with other teachers. When teachers recognize the value of sharing experiences and materials, the faculty moves toward a common point of view with regard to learning and curriculum. If a supervisor's work is effective, more teachers will find value in this joint planning.

14. *How many more pupils are being included in planning and evaluating?* The learning situation improves as the people involved in it have an opportunity to make their purposes clear and to make judgments about the success of their activities. A supervisor improves the learning situation as he or she assists teachers to gain the security and the techniques that make it possible for them to utilize the intelligence of pupils in making judgments about what is to happen and what has already happened. One of the barometers by which to judge a supervisor's productivity is the extent to which increased pupil-teacher planning is occurring.

15. *Is a larger percentage of the staff assuming responsibility for the improvement of the program?* Through individual efforts, a supervisor is able to effect some changes in the curriculum, but this effort is not enough. It is only as he or she works in such a way that more and more people begin to desire change and to assume responsibility for making it that a supervisory program has impact on a school system.

16. *Are staff meetings becoming more faculty directed?* If staff meetings remain the exclusive property of the administrators, changes of lasting significance are unlikely. If the administrator invites staff members to assume responsibility, and no teacher leadership emerges, then nothing happens except an increase in staff dissatisfaction. When a supervisor's work procedures are effective, the faculty gives more and more attention to the planning of meetings and to the use of meetings to make decisions concerning school policy. If only 25 percent of the staff is inter-

ested in making decisions concerning policy, it is difficult to make a judgment about the quality of the supervision. If next year, only the same 25 percent is interested in making decisions, it is apparent that the supervisory procedures being followed are not the kind that increase the staff's self-direction. If a supervisor is doing his or her job effectively, staff members become increasingly able to conduct their own meetings and to decide on policy. The staff becomes concerned with knowing limitations and possibilities and in making judgments concerning the next best steps in the situation.

17. *How many more teachers are using a wider range of materials?* A good learning situation is one that makes it possible for pupils to find materials and media through which they can learn better. In order to provide for differences in reading ability, the books available must cover reading levels of a number of grades. To make it possible for many youngsters to express themselves easily, the classroom should contain art materials and other media through which they may express how they feel about the experiences they have been having. To provide information, there should be references, filmstrips, tapes, and pictures available. If supervision has been effective, the teaching staff has sought to increase its acquaintance with, and skill in using, a variety of media. More teachers are making available to youngsters different ways of learning and sharing.

18. *How are students scoring on achievement tests?* The end result of all efforts is to increase the learning of children. Under ordinary circumstances, pupil achievement should be higher each year as the result of a supervisor's efforts. However, it is important to consider the external factors that bear on the school situation before judgments based on the achievement of youngsters are made. The nature of the community may have changed, and the intellectual environment of the homes may have become lower or higher. Decreased funds for schools may have deprived youngsters of instructional materials and lowered the teacher morale so that less learning for pupils results. However, if the situation has remained approximately the same, and if a supervisor's efforts have been successful, the achievement level of pupils will have been raised.

In spite of all the preceding questions, self-evaluation by the official leader is not enough. The leader must obtain the judgments of others in determining the revisions to be made in his or her procedures.

Supervisors' work should be evaluated as a part of the judgments concerning the total group effort. They are working within the group. Their function is to contribute to the group's accomplishment of its goals. Acceptance of this principle keeps the faculty from stating that the official leader is strong or weak. Rather, faculty members say, "We have achieved these goals but failed to reach those. Our supervisor has been very helpful on certain points and would strengthen us if he or she would put more emphasis on these other activities during the next few months."

If goals have been established, the only way to judge the success of the group and the supervisor is by the amount of progress made toward achieving the goals. The goals of the school are the criteria against which the work of the formal leader must ultimately be judged. Maintaining the status quo in a school program is inadequate unless it is being maintained in the face of constantly increasing difficulties.

In order to determine progress, it is necessary to know where the group starts. Some base line must be established. The program of the school must be accurately recorded so that the group will be able to determine exactly the amount of change that has taken place. Either the beginning of the school year, or the time at which the evaluative criteria are applied to the school program, may be used. The starting point chosen does not matter if it is recent enough to permit detection of change that is occurring under the impact of present activity. But some complete picture of existing conditions at the start of the project is essential.

As a group evaluates its work and that of its supervisor, it is necessary to determine the amount of change that has been produced in the direction of the group goals since the base line was established. How does the school program now differ from the school program at the previous date?

When the types and amount of change have been determined, the group is ready to make judgments. If no change has occurred, the judgment is obvious. If some change has been effected, the group must decide whether that progress is satisfactory in light of existing conditions. At this point the judgment becomes subjective.

Everyone involved in the situation—supervisors, teachers, parents, pupils, community groups—should be a part of the judgment process. The amount of change can be determined by individuals—a teacher, the principal, or an outside group—but the judgments about the amount of progress must be made by all concerned. Whether or not the supervisor desires this condition, it will occur.

Skillful supervisors devise situations for obtaining these judgments and use them in improving the school program. Unskillful leaders will pretend that they can ignore them and will find that they have missed an opportunity to build group spirit and solid backing for the program. They will wonder why opposition is developing in those whose judgments were not obtained and used.

The judgments that name areas of less-than-satisfactory progress will indicate the points where analysis and revision are needed, either in the work of the supervisor or of others in the group. The specific criteria by which a program and the official leader should be judged fall into four categories:

1. More responsible participation of students, teachers, and community members in the improvement of the program.
2. Enrichment of the school program through an increase in opportunities and activities for all.
3. Improvement of learning situations for students.
4. Greater contribution of the school to the improvement of community living.

Evaluation of a supervisor must be an evaluation of program development, with specific attention devoted to the procedures by which more group potential for progress can be released.

Supervisors who have formulated a theory to guide their action, and criteria to evaluate their success, will grow in skill and competency. They will use the results of their evaluation to test their theory and to identify the areas in which they need to search for new knowledge and insight and for additional courses of action from which to choose.

REFERENCES

ABBOTT, M., 1965. Unpublished Paper. Auburn, Ala.: Auburn University.

ABBOTT, M. G., and J. T. LOVELL, eds., 1967. *Change Perspectives in Educational Administration.* Montgomery, Ala.: Paragon Press.

ACHILLES, C. M., and D. NORMAN, 1974. "Communication and change in education," *Planning and Changing,* 5: 138–142.

ACHILLES, C. M., and L. W. HUGHES, 1971. "The supervisor as a change agent," *Educational Leadership,* 28: 840–843.

AINSWORTH, L. H., 1958. "Rigidity, insecurity and stress," *Journal of Abnormal and Social Psychology,* 56: 67–74.

ALLEN, D. W., 1971. "In-service teacher training: A modest proposal," *Improving In-Service Education,* ed. L. J. Rubin. Boston: Allyn & Bacon.

ALLEN, L. W., C. M. ACHILLES, and W. OWENS, 1978. "Study councils and the NDN: One link to better education," *Catalyst for Change,* 8: 14–15.

ALEXANDER, W. M., ed., 1969. *The High School of the Future: A Memorial to Kimball Wiles.* Columbus, Ohio: Chas. E. Merrill.

ALEXANDER, W. M., and R. J. HAVINGHURST, 1962. "Bases for curriculum decision," *National Elementary Principal,* 42: 8–12.

ALLINGHAM, R. B., et al., 1961. "How supervise instruction in the large urban secondary school?" *National Association of Secondary School Principals Bulletin,* 45: 7–11.

ALLUTTO, J. A., and A. BELOSCO, 1972. "Patterns of teacher participation in school system decision making," *Educational Administration Quarterly,* 9: 27–41.

AMERICAN ASSOCIATION OF SCHOOL ADMINISTRATORS, 1971. *Profiles of the Administrative Team.* Washington, D.C.: American Association of School Administrators.

AMIDON, E. J., and E. HUNTER, 1966. *Improving Teaching: Analyzing Verbal Interaction in the Classroom.* New York: Holt, Rinehart and Winston.

ANDERSON, J. G., 1968. *Bureaucracy in Education.* Baltimore, Md.: Johns Hopkins.

ANDERSON, R. C., et. al., 1969. *Current Research on Instruction.* Englewood Cliffs, N.J.: Prentice-Hall.

ANDERSON, R. H., 1966. *Teaching in a World of Change.* New York: Harcourt Brace Jovanovich.

ANDERSON, R., E. McPHIL, AND C. REAVIS, 1978. "Decentralization and clinical supervision—a functional blend," *Planning and Change,* 9: 42–48.

ANDERSON, L. R., and F. E. FIEDLER, 1964. "The effect of participatory and supervisory leadership on group creativity," *Journal of Applied Psychology,* 48: 227–236.

ARGYRIS, C., 1961. "Organizational leadership," *Leadership and Interpersonal Behavior,* eds. L. Petrullo and B. M. Bass. New York: Holt, Rinehart & Winston.

ARGYRIS, C., 1964. *Integrating the Individual and the Organization.* New York: John Wiley.

ARGYRIS, C., 1965. *Organization and Innovation.* Homewood, Ill.: Richard D. Irwin and the Dorsey Press.

ARGYRIS, C., 1970. *Intervention Theory and Method: A Behavioral Science Method.* Reading, Mass.: Addison-Wesley.

ARNSTINE, D., 1971. "Freedom and bureaucracy in the schools," *Freedom, Bureaucracy and Schooling,* ed. V. F. Haubrick. Washington, D.C.: Association for Supervision and Curriculum Development.

ARONSON, E., and B. W. GODLEN, 1962. "The effect of relevant and irrelevant aspects of communicator credibility on opinion change," *Journal of Personality,* 30: 135–146.

ASSOCIATION FOR SUPERVISION AND CURRICULUM DEVELOPMENT, 1975. *Needs Assessment: A Focus for Curriculum Development.* Washington, D.C.: Association for Supervision and Curriculum Development.

ASSOCIATION FOR SUPERVISION AND CURRICULUM DEVELOPMENT, 1962. *Perceiving Behaving Becoming.* Washington, D.C.: Association for Supervision and Curriculum Development.

ATKINSON, J. W., and D. BIRCH, 1978. *An Introduction to Motivation.* New York: D. Van Nostrand.

ATKINSON, J. W., and J. O. RAYNOR, 1978. *Personality, Motivation, and Achievement.* New York: Halstead Press.

ATKINSON, K., 1971. "Communication: Closing the widening gap," *The Clearing House,* 46: 27–31.

AYER, F. C., and A. S. BARR, 1928. *The Organization of Supervision.* New York: D. Appleton and Co.

BACHMAN, J. D., et. al., 1968. "Bases of supervisory power: A comparative study in five organizational settings," *Control in Organization,* ed. Arnold S. Tannenbaum. New York: McGraw-Hill.

BACK, K. W., 1951. "Influence through social communication," *Journal of Abnormal and Social Psychology,* 46: 9–23.

BAHRICK, G. P., 1954. "Incidental learning under two incentive conditions," *Journal of Experimental Psychology,* 47: 170–172.

BAIRD, J. E., Jr., and G. K. WIETING, 1979. "Nonverbal communication can be a motivational tool," *Personnel Journal*, 58: 607–625.

BALDWIN, T. L., and C. J. GARVEY, 1973. "Components of accurate problem-solving communications," *American Educational Research Journal*, 10: 39–48.

BALES, R. F., et. al., 1951. "Channels of communication in small groups," *American Sociological Review*, 16: 461–468.

BARNARD, C. I., 1938. *The Functions of the Executive*. Cambridge, Mass.: Harvard University Press.

BARNETT, H., 1962. *Innovation: The Basic of Cultural Change*. New York: McGraw-Hill.

BASKIN, S., 1962. "Experiment in independent study (1956–1960)," *Journal of Experimental Education*, 31: 183.

BASS, B. M., 1960. *Leadership, Psychology and Organizational Behavior*. New York: Harper & Row, Pub.

BASS, B. M., 1961. "Some observations about a general theory of leadership and interpersonal behavior," *Leadership and Interpersonal Behavior*, eds. L. Petrullo and B. M. Bass. New York: Holt, Rinehart & Winston.

BASS, B. M., and E. C. RYTERBAND, 1979. *Organizational Psychology (2nd ed.)*. Boston: Allyn & Bacon.

BATTEN, J. D., 1976. "Face to face communication," *The Personnel Administrator*, 21: 51–54.

BAVELAS, A., 1942. "Morale and the training of leaders," *Civilian Morale*, ed. G. Watson. Boston: Houghton Mifflin.

BAVELAS, A., 1950. "Communication patterns in task-oriented groups," *Journal of the Acoustical Society of America*, 22: 725–730.

BAVELAS, A., and P. BARRETT, 1951. "An Experimental Approach to Organizational Communication," *Personnel*, 27: 366–371.

BEAL, G. M., E. M. ROGERS, and J. M. BOHLEN, 1957. "Validity of the concept of stages in the adoption process," *Rural Sociology*, 22: 166–168.

BEATTY, P. J., 1977. "Dialogic communication in the supervision process: A humanistic approach," *Education*, 92: 226–232.

BEAUCHAMP, GEORGE A., 1978. "A hard look at curriculum," *Educational Leadership*, 35: 404–409.

BEKEROGLU, H., and T. GOREN, 1977. "Motivation, the state of the art," *Personnel Journal*, 56: 561–562.

BELLACK, A. A., et. al., 1968. "The language of the classroom," *Teaching: Vantage Points for Study*, ed. R. T. Hyman. Philadelphia: Lippincott.

BELLON, J., R. E. EAKER, J. O. HUFFMAN, and R. V. JONES, Jr., 1976. *Classroom Supervision and Instructional Improvement: A Synergetic Process*. Dubuque, Iowa: Kendall/Hunt.

BENNETT, J., and R. McKNIGHT, 1956. "Misunderstandings in communications between Japanese students and Americans," *Social Problems*, 3: 243–256.

BENNIS, W. G., 1966. *Changing Organizations*. New York: McGraw-Hill.

BENNIS, W. G., 1966. *Communication in Organizations*. New York: West Publishing Co.

BENNIS, W. G., 1973. "The Doppelganger effect," *Newsweek*, 82: 13.

BENNIS, W. G., K. D. BENNE, R. CHIN, and K. W. COREY, 1976. *The Planning of Change*. New York: Holt, Rinehart & Winston.

BENNIS, W. G., and E. H. SCHEIN, eds., 1966. *Leadership and Motivation: Essays of Douglas McGregor*. Cambridge, Mass.: M.I.T. Press.

BERGIN, A. E., 1962. "The effect of dissonant persuasive communications upon changes in a self-referring attitude," *Journal of Personality*, 30: 423–438.

BERKOWITZ, L., 1951. "Some Effects of Leadership Sharing in Small Decision-Making Conference Groups," (unpublished doctor's dissertation). Ann Arbor, Mich.: University of Michigan.

BERLO, D. K., 1960. *The Process of Communication.* New York: Holt, Rinehart & Winston.

BERMAN, L. M., ed., 1963. *The Nature of Teaching.* Milwaukee, Wisc.: University of Wisconsin.

BERMAN, L. M., 1968. *New Priorities in the Curriculum.* Columbus, Ohio: Chas. E. Merrill.

BERNE, E., 1973. *Games People Play.* New York: Ballantine Books.

BIDWELL, C. E., and J. D. KASARDA, 1975. "School district organization and student achievement," *American Sociological Review,* 40: 55–70.

BISHOP, L. J., 1976. *Staff Development and Instructional Improvement.* Boston: Allyn & Bacon.

BISHOP, L. J., and G. R. FIRTH, 1977. "New conceptions of supervision," *Educational Leadership,* 34: 572–575.

BLAKE, R. H., and E. O. HAROLDSEN, 1975. *A Taxonomy of Concepts in Communication.* New York: Hastings House.

BLAKE, R. R., et al., 1964. "Breakthrough in organization development," *Harvard Business Review,* 42: 133–155.

BLAKE, R. R., and J. S. MOUTON, 1976. "Strategies of consultation," *The Planning of Change,* eds. W. G. Bennis, K. D. Benne, R. Chin, and K. Carey. New York: Holt, Rinehart & Winston.

BLAU, P. M., 1956. *Bureaucracy in Modern Society.* New York: Random House.

BLAU, P. M., and R. W. SCOTT, 1962. *Formal Organizations: A Comparative Approach.* San Francisco: Chandler Publishing Co.

BLAU, P. M., 1963. "Bureaucracy in modern society," *Organizations: Structure and Behavior,* ed. Joseph A. Litterer. New York: John Wiley.

BLOOM, B. S., ed., 1956. *Taxonomy of Educational Objectives.* New York: Longmans, Grun, and Co.

BLUMBERG, A., and E. AMIDON, 1965. "Teacher perceptions of supervisor-teacher interaction," *Administrator's Notebook,* XIV.

BOAG, T. J., 1952. "The white man in the Arctic, a preliminary study of problems of adjustments," *American Journal of Psychiatry,* 109: 444–449.

BOBBITT, J. F., 1912. "The elimination of waste in education," *The Elementary School Teacher,* 12: 260.

BOBBITT, J. F., 1913. "Some general principles of management applied to the problems of city school systems," *Twelfth Yearbook of the National Society for the Study of Education, Part I.* Chicago, Ill.: University of Chicago Press.

BOBBITT, J. F., 1920. "The objectives of secondary education," *The School Review,* 28: 738.

BORMAN, E. G., J. PRATT, and L. PUTNAM, 1978. "Power, authority, and sex: Male response to female leadership," *Communication Monographs,* 45: 119–155.

BOVARD, E. W., Jr., 1951. "Group structure and perception," *Journal of Abnormal and Social Psychology,* 46: 398–405.

BRADLEY, P. H., 1978. "Power, status, and upward communication in small decision-making groups," *Communication Monographs,* 45: 33–43.

BRIMM, J. L., and D. TOLLETT, 1974. "How do teachers feel about inservice education?" *Educational Leadership,* 31: 521–525.

BRINER, C., and G. SROUFE, 1971. "Organization for education in 1985," *Educational Futurism 1985,* eds. W. G. Hack, et. al. Berkeley, Cal.: McCutchan Publishing.

BROWN, C. G., and T. S. COHN, 1958. *The Study of Leadership*. Danville, Ill.: The Interstate.

BROWN, R. W., and E. H. LENNEBERG, 1954. "Studies in linguistic relativity," *Journal of Abnormal and Social Psychology,* 49: 454–462.

BRUNER, J. S., 1961. "The act of discovery," *Harvard Educational Review,* 31: 21–32.

BRUNER, J. S., 1966. *Toward a Theory of Instruction*. Cambridge, Mass.: The Belknap Press of Harvard University Press.

BRUNER, J. S., 1973. *Beyond the Information Given*. New York: W. W. Norton & Co., Inc.

BUCHANAN, P. C., 1972. "Organizational development as a process strategy for change," *Educational Technology,* 29: 10–13.

BURNHAM, R., and M. KING, 1961. *Supervision in Action*. Washington, D.C.: Association for Supervision and Curriculum Development.

BURNHAM, R. M., 1962. "A neglected resource in the education of teachers," *The Journal of Teacher Education,* 13: 85–87.

BURNHAM, R. M., 1976. "Instructional supervision: Past, present and future perspectives," *Theory Into Practice,* 15: 301–305.

BURNS, J. M., 1978. *Leadership*. New York: Harper & Row, Pub.

BURNS, J. C., S. M. BLAKE, E. S. SCHELDON, and G. J. KLOPF, 1975. "Inservice for educational leadership," *National Elementary Principal,* 55: 74–80.

BURNS, M. L., 1977. "The effects of feedback and commitment to change on the behavior of elementary school principals," *The Journal of Applied Behavioral Science,* 13: 159–166.

BURRELL, D., 1976. "The teachers centre: A critical analysis," *Educational Leadership,* 33: 422–427.

BURTON, W. H., and L. J. BRUECKNER, 1966. *Supervision, a Social Process*. Englewood Cliffs, N.J.: Prentice-Hall.

CALDWELL, W. E., and F. LUTZ, 1978. "The measurement of principal rule administration behavior and its relationship to educational leadership," *Educational Administration Quarterly,* 14: 63–79.

CALLAHAN, R. E., 1962. *Education and the Cult of Efficiency*. Chicago, Ill.: University of Chicago Press.

CAMPBELL, R. F., and J. M. LIPHAM, eds., 1960. *Administrative Theory as a Guide to Action*. Chicago, Ill.: University of Chicago Press.

CAMPBELL, R. F., 1977–78. "A history of administrative thought," *Administrator's Notebook,* 26.

CARLTON, C. G., 1971. "The role of instructional supervisors as perceived by teachers and principals in selected Florida elementary schools," *Dissertation Abstracts International,* 31.

CARP, F. M., et. al., 1963. "Human relations knowledge and social distance set in supervisors," *Journal of Applied Psychology,* 47: 178–180.

CARTER, L. F., 1951. "Appointed leaders less authoritarian than 'natural' ones, study indicates," *Research Reviews*.

CARTWRIGHT, D., and Z. ZANDER, eds., 1960. *Group Dynamics: Research and Theory*. Evanston, Ill.: Row, Peterson.

CASTETTER, W. B., 1981. *The Personnel Function in Educational Administration*. New York: Macmillan.

CASWELL, H. L., and D. CAMPBELL, 1935. *Curriculum Development*. New York: American Book.

CATTELL, R. B., 1951. "New concepts for measuring leadership in terms of group syntality," *Human Relations,* 4: 161–184.

CHIN, R., 1976. "The utility of system models and developmental models for practitioners," *The Planning of Change,* eds. W. G. Bennis, K. D. Benne, R. Chin, and K. Carey. New York: Holt, Rinehart & Winston.

CHIN, R., and K. D. BENNE, 1976. "General strategies for effecting change in human systems," *The Planning of Change,* eds. W. G. Bennis, K. D. Benne, R. Chin, and K. Carey. New York: Holt, Rinehart & Winston.

CHOWDHREY, K. and T. NEWCOMB, 1952. The relative abilities of leaders and non-leaders to estimate opinions of their own groups," *Journal of Abnormal and Social Psychology,* 47: 51-71.

CHURCHMAN, D. A., 1979. "New approach to evaluating the implementation of innovative educational programs," *Educational Technology,* 19: 25-28.

CLARK, R. S., 1968. "A Study of the Relation of Instructional Supervision Behavior to Teacher Satisfaction and to Teacher-Pupil Relationships," (Ed. D. dissertation). Auburn, Ala.: Auburn University.

COCH, L., and J. R. FRENCH, 1948. "Overcoming resistance to change," *Human Relationships,* 1: 512-532.

COGAN, M. L., 1973. *Clinical Supervision.* Boston: Houghton Mifflin.

COGAN, M. L., 1976. "Rationale for clinical supervision," *Journal for Research and Development in Education,* 9: 3-19.

COHEN, A. R., 1958. "Upward communication in experimentally created hierarchies," *Human Relations,* 11: 41-52.

COHEN, A. R., 1962. "The effects of changes in communication networks on the behaviors of problem-solving groups," *Sociometry,* 25: 177.

COMBS, A. W., and D. Snygg, 1959. *Individual Behavior.* New York: Harper & Row, Pub.

COMMOSS, H. H., 1962. "Some characteristics related to social isolation of second grade children," *Journal of Educational Psychology,* 53: 38-42.

COOPERATIVE DEVELOPMENT OF PUBLIC SCHOOL ADMINISTRATION, ALBANY, NEW YORK, 1957. "Instructional staff administrators," *Organizing Schools for Effective Education,* eds. Daniel Griffith, et. al. Danville, Ill.: The Interstate, 1962.

CONRAD, M. J., K. BROOKS, and G. FISHER, 1974. "A model for comprehensive educational planning," *Journal of Planning and Changing,* 4: 3-14.

CORNELL, F., 1954. "When should teachers share in making administrative decisions?" *The Nation's Schools,* 53: 43-45.

CORWIN, R. G., and R. A. EDELFELT, 1976. *Perspectives on Organizations.* Washington, D.C.: American Association of Colleges for Teacher Education.

COURTRIGHT, J. A., 1978. "A laboratory investigation of groupthink," *Communication Monographs,* 45: 229-246.

COWLEY, W. H., 1928. "Three distinctions in the study of leaders," *Journal of Abnormal and Social Psychology,* 23: 144-157.

COWLEY, W. H., 1931. "The traits of face-to-face leaders," *Journal of Abnormal and Social Psychology,* 26: 304-313.

CUBBERLEY, E., 1916. *Public School Administration.* Boston: Houghton Mifflin.

CULBERTSON, J., 1959. "Recognizing roadblocks in communication channels." *Administrator's Notebook,* 7: 1-4.

CULBERTSON, J., 1976. "Educational leadership: The uses of adversity," *Theory Into Practice,* 15: 253-259.

CUMMINGS, L. L., and M. J. O'CONNELL, 1978. "Organizational innovation: A model and needed research," *Journal of Business Research,* 6: 33-50.

CUNNINGHAM, L. L., 1959. "The process of educational policy development," *The Administrator's Notebook,* 11: 1-4.

CUNNINGHAM, L. L., 1963. "Effecting change through leadership," *Educational Leadership,* 21: 75-79.

CUNNINGHAM, L. L., 1973. "Educational leadership: The curious blend," *Educational Leadership*, 33: 323–326.

CZAJKOWSKI, T. J., and J. L. PATTERSON, 1980. "Curriculum change and the school," *Considered Action for Curriculum Improvement,* ed. A. W. Foshay. Washington, D.C.: Association for Supervision and Curriculum Development.

DANCE, F. E. S., 1970. "The 'concept' of communication," *The Journal of Communication,* 20: 201–210.

DANLEY, W. E., Sr., and B. BURCH, 1978. "Teacher perceptions of the effective instructional leader," *The Clearing House,* 52: 78–79.

DAVIS, K. E., and C. C. FLORQUIST, 1965. "Perceived threat and dependence as determinants of the tactical usage of opinion conformity," *Journal of Experimental Psychology,* 1: 219–236.

DAVIS, K., and W. G. SCOTT, eds., 1964. *Readings in Human Relations.* New York: McGraw-Hill.

DAVITS, JR., R., and D. J. MASON, 1960. "Manifest anxiety and social perception," *Journal of Consulting Psychology,* 24: 554.

DEVANEY, K., 1976. "What's a teachers' center for?" *Educational Leadership,* 33: 413–416.

DILLON-PETERSON, B., 1981. *Staff Development/Organizational Development.* Washington, D.C.: Association for Supervision and Curriculum Development.

DOLL, R. C., 1962. "In-service training in communication," *Overview,* 3: 57.

DOLL, R. C., 1972. *Leadership to Improve Schools.* Worthington, Ohio: Charles A. Jones.

DOWIS, J. L., and O. DIETHELAM, 1958. "Anxiety, stress and thinking: An experimental investigation," *Journal of Psychology,* 45: 227–238.

DOWNEY, L. W., 1969. *The Task of Public Education.* Chicago, Ill.: Midwest Administration Center, University of Chicago.

DOYLE, W. J., and W. P. AHLBRAND, 1974. "Hierarchical group performance and leader orientation," *Administrator's Notebook,* 22: 3.

DRUCKER, P. F., 1970. *Technology, Management, and Society.* New York: Harper & Row, Pub.

DYER, W., R. MADDOCKS, J. MOFFITT, and W. UNDERWOOD, 1970. "A laboratory-consultation model for organizational change," *Journal of Applied Behavioral Science,* 6: 211–227.

DYKES, A., 1963. "Influencing the power elite," *The Education Digest,* 29: 28.

EAGLE, M., 1959. "The effects of subliminal stimuli of aggressive content on conscious cognition," *Journal of Personality,* 27: 578.

EASTERBROOK, J. AL, 1955. "The effect of emotion on cue utilization and the organization of behavior," *Journal of Abnormal and Social Psychology,* 51: 458–463.

EISENBERG, A., and R. R. SMITH, 1971. *Nonverbal Communication.* Indianapolis, Ind.: Bobbs-Merrill.

EISNER, E. W., 1980. "Future priorities for curriculum reform," *Educational Leadership,* 37: 543–556.

ELKIN, F., G. HALPERN, and A. COOPER, 1962. "Leadership in a student mob," *Canadian Journal of Psychology,* 16: 199–201.

EMMER, E. T., and G. B. MILLETT, 1970. *Improving Teaching through Experimentation: A laboratory approach.* Englewood Cliffs, N.J.: Prentice-Hall.

EPPERSON, D. C., 1962. "Stimulating teacher collaboration in the improvement of educational practice," *National Association of Secondary School Principals Bulletin,* 46: 45–49.

ESPOSITO, J. P., G. E. SMITH, and H. J. BURBACH, 1975. "A delineation of the supervisory role," *Education,* 96: 63–67.

ETZIONI, A., 1964. *Modern Organizations.* Englewood Cliffs, N. J.: Prentice-Hall.

ETZIONI, A., 1969. *The Semi-Professions and Their Organizations.* New York: Free Press.

FAST, J., 1970. *Body Language.* New York: Simon & Schuster.

FAYOL, H., 1971. "General principles of management," *Organizational Theory,* ed. D. S. Pugh. New York: Penguin.

FELDHUSEN, J. F., and H. J. KLAUSMEIER, 1962. "Anxiety, intelligence and achievement in children of low, average and high intelligence," *Child Development,* 33: 403-410.

FESTINGER, L., and H. A. HUTTE, 1954. "An experimental investigation of the effect of unstable interpersonal relations in a group," *The Journal of Abnormal and Social Psychology,* 49: 513-522.

FESTINGER, L., and J. THIBAUT, 1951. "Interpersonal communication in small groups," *Journal of Abnormal and Social Psychology,* 46: 92-99.

FESTINGER, L., J. TORREY, and B. WILLERMAN, 1954. "Self-evaluation as a function of attraction to the group," *Human Relations,* 7: 161-174.

FIEDLER, FRED E., 1976. "The leadership game: Matching the man to the situation," *Organizational Dynamics,* 4: 6-16.

FIEDLER, FRED E., 1979. "Responses to Sergiovani," *Educational Leadership,* 36: 394-402.

FIEDLER, FRED E., and W. A. T. MEAUWESE, 1963. "Leader's contribution to task performance in cohesive and uncohesive groups," *Journal of Abnormal Psychology,* 67: 83-87.

FINE, B. J., 1957. "Conclusion-drawing, communicator credibility, and anxiety as factors in opinion change," *Journal of Abnormal and Social Psychology,* 54: 369-374.

FIRESTONE, WILLIAM A., 1977. "Participation and influence in the planning of educational change," *Journal of Applied Behavioral Science,* 13: 167-183.

FIRTH, G., 1976. "Theories of leadership: Where do we stand?" *Educational Leadership,* 33: 327-331.

FISHER, W. P., and M. F. KLEIN, 1978. "Challenging simplistic beliefs about curriculum," *Educational Leadership,* 35: 390-393.

FLANDERS, N. A., 1951. "Personal-social anxiety as a factor in experimental learning situations," *Journal of Educational Research,* 45: 100-110.

FLANDERS, N. A., 1962. "Using interaction analysis in the in-service training of teachers," *Journal of Experimental Education,* 30: 313.

FLANDERS, N. A., 1963. "Teacher behavior and in-service programs," *Educational Leadership,* 21: 25-29.

FLANDERS, N. A., 1976. "Interaction analysis and clinical supervision," *Journal of Research and Development in Education,* 9: 47-57.

FLEISHMAN, E. A., E. F. HARRIS, and H. E. BURTT, 1955. *Leadership and Supervision in Industry.* Columbus, Ohio: Ohio State University, Bureau of Educational Research.

FLEMING, J. N., 1963. "An Analysis and a Comparison of the Decision-Making Processes in Two School Faculties," (unpublished doctor's dissertation). Gainesville, Fla.: University of Florida.

FOLTX, R. G., 1973. *Management by Communication.* Philadelphia, Pa.: Chilton.

FORSYTH, P. B., and W. K. HOY, 1978. "Isolation and alienation in educational organizations," *Education Administration Quarterly,* 14: 80-96.

FOSHAY, A., 1980. *Considered Action for Curriculum Improvement.* Washington, D.C.: Association for Supervision and Curriculum Development.

FRAZIER, A., 1963. "The new teacher—a new kind of supervision?" *Educational Leadership,* 21: 97-100.

FRAZIER, A., 1972. *Open Schools for Children.* Washington, D.C.: Association for Supervision and Curriculum Development.

FREY, W. P., 1979. "How to keep those new programs alive and well," *Educational Leadership,* 37: 208-210.

FURZE, B. W., 1975-76. "The career investments of public school superintendents," *Administrator's Notebook,* Vol. XXIV, 7.

GAGNE, R. M., and L. T. BROWN, 1961. "Some factors in the programming of conceptual learning," *Journal of Experimental Psychology,* 62: 313-321.

GAIER, E. L., 1952. "The relationship between selected personality variables and the thinking of students in discussion classes," *School Review,* 60: 404-411.

GARDINER, J. C., 1971. "Synthesis of experimental studies of speech communication feedback," *The Journal of Communication,* 21: 17-35.

GARDNER, J. W., 1965. "How to prevent organizational dry rot," *Harper's Magazine,* 231: 20-26.

GATES, P. E., K. H. BLANCHARD, and P. HERSEY, 1976. "Diagnosing educational leadership problems: A situational approach," *Educational Leadership,* 33: 348-354.

GELLERMAN, S., 1968. *Management for Motivation.* New York: American Management Association.

GETZELS, J. W., 1960. Theory and practice in educational administration: An old question revisited," *Administrative Theory as a Guide to Action,* eds. R. F. Campbell and J. M. Lipham. Chicago, Ill.: University of Chicago Press.

GETZELS, J. W., and E. G. GUBA, 1954. "Role, role conflict and effectiveness," *American Sociological Review,* 19: 164-175.

GETZELS, J. W., 1957. "Social behavior and the administrative process," *The School Review,* 45: 423-442.

GETZELS, J. W., J. M. LIPHAM, and R. F. CAMPBELL, 1966. *Educational Administration as a Social Process.* New York: Harper & Row, Pub.

GIBLIN, E. J., 1976. "Motivating employees: A closer look," *Personnel Journal,* 55: 68-75.

GILCHRIST, J. C., M. E. SHAW, and L. C. WALKER, 1954. "Some effects of unequal distribution of information in wheel group structure," *Journal of Abnormal and Social Psychology,* 49: 554-556.

GLASS, D. C., 1954. "Changes in liking as a means of reducing cognitive discrepancies between self-esteem and aggression," *Journal of Personality Psychology,* 32: 531-549.

GLICKMAN, C. D., 1981. *Developmental Supervision.* Washington, D.C.: Association for Supervision and Curriculum Development.

GOETZINGER, C., and M. Valentine, 1964. "Problems in executive interpersonal communication," *Personnel Administration,* 27: 24-29.

GOLDHABER, G. M., 1979. *Organizational Communication.* Dubuque, Ia.: Wm. C. Brown.

GOLDHAMMER, R., 1969. *Clinical Supervision.* New York: Holt, Rinehart & Winston.

GOLDHAMMER, R., R. H. ANDERSON, and R. J. KRAJEWSKI, 1980. *Clinical Supervision.* New York: Holt, Rinehart & Winston.

GOOD, T. L., and J. E. BRODY, 1978. *Looking in Classrooms.* New York: Harper & Row, Pub.

GOODLAD, J., 1969. In an address delivered in Connecticut.

GOODLAD, J., M. FRANCIS KLEIN, and Associates, 1970. *Behind the Classroom Door.* Worthington, Ohio: Charles E. Jones.

GOODLAD, J., and Associates, 1978. "Challenging simplistic beliefs about curriculum," *Educational Leadership,* 35: 390-393.

GOULDNER, A. W., 1954. *Patterns of Industrial Bureaucracy.* Glencoe, Ill.: Free Press.

GREER, E. S., 1961. "Human relations in supervision," *Education,* 82: 203-206.

GRIENER, L. E., 1973. "What managers think of participative leadership," *Harvard Business Review,* 51: 111-117.

GRIFFITHS, D. E., D. CLARK, D. R. WYNN, and L. IANNACCONE, 1962. *Organizing Schools.* Danville, Ill.: The Interstate.

GROBMAN, H. G., 1958. "The Public School Principal's Operational Behavior, Theory and Practice and Related School and Community Interactions Based on Data from the Investigations of the University of Florida CPEA Leadership Project," (unpublished doctor's dissertation). Gainesville, Fla.: University of Florida.

GROSS, N., and R. E. HERRIOTT, 1965. *Staff Leadership in Public Schools: A Sociological Inquiry.* New York: John Wiley.

GUBA, E. G., 1960. "Research in internal administration—what do we know?" *Administrative Theory as a Guide to Action.* Chicago, Ill.: The University of Chicago Press.

GUBA, E. G., 1968. "Diffusion of innovations," *Educational Leadership,* 25: 292-295.

GUELCHER, W., T. JACKSON, and F. NECHELES, 1970. *Microteaching and Teacher Training, a Refined Version.* Chicago, Ill.: University of Chicago Press.

GUETZKOW, H., and W. R. DILL, 1957. "Factors in the organizational development of task-oriented groups," *Sociometry,* 20: 175-204.

GUETZKOW, H., and H. A. SIMON, 1955. "The impact of certain communication nets upon organization and performance in task-oriented groups," *Management Science,* 1: 233-250.

GUILFORD, J. S., and D. E. GRAY, 1970. *Motivation and Modern Man.* Reading, Mass.: Addison-Wesley.

GUSTAD, J. W., 1962. "Communication failures in higher education," *Journal of Communication,* 12: 11.

GYLLENHAMMER, P. G., 1977. "How Volvo adapts work to people," *Harvard Business Review,* 55: 102-113.

GYNTHER, R. A., 1957. "The effects of anxiety and of situational stress on communicative efficiency," *Journal of Abnormal and Social Psychology,* 54: 274-276.

HACKMAN, R. C., and R. G. MOON, 1950. "Are leaders and followers identified by similar criteria?" *American Psychologist,* 5: 312.

HACKMAN, J. R., et. al., 1975. "A new strategy for job enrichment," *California Management Review,* 17: 62-70.

HAHN, C. P., 1961. "Collection of data for utilization in curriculum planning of the U.S. Air Force Academy," *Leadership and Interpersonal Behavior,* eds., L. Petrullo and B. M. Bass. New York: Holt, Rinehart & Winston.

HALE, W. T., 1961. "UICSM's decade of experimentation," *The Mathematics Teacher,* 54: 613-618.

HALL, E. J., S. S. MOUTON, and R. R. BLAKE, 1963. "Group problem-solving effectiveness under conditions of pooling versus interaction," *Journal of Social Psychology,* 1: 147-157.

HALL, E. T., 1959. *The Silent Language.* New York: Doubleday.

HALLWORTH, H. J., 1961. "Anxiety in secondary modern and grammar school children," *The British Journal of Educational Psychology*, 31: 281.

HALPIN, A. W., 1966. *Theory and Research in Administration*. New York: Macmillan.

HALPIN, A. W., and D. B. CROFT, 1963. *The Organizational Climate of Schools*. Chicago, Ill.: University of Chicago Press.

HARE, A. P., 1952. "A study of interaction and consensus in different sized groups," *American Sociological Review*, 17: 261–267.

HARRIMAN, B., 1974. "Up and down the communications ladder," *Harvard Business Review*, 52: 143–151.

HARRIS, B., 1975. *Supervisory Behavior in Education*. Englewood Cliffs, N.J.: Prentice-Hall.

HARRIS, B., 1976. "Supervisor competence and strategies for improving instruction," *Educational Leadership*, 33: 332–335.

HARRIS, B., 1977. "Altering the thrust of supervision through creative leadership," *Educational Leadership*, 34: 567–571.

HARRIS, B., 1980. *Improving Staff Performance through In-Service Education*. Boston: Allyn & Bacon.

HARRIS, B. M., and L. A. VALVERDE, 1976. "Supervisors and educational change," *Theory Into Practice*, 15: 267–273.

HARRIS, B., et. al., 1979. *Personnel Administration in Education*. Boston: Allyn & Bacon.

HARRISON, R. P., 1974. *Beyond Words: An Introduction to Nonverbal Communication*. Englewood Cliffs, N.J.: Prentice-Hall.

HARRISON, R., and B. LUBIN, 1965. "Personal style group composition and learning," *Journal of Applied Behavioral Science*, 1: 286–301.

HARLTEY, H. J., 1968. *Educational Planning-Programming-Budgeting*. Englewood Cliffs, N.J.: Prentice-Hall.

HAUN, H. T., 1975. "A Study of Work Satisfaction and Dissatisfaction among Selected Women Leaders in Higher Education," (unpublished dissertation). Knoxville, Tenn.: University of Tennessee.

HAYAKAWA, S. T., and W. DRESSER, eds., 1970. *Dimensions of Meanings*. Indianapolis, Ind.: Bobbs-Merrill.

HEBB, D. O. 1958. "The motivating effects of exteroceptive stimulation," *American Psychologist*, 13: 109–113.

HECKINGER, F. M., 1976. "Where have all the innovations gone?" *Today's Education*, 65: 81–83.

HEINICKE, C., and R. F. BALES, 1953. "Developmental trends in the structure of small groups," *Sociometry*, 16: 7–38;

HEMPHILL, J. K., 1949. *Situational Factors in Leadership*. Columbus, Ohio: Ohio State University.

HEMPHILL, J. K., D. GRIFFITHS, and N. FREDERICKSON, 1962. *Administrative Performance and Personality*. New York: Bureau of Publications, Teacher's College, Columbia University.

HEMPHILL, J. K., 1961. "Why people attempt to lead," *Leadership and Interpersonal Behavior*, eds. L. Petrullo and B. M. Bass. New York: Holt, Rinehart & Winston.

HERSEY, P., and K. BLANCHARD, 1977. *Management of Organizational Behavior*. Englewood Cliffs, N.J.: Prentice-Hall.

HERZBERG, F., 1968. "One more time: How do you motivate employees," *Harvard Business Review*, 46: 53–62.

HERZBERG, F., 1976. *The Managerial Choice: To be Efficient and to be Human*. Homewood, Ill.: Dow-Jones-Irwin.

HERZBERG, F., B. MAUSNER, and B. SNYDERMAN, 1959. *The Motivation to Work.* New York: John Wiley.

HICKS, J. A., and J. B. STONE, 1962. "The identification of traits related to managerial success," *Journal of Applied Psychology,* 46: 428–432.

HOFFMAN, L. R., E. HARBURG, and N. R. F. MAIER, 1962. "Differences and disagreement as factors in creative group problem solving," *Journal of Abnormal and Social Psychology,* 64: 206–214.

HOLDAWAY, E. A., 1978. "Facet and overall satisfaction of teachers," *Educational Administration Quarterly,* 14: 80–96.

HOMANS, G. C., 1950. *The Human Group.* New York: Harcourt Brace Jovanovich.

HORNSTEIN, H. A., D. M. CALLAHAN, S. FISCH, and B. A. BENEDICT, 1968. "Influence and satisfaction in organizations: A replication," *Sociology of Education,* 41: 380–389.

HOROWITZ, M. W., J. LYONS, and H. V. PARLMUTTER, 1950. "Induction of forces in discussion groups," *American Psychologist,* 5: 301.

HORTON, D., and R. R. WOHL, 1956. "Mass communications and para-social interaction, observations on intimacy at a distance," *Psychiatry,* 19: 215–230.

HOUSE, R. J., 1971. "A path goal theory of leader effectiveness," *Administrative Science Quarterly,* 16: 321–338.

HOUSE, R. J., and T. R. MITCHELL, 1974. "Path-goal theory of leadership," *Journal of Contemporary Business,* Autumn: 81–97.

HOY, W. K., 1978. "Isolation and alienation in educational organization," *Educational Administration Quarterly,* 14: 80–96.

HOY, W. K., and C. G. MISKEL, 1978. *Educational Administration: Theory, Research and Practice.* New York: Random House.

HOY, W. K., W., NEWLAND, and R. BLAZOVSKY, 1977. "Subordinate loyalty to superior, esprit, and aspects of bureaucratic structure," *Educational Administration Quarterly,* 13: 71–85.

HUNTER, M., 1979. "Teaching is decision making," *Educational Leadership,* 37: 62–67.

HUSEMAN, R. E., J. H. LAHIFF, and J. D. HATFIELD, 1976. *Interpersonal Communications in Organizations.* Boston: Holbrook Press.

HYMAN, R. T., 1975. *School Administrator's Handbook of Teacher Supervision and Methods.* Englewood Cliffs, N.J.: Prentice-Hall.

JAIN, H. C., 1973. "Supervisory communication and performance in urban hospitals," *The Journal of Communication,* 23: 103–117.

JANIS, I., and L. MANN, 1977. *Decision Making: A Psychological Analysis of Conflict, Choice, and Commitment.* New York: Free Press.

JAY, A., 1967. Management and Machiavelli: *An Inquiry into the Politics of Corporate Life.* New York: Holt, Rinehart & Winston.

JENKS, R. S., 1970. "Action-research approach to organizational change," *Journal of Applied Behavioral Science,* 6: 131–150.

JENNINGS, H. H., 1950. *Leadership and Isolation.* New York: Longman.

JOHNSON, R. I., M. SCHALKAMP, and L. A. GARRISON, 1956. *Communication: Handling Ideas Effectively.* New York: McGraw-Hill.

JOYCE, B. R., 1978. *Selecting Learning Experiences.* Washington, D.C.: Association for Supervision and Curriculum Development.

JOYCE, B. R., and B. SHOWERS, 1980. "Improving inservice training: The messages of research," *Educational Leadership,* 37: 379–385.

KALLEGIAN, V., P. BROWN, and I. R. WESCHLER, 1953. "The impact of interpersonal relations on ratings of performance," *Public Personnel Review,* 14: 166–160.

KASLOW, C., 1971. "Faculty receptivity to organizational change: A test of two explanations of resistance to innovation in higher education," *Journal of Research and Development in Education,* 10: 87–98.

KATZ, E., 1961. "The social itinerary of technological change: Two studies on the diffusion of innovation," *Human Organization,* 20: 70–82.

KATZ, R. L., 1974. "Skills of an effective administrator," *Harvard Business Review,* 52: 90–102.

KATZMAN, N., 1974. "Impact of communication technology: Promises and prospects," *Journal of Communication,* 24: 47–58.

KAY, E., and H. H. MEYER, 1965. "Effects of threat in a performance appraisal interview," *Journal of Applied Psychology,* 49: 311–317.

KELLEY, H. H., 1951. "Communication in experimentally created hierarchies," *Human Relations,* 4: 39–56.

KELLEY, H. H., and E. H. VOLKART, 1952. "The resistance to change of group anchored attitudes," *American Sociological Review,* 18: 453–465.

KELLY, E. C., and M. I. RASEY, 1952. *Education and the Nature of Man.* New York: Harper & Row, Pub.

KERSH, B. Y., 1958. "The adequacy of 'meaning' as an explanation for the superiority of learning by independent discovery," *Journal of Educational Psychology,* 49: 282–292.

KERSH, B. Y., 1962. "The motivating effect of learning by directed discovery," *Journal of Educational Psychology,* 53: 65–71.

KERSH, B. Y., and M. C. WITTROCK, 1962. "Learning by discovery: An interpretation of recent research," *Journal of Teacher Education,* 13: 461–468.

KESTER, S. W., and G. LETCHWORTH, 1972. "Communication of teacher expectations and their effects on achievement and attitudes of secondary school students," *Journal of Education Research,* 66: 51–55.

KETS de VRIES, and F. F. MANFRED, 1979. "Managers can drive their subordinates mad," *Harvard Business Review,* 57: 125–134.

KIESLER, C. A., 1963. "Attraction to the group and conformity to group norms," *Journal of Personality,* 31: 559–569.

KIMBROUGH, R. B., 1965. "Community power structure and curriculum change," *Strategy for Curriculum Change,* Washington, D.C.: NEA-ASCD.

KIMBROUGH, R. B., 1964. *Political Power and Educational Decision-Making.* Skokie, Ill.: Rand McNally.

KIMBROUGH, R. B., and M. Y. NUNNERY, 1971. *Politics, Power, Polls, and School Elections.* Berkeley, Cal.: McCutchan.

KIPNIS, D., and W. P. LANE, 1962. "Self-confidence and leadership," *Journal of Applied Psychology,* 46: 291–295.

KIRSCH, P. E., 1960. "Classroom visitation," *National Association of Secondary School Principals Bulletin,* 44: 34–39.

KITANE, H. H. L., 1962. "Adjustment of problem and nonproblem children to specific situations: A study in role theory," *Child Development,* 33: 229–233.

KITTELL, J. E., 1959. "An experiential study of the effect of external direction during learning on transfer and retention of principles," *Journal of Educational Psychology,* 48: 391–405.

KLIEBARD, H. M., 1971. "Bureaucracy and curriculum theory," *Freedom, Bureaucracy, and Schooling,* ed. V. F. Haubrick. Washington, D.C.: Association for Supervision and Curriculum Development.

KNEZEVICH, S. J., 1971. "Perspectives on the educational program in 1985," *Educational Futurism in 1985,* eds. W. G. Hack, et. al. Berkeley, Cal.: McCutchen.

KOEHLER, J. W., K. ANATOL, and R. APPLEBAUM, 1976. *Organizational Communication: Behavioral Perspectives.* New York: Holt, Rinehart & Winston.

KOOPMAN, R. G., A. MEIL, and P. J. MISNER, 1948. *Democracy in School Administration.* Englewood Cliffs, N.J.: Prentice-Hall.

KOTTER, J. P., 1977. "Power, dependence, and effective management," *Harvard Business Review,* 55: 125–136.

KRAJEWSKI, R. J., 1976. "Clinical supervision: To facilitate teacher self improvement," *Journal of Research and Development in Education,* 9: 58–66.

LANGWORTHY, R. L., 1964. "Process," *A Dictionary of the Social Sciences,* eds. J. Gould and W. L. Kolb. New York, Free Press.

LARSON, O. N., and R. J. MILL, 1958. "Social structure and interpersonal communication," *American Journal of Sociology,* 63: 497–505.

LAWLER, M., 1961. "New frontiers for supervision," *Educational Leadership,* 19: 82.

LAWRENCE, G., 1974. *Patterns of Effective Inservice Education: A State of the Art Summary of Research of Materials and Procedures for Changing Teacher Behaviors in Inservice Education.* Tallahassee, Fla.: Florida State Department of Education.

LEAVITT, H., 1951. "Some effects of certain communication patterns on group performance," *Journal of Abnormal and Social Psychology,* 46: 38–50.

LEE, I. J., 1952. *How to Talk with People.* New York: Harper & Row, Pub.

LEEPER, R. R., ed., 1965. *Role of Supervisor and Curriculum Director in a Climate of Change.* Washington, D.C.: Association for Supervision and Curriculum Development.

LEVIN, T., and R. LONG, 1981. *Effective Instruction.* Washington, D.C.: Association for Supervision and Curriculum Development.

LEWIN, K., 1939. "Experiments in social space," *Harvard Educational Review,* 9: 21–32.

LEWIN, K., 1943. "Forces behind food habits and methods of change," *The Problem of Changing Food Habits.* Bulletin of the National Research Council, No. 108.

LEWIN, I., 1944. "The dynamics of group action," *Educational Leadership,* 1: 195–200.

LEWIN, K., 1947. "Group decision and social change," *Readings in Social Psychology,* eds. T. M. Newcomb and E. L. Hartley. New York: Holt, Rinehart & Winston.

LEWIN, K., and R. LIPPITT, 1939. "An experimental approach to the study of autocracy and democracy: A preliminary note," *Sociometry,* 1: 292–300.

LEWIS, A. J., and A. MIEL, 1972. *Supervision for Improved Instruction.* Belmont, Cal.: Wadsworth.

LICATA, J. W., E. C. WILLIS, and C. M. WILSON, 1977. "Initiating structure for educational change," *NASSP Bulletin,* 61: 25–33.

LIKERT, R., 1961. "An emerging theory of organization, leadership, and management," *Leadership and Interpersonal Behavior,* eds. L. Petrullo and B. M. Bass. New York: Holt, Rinehart & Winston.

LIKERT, R., 1971. "The principle of supportive relationships," *Organizational Theory,* ed. D. S. Pugh. New York: Penguin.

LIKERT, R., and J. G. LIKERT, 1976. *New Ways of Managing Conflict.* New York: McGraw-Hill.

LIKERT, R., and J. G. LIKERT, 1978. "A method for coping with conflict in problem solving groups," *Group and Organization Study,* 3: 426–433.

LIONBERGER, H. F., 1961. *Adoption of New Ideas and Practices.* Cedar Falls, Iowa: Iowa State Press.

LIONBERGER, H. F., 1965. "Diffusion of innovations in agricultural research in schools," *Strategy for Curriculum Change.* Washington, D.C.: NEA-ASCD.

LIONBERGER, H. F., and R. R. CAMPBELL, 1963. *The Potential of Interpersonal Networks for Message Transfer from Outside Information Sources: A Study of Two Missouri Communities.* Columbia, Mo.: Agricultural Experiment Station, Research Bulletin 842.

LIONBERGER, H. F., and C. M. MILTON. 1957. *Social Structure and Diffusion of Farm Information.* Columbia, Mo.: Agricultural Experiment Station, Research Bulletin 631.

LIPPITT, G. L., 1955. "What do we know about leadership?" *National Education Association Journal,* 44: 556–557.

LIPPITT, G. L., ed., 1961. *Leadership in Action.* Washington, D. C.: National Education Association.

LIPPITT, G. L., 1979. "Responses to Sergiovani," *Educational Leadership,* 36: 394–402.

LIPPITT, R., 1965. "Roles and processes in curriculum development and change," *Strategy for Curriculum Change.* Washington, D.C.: NEA-ASCD.

LIPPITT, R., N. POLANSKY, and S. ROSEN, 1952. "The dynamics of power: A field of study of social influence in groups of children," *Human Relations,* 5: 37–64.

LIPPITT, R., J. WATSON, and B. WESTLEY, 1958. *The Dynamics of Planned Change.* New York: Harcourt Brace Jovanovich.

LIPPITT, R., and R. K. WHITE, 1943. "The social climate of children's groups," *Child Behavior and Development,* eds. R. G. Baker, J. S. Kounin, and H. F. Wright. New York: McGraw-Hill.

LIPPITT, R., and R. K. WHITE, 1947. "An experimental study of leadership and group life," *Readings in Social Psychology,* eds. T. Newcomb and E. Hartley. New York: Holt, Rinehart & Winston.

LITTERER, J. A., 1969. *Organizations.* New York: John Wiley.

LONSDALE, B. J., 1963. "The guise of supervision," *Educational Leadership,* 21: 69–74.

LOVELL, J. T., 1967. "A perspective for viewing instructional supervisory behavior," *Supervision: Perspectives and Propositions,* ed. W. H. Lucio. Washington, D.C.: Association for Supervision and Curriculum Development.

LOVELL, J. T., 1977. *Authority for Instructional Supervisors.* Washington, D.C.: Association for Supervision and Curriculum Development.

LOVELL, J. T., 1978. "Instructional supervision: Emerging perspective," *The Roles and Responsibilities of Instructional Supervisors,* ed. A. W. Sturgess. Washington, D.C.: Association for Supervision and Curriculum Development.

LOVELL, J. T., and M. S. PHELPS, 1976. *Supervision in Tennessee: A Study of the Perceptions of Teachers, Principals and Supervisors.* Tennessee Association for Supervision and Curriculum Development.

LOVELL, J. T., and M. S. PHELPS, 1977. "Supervision in Tennessee as perceived by teachers, principals, and supervisors," *Educational Leadership,* 35: 226–228.

LUCIO, W. H., ed., 1967. *Supervision: Perspectives and Propositions.* Washington, D.C.: Association for Supervision and Curriculum Development.

LUCIO, W. H., and J. D. McNEIL, 1969. *Supervision: A Synthesis of Thought and Action.* New York: McGraw-Hill.

LYDA, W. L., 1960. "A suggested conceptual system for decision-making in curriculum development," *Educational Record,* 41: 74–83.

LYONS, D. S., and C. M. ACHILLES, 1976. "The principal as a professional decision maker," *Educational Administration Quarterly,* Winter, 43–53.

MACDONALD, J. B., B. J. WOLFSON, and E. ZARET, 1973. *Reschooling Society: A Conceptual Approach.* Washington, D.C.: Association for Supervision and Curriculum Development.

MACKENZIE, G. N., 1964. "Curricular change: Participants, power, and process," *Innovation in Education,* ed. M. B. Miles. New York: Teacher's College Press.

MACKINNON, W. J., and R. CENTERS, 1957–58. "Social psychological factors in public orientation toward an outgroup," *American Journal of Sociology,* 63: 415.

MACY, J., Jr., L. S. CHRISTIE, and R. D. LUCE, 1953. "Coding noise in a task-oriented group," *Journal of Abnormal and Social Psychology,* 48: 401–409.

MANDLER, G., and S. B. SARASON, 1952. "A study of anxiety and learning," *Journal of Abnormal and Social Psychology,* 47: 166–173.

MARCH, J. G., and H. A. SIMON, 1961. *Organizations.* New York: John Wiley.

MARCH, J., ed., 1965. *Handbook of Organizations.* Chicago, Ill.: Rand McNally.

MARGULIES, N., P. L. WRIGHT, and R. W. SCHOLL, 1977. "Organization development techniques: Their impact on change," *Group and Organization Studies,* 2: 428–448.

MARKEY, O. B., and G. HERBKERSMAN, 1961. "An experiment in student responsibility," *The School Review,* 69: 169–180.

MARKOWITZ, S., 1976. "Dilemma of authority in supervisory behavior," *Educational Leadership,* 33: 367–372.

MARKS, A., J. P. GUILFORD, and P. R. MERRIFIELD, 1959. "A study of militancy leadership in relation to selected intellectual factors," *Leadership and Interpersonal Behavior,* eds. L. Petrullo and B. M. Bass. New York: Holt, Rinehart, & Winston.

MASLOW, A. H., 1943. "A theory of human motivation," *Psychological Review,* 50: 370–396.

MASLOW, A. H., 1954. *Motivation and Personality.* New York: Harper & Row, Pub.

MASLOW, A. H., 1971. "Theory Z," *The Further Reaches of Human Nature,* New York: Penguin.

MAXON, R. C., and W. E. SISTRUNK, 1973. *A Systems Approach to Educational Administration.* Dubuque, Iowa: Wm. C. Brown.

MAYO, E., 1933. *The Human Problems of an Industrial Civilization.* New York: Macmillan.

MAZZARELLA, J. A., 1980. "Synthesis of research on staff development," *Educational Leadership,* 38: 182–195.

McCALL, M. W., JR., and M. M. LOMBARDO, 1978. *Leadership: Where Else Can We Go?* Durham, N. C.: Duke University Press.

McCLELLAND, D. C., and D. H. BURNHAM, 1976. "Power is the great motivator," *Harvard Business Review,* 54: 100–110.

McCLEARY, L. E., 1968. "Communication in large secondary schools," *NASSP Bulletin,* 52: 48–61.

McCLINTOCK, C. G., 1963. "Group support and the behavior of leaders and non-leaders," *Journal of Abnormal and Social Psychology,* 67: 105–113.

McCLINTOCK, C. G., 1965. "Group support, satisfaction and the behavior profiles of group members," *British Journal of Social and Clinical Psychology,* 4: 169–174.

McGRATH, J. E., 1962. "The influence of positive interpersonal relations on adjustment and effectiveness in rifle teams," *Journal of Abnormal and Social Psychology,* 65: 365–375.

McGRATH, J. E., and I. ALTMAN, 1966. *Small Group Research.* New York: Holt, Rinehart & Winston.

McGREGOR, D., 1957. "The human side of enterprise," *Proceedings of the Fifth Anniversary Convocation of the School of Industrial Management.* Cambridge, Mass.: MIT Press.

McGREGOR, D., 1960. *The Human Side of Enterprise.* New York: McGraw-Hill.

McINTYRE, D. J., 1979. "Attitude change models: Meaning for principals," *NASSP Bulletin,* 63: 45–48.

McKEACHIE, W. J., J. D. POLLIE, and J. SPEISMAN, 1955. "Relieving anxiety in classroom examinations," *Journal of Abnormal and Social Psychology,* 50: 93–98.

MELNICK, Z. H., 1981. "Teacher Perceptions of Inservice Education Programs in Tennessee Public Schools," (unpublished doctor's dissertation). Knoxville, Tenn.: University of Tennessee.

MEREI, F., 1949. "Group leadership and institutionalization," *Human Relations,* 2: 23–29.

MERTON, R. K., 1940. "Bureaucratic structure and personality," *Social Forces,* 18: 560–568.

MIEL, A., 1946. *Changing Curriculum.* Englewood Cliffs, N.J.: Prentice-Hall.

MIEL, A., 1942. "In service education re-examined," *The National Elementary Principal,* 41: 6–11.

MILES, M., 1959. *Learning to Work in Groups.* New York: Teacher's College, Columbia University.

MILES, M., 1965. "Education and innovation: The organization as context," *Change Perspectives in Educational Administration,* eds. M. G. Abbott and J. T. Lovell. Auburn, Ala.: Auburn University.

MILES, M., 1971. *Innovation in Education.* New York: Teacher's College, Columbia University.

MILES, R. E., 1965. "Human relations or human resources," *Harvard Business Review,* 43: 148–163.

MILLER, H. E., and J. R. TERBORG, 1978. "Motivation, behavior, and performance: A closer examination of goal setting and monetary incentives," *Journal of Applied Psychology,* 63: 29–39.

MILLER, V., 1965. *The Public Administration of American School Systems.* New York: Macmillan.

MILLINGER, G. D., 1956. "Interpersonal trust as a factor in communication," *Journal of Abnormal and Social Psychology,* 52: 304–309.

MINTZBERG, H., 1979. *The Nature of Organizational Structure.* Englewood Cliffs, N.J.: Prentice-Hall.

MISKEL, C. G., 1977. "Principals' attitudes toward work and coworkers, situational factors, perceived effectiveness, and innovation effort," *Educational Administration Quarterly,* 13: 51–70.

MOELLER, G. H., and W. W. CHARTERS, 1966. "Relation of bureaucratization to sense of power among teachers," *Administrative Science Quarterly,* 10: 444–465.

MOHR, L. B., 1977. "Authority and democracy in organizations," *Human Relations,* 30: 919–947.

MOHRMAN, A. M., R. A. COOK, and S. A. MOHRMAN, 1978. "Participation in decision making: A multidimensional perspective," *Educational Administration Quarterly,* 14: 13–29.

MONTAGUE, E. K., 1953. "The role of anxiety in serial rote learning," *Journal of Experimental Psychology,* 45: 91–96.

MOORE, S. A., 1976. "Organizational inertia and resistance to change," *The Educational Forum,* 41: 33–36.

MOOS, R. H., and J. C. SPEISMAN, 1962. "Group compatibility and productivity," *Journal of Abnormal and Social Psychology,* 65: 190–196.

MORSE, J. J., and J. W. LORSCH, 1970. "Beyond Theory Y," *Harvard Business Review,* 48: 61–68.

MOSHER, R. L., and D. E. PURPLE, 1972. *Supervision: The Reluctant Profession.* Boston: Houghton Mifflin.

MYERS, A., 1962. "Team competition, success, and the adjustment of group members," *Journal of Abnormal and Social Psychology,* 65: 325–332.

MYERS, R., 1954. "The Development and Implications of a Conception of Leadership for Leadership Education," (unpublished doctor's dissertation). Gainesville, Fla.: University of Florida.

NATIONAL TRAINING LABORATORY IN GROUP DEVELOPMENT, 1953. *Explorations in Human Relations Training.* Washington, D.C.: NEA.

NEDD, A. N., 1971. "Attitudes toward change," *Administrative Science Quarterly,* 16: 259–268.

NELSON, H., et. al., 1956. "Attitudes as adjustment to stimulus, background and residual factors," *Journal of Abnormal and Social Psychology,* 52: 314–322.

NETZER, L. A., et. al., 1970. *Interdisciplinary Foundations of Supervision.* Boston: Allyn & Bacon.

NEWELL, C. A., 1978. *Human Behavior in Educational Administration.* Englewood Cliffs, N.J.: Prentice-Hall.

OBER, R. L., E. L. BENTLEY, and E. MILLER, 1971. *Systematic Observation of Teaching.* Englewood Cliffs, N.J.: Prentice-Hall.

OLIVA, P. T., 1976. *Supervision for Today's Schools.* New York: Thomas Y. Crowell.

OLIVERO, J. L., 1976. "Helping teachers grow professionally," *Educational Leadership,* 34: 194–200.

OLSON, A. R., 1960. "Organizing a faculty for curriculum improvement," *National Association of Secondary Schools Bulletin,* 44: 94–97.

ORLOSKY, D., and O. SMITH, 1972. "Educational change: Its origins and characteristics," *Phi Delta Kappan,* 53: 412–414.

OUCHI, W. G., 1981. *Theory Z.* New York: Avon Books.

OWENS, R. G., 1980. *Organizational Behavior in Schools.* Englewood Cliffs, N.J.: Prentice-Hall.

OWENS, R. G., and C. R. STEINHOFF, 1976. *Administering Change in Schools.* Englewood Cliffs, N.J.: Prentice-Hall.

PALERMO, D. A., A. CASTANEDA, and B. R. McCANDLESS, 1956. "The relationship of anxiety in children to performance in a complex learning task," *Child Development,* 27: 333–337.

PASCOE, D., 1963. "Three concepts of democratic district leadership," *Educational Leadership,* 21: 89–92.

PATTERSON, J. L., and T. J. CZAJKOWSKI, 1979. "Implementation: Neglected phase in curriculum change," *Educational Leadership,* 37: 204–206.

PEABODY, R. L., 1969. "Perceptions of organizational authority: A comparative analysis," *Organizations: Structure and Behavior,* ed. Joseph A. Litterer. New York: John Wiley.

PETRULLO, L, and B. M. BASS, 1961. *Leadership and Interpersonal Behavior.* New York: Holt, Rinehart & Winston.

PHEYSEY, D., R. L. PAYNE, and D. PUCH, 1971. "Influence of structure at organizational and group levels," *Administrative Science Quarterly,* 16: 61–73.

PHILLIPS, B. N., 1955. "An experimental study of the effects of cooperation and competition, intelligence and cohesiveness on the task efficiency and process behavior of small groups," *Thesis Abstract Series #6.* Bloomington, Ind.: Indiana University.

PIPER, D. L., 1974. "Decision making: Decisions made by individuals vs. those made by group consensus or group participation," *Educational Administration Quarterly,* 10: 82–95.

POLANSKY, N., R. LIPPITT, and F. REDL, 1950. "An investigation of behavioral contagion in groups," *Human Relations,* 3: 319–348.

PORTER, L. W., E. LAWLER, and J. R. HACKMAN, 1977. *Behavior in Organizations.* New York: McGraw-Hill.

PRATT, W. E., and D. G. McGAREY, 1958. *A Guide to Curriculum Improvement in Elementary and Secondary Schools.* Cincinnati, Ohio: Public School Publishing.

PRENTICE, D. S., 1975. "The effects of trust-destroying communication on verbal fluency in the small group," *Speech Monographs,* 42: 262–270.

PRESTON, M. G., and R. K. HEINTZ, 1949. "Effects of participatory vs. supervisory leadership on group judgment," *Journal of Abnormal and Social Psychology,* 44: 345–355.

PRYER, M. W., A. W. FLINT, and B. M. BASS, 1962. "Group effectiveness and consistency of leadership," *Sociometry,* 25: 391–397.

PUCKETT, D. W., 1963. "The status and function of the general school supervisor in selected Arkansas schools," *Dissertation Abstracts International,* 23: 27–58.

PULLEY, J. L., 1975. "Principal and communication: Some points of interference," *NASSP Bulletin,* 59: 50–54.

PURKEY, W. W., 1978. *Inviting School Success.* Belmont, Cal.: Wadsworth.

READ, W. H., 1962. "Upward communication in industrial hierarchies," *Human Relations,* 15: 3–16.

READER, N., and H. B. ENGLISH, 1947. "Personality factors in adolescent female friendships," *Journal of Consulting Psychology,* 11: 212–220.

REBER, R. W., and G. E. TERRY, 1975. *Behavioral Insights for Supervision.* Englewood Cliffs, N.J.: Prentice-Hall.

REDDIN, W. J., 1970. *Managerial Effectiveness.* New York: McGraw-Hill.

REDDIN, W. J., 1970. "An integration of leader-behavior typologies," *Group and Organizational Studies,* 2: 282–295.

REEVES, J. M., and L. GOLDMAN, 1957. "Social class perceptions and school maladjustment," *Personnel and Guidance Journal,* 35: 414–419.

REGER, R., 1962. "An attempt to integrate a group isolate," *Journal of Educational Sociology,* 36: 154.

REITZ, H. J., 1977. *Behavior in Organizations.* Homewood, Ill.: Richard D. Irwin.

REVANS, R. N., 1964. "Standards for morals: Cause and effect," cited in T. J. Sergiovanni and R. J. Starratt, *Emerging Patterns of Supervision: Human Perspectives.* New York: McGraw-Hill, 1971.

RICHMAN, B. M., and R. M. FARMER, 1976. *Leadership, Goals, and Power in Higher Education.* San Francisco: Jossey-Bass.

ROBBINS, S. P., 1976. *The Administrative Process.* Englewood Cliffs, N.J.: Prentice-Hall.

ROBERTS, A. D., 1975. *Educational Innovation: Alternatives in Curriculum and Instruction.* Boston, Mass.: Allyn & Bacon.

ROBERTS, K. H., and C. A. O'REILLY, 1974. "Failures in upward communication in organizations: Three possible culprits," *Academy of Management Journal,* 17: 205–215.

ROETHLISBERGER, F. J., and W. J. DICKSON, 1947. *Management and the Worker.* Cambridge, Mass.: Harvard University Press.

ROGERS, C. R., 1961. *On Becoming a Person.* Boston: Houghton Mifflin.

ROGERS, C. R., 1969. *Freedom to Learn.* Columbus, Ohio: Chas. E. Merrill.

ROGERS, C. R., 1971. "Can schools grow persons?" *Educational Leadership,* 29: 215-217.

ROGERS, E. M., 1962. *Diffusion of Innovations.* New York: Free Press.

ROGERS, E. M., and F. SHOEMAKER, 1971. *Communication of Innovations.* New York: Free Press.

ROGERS, E. M., and R. A. ROGERS, 1975. "Organizational communication," *Communication and Behavior,* eds. G. J. Hanneman and W. J. McEwen. Reading, Mass.: Addison-Wesley.

ROGERS, R. E., 1975. *Organizational Theory.* Boston, Mass.: Allyn & Bacon.

ROGERS, V. R., 1976. "Why teachers centers in the U.S.?" *Educational Leadership,* 33: 406-412.

RUBIN, L., 1976. *The Future of Education: Perspectives on Tomorrow's Schooling.* Boston, Mass.: Allyn & Bacon.

RUBIN, L., 1978. *The In-Service Education of Teachers.* Boston, Mass.: Allyn & Bacon.

RUNKEL, P. J., 1956. "Cognitive similarity in facilitating communication," *Sociometry,* 19: 178-191.

RUSSELL, E. B., and J. R. WARMBROD, 1977. "Change orientation of educators: A potential tool for change advocates in state-level educational agencies," *Journal of Research and Development in Education,* 10: 50-62.

SAND, O., et. al., 1960. "Components of the curriculum: Curriculum decisions in secondary education," *Review of Educational Research,* 30: 233-237.

SANFORD, A. C., G. T. HUNT, and H. J. BRACEY, 1976. *Communication Behavior in Organizations.* Columbus, Ohio: Chas. E. Merrill.

SARGENT, J. F., and G. R. MILLER, 1971. "Some differences in certain communication behavior of autocratic and democratic leaders," *Journal of Communication,* 21: 233-252.

SAVAGE, R., 1967. "A Study of Teacher Satisfaction and Attitudes," (unpublished doctor's dissertation). Auburn, Ala.: Auburn University.

SAYLES, L. R., 1979. *Leadership.* New York: McGraw-Hill.

SCHEIN, E., 1976. "Process consultation," *The Planning of Change,* eds. W. G. Bennis, K. D. Benne, R. Chin, and K. Carey. New York: Holt, Rinehart & Winston.

SCHEIN, E. H., and W. G. BENNIS, 1965. *Personal and Organizational Change through Group Methods: The Laboratory Approach.* New York: John Wiley.

SCHMIDT, G. L., 1976. "Job satisfaction among secondary school administrators," *Educational Administration Quarterly,* 12: 68-86.

SCHNEIDER, J. E., 1971. "Mind to mind communication: Nonverbal influences?" *Theory Into Practice,* 10: 259-263.

SCHRAG, C. C., and O. N. LARSEN, 1954. *Sociology.* New York: Harper & Row, Pub.

SCHULTZ, W. C., 1961. "The ego, FIRO theory and the leader as completer," *Leadership and Interpersonal Behavior,* eds. L. Petrullo and B. M. Bass. New York: Holt, Rinehart & Winston.

SCOTT, L. K., 1978. "Charismatic authority in the rational organization," *Educational Administration Quarterly,* 14: 43-62.

SCOTT, W. G., 1975. "Organization theory," *Theories of Organization,* ed. H. L. Tosi. Chicago, Ill.: St. Clair Press.

SEAGER, G. B., Jr., 1979. "Diagnostic Supervision," (a paper presented at the National Conference of the Council of Professors of Instructional Supervision).

SELZNICK, R., 1949. *T.V.A. and the Grass Roots.* Berkeley: University of California Press.

SERGIOVANNI, T. J., 1967. "Factors which affect satisfaction and dissatisfaction of teachers," *Journal of Educational Administration,* 5: 66–82.

SERGIOVANNI, T. J., 1976. "Toward a theory of clinical supervision," *Journal of Research and Development in Education,* 9: 20–29.

SERGIOVANNI, T. J., and R. J. STARRATT, 1971. *Emerging Patterns of Supervision: Human Perspectives.* New York: McGraw-Hill.

SERGIOVANNI, T. J., and R. J. STARRATT, 1979. *Supervision: Human Perspectives.* New York: McGraw-Hill.

SEXTON, M. J., and K. D. D. SWITZER, 1977. "Educational leadership: No longer a potpourri," *Educational Leadership,* 25: 19–21.

SHARPLES, B., 1975. "Rational decision making in education: Some concerns," *Educational Administration Quarterly,* Spring: Vol. 11, 55–65.

SHAW, M. E., 1954. "Some effects of unequal distribution of information upon group performance in various communication nets," *Journal of Abnormal and Social Psychology,* 49: 547–553.

SHAW, M. E., 1955. "A comparison of two types of leadership in various communication nets," *Journal of Abnormal and Social Psychology,* 50: 127–134.

SHAW, M. E., 1963. "Some effects of varying amounts of information exclusively possessed by a group member upon his behavior in the group," *Journal of General Psychology,* 68: 71.

SHAW, M. E., G. H. ROTHSCHILD, and J. F. STRICKLAND, 1957. "Decision processes in communication nets," *Journal of Abnormal and Social Psychology,* 54: 323–330.

SHETTY, Y. K., 1978. "Managerial power and organizational effectiveness: A contingency analysis," *Journal of Management Studies,* 16: 176–186.

SIMON, H. E., 1975. *The New Science of Management Decision.* Englewood Cliffs, N.J.: Prentice-Hall.

SIMON, H. E., 1976. *Administrative Behavior.* New York: Free Press.

SPEARS, H., 1957. *Curriculum Planning through In-Service Programs.* Englewood Cliffs, N.J.: Prentice-Hall.

STEINER, I. D., and E. D. ROGERS, 1963. "Alternative responses to dissonance," *Journal of Abnormal and Social Psychology,* 66: 128–136.

STERLING, T. D., and B. G. ROSENTHAL, 1950. "The relationship of changing leadership and followership in a group to the changing phases of group activity," *American Psychologist,* 5: 311.

STITH, M., and R. CONNOR, 1962. "Dependency and helpfulness in young children," *Child Development,* 33: 15–20.

STOGDILL, R. M., 1950. "Leadership, membership and organization," *Psychological Bulletin,* 47: 1–14.

STOGDILL, R. M., 1957. *Leader Behavior: Its Description and Measurement.* Columbus, Ohio: Bureau of Business Research, College of Commerce and Administration, Ohio State University.

STOGDILL, R. M., 1974. *Handbook of Leadership.* New York: Free Press.

STRICKLAND, L. H., E. E. JONES, and W. P. SMITH, 1960. "Effects of group support on the evaluation of an antagonist," *Journal of Abnormal and Social Psychology,* 61: 73–81.

SUCHMAN, J. R., 1961. "Inquiry training: Building skills for autonomous discovery," *Merill-Palmer Quarterly of Behavior and Development,* 7: 147–169.

SUGG, W. B., 1955. "A Study of the Relationship between Program Development and the Working Patterns of School Principals," (unpublished doctor's dissertation). Gainesville, Fla.: University of Florida.

SULLIVAN, C. G., 1980. *Clinical Supervision.* Washington, D.C.: Association for Supervision and Curriculum Development.

SUSSMAN, L., 1975. "Communication in organizational hierarchies," *Western Speech Communication Journal,* 39: 191–199.

SWEARINGEN, M. E., 1960. "Identifying needs for in-service growth," *Educational Leadership,* 17: 332–335.

TABACHNICK, B. R., 1962. "Some correlates of prejudice toward negroes in elementary age children," *The Journal of Genetic Psychology,* 100: 193–204.

TANNENBAUM, R., I. WESCHLER, and F. MASSARILS, 1959. *Leadership and Organization.* New York: McGraw-Hill.

TANNENBAUM, R. I., 1961. *Leadership and Organization: A Behavioral Science Approach.* New York: McGraw-Hill.

TANNENBAUM, R. I., and W. H. SCHMIDT, 1973. "How to choose a leadership pattern," *Harvard Business Review,* 51: 162–164.

THIBAUT, J., 1950. "An experimental study of the cohesiveness of underprivileged groups," *Human Relations,* 3: 25–78.

THOMPSON, D. E., 1971. "Favorable self-perception, perceived supervisory style, and job satisfaction," *Journal of Applied Psychology,* 55: 349–352.

THOMPSON, V. A., 1961. *Modern Organizations: A General Theory.* New York: Knopf.

TOSI, H. L., 1975. *Theories of Organization.* Chicago, Ill.: St. Clair Press.

TOSI, H. L., and S. J. CARROLL, 1976. *Management: Contingencies, Structure and Process.* Chicago, Ill.: St. Clair Press.

TUBBS, S. L., and S. MOSS, 1977. "Organizational communication," *Human Communication.* New York: Random House.

TURNER, R. H., 1978. "The role and the person," *American Journal of Sociology,* 84: 1–23.

TYLER, R. W., 1950. *Basic Principles of Curriculum Instruction.* Chicago, Ill.: University of Chicago Press.

TYLER, R. W., 1978. "Accountability and teacher performance: Self-directed and external-directed professional improvement," *The In-Service Education of Teachers,* ed. L. Rubin. Boston: Allyn & Bacon.

VALENTINE, J. W., B. L. TATE, A. T. SEAGREN, and J. A. LAMMEL, 1975. "Administrative verbal behavior: What you say does make a difference," *NASSP Bulletin,* 59: 67–74.

VEIGA, J. F., and J. N. YANOUZAS, 1979. *The Dynamics of Organization Theory.* New York: West Publishing Co.

VROOM, V. H., 1970. "The nature of the relationship between motivation and performance," *Management and Motivation,* eds. V. Broom and E. L. Deci. New York, Penguin.

WALBERG, H. J., ed., 1974. *Evaluating Educational Performance.* Berkeley, Cal.: McCutchan.

WATERHOUSE, I. K., and I. L. CHILD, 1953. "Frustration and the quality of performance: III. An experimental study," *Journal of Personality,* 21: 298–311.

WATSON, D., and B. BROMBERG, 1965. "Power communication and positive satisfaction in task-oriented groups," *Journal of Personality and Social Psychology,* 2: 859–964.

WEIGAN, J., ed., 1971. *Developing Teacher Competencies.* Englewood Cliffs, N.J.: Prentice-Hall.

WHITE, R., and R. LIPPITT, 1960. "Leader behavior and member reaction in three social climates," *Group Dynamics,* eds. D. Cartwright and A. Zander. Evanston, Ill.: Row Peterson.

WHITMAN, R. M., and D. STOCK, 1958. "The group focal conflict," *Psychiatry,* 21: 269–276.

WHYTE, W. F., 1943. *Street Corner Society*. Chicago, Ill.: University of Chicago Press.

WICK, J. W., and D. L. BEGGS, 1971. *Evaluation for Decision Making in the Schools*. New York: Houghton Mifflin.

WILEN, W. W., and R. KINDSVATTER, 1978. "Implications of research for effective in-service education," *The Clearing House*, 51: 392–396.

WILES, J., and J. BONDI, 1980. *Supervision, a Guide to Practice*. Columbus, Ohio: Chas. E. Merrill.

WILES, K., 1950. *Supervision for Better Schools*. Englewood Cliffs, N.J.: Prentice-Hall.

WILKENING, E. A., 1956. "Roles of communicating agents in technological change in agriculture," *Social Focus*, 34: 361–367.

WILKINS, E. J., and R. DECHARMS, 1962. "Authoritarianism and response to power cues," *Journal of Personality*, 30: 439–443.

WILSON, L. C., 1971. *The Open Access Curriculum*. Boston: Allyn & Bacon.

WILSON, L. C., et. al., 1969. *Sociology of Supervision*. Boston: Allyn & Bacon.

WOODS, T. E., 1967. *The Administration of Educational Change*. Eugene, Ore.: University of Oregon.

YARBROUGH, V. E., 1975. "Teacher growth: The field services cluster," *Educational Leadership*, 32: 335–338.

YEATTS, E. H., 1976. "Staff development: A teacher-centered in-service design," *Educational Leadership*, 33: 417–421.

YOUNG, J. and J. EMANUAL, 1977. "Using the 'grapevine' as a problem-solving tool," *NASSP Bulletin*, 61: 46–48.

ZALTMAN, G., D. FLORIA, and SIKARSKI, 1977. *Dynamic Educational Change*. New York: Free Press.

ZANDER, A., and A. R. COHEN, 1955. "Attributed social power and group acceptance: A classroom experimental demonstration," *Journal of Abnormal and Social Psychology*, 51: 490–492.

INDEX